The Mystery of the THREE KINGS

THE LOST ANCIENT UNDERSTANDING

Vatican Document Proves
One of the Largest Blunders
In Church History

A Documented Journey From
Ophir, Tarshish & Sheba, Philippines

ORIGIN? WHEN? WHAT STAR? WHAT IS A MAGI?
THEIR NAMES & NUMBER? WHEN WAS JESUS BORN?
AN ENTIRE PARADIGM ONCE KNOWN NOW RESTORED.

Timothy Schwab
Anna Zamoranos, Lisa George

CONTRIBUTORS
VIVIEN CRUZ, RICHIE B. CUBOS, ZEN GARCIA, MARVIN & ARLENE LEONARDO

Vatican Document Translation From
*"**Revelation of the Magi: The Lost Tale of the Wise Men's Journey to Bethlehem.**"*
By Brent Landau. HarperOne, An Imprint of Harper-Collins Publishers. New York. 2010.
Chapters and Verses noted in each reference. Out or respect, we will only publish excerpts of the translation and will not publish this text in its entirety. We encourage everyone to attain a copy of Landau's full translation on Amazon and other outlets. Our use of these fragments is in accordance with the Fair Use Act.

Library Of Congress Control Number: 1-14436697531
ISBN Number: 979-8-346-12032-2

To order additional copies of this book, contact:

www.OphirInstitute.com
The God Culture
TheGodCulture@gmail.com
Facebook: The God Culture - Original
www.TheGodCulture.com

NOTE: Why Foreward vs. the traditional foreword? As The God Culture represents an adjusting of traditional history, geography and bible interpretation, they wanted something more from the opening words that sets the tone appropriately. They employ a sort of literary double entendre in using the word Foreward, reviving an Old English word far more significant. Foreward means: to keep, guard, vanguard, protect, tend. It denotes a warding of evil in a sense. This work also strives to move people forward out of the Dark Ages, which persist. For this book, that is the title chosen very appropriately in raising the curtain on this work.

Contents

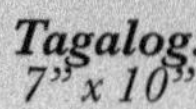

The Full Case:
6" x 9" Paperback

Tagalog:
6" x 9" Paperback

Ilokano:
6" x 9" Paperback

Coffee Table Book:
10" x 12" Hardcover

Three Kings:
7" x 10"

**Garden of Eden
Revealed:** *7" x 10"*

Apocrypha: Vol. 2:
7" x 10"

REST: Sabbath:
6" x 9" Paperback

▶ **YouTube** *The God Culture*   f *The God Culture - Original*

www.OphirInstitute.com

Foreward BY LISA GEORGE, BED, MSCP

The people of the Philippines have endured more hardships as a whole culture than any other on earth. It is with this knowledge, and witnessing their struggles firsthand, that drew our interest to research of their origins before the arrival of the Spanish on the ancient archipelago. No other national group has expanded to reside peacefully in every nation, often working abroad in menial and laborious occupations that westerners depend on, but pay little for their friendly services.

In Hawaii, thousands of Filipinos were originally a part of organized slave labor camps, developed and recruited by Dole, Del Monte, and C & H companies, directly from their home countries, and boarded ships that offered free travel and lodging for single, healthy men. They resided in tiny shacks within camps, on Oahu, Maui, and Kauai, and their pay averaged about ten cents per day for the laborious field work of planting, watering, harvesting, and processing fresh pineapple and sugar cane. These migrant workers saved what little money they could, and sent a large part of their paychecks to their families back in the Philippines. The majority of these workers were from Ilocos Norte, Luzon, and eventually would bring their families to live in Hawaii as well, often expanding their travel and work to include agricultural fields in California. It is no secret that Filipinos have excellent skills in tending to plants.

We have visited over one hundred foreign countries via cruise ship in the past two decades, and have encountered Filipinos working in every one of them. They are the waiters, chefs, and housekeeping staff on board during the day, and the entertainment crew in the evenings. They are the restaurant and hotel staff, the call center voices, the care-givers for children, elderly and disabled. Their welcoming, beautiful smiles and friendly dispositions make their personalities excellent for these positions.

After living in a Filipino family for most of my life, I learned to appreciate the safety and stability within their family units that was lacking in typical USA families. Instead of sending their children away upon reaching adulthood, they embraced their young adults, providing rent-free living in an additional home, located within the family compound, until young couples saved enough money to provide their own shelter and food. It was comforting to know that if I became too sick to work, or care for my house or children, that we would not have to live on the street, as part of a Filipino family. They rarely sent their elderly to live in an elderly care home; rather, they were the caretakers of numerous elderly and foster homes that I worked with here in Hawaii. Their customs seemed biblical, and I didn't understand why until recently.

In 2018, during a certain broadcast of a large Youtube channel which we used to enjoy, the host described a familiar story of the wise men who traveled from the East to Bethlehem, to see the long-awaited Messiah. Having a sarcastic tone, the host also mentioned some recent ridiculous research by another ministry on Youtube, that claimed to prove these kings journeyed from the Philippines to Israel, where Messiah was born. I sat upright and asked my Filipino husband to rewind the video, so that we could take note of where this information was located. We immediately looked for the ridiculous channel, and stumbled upon *The God Culture.*

Ever since that day, we have binge watched hundreds of TGC videos, read every one of their published works, purchased their writings for friends and family, and did our own research on the history of the Philippines. We have arrived at the same conclusions as *The God Culture* team, proving their research is definitely NOT ridiculous. We prayed for more truth to be revealed since, and Yah is faithful.

Last year, we were introduced to an obscure little book that had been fairly recently translated to English by Brent Landau, Revelation of the Magi. Our friend and author, Zen Garcia, an authority on ancient writings, shared a summarizing version of it with us, and we immediately knew that the book would be a wonderful addition to the research done by *The God Culture.* With the prior knowledge of the origin of the Kings of the East, it was easy to realize that the Magi were one and the same holy men who traveled to Bethlehem.

During our latest visit to the Philippines, which we now call Ophir, Sheba, and Tarshish, I brought a copy of *Revelation of the Magi* to share with *The God Culture* team in person, so that they would have even more evidence for the excellent research they had already discovered. It was an amazing journey to embark upon, as we were able to attend a huge conference, get to know the team, and travel to the Mount of the East, Mount Hibok Hibok, ourselves. We thank the Most High for continuing to fulfill prophecy in the end times, while we explore this ancient land, as described in Daniel 12:4, "Many shall travel back and forth (as mariners on the sea), and knowledge will increase (in the last days)." (Strong's Concordance)

Who transformed the wealthiest nation in history into a Third World country?
Illustration extracted from: Bagay, Nicolás De La Cruz, Engraver, and Pedro Murillo Velarde.
A Hydrographical and Chorographical Chart of the Philippine Islands.
[Manila: Publisher Not Identified, 1734] Map. U.S. Library of Congress. Public Domain.
https://www.loc.gov/item/2021668467/.

AdobeStock.
The Real
Queen of Sheba

Introduction

In 2017, *The God Culture* released its viral *Solomon's Gold Series* on YouTube, followed by two international books, documenting this position in research, also supported by a 300-page Sourcebook. As study deepened, they found the *Gospel of Matthew* was not the only Biblical source of the account of the Magi. Instead, King David provided us with geography of these Kings, documenting they were, in fact, Kings even. Every year, around Christmastime, we see articles and listen to sermons that are oblivious to these Bible facts, in ignorance of scripture. Those are not Biblical positions.

This understanding is not new, but an ancient view, known for thousands of years, which never should have been lost. One would struggle to find a single scholar who even knows this truth, unless they are a viewer or reader of *The God Culture* positions. However, when we conducted a conference in Davao City, Philippines in 2024, friends from Hawaii arrived with a book, reviewed on Zen Garcia's U.S. radio and social media program, that affirmed these findings with incredible strength. Though these notable Kings commenced their journey from the Philippines indisputably in scripture, we now have in our possession, a recent English translation of a Vatican Library document which fully affirms this revelation. This is not a fragment and not small.

According to the translator, ***Revelation of the Magi (RoTM)***, from the Vatican Library, is dated as early as the second century A.D. It was recently translated to English for the first time, from the Syriac language, and published by Harper-Collins Publishers in 2010. This monumental document was translated and released by Brent Landau with the assistance of numerous Harvard, Cambridge and other university professors.[1] Though not a firm date, Landau proves this document existed at least prior to 500 A.D., which is really all one needs to know. This means it preceded the Catholic legend of Caspar, Melchior, and Balthasar as false, fabricated names as well as the spurious narrative of their deriving from Persia, Arabia, and India as is still claimed in ignorance. This writing lists their names as well as their land of origin, and none match the newer legend. This is not a Biblical fact, but is against what the Bible teaches, and is hiding their region of the Magi's ancestry. These fraudulent names should never be repeated by any church.

The Catholic Church has known this legend was false from its inception, covering up the true land for some apparently nefarious reason. Why would they not want us to know the Wise Men came from the Philippines? Is it because they conquered that region, stealing its resources for centuries? We all know Spain was part of the Holy Roman Empire, as was the United States, who would conquer the Philippines after that. The Treaty of Paris of 1783 clarifies that the King of England and the

United States of America, was also, Arch-Treasurer and Prince Elector for the Holy Roman Empire, led by the Pope, ultimately.[1] Would this mean the Catholic Church knew it was stealing the very same resources from the same land of the 3 Kings, which also happens to be the land over the Garden of Eden, even according to this Vatican Library document? Or even greater, would this indict the Catholic Church as not actually bringing Jesus *(Yahusha)* to the Philippines, but suppressing the original, authentic Biblical religion of a land connected in relationship to Him for at least 1,500 years prior? This Vatican document answers that question in the affirmative. What does this say of the Catholic Religion, when it squashes the actual practice of the Bible and replaces it as a clear counterfeit? Well, we certainly do not expect nor wish for the Pope's endorsement of this research. However, prove all things and hold fast that which is good *(1 Th. 5:21)*.

This is no surprise, as they do not want us to know the land of Ophir, Sheba, Tarshish and the Garden of Eden also have been found in the Philippines for over 6,000 years of valid history and geography. This included the famous map of Cosmas the Indian Voyager, a Catholic monk and merchant traveler who mapped Paradise *(Garden of Eden)* in the Philippines in 550 A.D.[2] in his book **Christian Topography** *[p. 14]*. This map has been catalogued and known in the Vatican Library, St. Catherine Monastery in Sinai, and Laurenziana Library in Florence for more than 1,000 years.

In his written directions, Cosmas defines the map as one would exit the Indian Ocean and hang a left, with the Garden of Eden just to the right. One is not a scholar when they do not know basic directions; that the exit is at the Malay Peninsula, and one turns North into the South China Sea from there. The islands to the East of that are known as the Philippines archipelago; let us not pretend they know their left from right, even. Those directions are also affirmed in **Revelation of the Magi.**

The renown Catholic, Isidore of Seville offered much geography in his chronicles. His 600 A.D. map[2] defines Paradise *(Garden of Eden)* in the Philippines southeast of *Serices*, which is South China *[p. 15]*. *Tylos* or *Thilis*, the Isle of Pearl is in the same region, which proves to be Palawan. It is befuddling that anyone calling themselves academic struggles with that. Chryse and Argyre are islands in the same archipelago once again. This is a common theme throughout history, yet missed by most PhDs who simply have never conducted true research on this topic.

In 650 A.D., the Italian Ravenna Map[2] *[p. 16]* also labels the large island of the Philippines Southeast of China in the South China Sea as *"Paradise"* with the isles of Chryse *(Greek for Ophir)* and Argyre *(Greek for Tarshish)* nearby in the same archipelago we call the Philippines today. Catholic history knew this was never a mystery.

---

[1] *Facsimile of Original Treaty of Paris 1783 from the U.S. Senate can be downloaded at: www.senate.gov/artandhistory/history/resources/pdf/TreatyofParis1783.pdf.*
[2] *All maps in full color, high resolution in Garden of Eden Revealed: The Book of Maps. Schwab/ Zamoranos. 2024. www.OphirInstitute.com.*

The Catholic Beatus of Liébana, a Spanish monk, theologian, and author created a mapping perspective which continued for centuries. The 800 A.D. publishing is included on page 17.[2] In *Garden of Eden Revealed: The Book of Maps*,[2] there are several for review, including a 787 A.D. map[2] from the Spanish monk, preserved in the Monastery of Silos since 1109. It locates Paradise, Chryse and Argyre in the area of the Philippines. This was no enigma to the Catholic paradigm. A similar view is found on maps in 970, 975, 1047, 1086, 1175, 1185, 1220 and more.[2]

This thinking was not new at all in the sixth century, but a continuation of the geography set forth in 1 Enoch *[p. 120]*, Jubilees *[p. 118]*, and Words of the Archangel Michael *[p. 121]* found in the Dead Sea Scrolls, which all coalesce with Genesis 2, and assist in explaining it, as they should. Enoch even defines the *Seven Mountains of Eden*, which parallel the seven islands of Visayas, Philippines in geographic orientation and in his resource descriptions. Of course, Genesis 2 defines this land of Havilah where Adam and Havah *(Eve)* dwelled by three resources (the Philippines leads the world in history in all three); gold, pearl and the onyx stone. The fragment from the Archangel Michael defines this migration of the holy sons of Joktan, including Ophir, Sheba and Havilah, to the *Nine Mountains of Eden*, which would be to add Luzon and Mindanao. It also provides geography fitting to the Philippines in whole, including the mention of the place where Gabriel resides on earth. This is confirmed in 1 Enoch as the Garden of Eden *[1En. 20]*.

Enoch and Michael were eyewitness observers. No modern scholar is. They may attempt to disparage those texts, just as some will attack the ***Revelation of the Magi***. However, these books vet as valid and valuable, regardless of whether one inducts them into their Bible canon. They are valid history as fact, and their accuracy is confirmed in many ways, which is the greatest criteria of truth.

The Greeks offer markers for the land of Chryse *(Gold of Ophir and the Garden)* over the 800 or so years of their Empire, as they inherited the route of the ships of Tarshish, who was a Greek. This thinking led to the T-O Map perspective, in which Paradise was located by the Tropic of Cancer to the East of mainland Asia.[2] That proves to be the Philippines, as this was known Bible exegesis all along.

It continued to be understood in 43 A.D. by Pomponius Mela *[p. 85]*,[2] a Roman who preserved that route from the "olden writers" of Greece, in his own words. His work was used, until at least the year 1500 and beyond.[2] As it is first identified geographically and scientifically in Genesis 2, this is exactly what one would expect. In 50 A.D., The Periplus of the Erythraean Sea *[p. 86]*[2] pinpoints the same. In 90 A.D., Josephus[2] interpreted the Hebrew in Genesis 2 to read that the Garden was planted in the East. Josephus and the rest all understood Israel is not the East in the Bible perspective. Much of the Bible was written in Israel, and it is certainly a laughable proposition that one writing in Israel meant the land of Israel, when they define the Garden planted in the East. The Latin word used is *Orient* because it is the Far East.

Dyonisius the Tourist affirms this in 124 A.D. *[p. 87][2]* as did African scholar, Lucius Caecilius Firmianus Lactantius,[2] who wrote **Divine Institutes** in 310 A.D. He defined the Garden of Eden in the regions of the East *(2.13)* meaning Far East. The real question is: Who lost the Land of Gold and Garden of Eden? The same scholars displaced the Magi and forgot from where they came; yet, this was known.

The Vatican was aware the Garden of Eden was in the Philippines, which is why it approved the sending of explorers, such as Columbus and Magellan, to locate these famed isles in the Philippines.[2] Their journals and notes affirm that they were seeking the Land of Gold of King Solomon known as Ophir *(Chryse in Greek)* and Tarshish *(Argyre in Greek)* as well as the Garden of Eden in the same region.[2] Columbus even equated the Chinese name of the Isles of Gold, reported by Marco Polo as Zipangu, as this very same existence of Ophir. He followed maps, and likely created his own, pinpointing these in the Philippines.[2] The National Library of France studied that 1490 Columbus Map for about thirty years before concluding and authenticating it was the work of the Columbus brothers in 1490 *[p. 18].*[2]

Of course, this is also affirmed in the two maps Columbus used[2] to plot his course for the Philippines, according to his own words in his journal, as Ophir, Tarshish, and the Garden of Eden. These included the first globe map of the world ever created–the 1492 Portuguese government-commissioned Behaim Globe*[p. 23].*[2] Though German in nativity, Behaim lived in Portugal at that time and was hired to construct this sphere by Portuguese King João, according to Cambridge University's Whipple Museum of History.[3] He raised additional funding from his home country in his three-year stay there, but this map included the Portuguese government exploration data, representing the government position and record.

The second was a 1474 Map of Paolo Dal Pozzo Toscanelli *[p. 22],*[2] a Catholic mathematician, astronomer, and cosmographer from Florence (according to Catholic.com). These both label *Chryse* and *Zipangu* as essentially Luzon Island in the Philippines, southeast of China, East of Indochina, and Northeast of Borneo. On the Behaim Globe, Mindanao, Philippines is labeled *Argyre*, the Greek name for Tarshish, as the land of silver. He included *Thilis*, the ancient name for the Isle of Pearl, which is essentially Palawan, who still boasts the largest pearls on Earth to this day. Anyone calling themselves a scholar, or even a cartographer, who does not know that is the Philippines, would have to be a dunce. Certainly, they cannot read a map if they are unable to conclude such.

This is even written into contracts by the King of Spain, as an emissary of the Pope, such as the hiring of Sebastian Cabot in 1525,[1] where the King knew he was

---

[1] *"Magellan's voyage around the world; three contemporary accounts [by] Antonio Pigafetta, Maximilian of Transylvania [and] Gaspar Correa." Charles E. Nowell, Northwestern University Press, 1962. p. 21-22.* [2] *Garden of Eden Revealed: The Book of Maps. Schwab/Zamoranos. 2024. www.OphirInstitute.com.* [3] *"Katie Taylor, 'A brief history of globes' University of Cambridge, Whipple Museum of the History of Science. University of Cambridge, 2009.*

not living in Tarshish, regardless of illiterate Rabbi babble followed in modern scholarship. Spain knew it was never Tarshish. This contract for hire firmly located Ophir and Tarshish North of Indonesia and South of China in a written government document. Spanish Government Document No. 98 even provides details, that when mapped, also lands in the Philippines as Ophir and Lequios, as well as Tarshish, just as Columbus and Magellan had found in their research. Historians, such as Father Francisco Colin, continued to refer. to the Philippines as Ophir and Tarshish.

*"And that this was really so, and that the **principal settler of these archipelagoes [Philippines] was Tharsis, son of Javan**, together with his brothers, as were **Ophir and Hevilath** (Havilah/Hawilat) of India, we see in the tenth chapter of Genesis..."* –Father Francisco Colin, 1663 [1]

Indeed, other Catholic scholars recount the same, such as António Galvão, whose work was published in English in 1601.[2] Galvão served as a Governor and Captain in the Holy Roman Empire. Before 1627, Dominican Gregorio Garcia of the Catholic Order wrote of the Philippines as Ophir and Tarshish.[3] Even a former Prime Minister of the Philippines, who was also a poet and novelist, Pedro Alejandro Paterno y de Vera Ignacio, recorded in 1891 that the Philippines was Ophir.[4] He was also awarded the Order of Isabella the Catholic in 1893, and was the first Filipino Director of Museo Biblioteca de Filipinas, the National Library. These are but a few examples that the Catholic Church was aware the Philippines was this Ancient Land of Gold, the Garden of Eden, and the home of the Magi. Any claim this was ever an actual mystery is illiterate to history.

As some demand archaeology from ancient gold mining, which required no equipment that would leave an archaeological signature,[5] let us not pretend they are behaving logically, nor even as adults. The application is gold, and the Philippines ranks number 2 in untapped gold deposits in the ground,[6] and number 1 in history. South Africa is very new to the gold arena, not even having a gold rush

---

[1] *'The Philippine Islands, 1493-1898 - Volume 40 of 55, 1690-1691." By Francisco Colin, Francisco Combos, Gaspar de San Aguston and Dominican Gregorio Garcia locating Ophir in Moluccas and the Philippines. Edited By: E.H. Blair J.A. Robertson. Appendix: Ethnological Description of the Filipinos. Chapter IV. ebook: p. 38.* [2] *"The Discoveries of the World, from Their First Originall Unto the Yeere of our Lord 1555." By Antonio Galvão. Corrected, Quoted and Now Published in English. By Richard Hakluyt. Londini. 1601. p. 8.* [3] *"Origen de los indios de el Nuevo Mundo e Indias Occidentales." By Gregorio Garcia. Con Priveligio. p. 37.* [4] *"Philippine Progress Prior to 1898." By Austin Craig and Conrado Benitez. Of the College of Liberal Arts Faculty of the University of the Philippines. Philippine Education Co., Inc., Manila, 1916. p. 92. Citing Works on Conjectural Anthropology, Former Prime Minister Pedro A. Paterno. Mojares 2006. p. 85.* [5] *"Gold in early Southeast Asia." By Anna T. N. Bennett. ArcheoSciences, 33. 2009, 99-107.* [5] *a. "Miners Shun Mineral Wealth of the Philippines." By Donald Greenlees. NY Times. May 14, 2008. Citing The Fraser Institute. b. "Trillion – Dollar Philippine Economic Goldmine Emerging From Murky Pit." By Ralph Jennings. Forbes Magazine. Apr. 5, 2015.*

A map of the world by Cosmas Indicopleustes "Indian Voyager" in a medieval manuscript of the "Christian Topography": Rome, Biblioteca Apostolica Vaticana, Vat. gr. 699, fol. 40v. Wikimedia Commons. Public Domain. Randall wrote that Cosmas "had great popularity among even the educated till the twelfth century." See John Herman Randall, Jr., The Making of the Modern Mind: A Survey of the Intellectual Background of the Present Age (Boston: Houghton Mifflin, 1926), 23.

THE BIBLE ONCE INCLUDED AN ACCURATE MAP TO THE GARDEN OF EDEN IN THE PHILIPPINES! COSMAS' MAP OF THE EARTH ONCE APPEARED IN THE CODEX SINAITICUS GRAECUS 1186, FOL. 66V NOW AT ST. KATHERINE'S MONASTERY, SINAI.

Cosmas was likely an eyewitness observer to the areas of Southeast Asia as he pictures "The hog-deer I have both seen and eaten." In Greek, this is χοιρέλαφον: babyrousa. babi is the Malay and Indonesian word for 'pig' and rusa means 'deer'. This genus of pigs is present only in the Indonesian islands of Sulawesi, Lembeh, Sula, Malenge and Buru. The Garden is beyond there to the Northeast in the Philippines. Those claiming he did not have knowledge that far cannot read. This was not the Indian variety!

Cosmas illustration of the pig-deer he saw and ate. The Indian hog-deer looks like a deer.

Babyrousa togeanensis from Indonesia. Wikimedia Commons. Public Domain.

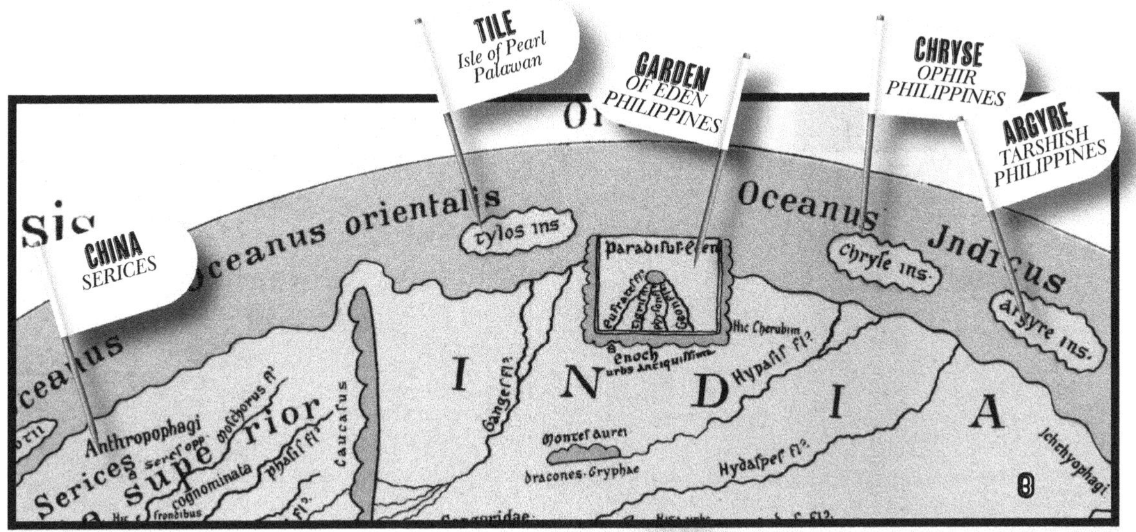

Miller Mappaemundi VI.
Taf: 2.

Weltkarte des Isidor von Sevilla. Mappae Mundi Bd. Vi. "Rekonstruierte Karten."
Reconstructed in 1898 by Dr. Konrad Miller. [3]

Reconstruction of a mappa mundi from the notes of an anonymous geographer from Ravenna (Italy), c. 650 AD, also known as the "Ravennate" mappa mundi. The reconstruction was printed in Konrad Miller (1898) 'Mappaemundi: Die ältesten Weltkarten, Stuttgart: Roth'sche. Volume VI, table 1. The map is unusually gridded by a rare 24-wind compass (or, more precisely, a classical 12-wind compass strangely partitioned into "day" and "night" segments, yielding 24 rays.). Wikimedia Commons. Public Domain. Note: Enoch's mindset is also foud here.

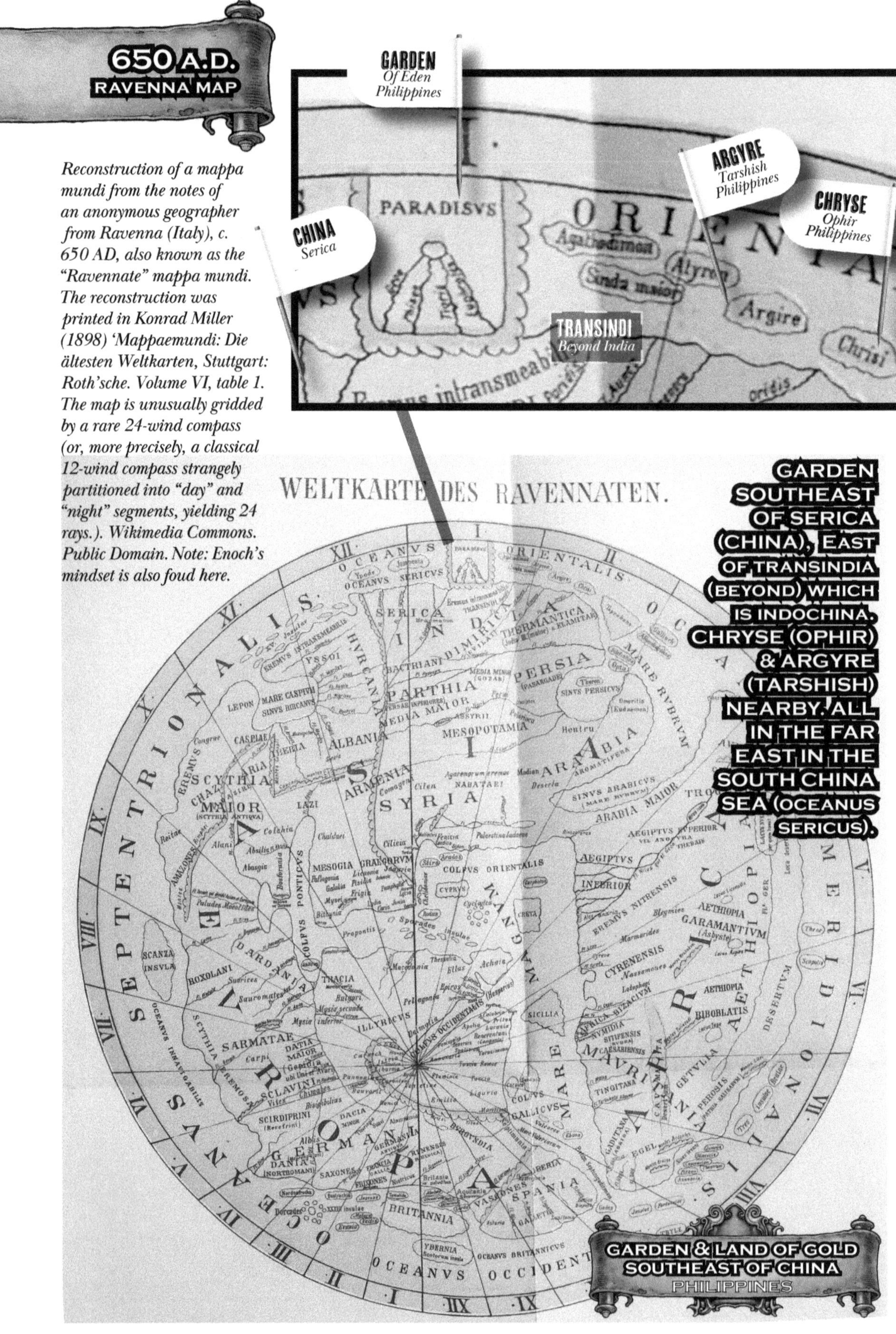

GARDEN OF EDEN ISLE BY SOUTH CHINA (SERES) WITH ARGYRE AND CHRYSE WITH THE RIVERS FROM EDEN SOUTHEAST OF CHINA. GANGES FLOWS INTO INDIAN OCEAN. THIS INDIA IS INDOCHINA BEYOND GANGES.

*East of the Garden of Eden, a text evokes India "**famous for its gems and elephants… where gold and silver abound**. The land, it is said, **produces two crops a year**. There are men of all colours, huge elephants and dragons, as well as monoceross, parrots, ebonywood, cinnamon… These are all native resources to the Philippines including elephants as their bones are found there as well as dinosaur or dragon bones. However, if in fact mythical creatures were intended, they aren't found anywhere else either. Translation by Bibliothèque nationale de France.*

THE WIND SHIFTS FROM SOUTH TO EAST DENOTING THE MALAY TIP.

750-800 A.D. Beatus Map from the Spanish monk Beatus of Liébana, produced in Saint-Sever Abbey, France. Inset enlargement from Konrad Miller's 1895 reconstruction. The map is faced eastwards, and not northwards, as usual in modern cartography. For this reason, it is said that the map is oriented. Wikimedia Commons. Public Domain. Hi resolution inset licensed thru Alamy.

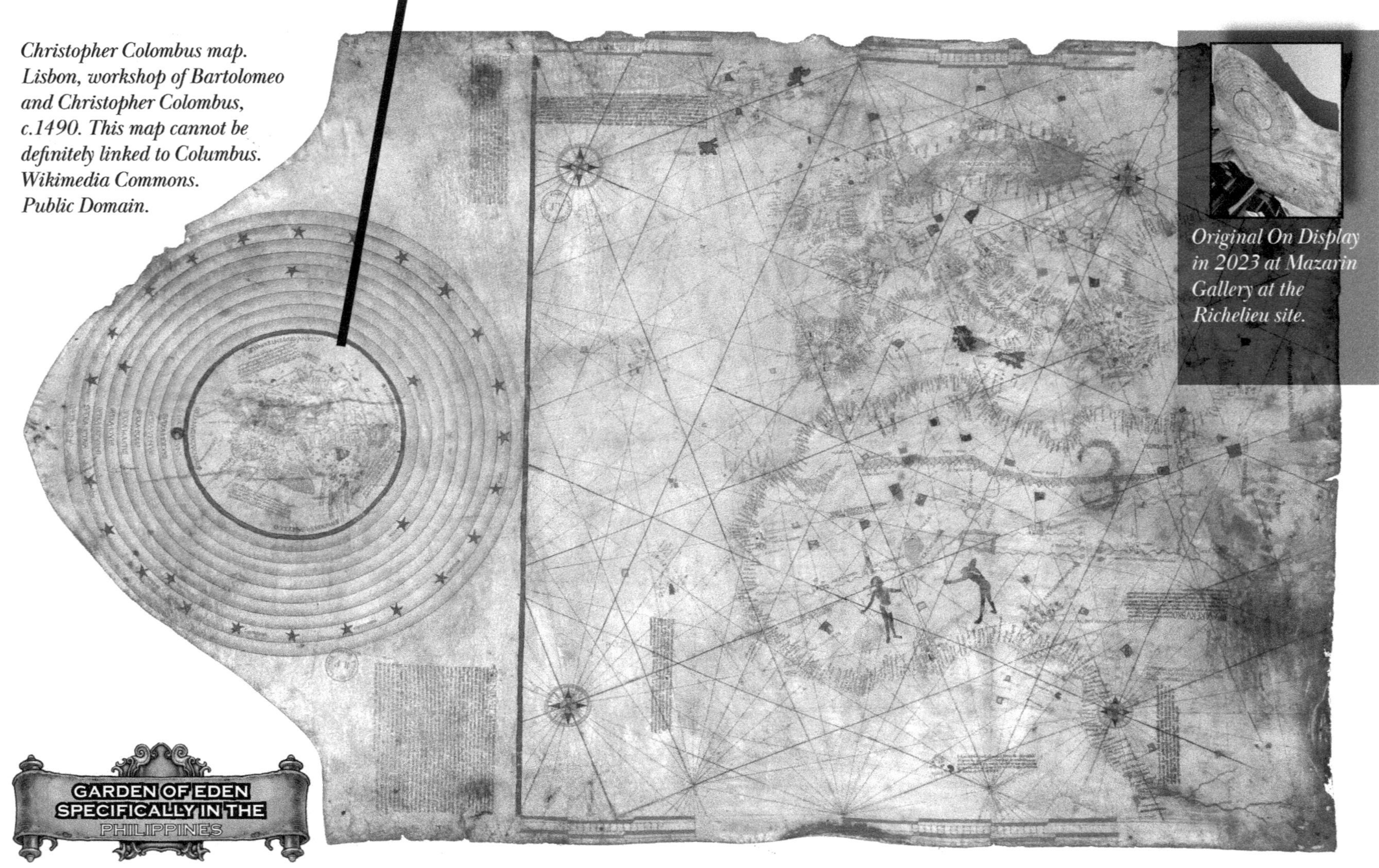

Christopher Colombus map. Lisbon, workshop of Bartolomeo and Christopher Colombus, c.1490. This map cannot be definitely linked to Columbus. Wikimedia Commons. Public Domain.

Original On Display in 2023 at Mazarin Gallery at the Richelieu site.

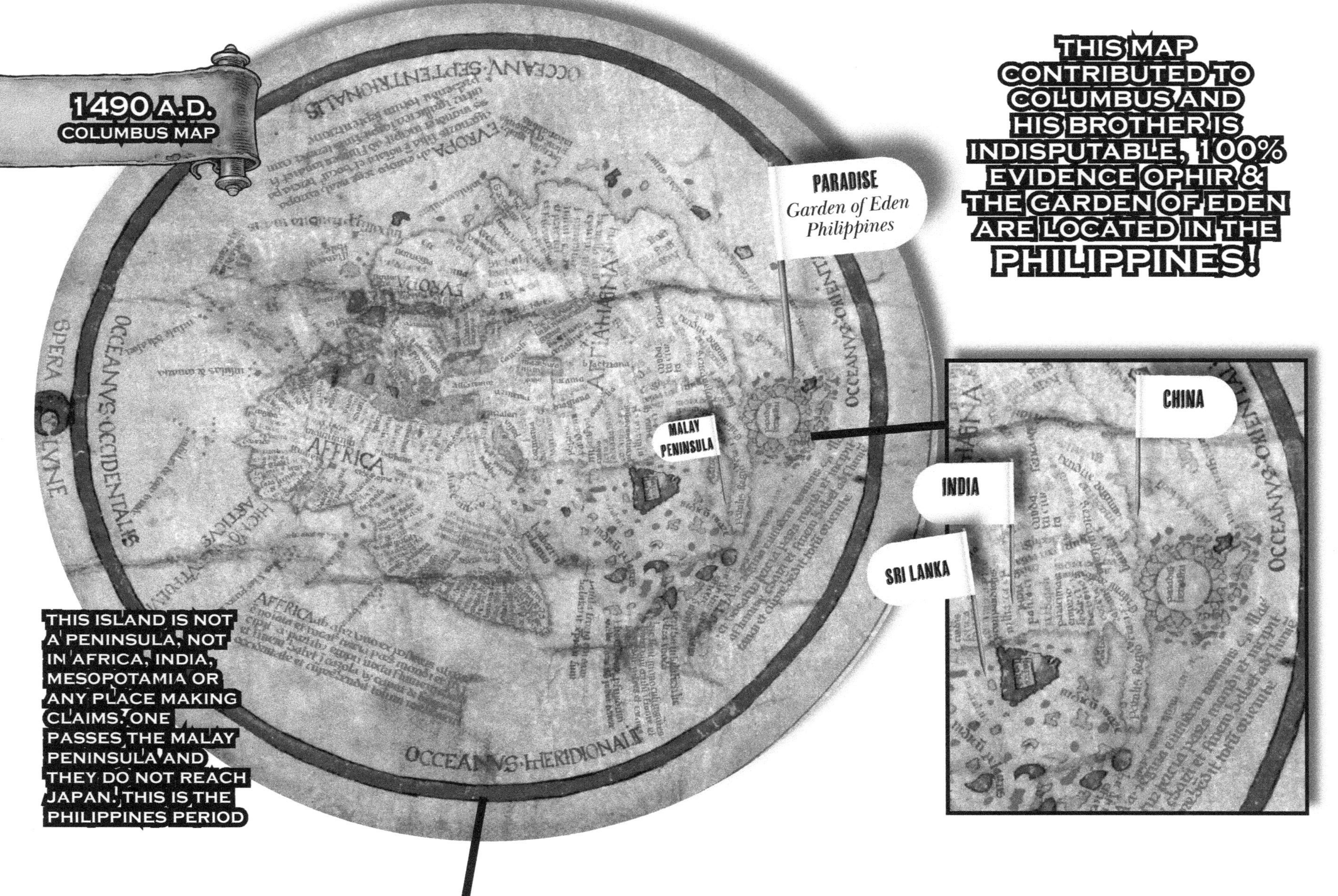

1490 A.D.
COLUMBUS MAP
THIS MAP CONTRIBUTED TO COLUMBUS AND HIS BROTHER IS INDISPUTABLE, 100% EVIDENCE OPHIR & THE GARDEN OF EDEN ARE LOCATED IN THE PHILIPPINES!
PARADISE
Garden of Eden
Philippines
THIS ISLAND IS NOT A PENINSULA, NOT IN AFRICA, INDIA, MESOPOTAMIA OR ANY PLACE MAKING CLAIMS. ONE PASSES THE MALAY PENINSULA AND THEY DO NOT REACH JAPAN. THIS IS THE PHILIPPINES PERIOD
MALAY PENINSULA
CHINA
INDIA
SRI LANKA
OCEANV SEPTENTRIONALIS
EVROPA
ASIA MAGNA
AFRICA
SPERA CLYNE
OCCEANVS OCCIDENTALIS
OCCEANVS HERIDIONALE
OCCEANVS ORIENTALIS

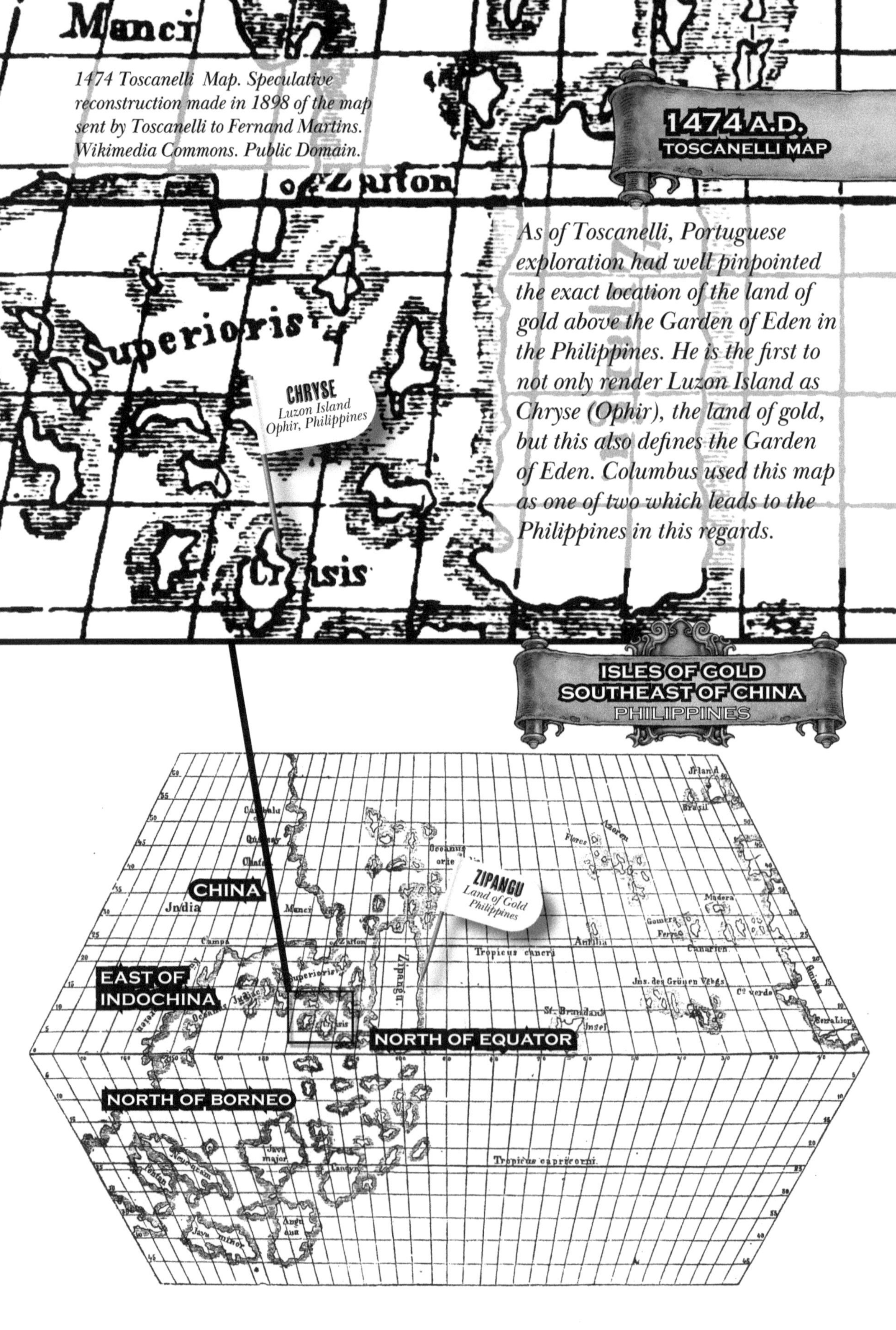

1474 Toscanelli Map. Speculative reconstruction made in 1898 of the map sent by Toscanelli to Fernand Martins. Wikimedia Commons. Public Domain.

As of Toscanelli, Portuguese exploration had well pinpointed the exact location of the land of gold above the Garden of Eden in the Philippines. He is the first to not only render Luzon Island as Chryse (Ophir), the land of gold, but this also defines the Garden of Eden. Columbus used this map as one of two which leads to the Philippines in this regards.

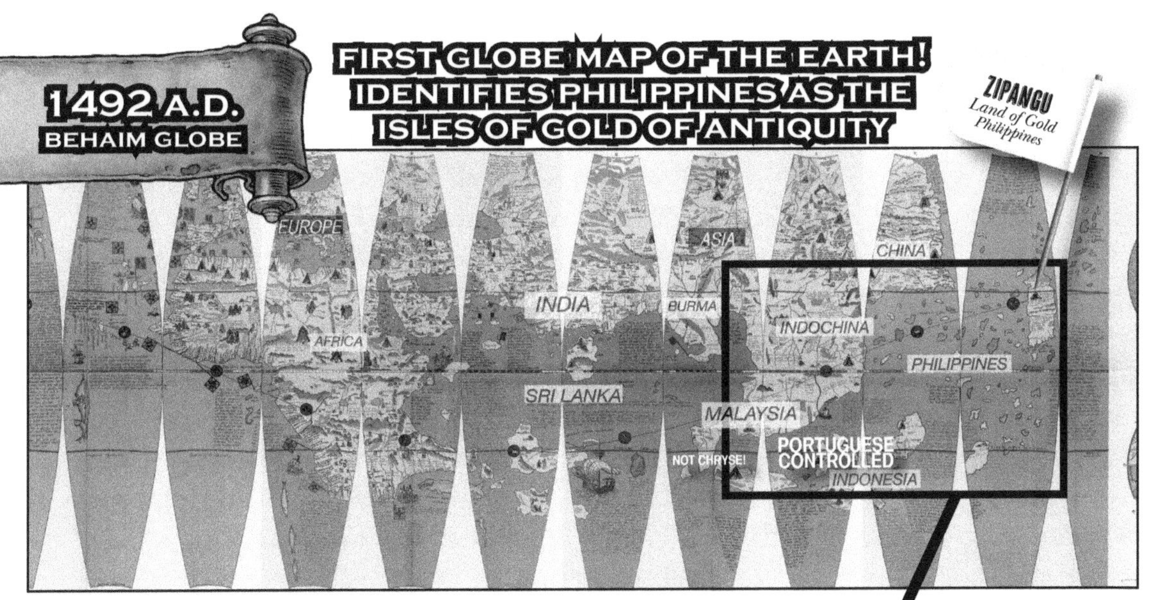

A modern facsimile of Martin Behaim's
1492 Erdapfel map. Behaim Globe (1492–
1493) Ernst Ravenstein: Martin Behaim.
His Life and his Globe. London 1908.
Wikimedia Commons. Public Domain.

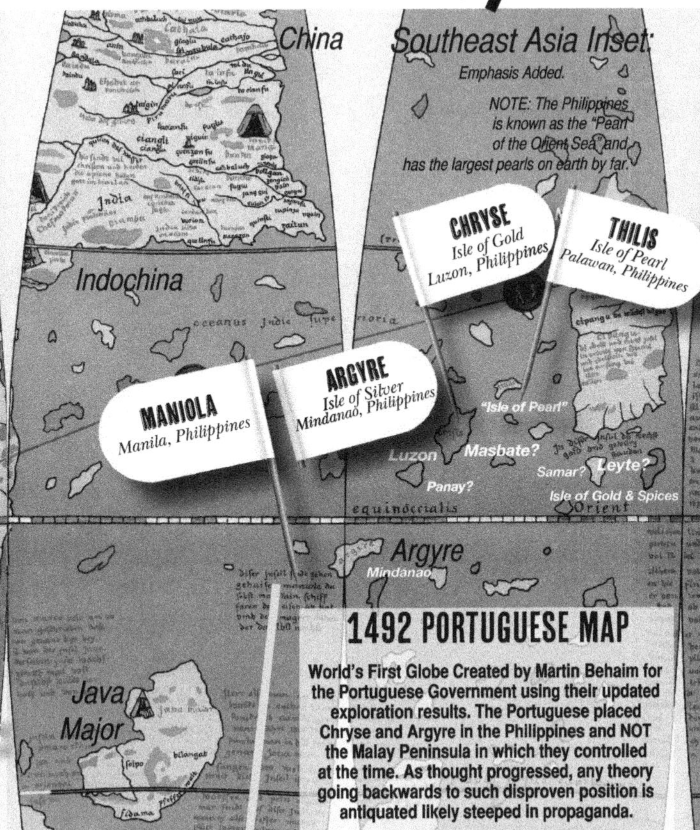

1492 PORTUGUESE MAP

World's First Globe Created by Martin Behaim for
the Portuguese Government using their updated
exploration results. The Portuguese placed
Chryse and Argyre in the Philippines and NOT
the Malay Peninsula in which they controlled
at the time. As thought progressed, any theory
going backwards to such disproven position is
antiquated likely steeped in propaganda.

This map also discusses the legendary Maniola in the text block right next to Argyre.
This is debate this writing will not enter but it sure seems very close to Manila in name.

until 1886.[1] The study we cite is not gold production, (which is meaningless), but instead the actual gold in the ground. Even though China is a major gold producer, at over 30 times the size of the Philippines, it still has less untapped gold in the ground than does the Philippines. That is no contest.

However, alluvial gold deposits define the ancient narrative without modern equipment. Massive deposits must exist in these isles of antiquity, which is why South Africa, (which is not isles and exists in Ham's territory) wrongly fails such a test quickly. Indeed, the Land of Gold is documented by Pomponius Mela *(43 A.D.)*[2] and Solinus *(300 A.D.)*[3] to possess gold and silver literally in its soil. This perfectly fits the Philippines, which has valid history from Pigafetta[3] in two accounts, where he witnessed a valley of gold on the ground, (not in the mountains), and the King of Butuan brought a large gold nugget to Magellan that he acquired by simply seeking in the ground.[4] The abundance is documented all over the Spanish writings in the 16th and 17th centuries. Local, oral legends in the Philippines also detail such.

Finally, this King of Butuan also boasted of his palace of gold, fitting the Marco Polo account of Zipangu, which has never been Japan.[4] The colonialists even renamed that country in fraud, as it still calls itself Nippon/Nihon. Those Isles of Gold must be Southeast of South China, and only the Philippines has the resources mentioned in this land, not Japan.[5] Even cannibal legends persist in Zipangu, and Japan has no such legends, while the Philippines has many, even chronicled by the Chinese.[5] That is another completely unacademic position easily obliterated with real examination.

The Queen of Sheba from the Philippines

Also, the nativity of the Queen of Sheba, who brought gold and other gifts to Solomon, is very well preserved in scripture. However, the entirety of modern scholarship generally holds that she originated in Ethiopia, as they forget there are two Shebas in Genesis 10. They ignore one and call that scholarship. We do not. This requires an unschooled view, or at least the wrong school, that has never inspected even the basics of her story. This royal came to Solomon after hearing

---

[1] *Department of Archeology, University of Cape Town Rondebosch 7701. By Duncan Miller, Nirdev Desai & Julia Lee-Thorp. South Africa Archeology Society Doodwin Series 8, 91-99, 2000. University of the Witwatersrand, Johannesburg. p. 1-2.* [2] *"Pomponius Mela, Chorographia Bk II, from Pomponius Mela's Description of the World." Translated by Frank E. Romer. University of Michigan Press. 1998. Sections 3.67-3.71.* [3] *Solinus, Polyhistor, 52.17 -ca. 300 CE.* [4] *"The First Voyage Round the World by Antonio Pigafetta." 1522, translated by Lord Stanley of Alderley. p. 40, 110, & 114. "Magellan's Voyage Around the World By Antonio Pigafetta" By James Alexander Robertson. Vol. 1. U.S. 1906. pp. 111, 117-119.* [5] *All maps in full color, high resolution in Garden of Eden Revealed: The Book of Maps. Schwab/Zamoranos. 2024. www.OphirInstitute.com.*

about his wisdom and the name of His Elohim in her own land of Ophir *(Genesis 10:1, 6)*. Her story is a continuation of Solomon's building a navy on the Red Sea *(9:26)*. They go to Ophir to fetch gold and resources *(9:28)*. AND then, the Queen of Sheba hears from whom *(10:1)*? She is visited by Solomon's navy in Ophir *(9:28)* as that is Sheba from Shem *(10:25-30)*, never Ham. She must be from Ophir's family, and Ophir is the key. There is only one Ophir in all of scripture *(10:25-30)*, and he is progeny of Shem, who migrated with his brothers (including Sheba), to the Philippines. Thus, Sheba, whose offspring later produced a royal Queen, is not the Sheba from Ham!

1 Kings 10:1 KJV
And when the queen of Sheba heard of the fame of Solomon concerning the name of the LORD, she came to prove him with hard questions.

This Queen was educated in the covenant, giving Biblically to the Temple, bringing the same resources from the same land that Adam offered in his first sacrifice, and that the Wise Men brought to the feet of Messiah *(1 Ki. 10:10)*. These are not coincidences. She offered this oblation of gold, frankincense, myrrh and jewels at the same time as Solomon's navy presented their acquisitions of the same resources as Sheba *(1 Ki. 10:10-11)*. This is because they went to Ophir, Sheba and Tarshish, which are all part of the same archipelago, as this Queen descended from Ophir's brother: Sheba.

After presenting her offerings, the Queen of Sheba left, with no affair and no child. Solomon was wise and holy at this time, as well as happily married to an Egyptian royal. Read Song of Solomon and this is obvious. No, the Queen of Sheba is not the black wife of Solomon there *(Song of Sol. 1:5-6)*. That is his Egyptian wife; there is another illiteracy attempted. Some confuse Solomon with her, claiming he said he was black and comely, when that was her writing. He was not having affairs at that time, when the Temple was being built, which again, is not scripture. There is no credible record that Solomon and the Queen of Sheba ever had an affair. It is a shameful occult legend that should never enter the halls of Bible scholarship. It comes from the occult *Kebra Nagast*[1] in Ethiopia and is picked up in the fraudulent Quran, as well as the newer Talmud. Neither are scripture in any sense, and both are riddled with occult inaccuracies.

When we find satanic narratives infiltrating Bible scholarship, we rebuke such positions as illiterate. A Bible scholar could not be more so when they infuse the occult and never bother to research it. It does not matter what PhD came before them, this is always stupid. It doesn't matter when a consensus to be dull is reached. A pile of idiocy is just more illiteracy. We must prove all things in this age.

In the case of the Queen of Sheba, the Ethiopian claim comes from the *Kebra Nagast*.[1] In this fraudulent legend, their Queen had the legs and hoof of a goat.

That's Ma-a-a-a-d! This reaches the definition of insane when modern scholars accept that Solomon not only entertained a Nephilim hybrid goat lady, but he also supposedly slept with her, and fathered a nice little hybrid goat child with her. Now you can see why we use such strong rebuke. King David fought to rid the land of Nephilim and now they supposedly enter into his bloodline through his son, at a time when Solomon is recorded in scripture as holy. This is not Biblical at all. The Bible says the Queen of Sheba came, questioned, gave and went.

Also, the Prophet Jeremiah really nails this geography in a passage where he associates the frankincense of Sheba with that of sugarcane. This is a massive problem for the legend from Ethiopia, from the wrong son of Noah and wrong territory. Ethiopia did not even grow sugarcane until it was introduced in the sixteenth century.[2] However, the Philippines has had native sugarcane since at least 1,000 years before King Solomon, according to the Republic of the Philippines Agricultural Department.[3]

Jeremiah 6:20 KJV
To what purpose cometh there to me incense (בונה: lᵉbôwnâh: frankincense) from Sheba, and the sweet cane from a far country? your burnt offerings are not acceptable, nor your sacrifices sweet unto me.

Yes, the Philippines has incense from the Pili tree labeled *"poor man's frankincense."*[3] Manila elemi comes from the Pili tree and Egyptian archaeology proves that the frankincense and myrrh of ancient Egypt in Bible times tests scientifically as elemi.[4] Neither are what we call frankincense nor myrrh in modern times, specifically. Either could work, but the terms are more inclusive than claimed by Rabbis who do not represent the Bible paradigm. Messiah called that "leaven."

However, no guessing is necessary on this topic. Sheba is mapped in the Philippines as Sheba/Saba/Seba Island; rendered as Saba or Seba Dibae *(island in sanskrit and "Is it?" in Tagalog)*. We find this on maps for more than 6 centuries, from at least 1100 to 1752 *[pp. 26-29]*. *The God Culture* team has overwhelmingly proven the Ancient Land of Gold, known as Ophir, Sheba and Tarshish and the Garden of Eden region in the modern Philippines. Though we did not remake this position

---

[1] *"The Queen Of Sheba." By Michael Wood. BBC News. Last updated 2011-02-17.* [2] *"Research Article: Sugarcane Landraces of Ethiopia: Germplasm Collection and Analysis of Regional Diversity and Distribution." Hindawi Advances In Agriculture, Aug. 14, 2018. Vol. 2018, Article ID 7920724, 18 pages.* [3] *Sugar Regulatory Administration. Republic of the Philippines. Department of Agriculture. Retrieved Dec. 17, 2019.* [4] *a. "Poor Man's Frankincense" Manila Elemi. "Young Living sees growing demand for essential oils." By Zsarlene B. Chua. Business World. Apr. 22, 2019. b. "Canarium luzonicum. Manila Elemi." Stuart Xchange. Godofredo U. Stuart Jr., M.D. Updated June 2017. c. "Perfumery Material: Elemi." By Elena Vosnaki. Perfume Shrine. Dec. 2012.*

here, except in brief, it will serve to interpret these famed locations from which the Wise Men, described in the *Book of Matthew* originated. This geography has always been in scripture and never a true mystery to the ancient record. It is the new, strange doctrine which lost it. The *Gospel of Matthew* is not even the first account of these Wise Men who were prophesied in the Psalms of David as Kings, even documented in songs about the topic, and all along the Vatican had possessed a document which affirms this research, fully. All of the evidence will be presented together here in this writing.

The last topic for consideration is the Land of the Garden of Eden, also found in the Philippines, as demonstrated here in the Introduction, through maps, as well. Indeed, we know this is a lightning rod for some who demand a political view called Zionism, that does not originate in any scripture. Replacing Biblically-established doctrine with a new, political platform undermines their credibility and wreaks of propaganda. Israel, which was defiled for thousands of years before Abraham, was somehow a Holy Land? Can they read at all? No pastor should be a Zionist when they are told to believe the Rabbis over what the Bible clearly says. A Filipino pastor who does such, is simply another colonial propagandist, leading their people back into slavery. Ancient Israel was the origin of the "Watcher/Fallen Angel Oath," and their offspring, the Nephilim, from the days of Jared, the 5th generation from Adam to the Flood. Shortly after the Deluge, there were again giants defiling the land, even in the days of Abraham and beyond. That is what scripture says. If a Rabbi disagrees with scripture, (about 15% of Judaism does not agree with Zionism either), then, that is no Bible scholar, and not one who deserves attention.

Indeed, the first question that arises at this point is: What about the Rivers from Eden? Aren't they in Mesopotamia? That is the Occult Creation Myth, not the Bible which places the Garden in the Far East. Isn't one of these Rivers the Tigris? Well, not even remotely, as that is a replacement word, not a translation, and it is fraud. The Hebrew word is Hiddekel, and that river is East of Assyria. What Bible scholar does not know that the Tigris is the Western boundary of Ancient Assyria in Bible times, and thus, cannot be East of Assyria, defining the West. That is illiterate. All 5... Oops!... Scholars cannot read, claiming there are four, as they missed the largest source river, which is still Nahar *(נהר)*, (not from snow caps, a geyser, a spring, or a lake). When a scholar cannot follow simple words in definition, they are useless on such a topic. For those thinking the Gihon Springs could be the Gihon River, they must apply simple logic that Zionists do not bother with. They must understand what a river is and what a spring is as confusing those is very obtuse especially when the Gihon River surrounds the whole land of Ethiopia. When they require you to move Ethiopia into Israel, run away. We cover this in both books and our *Rivers from Eden Series.*

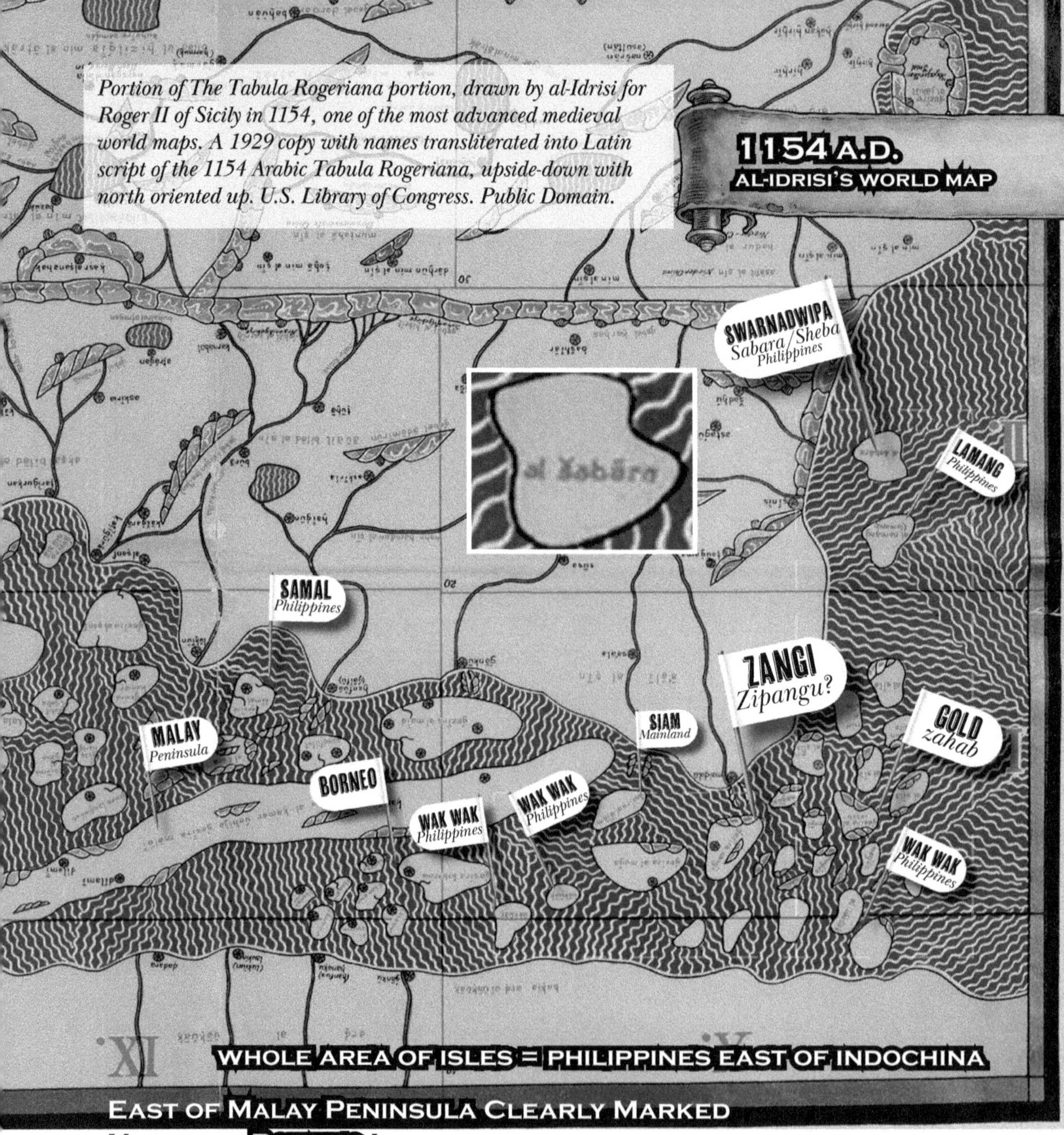

EAST OF MALAY PENINSULA CLEARLY MARKED
NORTH OF BORNEO IDENTIFIED

PHILIPPINE ISLES LABELED ZANGI (ZIPANGU), 3 AS WAK WAK MUSLIM LAND OF GOLD, ZAHAB AS GOLD ISLE IN ARABIC/HEBREW, WITH SAMAL TOO FAR SOUTH, AND LAMANG PHILIPPINES.

SABARA, THE INDIAN SWARNADWIPA IS LIKELY THE SAME AS SHEBABIBAE OR SHEBA, THAT COULD ALSO BE THE ORIGIN OF THE CHINESE ISLE OF GOLD NAMED SHEBO/SHEPO THE MUSLIMS CALL ZABAG. NORTH CHINA IS LABELED JUST ABOVE THE MOUNTAIN RANGE AT THE TOP AS SIN OR SINA LABELED MULTIPLE TIMES.

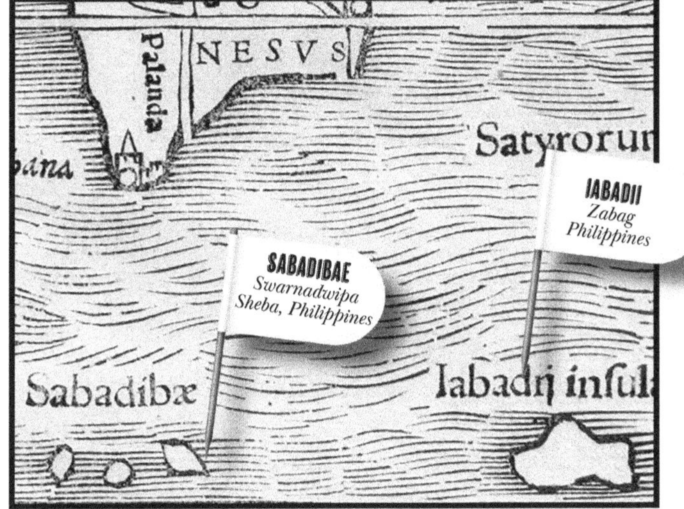

Sabadibae. Portion of 1545 Tabula Asiae XI. Ptolemy, 2nd cent. Geographia universalis.Heinrich Petri. Wikimedia Commons. Public Domain.

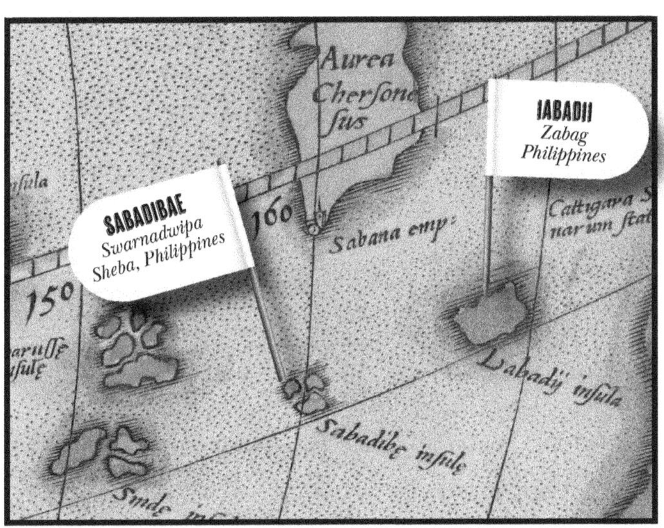

Sabadibae. Portion of Universalis Tabul Iuxta Ptolemaeum. 1578 Ptolemy, 2nd cent. Tabulae geographicae. Coloniae Agrippinae typis Godefridi Kempensis, 1578. Wikimedia Commons. Public Domain.

Portion of Typus Orbis Terrarum Ad Imitationem Universalis Gerhardi Mercatoris. Circa 1600. Matthias Quad / Johann Bussemachaer. Wikimedia Commons. Public Domain.

68

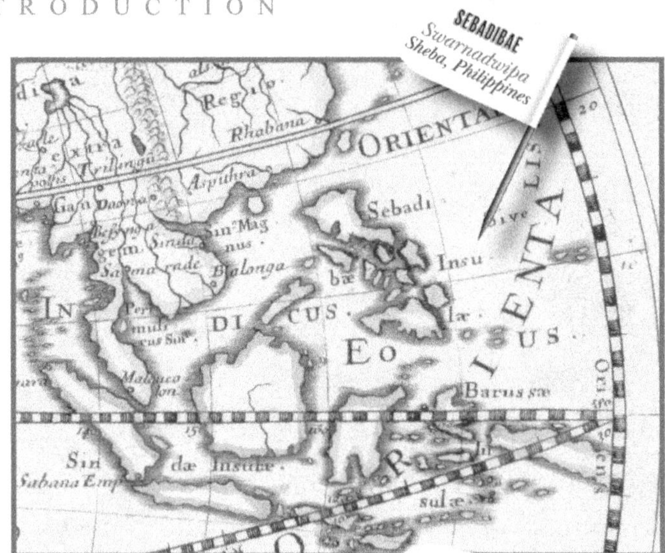

Portion of 1657 Orbis vetus et orbis veteris utraque continens, terrarumq[ue] tractus arcticus et antarticus ex Platone, Theopompo sive Aeliano, Manilio &tc. U.S. Library of Congress. Public Domain.

69

Nicolas Sanson. Portion of "Mappe-Monde, ou Carte Generale Du Monde." Paris: N. Sanson, 1651. Published in 1695. 14 x 21. Engraving. Original hand color. Hemispheres of Earth. Wikimedia Commons. Public Domain.

70

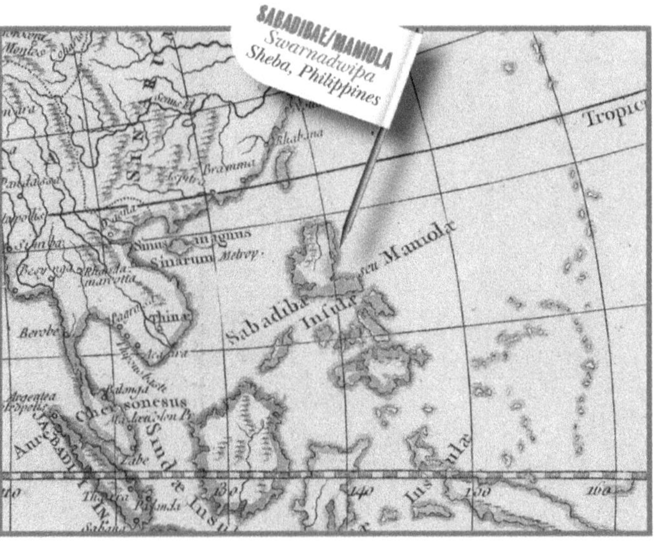

Robert De Vaugondy, Didier, Cartographer. Portion of Map of the Old World. Paris: Didier Robert de Vaugondy and Antoine Boudet, 1752. U.S. Library of Congress. Public Domain.

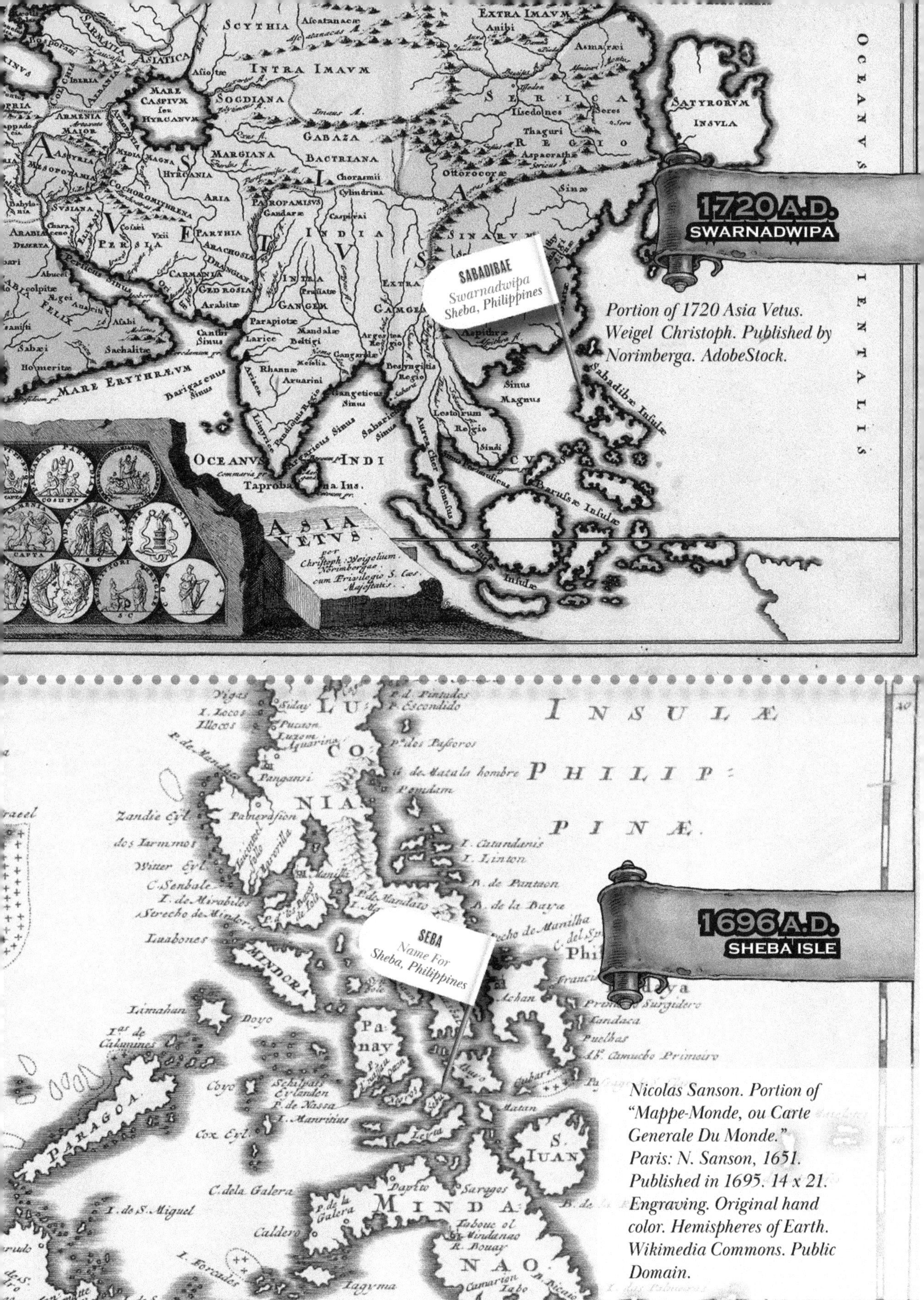

Portion of 1720 Asia Vetus. Weigel Christoph. Published by Norimberga. AdobeStock.

Nicolas Sanson. Portion of "Mappe-Monde, ou Carte Generale Du Monde." Paris: N. Sanson, 1651. Published in 1695. 14 x 21. Engraving. Original hand color. Hemispheres of Earth. Wikimedia Commons. Public Domain.

Detail from a Neapolitan presepe, currently on display in Rome.
By Howard Hudson (2006),
Wikimedia Commons. Public Domain.

Chapter 1: The Magi According to Matthew

The account of the Magi, as described in the *Gospel of Matthew*, has been assessed repeatedly by scholars in the past few centuries. The overall conclusion is that Matthew's account leaves huge gaps of time within the story. As researchers of truth, we agree with this particular assessment, as you will see evidence of throughout this chapter. However, Matthew's narrative describing the traveling Wise Men is not alone, even in modern Bible Canon. It is pitiful that some scholars pretend to speak as experts on a topic they obviously have not conducted in-depth research on. In this chapter, we will first review the story, and then build a foundation on what scripture actually says, identifying what elements are already deviating from the truth in modern scholarship, and leading to erroneous conclusions.

Matthew 2:1-2 KJV
*Now when Jesus was born in Bethlehem of Judaea in the days of Herod the king, behold, there came wise men from the east to Jerusalem, Saying, Where is he that is born **King of the Jews?** for we have seen his star in the east, and are come to **worship him**.*

We will cover the timing of Herod's reign and death in a later chapter. However, we know Herod had to be alive for this account. As far as *Jews*, there is no such people, nor word ever rendered in either Hebrew or Greek Bibles. The letter "J" cannot even be considered in ancient Hebrew, Greek, Aramaic, Latin, Old French, Old German, nor Old English until the 1500s or so. No Bible should ever include this word, especially since the word is Yahudi, in both Hebrew and Greek, consistently. This is a literal identification of Yah's people, which no one rational or logical would ever reduce to the word "Jew." The King of the Yahudim is the King of Yah's People, which was never solely Israel. In the Exodus, Moses well declares one law for the native-born Israelite from Jacob, as well as the stranger who dwelled among them *(Ex. 12:49; Num. 15:16)*. It is truly fiction to set up a race as superior in any sense. That is called racism in any other context. The Jewish master race principle is one of the synagogue of satan, who say they are Yahudim and are not but do lie *(Rev. 2:9, 3:9)*.

Greek: Ἰουδαίων: *Yahudi, Yahudiahs plural.*
Hebrew: יהודי *or* ביהודי: *Yahudi, Yahudim plural. Jer. 34:9 ; Zec. 8:23.*

Notice, the Magi came to worship the Messiah. The Magoi of Babylon and Persia, who were not even prominent in that era anymore, would have desired to kill him and certainly were not known as worshippers of the Bible. Those fabricating a story of their conversion in the days of Daniel fail to read the New Testament, which still rebukes those Magoi as sorcerers *(Acts 13:6, 8)*. We all know how they attacked Daniel. How much more for the Messiah? Worse, who was the dunderhead who forgot that they included Saudi Arabia and India as part of their list, when these nations have no evidence of a Magoi cult? It is the same with the bones the Catholic Church claims to have in fraud, yet, all from Persia, forgetting their own stupidity requires three different nations. They cannot even meet their own criteria.

The Magi were a group of dedicated worshippers on a level that, you will see, is that of covenant. They knew the Bible and kept this tradition of worship, regarding the coming Star of the Messiah, for many centuries. We will also break down what this Star of Messiah was in an upcoming chapter, and revelation will abound.

Matthew 2:3-6 KJV
*When Herod the king had heard these things, he was troubled, and all Jerusalem with him. And when he had **gathered all the chief priests and scribes** of the people together, he demanded of them **where Christ should be born**. And they said unto him, In **Bethlehem** of Judaea: for thus it is written by the prophet, And thou Bethlehem, in the land of Juda, art not the least among the princes of Juda: for out of thee shall come a Governor, that shall rule my people Israel.*

Herod was threatened by a true King indeed. Notice, he gathered ALL the chief priests and scribes. He was not aware of any Star that appeared in his dominion. If there were a "Star of Bethlehem" (which is never mentioned even once in any scripture), he and his astronomers/astrologers would have seen it. He knew nothing, because the Star did not appear in Israel until after the Wise Men came. It appeared only in the Far East, initially. At this time, after the Hasmonean Assault and Dynasty period, these were Pharisees, etc. from the Sanhedrin, from what Jesus *(Yahusha)* defined as the Synagogue of Satan *(Rev. 2:9, 3:9)*. They were not actual Levites, but replacements, according to the Dead Sea Scrolls. They were not legitimate Temple Priests, and they were not on the list for those to be informed by Yahuah, obviously. They did not see a Star, and were not entitled to see it. They did, however, know where Messiah would be born in Bethlehem. They did not care, as there is no offer in the narrative for them to accompany the Magi. When Messiah launched His ministry, He did not do so at the Jerusalem Temple they defiled. Instead, they attempted to murder Him and ultimately demanded His execution, declaring the Son of Yahuah sinful. He was not. They were and still are to this day.

Matthew 2:7-8 KJV
*Then Herod, when he had **privily called the wise men**, enquired of them diligently **what time the star appeared**. And he sent them to Bethlehem, and said, Go and search diligently for the young child; and when ye have found him, **bring me word again**, that **I may come and worship him also**.*

Obviously, Herod had no intention of worshipping what he anticipated as a rival. The Wise Men will understand this later. He wanted to know exactly what time of year the Star appeared, and how long ago. We know, from reading scripture, that he moved against children of that age and below just to make sure he killed this King. He'll fail, but in verse 16, this is the timing he will use to determine he needed to murder all children in that area that were two years of age and younger. The Wise Men will not return.

Matthew 2:9-11 KJV
*When they had heard the king, they departed; and, lo, **the star, which they saw in the east, went before them**, till it came and **stood over where the young child was**. When they saw the star, they rejoiced with exceeding great joy. And when they were come into the house, they saw the young child with Mary his mother, and **fell down, and worshipped him**: and when they had **opened their treasures, they presented unto him gifts; gold, and frankincense, and myrrh.***

The Star was not a constellation or planetary alignment, as it could move from Jerusalem to Bethlehem. Stellarium software cannot find this Star. Its full route was from the Philippines, where it first appeared, into the Indian Ocean where the Magi followed it in their ship, for almost 2 years. When one learns, they originated in the Far East, this makes sense. They headed around Africa, into the Mediterranean, and finally arrived in Israel. The Star seemed to disappear at that point and reappear in the narrative (which will be affirmed). This is why they rejoiced, because they had not seen the Star since they arrived, and the journey would then continue. They would not have gone to Herod for directions if the Star had shown at that time. They would not have needed his help.

Led to Bethlehem, they met the Son of Yahuah they long awaited to worship. They fell down and presented their gifts from the treasury they curated since the days of Adam. Yes, Magi precede even the Flood in practice, and confusing them with sorcerers is lame. We will get to that. This account is far more beautiful, holy and even historic than any scholar has ever realized.

Unfortunately, there are nativities on display with Wise Men present. That is illiterate. This was two years later. Messiah was a toddler, not a newborn. Herod killed those based on the timing of when the Magi saw the Star, which they informed him was two years earlier. This Greek word is not specific to age. Though it could be a newborn, (as eight-day-old John the Baptist is described in John 1:52), it is routinely used to describe a young child, even up to at least 12 years of age (such as in Mark 5:39-42, referring to Jairus' daughter). However, such specificity is not needed in the word, as Matthew is clear; the Wise Men told Herod the Messiah was 2 years old *(v. 16)*. This word and translation use is fine.

παιδίον: paidíon, pahee-dee'-on; neuter diminutive of G3816; a childling (of either sex), i.e. (properly), an infant, or (by extension) a half-grown boy or girl; figuratively, an immature Christian:— (little, young) child, damsel (G3813).
child (25x), little child (12x), young child (10x), damsel (4x).

Matthew 2:12-13 KJV
*And being warned of God in a dream that they should **not return to Herod**, they departed into their*

own country another way. And when they were departed, behold, the angel of the Lord appeareth to Joseph in a dream, saying, Arise, and take the young child and his mother, and flee into Egypt, and be thou there until I bring thee word: for Herod will seek the young child to destroy him.

Is this the end of their story? No. We will get to that. This was their ministry over centuries time. They were the keepers of the secret of the Star of the Messiah, which is His light, not an angel, and not something routinely found in the sky. They were to be informed, and few were. These Magi were truly righteous priests in their own right. They brought the wealth that Jesus *(Yahusha)* would need to start His ministry. The angel warned them not to return to Herod, so they left and returned to their homeland. Matthew has no need to continue the narrative and would not be privy to such information beyond.

Also, let us clear up another inept criticism from scholars who cannot seem to read. Joseph was then warned in a dream, and fled to Egypt, away from Herod's coming massacre. Luke never says that did not happen. He just picks up later in the story when they return to Nazareth, which agrees with Matthew. There is no conflict nor disagreement in the two accounts. That is scoffing, not scholarship. He also does not provide the account of the Wise Men, and may not have even known it (which is not a requirement anyone should place on him). This kind of gnat straining in a false paradigm destroys the credibility of scholars who attempt such, as they also try to attack the Bible. If they only researched it out a little and used some common sense, they would never write such nonsense.

Matthew 2:16-18 KJV

*Then Herod, when he saw that he was **mocked of the wise men**, was exceeding wroth, and sent forth, and **slew all the children** that were in **Bethlehem**, and in all the coasts thereof, from two years old and under, according to the time which he had diligently enquired of the wise men. Then was fulfilled that which was spoken by Jeremy the prophet, saying, In Rama was there a voice heard, lamentation, and weeping, and great mourning, Rachel weeping for her children, and would not be comforted, because they are not.*

Somehow, tradition has completely ignored this passage in timing. The Magi were not there for the birth of Jesus *(Yahusha)*. Herod recognized the child had already been born and he killed two-year-old children and under. This age specifically represents the time which the Magi had said they saw the Star, and He was born, which was two years earlier. We are not given their answer to Herod's inquiry earlier, but we are here, as that is his basis for the two years and under. It was *"according to the time which he had diligently enquired of the wise men."* Matthew is very clear; this period when they saw the Star was 2 years earlier. Any nativity scene that includes these Wise Kings, is oblivious to scripture. They were not there.

This begs the question, why did it take them so long to arrive in Bethlehem? It would not make any sense for those supposed sorcerers in Persia, Arabia and India to even be notified of our Savior's birth. Persia's capital in the first century B.C. was Persepolis, Iran about 2,100 km. away from Jerusalem. The best way for such a travel would likely have been the camel, though the narrative does not have camels specifically. That is because the Magi took ships instead. Estimates of camel speeds are typically between 40-48 km. per day. Even the slower estimate would have them arrive in about 53 days (7.5 weeks). Does 53 days equal two years now? Scholars really should consider a little test before writing anything. This fails every possible test for accuracy. For the scholar who fabricated the fictitious theory that the Magi were delayed, yet provides no credible historic source for such a stupid claim, grow up and act like an adult.

Imagine, the Magoi of Persia heard of the birth of the Son of Yahuah and Savior of the world, but decided to wait almost 2 years to arrive on an 8-week journey. They would seem to not be very motivated to embark upon such a journey, and already fail the test of one deserving to be notified. This is ridiculously awry. The prospect from Saudi Arabia (whose title of 'Magoi' is not even appropriate), was much closer to Israel, and therefore fails each authenticity test even more so.

India is about twice the distance from Israel as Persia, and it still fails the location-based tests. It is about 4,500 km. to Jerusalem from there. Travel time would take about 180 days, based on our research, or just under 6 months. That is not two years. Go ahead and find a reason to double the estimate, and it still fails on all accounts. We know for certain the Magi traveled no less than a year, according to the **Revelation of the Magi** account, which we will cover. The *Gospel of Matthew* account holds the record of time, and his account says it was 2 years. Hopefully, we will all believe Matthew over a modern scholar.

If planning a trip from the Philippines, this would have to occur by boat. If the Kings, sons of Kings, and Wise Men met in the Visayas region; perhaps in Cebu, or nearby, they would have a much longer travel, justifying the two years. The Red Sea Port, at Ezion-Geber, was not available to Israel in that age. One would have to circumnavigate Africa, which the Greeks had already executed for more than 800 years at that point. There was no Suez Canal option then. In the first century B.C., a ship hugging the coasts (as was their custom in practice), would travel around three to four knots. At four knots, even with no breaks, one would arrive over 8,000 nautical miles away in Capetown, South Africa in about 100 days (according to Ports.com). As they were relying on wind and rowing in that age, they would need breaks in between, and typically they would not sail at night.

South Africa to Tanger, Morocco would be another 5,700 nautical miles. Let's add another 58 days to equal 158 days, so far. Finally, the last leg of the journey from Morocco to Tel Aviv, Israel would be another 2,300 nautical miles, or about 23 days at sea. The grand total at sea, without breaks, would be somewhere around 181 days just in sea travel alone. One would need to at least double that, based on the ancient methods of not sailing at night, which would essentially be a year at sea.

One would add even more time if storms were encountered, and ships dock at coastline harbors to avoid damage to the vessel. Along with stops to trade for supplies, repairs, etc. this would likely add 6 more months. Thus, travel time could be around a year and 4 months to arrive on the coast of Israel. Then, they needed to travel to Jerusalem, (about 66 miles away), where they stayed, awaiting instructions and directions. They went to Herod during that time.

Revelation of the Magi times them arriving in Jerusalem about two months before the birthday of Jesus *(Yahusha)*. We will cover that. Thus, total travel time was a journey of one year and ten months from the Philippines to Jerusalem. They waited there, and then they headed to Bethlehem, when the Star reappeared, a journey of only around ten miles or so. Of course, such a journey would also require planning before departure, which we did not account for in this rough math. The point is, the travel from the Philippines coalesces with the account from the *Book of Matthew*. All other times and locations fail miserably.

This is not cryptic. Reason tells us these worshippers of Yahuah must have a connection to Israel and its religion, and relationship to Yahuah, yet they were located in the Far East. That Biblical land is widely known as Ophir, Sheba, and Tarshish as King David defined as well as the Garden of Eden, in the Philippines. It may actually be the only place on Earth who truly allied with the original Tribes of Israel. Solomon went there to retrieve gold for the Temple. The Queen of Sheba came from that same region in the Philippines, offering the same gifts as Solomon's navy at the same time. Miraculously, these are the same offerings brought by the Three Kings in the *Gospel of Matthew*. That is no coincidence. In fact, these items are mentioned in Adam's first sacrifice, upon exile from the Garden, to this same land of Havilah/Elda, which would become known as Ophir, Sheba and Tarshish, Adam offered gold, frankincense, and myrrh. He is also the origin of the Magi practice as he was first to set aside these resources for the Messiah.

This Queen's story is bookended by the journey to Ophir to fetch gold, and the offering of these gifts by Hiram, Solomon's admiral, the same time with the Queen of Sheba. That is not India, nor Persia, nor Arabia. That is why the Magi did not show up at the birth, but two years later.

Jeremiah 31:15 is also invoked by the *Book of Matthew* in this story as prophesying of this event when Herod murdered so many children. When the passage quotes such a verse with attribution to the prophet, it is not logical to claim the account is not found anywhere else in scripture, when Matthew says it was. However, King David is completely accurate about the Wise Men in his geography; that is indisputable. We will cover that next.

Unfortunately, it is not just the Catholic Church who has completely corrupted the Christmas narrative. John Calvin is guilty of the same in ignorance. He chose a narrative of complete illiteracy regarding the Magi. In his gross ignorance, Calvin accuses the Catholic Church of such on the topic, but he, too, follows their fictitious narrative. This is a puppet show with a contrived debate over nothing in which both sides are full of error. They were Kings, indeed, according to King David, as well as *Revelation of the Magi*.

"But the most ridiculous contrivance of the Papists on this subject is, that those men were kings... Beyond all doubt, they have been stupefied by a righteous judgment of God, that all might laugh at [their] gross ignorance." –John Calvin[1]

Finally, where and when did this Catholic account of Melchior, Caspar, and Balthazar originate? Even Wikipedia credits two eighth-century writings, both from an original sixth century manuscript. This is more than a century after the definitive, documented origin of *Revelation of the Magi* we will cover. The Catholic Church knew the Persian connection was fiction, and the church leadership is still aware of their fabrications to this day.

These names first appear in an eighth century religious chronicle, Excerpta Latina Barbari, which is a Latin translation of a lost Greek manuscript probably composed in Alexandria roughly two centuries earlier. Another eighth century text, Collectanea et Flores, which was likewise a Latin translation from an original Greek account, continues the tradition of three kings and their names and gives additional details.[2]

These same intellectual children attempt etymologies from the *Acts of Thomas*, noting an Indian king, who lived long after the Wise Men were likely dead, and that king did not embrace Thomas in the Gnostic account. If he were a Magi or descended from one, he would have known whom Thomas was and embraced him. Also, how can they not even read his name to see it doesn't match? He was the first king of his name, and not even in power at the time of the Magi.

It has nothing to do with the visit of the Magi a century before. In fact, the name does not even connect. Scholars claim Gondophares I is Caspar, but that is ridiculous. He is also not Gudaphar, which is Hebrew, and includes the name Ophir. Duh! They were looking in the wrong country because they lost the home of the Magi, the Land of Gold, and the Garden of Eden. When these scholars of the Vatican, as well as Protestants, have no foundation, they have nothing to share that is credible. It is as if they wish to drive a car with no road and no tires. They lead nowhere. However, the ancient Wise Men lead us to the very land of prophecy.

---

[1] *Calvin, John. Calvin's Commentaries, Vol. 31: Matthew, Mark and Luke, Part I, tr. by John King. Retrieved 2010-05-15. Quote from Commentary on Matthew 2:1–6.* [2] *"Biblical Magi." Wikipedia. Retrieved Oct. 2025. Credibly citing: a. Excerpta Latina Barbari, page 51B: "At that time in the reign of Augustus, on 1st January the Magi brought him gifts and worshipped him. The names of the Magi were Bithisarea, Melichior and Gathaspa." b. Hugo Kehrer (1908), Die Heiligen Drei Könige in Literatur und Kunst (reprinted in 1976). Vol. I, p. 66. Online version. c. Collectanea et Flores in Patrologia Latina. XCIV, page 541(D) Online version.*

Propaganda Map Fails!

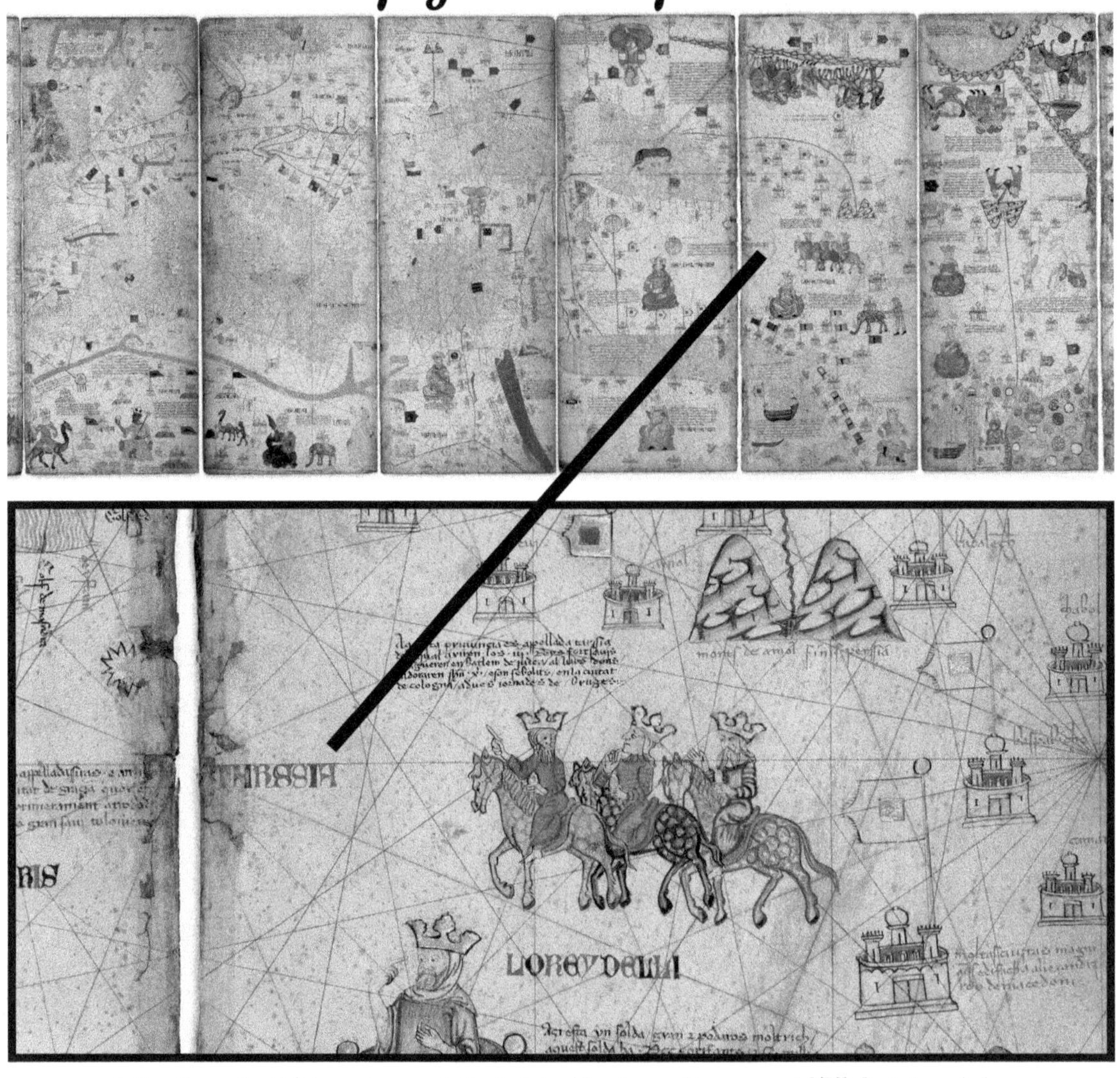

Atlas from the 14th century attributed to Abraham Cresques. 1375 Catalan Atlas.
Wikimedia Commons. Public Domain.

This is a Jewish propaganda map that places Tarshish in Persia with the three kings coming from there. Why? Psalm 72 defines the kings of Tarshish, the isles (Ophir), and Sheba bringing offerings to the Messiah. So why not just change maps and history to fit an illiterate theory with no basis? Solomon built a navy to go to Central Asia? Really? In the Talmud, Jews are encouraged to deceive the goyim in such ways, and this is clear propaganda of the most inept kind. The problem is this is illiterate as there is not even a claim that Persia is Tarshish for obvious reasons. Tarshish is an island (Is. 23:6, 60:9; Ps. 72:10). Oops! One would think a cartographer would know Central Asia is not an island, nor is Tartessus, Spain. Tarshish has resources native to the Philippines and Southeast Asia, not found in Persia, nor in the even worse guess; in Spain. Tarshish is mapped over thousands of years in the Philippines and never credibly in Persia, nor Spain. When the king of Spain hired explorers to go to Tarshish in the Far East, how is it scholarly to claim Spain or Persia was Tarshish?

Chapter 2: David's Prophecy of the Magi: Geography Few Scholars Even Know

We Three Kings of Orient Are By John H. Hopkins, Jr. (1857) [1]
We three kings of Orient are;
bearing gifts we traverse afar,
field and fountain, moor and mountain,
following yonder star.

Refrain:
O star of wonder, star of light,
star with royal beauty bright,
westward leading, still proceeding,
guide us to thy perfect light.
– United Methodist Hymnal, 1989

What did John Hopkins mean when he wrote the Magi originated in the Orient in *We Three Kings of Orient Are?* He was not just a songwriter, but a theologian known as an ecclesiologist in the 19th century. He would have been purposeful in such usage, and he was. Where did he get this knowledge from? From "scriptural references" (at Hymnary.org), Hopkins used Psalm 72:10 as the basis for this theology. [1] We will show you the Bible has always identified this region very well. Why had something that had never been an enigma in scripture to the ancients appear so vague and reinterpreted in Bible scholarship, when there is a direct reference that never led to Persia, Arabia, nor India as the origin of the Magi? That is a fabricated fiction by the Catholic Church in the 6th century.

Even the famous Christmas song *O Holy Night* [1] includes *"Wise Men from Orient land"* but whomever wrote that did not even read *The Gospel of Matthew* very well. The Wise Men were not there for the birth on that holy night, but two years later. However, that illiteracy is repeated by many scholars today. Their Star came with them from the East where it first appeared. It did not originate in Bethlehem and was not there at the birth, according to *The Gospel of Matthew* and the Vatican document we will reveal. However, one can find Hopkins repeats the Wise Men are from the Orient in his Spanish version *Del Oriente Somos Los Tres* [1] as well. What is the Orient in this context to Hopkins? No guessing is required.

He defines the term *Orient* in another song he wrote that reveals he knew what modern scholars have lost–the Psalm 72 geography of the Magi's origin. It is not Persia, Arabia nor India. This is why Paul, one of the foremost theologians of all time, admonished us to "...prove all things, hold fast that which is good" *(1 Th. 5:21).* There has been faulty deceptive evil out there, and it is moldy leaven in some cases,

---

[1] *hymnary.org.*

2,000 years old. The thinking that this illiterate tradition somehow gains credibility because it survived untested by so many for so long, is only evidence of a paradigm that has failed us all and remains broken. Why are they hiding this land?

When from the East the Wise Men Came By John H. Hopkins, Jr. (Adopted 1892) [1]
1 When from the East the wise men came,
Led by the Star of Bethlehem,
The gifts they bro't to Jesus were
Of gold, and frankincense, and myrrh.
2 Bright gold of Ophir, passing fine,
Proclaims a King of royal line;
For David's son in David's town,
Is born the heir of David's crown.

How did Hopkins, a 19th century theologian know the Wise Men originated in the Isles of Ophir in the Far East? He was reading his Bible. It is hard to believe practically an entire gaggle of PhD's missed the prophecy of the Wise Men from King David in Psalm 72, which offers geography contrary to their current positions, based on fiction. We can expose the leaven which obscures their thinking. We are presenting the ancient understanding of the Magi's origin, because the modern view is based on Catholic fiction from the 6th century, and does not align with the Bible. Their false doctrine has since been embraced by the entire world. Tradition becomes dangerous when it is erroneously based.

Psalm 72:10-15 KJV
The kings of Tarshish and of the isles shall bring presents: the kings of Sheba and Seba shall offer gifts. Yea, all kings shall fall down before him: all nations shall serve him. For he shall deliver the needy when he crieth; the poor also, and him that hath no helper. He shall spare the poor and needy, and shall save the souls of the needy. He shall redeem their soul from deceit and violence: and precious shall their blood be in his sight. And he shall live, and to him shall be given of the gold of Sheba: prayer also shall be made for him continually; and daily shall he be praised. There shall be an handful of corn in the earth upon the top of the mountains; the fruit thereof shall shake like Lebanon: and they of the city shall flourish like grass of the earth. His name shall endure for ever: his name shall be continued as long as the sun: and men shall be blessed in him: all nations shall call him blessed. Blessed be the LORD God, the God of Israel, who only doeth wondrous things. And blessed be his glorious name for ever: and let the whole earth be filled with his glory; Amen, and Amen. The prayers of David the son of Jesse are ended.

---

[1] *hymnary.org. The Hymnal: revised and enlarged as adopted by the General Convention of the Protestant Episcopal Church in the United States of America in the year of our Lord 1892.*

מֶלֶךְ: *melek; a king:–King, royal (H4428).*

First, King David said the Wise Men would be Kings. That's right. Every scholar who has written a book, article or blog on this topic, claiming they were not Kings (because Matthew uses the word Magos), proves to be indoctrinated and uneducated. Somehow, they conclude a King could not be a Wise Man, proving they have never actually tested the narrative, nor do they truly know Hebrew or English, apparently. Anyone claiming *The Gospel of Matthew* is the only mention of the Magi story, is not qualified to teach this topic. King David also provides geography, in his book of Psalms, that has never been questioned by scholars, legitimately. David also preserves the origin of the Magi as Tarshish, which our research proves is Mindanao, Philippines *(see Introduction)*. The isles are clearly Ophir by association, and that is the entire archipelago, as well as a direct reference mapped as Luzon Island, Philippines *(see Introduction)*.

Sheba, from where the Queen of Sheba derives, is recorded on maps as Cebu/Sebu or Visayas, Philippines *(see Introduction)*. Seba in Hebrew is Saba or Sabah, (which scholars seem oblivious to), is found in the ancient Philippines, now part of Malaysia on maps. Those supposed scholars that claim Sheba is the Sabaeans in Yemen have never researched even a shallow amount of Biblical and historic accounts on this. They do not even realize their wordplay reveals only ignorance. The Bible calls those Sabaeans and never Sheba. Oops! The etymology of Sabaeans is not even Sheba, but derives from Seba, the uncle of Sheba in Ham's lineage, according to Josephus.

"Sabas (Seba in Latin, not Sheba), who founded the Sabeans (Yemen)"
–Flavius Josephus, Antiquities, Book 1, 6.2

The Sabaeans are recorded many times in scripture, but never called Sheba even once. It is true the Hebrew form of Sheba is S-B-A and Saba could indeed be an appropriate rendering, perhaps. However, the Philippines has a Sabah, a territory mapped in Malaysia today. Government authorities continue to maintain that land is the Philippines. Regardless, it certainly was in ancient times. The Philippines also has one of its most abundant fruits—saba. Thus, the notion that only Yemen (on all of Earth), could be the Sheba of the Queen of Sheba, based on shabby Scholar Scrabble, is nonsensical, especially when the Sabaeans do not even descend from that other Sheba, from Ham, who is not affiliated whatsoever with the account. That is the only evidence they present. That is not a position, and not a hypothesis.

Indeed, *Havilah* is mentioned in Genesis 10 as the name of Ham's offspring, but is also the name of Shem's progeny. Scholars seem to forget that Ophir and Sheba (from Shem's bloodline) also have a brother named Havilah, who is the only Havilah that could fit the Queen of Sheba's geography. These sons of Shem never lived in Saudi Arabia nor India, and though they lived in Eastern Iran initially, they migrated to the Far East in about 2,300 B.C. They were in the Philippines together in the days of the Queen of Sheba. There is no claim or position in any sense that Sheba came from Persia. These are isles in scripture, not in Central Asia.

Indeed, Arabia is Shem's territory with Ham's descendants controlling it, which makes them cursed according to Noah's division of the Earth from the *Book of Jubilees* 8-9. Seba means *"to take captive"* or *"splinter."*[1] When coupled with another territory such as Sheba, it is territory, splinter, or in essence captive of Sheba; belonging to it. The Queen of Sheba must descend from Shem's Sheba, the brother of Ophir, never the one from Ham (who is not even in the lineage of the Sabaeans). These are not scholars on this topic. They fumble every aspect of the narrative in ignorance. Thus, Seba is Sheba as it is Sheba's territory.

What we have here are specifically three territories of leadership, in which at least six kings came to worship the Messiah, bearing gifts, 2 years after His birth. They were following the Star that appeared in the East, not in Bethlehem, that the Pharisees did not see in Israel (according to the *Gospel of Matthew*). Although there is a minimum of six in total (as 'these' is plural), there are exactly three leaders among the Kings, even in Psalm 72: Tarshish, Ophir *(the isles)*, and Sheba. This explains why Hopkins wrote *We Three Kings of Orient Are.* 3 Kings has precedence and is actually accurate when one understands the account and paradigm of the land associated. He did not actually err on that point in the song; modern scholars do. He clearly knew how to read at least Psalm 72. All of this will be confirmed and further explained in the ancient Vatican document; ***Revelation of the Magi,*** recently translated into English. These references tie together and affirm each other. This is what happens when one discovers the truth. We pray that all scholars will one day awaken to truth, as we have.

What gold is given to Jesus *(Yahusha)?* The Gold of Sheba, just as Hopkins described the bright gold of Ophir. This is the Sheba associated with Ophir and Tarshish, as King David wrote prophetically, as well as in historical songs we have reviewed. The recent Vatican manuscript will confirm our research, which is not debatable. Who cares what a scholar said, when they are not able to even read or understand writings from even 1000 years ago?

First, one must address the beginning of Psalm 72 in the King James Version, which appears also in the original, authorized 1611 version, the Brenton Greek Septuagint, and the Geneva Bible as *"[[A Psalm for Solomon.]]"* or *"[[For Solomon.]]."* We have a massive issue with the rendering in double brackets being interpreted that this is a prophecy of Solomon as that is NOT there. He fails on many levels many times as this son of David is the one and only Messiah. Notice, Hopkins referred to the Messiah as a son of David which we all know is appropriate as he descended from

---

[1] *"Sheba."* שבה *(shaba/sabah) "to take captive;"* שבא *(seba/saba) "used in the Aramaic Talmud to mean splinter." Abarim Publications.*

him indeed. It says David wrote the Psalm "FOR Solomon," not that Solomon is the subject, which he cannot be, as only the Messiah fits the description in this passage.

The likely origin of this gross interpretation and blasphemy is the Catholic Bible. In the version from the United States Conference of Catholic Bishops, they remove the brackets and render "Of Solomon" replacing "FOR." They were changing the text in fraud. A Psalm written for Solomon to understand is certainly not the same as inserting Solomon as the Messiah and subject, which can be easily tested. David did not write for Solomon to know whom he was to be, but wanted him to know of the Messiah from his lineage. This becomes very obvious, as there are multiple Messianic prophesies in the passage that never fit Solomon, and they are not just a few, but many that would make this misinterpretation impossible, or at least one would think.

From verses 10-15 alone, we find that this son of David cannot be Solomon. Solomon could not save souls nor redeem souls. Only Messiah can. We are aware that Zionism attempts to stretch Solomon's exploits in error, but 1 Kings 10:15 and 2 Chronicles 9:14 define Solomon's territory as only the "Kings of Arabia" and "Governors of Israel" paying tribute. ALL nations and ALL kings never bowed to Solomon and never served him, and never will. Zionism is not a Bible position but a government ideology, having no association with scripture in any sense. It has a racist platform that attempts to place Jewish blood above all others. The Bible never does. It is unfortunate that racist political ideology has crept into modern Bible scholarship. However, let us go backwards to the beginning of Chapter 72.

Psalm 72:1-9 KJV
*[[A Psalm for Solomon.]] Give the king thy judgments, O God, and thy righteousness unto the **king's son**. He shall **judge** thy people with **righteousness**, and thy poor with judgment. The mountains shall bring **peace** to the people, and the little hills, by **righteousness**. He shall judge the poor of the people, he shall **save the children of the needy**, and shall **break in pieces the oppressor**. They shall fear thee **as long as the sun and moon endure, throughout all generations. He shall come down** like rain upon the mown grass: as showers that water the earth. In his days shall the righteous flourish; and abundance of peace **so long as the moon endureth**. He shall have dominion also **from sea to sea, and from the river unto the ends of the earth**. They that dwell in the wilderness shall bow before him; and his enemies shall lick the dust.*

In addition to this being written for Solomon to understand, not being a prophecy of Solomon, this continues to be profoundly obvious that Solomon cannot be the topic here. Solomon did judge and at times in righteousness indeed, but he was never the righteous judge and did not stay on course. Only Jesus *(Yahusha)* is the righteous judge. He will bring peace to the people by righteousness, and Solomon failed. No earthly king can bring the lasting peace of the Day of Judgment.

Only Jesus *(Yahusha)* is prophesied to break the oppressor into pieces *(Ps. 2:9)* which David knew, since he wrote that too. Solomon did not champion the needy either, necessarily. The timeline is even established here for this future son of David, as He will be feared as long as the sun and moon endure, which is the Day of Judgment. It affirms itself that this is throughout all generations. Indeed, Solomon remains respected but not feared, not worshipped, not prayed for, and not alive. That would be ridiculous as well as blasphemous in assumption.

Solomon did not come down, but Messiah did. Solomon never controlled sea to sea to the ends of the Earth. He traded with Ophir in the Far East, but never had dominion over it. Messiah will. There is nothing literate about changing this passage in interpretation, to refer to King Solomon as the subject of this prophecy. Only One could fill those shoes; the Messiah. Therefore, when this son of David would be born, the Kings of Tarshish, Ophir and Sheba would come to bring him gifts. It is certainly not academic to claim the Queen of Sheba was actually a King, and what Kings did the Queen of Sheba in Solomon's days bring with her? Have they ever read the story? Not one king came with her and there would have to have been at least 6, to match David's prophecy. However, these territories do not even have a claim in Persia. The false attempt to insert Saudi Arabia (where Ophir never lived) and India (which fails every geographical test), have never been coherent readings of any passage. Most commentaries even forget there are three regions involved that they cannot even put together.

The Three Kings were three leaders by precedence and yes, they were Kings. They originated in Ophir, Sheba and Tarshish in what we call the Philippines today. We have already proven this connection in previous research, and have proved it in this book, thus far. However, review our full position in ***The Search for King Solomon's Treasure: The Lost Isles of Gold and Garden of Eden [5]*** and ***Garden of Eden Revealed: The Book of Maps [6]***, as well as our video teachings in our *Solomon's Gold Series, Find the Garden of Eden Series, Garden of Eden Revealed Map Series*, and *When Was Jesus Born? Series*. Additionally, once we discovered the newly translated Vatican Library document, ***Revelation of the Magi***, this now becomes fully proven, and the Vatican is exposed, as they had this evidence all along.

Bible Translation Gone Wild!

In Verse 10, the *English Catholic Public Domain Version (CPDV)* already changes Sheba to Arabia in illiteracy. Again, Sheba from Ham is the wrong Sheba (who must be from Shem), but even so, that wrong Sheba is Ethiopia, not Yemen or Arabia. The *CPDV* changes the narrative again, concerning the gold of Sheba. In Verse 15, it replaces Sheba with Arabia (in bad geography and Biblical exegesis). Why Arabia? First, Arabia is not isles. Is the Catholic Church perhaps trying to hide something here?

In the *Contemporary English Version, Second Edition (CEV)*, we see apparent fraud that leads to a colonial mindset of a conqueror, which the Pope's position has always favored. The Magi no longer bring an offering to the Messiah in this poor rendering. Instead, they are paying taxes to a conqueror (which Solomon never was), and Jesus *(Yahusha)* most certainly never was. This is illiterate propaganda on the worst level, not inspired scripture. To insert their evil doctrine of killing, stealing and destroying, they blaspheme the Messiah. *Satanic* is the only truly appropriate way to assess this kind of action and the Catholic Church is cursed as a result. No wonder the Pope espouses a Doctrine of Infallibility which contends when scripture disagrees with him; the Bible is wrong, and the Pope is right. Only satan would declare such.

Psalm 72:10-11 CEV
*Force the rulers of Tarshish+ and of the islands **to pay taxes to him**. **Make** the kings of Sheba and of Seba+ bring gifts. **Make** other rulers bow down and all nations serve him.*

Who would take these words from the Hebrew and completely rewrite the text in the Nephilim doctrine of conquest. That is not new to the Catholic Church but has existed since its inception. The word "force" is not used in this passage, nor is "taxes," and the word "make" (also meaning force), is a ridiculous way to view a passage about rulers bringing gifts to the Messiah to fuel His ministry. This requires a very twisted, even insane, scholarship of the inept. They do not have the slightest understanding of who the Messiah was and is. Even inserting Solomon as a conqueror would be terrible and erroneous, as he was never a conqueror. All Kings never served him, never worshipped him, never bowed down to him, but only the Kings of Arabia, which is likely why the Catholic Church changed the isles to Arabia in complete ignorance. However, it fails to pass translation accuracy tests, horribly.

Presents in Psalm 72:10 in Hebrew:
minchâh, min-khaw'; from an unused root meaning to apportion, i.e. bestow; a donation; euphemistically, tribute; specifically a sacrificial offering (usually bloodless and voluntary):–gift, oblation, (meat) offering, present, sacrifice. (H4503)

Offer Gifts in Psalm 72:10 in Hebrew:
אֶשְׁכָּר: *eshkâr: a gratuity:–gift, present. (H814)*

We find this insertion of altered doctrine in the *Latin Vulgate (VUL)* as "Arabiae et Saba" in Verse 10, in fraud. *Brenton's English Septuagint (BES)* does the same. The Jesuit Douay-Rheims 1899 American Edition follows this same Catholic propaganda, but of course, the Jesuits embedded themselves within and as the conquerors controlling the Philippines, which continues in some forms to this day.

That is no surprise. Neither has any such precedence.

However, if we go to the Philippines and take a look at their Tagalog Bibles, the deception becomes even greater in some mistranslated passages. In the *Magandang Balita Biblia* Awit *(Psalm)* 72:1 errs immediately, claiming "Panalangin para sa Hari: Katha ni Solomon" or "Prayer for the King: Legend of Solomon." How do they evolve from a message for Solomon apparent in the original Hebrew, *1611 KJV* and *Geneva Bible* to this being a prayer for, prophecy about, and even legend of Solomon? Well, clearly, whomever did so cannot read, as the passage disqualifies King Solomon as this King, directly, several times. No one can be this stupid.

Then, we have a major sin perpetrated by the Philippine Bible Society, who published their Tagalog, version-changing scripture, in inept exegesis. How exactly can their claim to have translated from the Masoretic Text lead to their changing words completely. The Society must have written their own. Understand, *Ang Biblia Dating (1905)* does not make these changes but adheres to the KJV translation.

Awit (Psalm) 72:10-11 Magandang Balita Biblia(Tagalog)
Mga haring nasa pulo at naroon sa **Espanya**, *maghahandog ng kaloob upang parangalan siya. Pati rin ang mga hari ng* **Arabia** *at* **Etiopia**, *may mga kaloob ding ibibigay sa kanya.*

Even Spanish Bibles do not make the assertion that Tarshish is Spain. The King of Spain, even in writing, is on record as locating Tarshish in the Far East in the Philippines, and never in their homeland. Tarshish being identified as Spain is propaganda-based, not a theory or truth. They do often identify Sheba as Saba, but Spanish maps show the Philippines as Saba Island*(s)* for centuries *(See Introduction)*. Claiming Yemen is the only place Saba ever existed as the only option is not scholarship. In Ancient Hebrew, it is translated to English as S-B-A, for which 'Saba' is a fine translation. It appears that the basis for this particular Tagalog Version is the *Good News Translation,* which renders Spain for Tarshish, though that was gross negligence all along.

The *New Living Translation (NLT)* makes an admission in Verse 10 that Sheba and Seba represent "Eastern Kings." Where are the illiterates who think King David wrote this from Israel and called Yemen: *East?* Worse, there are those who try to insert Africa into this formula, yet, when did Africa move East of Israel? It also tried to change the word *isles* to *coasts*, as do other, newer translations, which are all based on the 19th century, Westcott and Hort manuscripts. These occult-admitted translators write in their own letters that their corrupt manuscripts were 'meant to change the Bible'. They did. The NLT also introduces the Catholic fraud "Of Solomon" in Verse 1.

The Hebrew Names Version actually explains the paradigm of Chapter 72 from a Hebrew perspective, and is likely the most accurate in that regard. The Chapter was not actually written to, for, or even about Solomon. It was written BY Solomon,

"By Shlomo", which actually makes the most sense. Perhaps Solomon actually wrote this. He did not prophecy of Himself in the third person, if so. However, they then render Yiddish as Sheva and Seva, replacing the well-established "Bet" with "Vet." There are no such rules in ancient Hebrew, Greek, Aramaic, nor Latin, as none of these languages even contained a letter "V" until around the 1500's, when Ashkenazi Jews migrated into Europe, speaking an infused language, that has never represented Biblical Hebrew appropriately. Even those who seem to understand get distracted with Pharisee leaven. *The Complete Jewish Bible* follows this pattern, rendering Yiddish instead of Ancient Hebrew, but also projects Solomon as the author of the chapter in question, which seems probable.

Produced in 1995 by God's Word to the Nations Bible Society, their *GOD'S WORD Translation* also picks up on Psalm 72 as authored by Solomon. The Orthodox Jewish Bible conflicts the reader with the Catholic insertion "Of Solomon" instead of using "for," or "by" as the other Jewish creations, the KJV and really the far more credible translations. The *Orthodox Jewish Bible* also expresses Yiddish into the text, with "Sh'va and S'va" instead of "Sheba and Seba". No such characters exist originally, as the letters cannot be rendered.

The *Wycliffe Bible* expressed this was written "To Solomon" not that it is a prophecy about him, which it cannot be, regardless of the wording of any translation, no matter what. However, it then heads towards fraudulence, in verses 10 and 15, with Sheba placed in Arabia, using faulty logic.

In other words, the above named Bible versions are riddled in Pharisee leaven and lousy research. These are not theories (which do not belong in Bibles, regardless). They are deception and confusion, which make the Bible harder to read with no credible precedence. This is why so many concordances and Bible scholars continue to express opinions in ignorance. They know scholarship on the topic sometimes, but have not bothered to test it in the slightest. It should not be so difficult. They should know the text rather than position themselves as the blind leading the blind. King David wrote of geography, and he did not intend for those firm directions to be flexible nor changing with the wind of interpretation by those who cannot even read or tell directions, it seems.

Ancients Knew the Magi Were Kings:

Anyone quoting a Church Father, who was not aware of Psalm 72, is too uninformed to hold a position on this. King David said, "the Kings of Tarshish, and the isles (Ophir), and the Kings of Sheba and Seba..." Those add up to at least 6 Kings. In *Revelation of the Magi,* we are given their names, and there are actually 12, but not all 12 are Kings. In fact, the writing remedies this entire track of scoffing. They were broken into 3 categories: Some were Kings; at least six of them, according to King David. Some were princes (or sons of Kings), and some were Wise Men.

That seems pretty simple, and all of these accounts coalesce. We break down their names, with many originating in the Filipino languages even as well as Hebrew in a later chapter. The land of the Far East was the land of their nativity, where the word Magi originates. Contrary to popular belief and teaching, it is not a Greek word. In King David's case, he did not use some questionable word, leaving any remote room for any other meaning, period. He used the well noted Hebrew word for King, which was used to address himself. Duh!

מלך: *melek, meh'-lek; from H4427; a king:–King, royal (H4428).*

This word in Hebrew is the word for "King" in Bible translation. Of the 2,523 times it is used in the King James Version, it is "King" 2,519 times and "royal" two times. Kings are male, and as a royal refers to Kings or princes, the Bible is consistent with *Revelation of the Magi.* The other 3 uses are names of Kings, and once interpreted as Moloch, which is Ba'al, a god and king of those who serve him. Anyone claiming to be a Hebrew scholar, who takes this word elsewhere, when it is King, 100% of the time, is no scholar. Even the root word denotes King, Queen, reign (of a ruler), and not Magi or Wise Men. For the *Catholic Encyclopedia* to dismiss that, (as if they have such right), is witchcraft. However, this fraudulent encyclopedia does so again, when it tells us no one ever thought they were Kings. Of course, this is after they admit King David wrote they were Kings. He coincidentally knew what a King was, and he was not confused. They are.

"No Father of the Church holds the Magi to have been kings." – Catholic Encyclopedia

This is an admission, which maybe the author should have thought out before placing it in writing. The Catholic Church just admitted King David is not a father of their religion. Though not the intent of the author, that is what he wrote. Ouch! Unfortunately, they cannot even tell the truth in things like this when they attempt to cover their tracks. The same article in the *Catholic Encyclopedia* cites Church Fathers who did in fact define the Magi as Kings, [such as Caesarius of Aries, in his *Sermo 139 (PL,39. 2018)]*.

They also claim Psalm 72 is not about geography, and we should pay no attention to the exact geography offered in the passage. Let us just ignore that because it is inconvenient for their position? No, thank you. Maybe we should force them to offer a real position, or remain quiet on the topic, and stop deceiving people. At the top ranks of the RCC, the leaders are knowingly perpetrating this false information, and we will show you why, in a later chapter.

Tertullian (*"Adv. Marcion."*, *III, xiii*) guessed they were "well-nigh" Kings, meaning they were *almost* Kings. We covered the Hebrew word and it is the word *King*, not *almost* king. Why would that even be a point in the first place? Tertullian just disagreed with King David in the *Book of Psalms*, or almost…? One has to love the vague language of scholars who cannot commit to a position because they have not researched the subject. Quoting them, still not testing, is even worse. Let us not treat the guy as *almost* credible in Bible exegesis. They may hold Tertullian as a Church Father, but he is nothing to King David, who was a true prophet and celebrated author of part of our Bible. Tertullian was not! However, he had no knowledge of the true origin of the Magi, and the fact the word is not even Greek in derivation. Tertullian's not knowing is not a position.

Pliny the Elder chronicles about fictional Magi who were great magicians, as if he held a position at Disney. He knew nothing of the account. John Calvin was illiterate on the topic and would scoff at anyone that would call them, *The 3 Kings*, as scholars ridicule today in ignorance. Anyone claiming that in 440 B.C., Herodotus wrote about the Magi of the first century is no academic in any sense. The Persian Magoi were no longer in power, nor a force at that time, and how is it they get away with ignoring that Arabia and India had no Magi either? All three territories would have to qualify, yet, in their own view, they already know they are over 60% wrong, even though we know their inaccuracy is 100%. These are incoherent ramblings, not positions set in research of any kind.

The Catholic Church Knows It Has No Bones of the Magi!

This also means those at the highest levels of the Catholic Church are well aware that they do not have the bones of the Magi, who did not originate in Persia, Arabia, or India. The RCC claims to have their remains in Cologne today. They would have discovered these bones in Persia, supposedly, yet even their own legends are aware there are 3 different locations, and some include a 4th. All are erroneous and easily disproved. So, they forget in their own embellishment (in fraud), that they are supposed to represent all 3 areas, at least. What a dumbfounding claim. They got them from the wrong country, and they knew better. Certainly, Constantine's mom did not, as she rendered the most idiotic geography and supposed archaeology we have found. She was no scholar, and seemed challenged to even read the narratives. No one should have expected her to understand, but when she made such claims, she had to have answers. She had none. They still have none on those topics.

The cathedral of Cologne contains what are claimed to be the remains of the Magi; these, it is said, were discovered in Persia, brought to Constantinople by St. Helena, transferred to Milan in the fifth century and to Cologne in 1163 (Acta SS., I, 323). –Catholic Encyclopedia

Isaiah 60: Birth of Messiah or Lost Tribes Return in the Last Days?

One of the poorest interpretations we have seen is the claim that Isaiah 60 refers to the birth of Messiah. In this chapter, Isaiah makes a promise in prophecy to the Lost Tribes of Israel, that they will be returned by the Ships of Tarshish in the Last Days *(60:9)*. That is not the birth of Jesus *(Yahusha)* and neither is Psalm 68:29 (as some scholars have confused), as that is a prophecy of the days of Solomon. How exactly can a Bible scholar confuse these? They do not read clearly, even in full sentences. Once again, this appears Catholic in origin, and that paradigm seems to manipulate scripture whenever it does not fit their overall view. When the Ships of Tarshish, Philippines bring the return of the Lost Tribes, bringing their silver and gold along with them, they will stand against the world order, including the Catholic Church. Those that are not aware of the rich shipbuilding history of the ancient Philippines, with ships as large as the Spanish, are not exactly credible.

Isaiah 60:1-22 KJV

*Arise, shine; for thy light is come, and the glory of the Lord is risen upon thee. 2 For, behold, the darkness shall cover the earth, and gross darkness the people: but the Lord shall arise upon thee, and his glory shall be seen upon thee. 3 And the Gentiles shall come to thy light, and kings to the brightness of thy rising. 4 Lift up thine eyes round about, and see: all they gather themselves together, they come to thee: **thy sons shall come from far**, and thy daughters shall be nursed at thy side.*

*5 Then thou shalt see, and flow together, and thine heart shall fear, and be enlarged; because the abundance of the sea shall be converted unto thee, the **forces of the Gentiles shall come unto thee**.*

*6 The multitude of camels shall cover thee, the dromedaries of **Midian** and **Ephah**; all they from **Sheba** shall come: **they shall bring gold and incense**; and they shall shew forth the praises of the Lord. 7 All the **flocks of Kedar** shall be gathered together unto thee, the **rams of Nebaioth** shall minister unto thee: they shall come up with acceptance on **mine altar**, and **I will glorify the house of my glory**. 8 Who are these that fly as a cloud, and as the doves to their windows? 9 **Surely the isles shall wait for me, and the ships of Tarshish first, to bring thy sons from far, their silver and their gold with them**, unto the name of the Lord thy God, and to the Holy One of Israel, because he hath glorified thee. 10 And the **sons of strangers shall build up thy walls**, and **their kings shall minister unto thee**: for in my wrath I smote thee, but in my favour have I had mercy on thee. 11 Therefore **thy gates shall be open continually**; they shall **not be shut** day nor night; that men may bring unto thee **the forces of the Gentiles, and that their kings may be brought**. 12 For the nation and kingdom that will not serve thee shall perish; yea, those nations shall be utterly wasted. 13 The glory of **Lebanon** shall come unto thee, the **fir tree**, the **pine tree**, and **the box** together, to **beautify the place of my sanctuary**; and I will make the place of my feet glorious. 14 **The sons also of them that afflicted thee shall come bending unto thee; and all they that despised thee shall bow** themselves down at the soles of thy feet; and they shall call thee; The city of the Lord, The Zion of the Holy One of Israel.*

*15 Whereas thou has been forsaken and hated, so that no man went through thee, I will make thee an eternal excellency, a joy of many generations. 16 Thou shalt also suck the **milk of the Gentiles**, and shalt suck the **breast of kings**: and thou shalt know that I the Lord am thy Saviour and thy Redeemer,* *the mighty One of Jacob. 17 For **brass** I will bring **gold**, and for iron I will bring **silver**, and for wood brass, and for stones **iron**: I will also make **thy officers peace**, and **thine exactors righteousness**. 18 **Violence shall no more be heard in thy land**, wasting nor destruction within thy borders; but thou shalt call thy walls Salvation, and thy gates Praise. 19 The **sun shall be no more thy light by day**; neither for brightness shall the moon give light unto thee: but the **Lord shall be unto thee an everlasting light**, and thy God thy glory. 20 Thy sun shall no more go down; neither shall thy moon withdraw itself: for the Lord shall be thine everlasting light, and **the days of thy mourning shall be ended**. 21 Thy people also **shall be all righteous**: they shall **inherit the land for ever**, the branch of my planting, the work of my hands, that I may be glorified. 22 A little one shall become a thousand, and a small one **a strong nation: I the Lord will hasten it in his time**.*

Do scholars not know that the Southern Kingdom was still in Judaea at that time? Where are the Lost Tribes that returned with the Magi as well? Of course, that did not happen. Also, the passage quoted above is where some scholars and translations insert camels into the Magi account erroneously. There are none in the *Gospel of Matthew*, nor in Psalms. This passage is a reference to the End Times. *Strangers* will build up their walls, yet, oddly, these scholars seem to be unaware that just a few decades after Jesus' *(Yahusha's)* ascension, Jerusalem and the Temple were destroyed, not to be rebuilt to this day, for the Temple. Surely, they jest.

These unbelievers, seem to have missed an important concept; the Kings of the nations who arrive at that time will be enemies of Israel. They also ignore the geography in the passage, as the Ships of Tarshish return the Lost Tribes. Indeed, in this story, Saudi Arabia also arrives, but not in the birth account. Even Lebanon is mentioned as coming to bring trees. What trees did the 3 Kings bring? Have they ever read this full chapter? Have they ever read the accounts of the Magi?

How can they claim Israel was so safe in the days of Jesus *(Yahusha)* that the gates would always be opened (when that is not true). The Romans conquered Israel at that time. Add that to the missing 10 tribes of the Northern Kingdom who still are not in Israel. The sons of those who afflicted Israel will come to bow before them. This is repeated by Jesus *(Yahusha)* in Revelation 3:9-10 when he refers to the Synagogue of Satan doing so. The Magi were not such. When did the Philippines afflict Israel, ever? Even if this were Persia, when did Persia afflict Israel when they liberated them? Persia even assisted in funding the rebuilding of the temple.

Where is the brass and iron in the Magi accounts? Those were not brought at Messiah's birth. What scholar thinks that violence ended in Judaea in the first century? Jerusalem was sacked by Rome and the Temple destroyed in 70 A.D. Isaiah would be mistaken in his prophecy, were it meant for that time period. Isaiah was NOT wrong. When the sun and the moon disappear, it is near the Day of Judgement. Scholars know this, but cannot seem to read this particular chapter, quoted above, in context. How did they assume that the first century saw no more mourning and until this time? Israel did not become a strong nation under Rome in that era; but would be crushed by them. That would be a ridiculous assumption.

Church Art Gone Wrong!

Who thought it appropriate to include the eight pointed Star of Ishtar with eight rays of light as powering Mithra, claiming this to be Messiah's birth on the wrong day of the year, with erroneous Magi of the wrong races arriving two years too soon? Why are these stingy Kings only bearing little tiny gifts when they are supposed to be from the Land of Gold and resources? Why does Mary have a sun god circle around her head, and why is she a white non-Hebrew with a white child? Did the artist really believe that Roman soldiers attended this monumental event? There is not a single accurate point to this fresco and the Catholic Church affirms it as art. When will the Catholic Church find artists who can actually read?

Zurich, Switzerland - July 1, 2022:
The fresco of Three Magi in the church
Pfarrkirche Liebfrauen by Fritz Kunz (1906).
AdobeStock.

Chapter 3: Vatican Document Finally Released in English

Did you ever wonder why the Bible has so little detail of this famous account of *The Gospel of Matthew's* Wise Men? In addition to scholars ignoring Psalm 72 (which they clearly have difficulty reading plain Hebrew and English), imagine if a document was found in the Vatican Library that affirms exactly what King David wrote? Songs, and even artwork have expressed this truth for centuries. Would Bible scholars then take a position opposite the affirmed Word? We wish we could say that answer was "no way!" However, this is the norm in a paradigm of scoffing and unbelief who scantly researches, yet draws uneducated conclusions based on elementary level study, if that. The entire Christmas story is in danger of reading as fiction because of their embellishment and additives *(leaven)*. One cannot undermine their faith any worse, than to attack the very foundation of the Messiah's birth. Let us be clear, it is the church who has done so. There is no Bible passage which ever condones that behavior, but hundreds that condemn it.

In 2010, Brent Landau published the first English translation of a long-standing Vatican document he titled ***Revelation of the Magi (RotM).*** His translation appears solid, and we only publish portions in this writing out of respect. We encourage everyone to read the full translated text he has published. His interpretations are unresearched, but he does understand the extreme Orient was never Persia. Landau speculates that the originating land is China, because he is uneducated on maps of the first century, nor much history that well documents the end of the East as the islands in the South China Sea (known today as the Philippines), known in history as Ophir, Sheba, Tarshish and the Garden of Eden *(See Introduction)*. These lands are very clearly expressed as isles throughout history and the Bible, and are not China.

However, Landau renders the chain of custody of ***Revelation of the Magi*** in his research, which validates this as affirmation of the geography King David expressed in Psalm 72. The original text is preserved in the Syriac language used by early ekklesias, and there are few even capable of translation. Worse, modern scholars shy away from anything that does not already fit their current paradigm. That is likely the largest reason this manuscript went untranslated for more than 1,000 years, as it was in the possession of the Catholic Church.

The existing manuscript at the Vatican Library today was copied down at the Zuqnin monastery in southeast Turkey by an anonymous monk, and referred to by some as ***Chronicle of Zuqnin.*** This erroneous title has no merit, but understand that this particular monastery is well noted, containing several other ancient texts, as a rule. This document was then relocated to another monastery in the Egyptian

---

"Revelation of the Magi: The Lost Tale of the Wise Men's Journey to Bethlehem."
By Brent Landau. HarperOne, An Imprint of Harper-Collins Publishers. New York. 2010.

desert, and in the late eighth century, G. S. Assemani transferred the document to the Vatican Library in Rome, where it remains today. In 1950, the Vatican finally translated *Revelation of the Magi* into Italian and just recently, in 2010, Landau produced this first translation into English. It is a revelation of epic proportions, indeed. As Landau admits, this manuscript is securely dated to the eighth century, but he conducts further research, expressing a far earlier date that this text was known and quoted. That anonymous monk was not the author of this far more ancient document.

Theodorus bar Kōnī *(Konai/Konay)*, an Arabian Christian author of the 8th century, from Kaškar in Mesopotamia, also cites very specific detail from *Revelation of the Magi.* We do not receive the information of the arrival month of the Magi in Jerusalem anywhere else. We do know the *Gospel of Luke*, especially preserves Messiah's birth date well, in June, on the Day of Covenant Renewal: Feast of Shavuot *(See Chapter 10).* However, the Magi arrived in Jerusalem, not Bethlehem, in April, according to bar Konai *(Landau, Footnote 11).* Where did he learn that? It only exists one place which anyone has discovered, *Revelation of the Magi.*

Encyclopedia Brittanica and many other sources backdate the Catholic Church's Epiphany celebration of the Wise Men as January sixth, beginning around 354 A.D. or so in Rome with the East celebrating it even earlier. Thus, April is not a Catholic observance in date in origin. This document is not Catholic. Of course, they have the wrong time of year for the birth as well. Though the original writing of bar Kōnī is out of print, he is quoted by scholars since, as holding this position.

Why would the Magi arrive in April? That is the first Hebrew month of Abib *(Nisan)* when those in covenant observe the Spring Feasts of Passover, Unleavened Bread, and the First Fruits Offering. They did not arrive the year Jesus *(Yahusha)* was born, according to *The Gospel of Matthew*, but two years later, which *Revelation of the Magi* concurs in timeline. In April, these Wise Men arrived, but that is not the birth of Messiah. They met with Herod (as both texts agree), who would then kill Bethlehem children later, around the age given for the birth of Messiah, 2 years earlier.

The Magi then traveled from Jerusalem to Bethlehem to present their offerings and worship the Son of Yahuah. They celebrated His birthday on Shavuot in early June *(See Chapter 10).* This timeline aligns perfectly with our research, and this disproves those claiming these Wise Men waited for a year and 10 months to make a two-month journey. No logic progresses in that direction.

RotM 11:6 And just like the moon looks in the daytime in the days of Nisan, when the sun rises and it is absorbed in its light, so also did the sun seem to us when the star rose over us.

When the Star first appeared to the Magi in the Far East, they wrote it was as the sun in Springtime. The translator, Landau, assumes that is the month Nisan, but he admits in his margin note, it can also be interpreted "in Springtime." This coming Spring in Israel, 2025, will begin on March 20th and end June 21st. Indeed, this includes the month of Nisan/Abib as well as the second month of Zif and third month, which Babylonian name is Sivan. The best fit in the timeline for Messiah's birth would be the Feast of Shavuot in early June, which is still Spring. This is affirmed later in *Revelation of the Magi.*

Landau could not figure out the dynamic of the moon in the daytime being absorbed by the sun's light, because he did not understand the region involved. The sun in the Philippines is hottest and brightest in the months of April and May or Nisan/Abib and Zif. Indeed, the moon is out during the daytime around the world, several times of the year. However, this is a specific reference to the land where the sun actually rises, according to history and the *Book of 1 Enoch (See Introduction).* This region is literally considered *"subsolanus"* on several ancient maps, as the place where the sun and the East Wind originate. That was their perspective in the first century. Though places like the U.S. experience the hottest sun in summer, the Philippines' hottest months of the year are April/Abib/Nisan and May/Zif. Having said that, June remains almost as hot there, and the same dynamic really exists from April to June, which matches the appropriate translation of *Springtime.*

This is then, further affirmed in the arrival of the Magi at Jerusalem. It would be Springtime again, thus, at least a year passes in time during the course of the Magi's long journey. *The Gospel of Matthew* cites 2 years, and this manuscript affirms their arrival, as being at least a year after the birth of Messiah. The extra time is accounted for, as the Wise Kings' location was so far away, and they had quite a long trip to reach Israel. Otherwise, if they were so close as Persia and Arabia, it would be utterly ridiculous to imagine their waiting a year and 10 months to begin the journey, when Messiah was already born. Horsefeathers! Various Bible commentaries try to explain this time lapse away, speculating that there must have been some reason the Magi were detained, with no valid textual evidence ever explaining a reason. This points to witchcraft, not scholarship.

RotM 17:1 And when we arrived in the region of Jerusalem, in the month of flowers...

Anyone who is familiar with Israel knows the flowers bloom there from late January to late April, essentially. Match that to the Springtime reference when the Star appeared, which would discount January thru late March landing on Abib/Nisan for their arrival. Remember, this is when the Magi arrived in Jerusalem, not the birth, which is only slated as Springtime in the text. They met with Herod and officials first, as they were trying to figure out exactly where they would go until the Star appeared again, and guided them; at which they rejoiced.

The Magi tarried in Jerusalem from the end of Abib until closer to Shavuot. Then, these Kings ventured to Bethlehem, arriving for the birthday on Shavuot of the growing toddler, Jesus *(Yahusha)*. This still tracks with the Springtime and our finding of the birth of Messiah on Shavuot *(See Chapter 10)*. However, it also confirms that bar Kōnī was aware of the *Revelation of the Magi* when he expressed they came in April/Nisan/Abib. He also specifically mentioned the "month of flowers", directly quoting the text in *Mimra 7.17*. That date in month is not found anywhere else that we are aware of, except in *Revelation of the Magi*.

With a second witness from the eighth century era, this can be further enhanced beyond on this same track. Clement of Alexandria notes in *The Stromata*,[1] written around 198 A.D., that there were those in his era who believed Messiah was born in April. He uses the Egyptian month Pharmuthi which is from April 9 to May 8 on the Gregorian calendar, with the dates correlating to about April 20-21, according to Landau. No doubt that is the same date of when the Magi arrived, though this view forgets that they did not immediately get to Jesus *(Yahusha)*.

*"Further, others say that **He (Our Savior) was born on the twenty-fourth or twenty-fifth of Pharmuthi.**"*[1]

The fact that this mindset can be traced back that far affirms that *Revelation of the Magi* was known in 198 A.D. This is far more likely, because, as the text declares, it was originally written by the Magi themselves. No, we do not have the original which would have likely been written in Ancient Hebrew. In other words, Filipinos wrote their historic account from the Philippines, affirming the Bible story of the Magi, and scholars apply racism in dismissing this. We will not.

For those demanding this historic document be found in the Philippines, perhaps they should educate themselves. No history written by Filipinos survived the Catholic onslaught in conquest. No, not one single paragraph remains which tells us much. There must have been some of major importance for the Vatican to have them hidden or destroyed. For instance, this text proves the Vatican did not bring Jesus, but the Philippines had already maintained a relationship with Him, at least in part, from the time of His birth. The Apostle Thomas arrived in this ancient land long before the Catholic Church and their Jesuit explorers ever landed on their shores, 1400 years later. Oops! We still have ample documents from the conquerors, explorers, and the Chinese, Indians, and Greeks. We even have detailed maps over 6000 years old, but the local history was eliminated. Though Filipinos were noted to be literate, reading and writing in their own language, as many as one hundred percent in some areas, written historical documents are gone; or perhaps more are hidden in the bowels of the Vatican Library.[2] They were there.

---

[1] *Clement of Alexandria, The Stromata, Book I, Chapter 21, 198 A.D.* [2] *a. "Baths in 16th Century Philippines." By Beth Ocampo. Philippine Daily Inquirer. July 30, 2013. b. "When Did Philippine History Begin? " American Historical Association.*

There is no need to induct *Revelation of the Magi* into Bible Canon, which we have never suggested. It vets as a valid secondary support in history and that is all any of us needs. It proves *The Book of Matthew* was accurate, as well as King David's writings. However, as an historic text, it affirms *The Gospel of Matthew, The Book of Psalms*, and *The Book of Jeremiah*, in geographical concepts, the origin of the word 'Magi' (which is not Greek), and the names of the Wise Kings, which can all be tested for accuracy. Its content is not sketchy, as other later occult writings that quote it, and veer into other occult directions such as **The Book of the Cave of Treasures, The Book of the Bee**, and the **Fourth Book of Adam and Eve.** All these writings use elements from **Revelation of the Magi**, proving it was in circulation. When an author supports the occult over the Bible, and ignores historic support that affirms the Bible account as it is written, that is the worst of scholarship.

In **Revelation of the Magi**, Landau also translated a Latin text titled *Opus Imperfectum in Matthaeum* into English.[1] Now, that is helpful scholarship. Though unproven, it is believed by many that John Chrysostom penned this in the fourth century. This copy is a sixth century writing in the church with supporting detail for the *Book of Matthew*. In the excerpt, the author directly retells the account from **Revelation of the Magi**. It uses the account in large portion over two pages.

It is clearly the same account, as it includes the word 'Magi' (which is not Greek, but originates in the land of the Wise Kings of the Far East). It refers to Adam's prophecy from Seth; the geographic markers are all the same, the account of the Star is a match, the miracle of their food not running out but replenishing on the two-year journey, and the Apostle Thomas visiting the Far East in the Philippines. There is no doubt; the origin of this account in full is **Revelation of the Magi.** As this text was quoted in large portion in the sixth century, it existed before the Catholic fiction of Melchior, Balthasar and Caspar, also proving their geography wrong.

As a Syriac expert, Landau also believes the language used (such as "Holy Spirit" in the feminine form), demonstrates a practice that occurred in Syriac writings from the second to the fourth centuries. Beginning in the fifth century, that practice was abandoned, according to him. This may well be another compelling point that leads to an origin prior to the fifth century.

Indeed, there are other so-titled Infancy Gospels in the Early Church. However, those are clearly drawing one away from scripture rather than to it. In this case of **Revelation of the Magi**, we find it confirms Matthew as well as Psalm 72, as it should. We are not looking to conduct a counsel to vote it into Biblical Canon, but those who ignore history are destined to repeat it. Test this for yourself; you will find there is nothing in the content of **Revelation of the Magi** that is bothersome.

---

[1] *Opus Imperfectum in Matthaeum." From Migne's Patrologia Graeca, vlume 56, columns 637-638. "Revelation of the Magi: The Lost Tale of the Wise Men's Journey to Bethlehem." By Brent Landau. HarperOne, An Imprint of Harper-Collins Publishers. New York. 2010. pp. 103-105.*

Anything appearing so initially, can be taken to scripture and affirmed.

For any scholar (such as Landau), to claim that the story of the Magi in *The Book of Matthew* is not based on an historical event, requires a scoffing unbelief in the Bible. This is due to their not having tested it, but they sit in the seat of the scornful, unable to vet things as they are supposed to. This account does not appear in the other writings of the Apostles because the Magi are from the Far East, far removed from them. Expecting they must be is to apply a false litmus test already set to fail (which test is useless and can only have a false outcome). That is how one remains boxed into their current paradigm. It is unscholarly in practice.

One will also find what Landau terms Infancy Gospel X,[1] written in the mid to late second century, also has details that match **Revelation of the Magi.** Of course, in typical scholarly circular reasoning, he was unable to figure out which was the origin. A normal lay person could read and assess the obvious, but Landau chooses not to believe **Revelation of the Magi** could be the source, (or at least he refuses to commit, employing the scholarly side-step). Scholarly translators fear other scoffers, especially their peers, who love to quote and mock every committed stance not in agreement with their reviews. However, the Infancy Gospel X is not a valid record of history, but is a commentary by an early church father offering commentary. It is amazing how many scholars cannot perceive the difference between that, and a detailed account written by the Magi themselves. They will equate the two, which is erroneous.

Even in logic, when you have a 50-page detailed document, purporting to be from the first century, written by the Magi themselves, does it derive from a paragraph or little detail in comparison, written in the second century? Or is it the other way around? He calls this the "*obscure apocryphal Infancy Gospel*" and then equates it in weight, to a much more complex account with great detail. That is a dishonest assessment. In critical scholarship, such embellishment is typical and expected, as Pharisees were known to add leaven, according to our Messiah. Prophets and Apostles did not add leaven, in the form of embellishments and commentary. Normal folks reject that as unethical. What they are doing is undermining any thought of the text being credible with a mindset that causes any test to fail before they begin. That trap has now been released.

Sure, **Revelation of the Magi** also is not scripture, but it vets as historically valid, where the Early Church Father vets as those who crept in unawares. Scholars seem to also remain unaware of such infiltration after over 2,000 years. This same community of intellects demands the original text, in a paradigm that they well know is documented to copy scrolls over routinely, so they would not lose the

---

[1] *a. "Latin Infancy Gospels." M.R. James. Cambridge: Cambridge University Press, 1927.*

b. "Apocrypha Hiberniae I: Evangelia Infantiae." M. McNamara. Corpus Christianorum Series Apocryphorum 13-14. 2 vols. Turnhout: Brepols, 2001.

content. They demand all originals to prove when they were written, which is illiterate. Translators and historians have been dating copies found as the date of original authorship, which is dishonest.

Bear in mind, this is the same scholar who claims *Revelation of the Magi*'s first-person section offers a *complete avoidance of the proper name "Jesus Christ"*. The section in the book with the Apostle Thomas mentions it several times, but Landau discounts all of those. Ironically, that particular account actually completes the work of the Magi; even fulfilling their own prophecy. He claims this means it must have been added. Just as with the *Wisdom of Sirach*, where three generations authored the book close to this same era, this record was indeed written by multiple Magi. That doesn't discount anything, and the demand for one author in a group of holy priests, is nonsense.

Brent Landau is a Bible scholar who does not seem to know that *Jesus Christ* is not a proper name, but an improper manipulation of *Yahusha Messiah*. He does not even realize that there is no 'J' in ancient Hebrew, and that the actual name of *Yahusha* means: *Yah is salvation*. He also fails to realize that when he personally translated to English, the Hebrew word for *salvation* multiple times, he should have returned to Hebrew and rendered it as *Yahusha* or at least, *Yahshua*. That is the proper translation for *salvation*, and Bible scholars with as much formal education and experience translating as Landau has, should know better. We cover this concept in an upcoming chapter, with examples. He translated it into the English *salvation*, when it is clearly the name of the Messiah, meaning *salvation*. There is nothing wrong with translating it in this way, but failing to realize the proper translation of Messiah is *salvation* is illiterate especially when criticizing such.

There are many examples, but a perfect sample is his translating *"And the faith of salvation increased in the land of the East in those who heard (28:6)."* That is the name *Yahusha!* Perhaps he should try reading the New Testament, written at that same time, as we all know this would read, "the faith of, or in (same Hebrew word) *Yahusha*, increased in the land...." He continues with other similar word translations, such as, "The will of complete *salvation...(21:2)*," "This great gift and light of *salvation... (23:3),"* and, "...of the voice of *salvation...(25:1)*." These are all better left in Hebrew, as *Yahusha*, and are the same thing, regardless. Even in the section that features the Apostle Thomas, where *Jesus Christ* is mentioned several times, the Apostle definitely spoke of *Yahusha* by name, "I was sent in *salvation...(Yahusha!) (29:6),"* and "...the birth of *salvation... (Yahusha!) (30:2-9)."* There are no issues with leaving the translation *salvation*, as His name is the same. However, to not realize he stepped all over the Messiah's name, and then uses that ignorance to criticize, does not rise to an academic position. It is extremely sad that seminaries are so lacking in their training.

Landau also attempts to claim that *Revelation of the Magi* borrowed from the Apostle Paul, the Apostle John, and even the *Book of Revelation*. Would that not be an indication of something credible in the Bible paradigm? Somehow, he even claims the Magi would have died a decade before these were written, which is lousy speculation based on nothing. He could not know when the Magi who visited the Messiah died, especially not in Asia, where people tend to live longer than anywhere else in the world. He also fails to recognize the Magi are a group, and wrote this as a community, including the sons of those who journeyed, who would have heard the firsthand accounts. Of course, he fails to realize they knew these things before they happened in prophecy, from Adam through Seth and Enoch.

However, when the Apostle Thomas came, would he not speak in similar terms to Paul and John? The notion that he would not is ridiculous, and this is not a point. He does not know and cannot conclude this. Indeed, the language is similar and that is only affirmation that *Revelation of the Magi* is truly written in the Biblical perspective and paradigm by honest men. It is also evidence that the Apostle Thomas did, in fact, visit them as well. Landau refuses to even consider such.

In the eleventh century, Nestorian Bishop Shelêmôn or Solomon released *The Book of the Bee,*[1] indisputably quoting *Revelation of the Magi* on many points. Notice, that is far too late to be considered scripture, and when one reads it, it is clear the author was no scholar on the topic, and did not have an even elementary grasp. He copied the names of the Magi from *Revelation of the Magi*, creating this corrupt manipulation in *The Book of the Bee*. Even the number of twelve Kings is repeated. Also, they are Kings in that text as well. In other words, he had read it, as it was published many centuries prior, in Catholic monasteries, and in the Vatican, at that point. Otherwise, he recounted others who had read it.

Most of the names he lists are right out of *Revelation of the Magi* in origin. However, this scholarly Bishop from Mesopotamia had to inject the names of the Magi, traveling from Persia, where he resided. That was already the Catholic position in ignorance, and he simply followed that leaven, changing the view. He directly uses *Revelation of the Magi* in Chapters 38 and 39, and then changes the text to lead elsewhere, which is typical in the arena of corrupt scholarship.

He begins Chapter 38 with, *"SOME say that that star appeared to the Magi simultaneously with the birth of our Lord."* Who is SOME? Some say the moon is made of cheese, but is that credible? It is a reference to *Revelation of the Magi* and those recounting it. He fabricates there was "some accidental delay" in a weak attempt to explain the error of Persian Kings waiting one year and 10 months to take a two-month journey and visit the Messiah. Scholars and scribes make up stories that are not found within the text they are translating, to justify their ignorance.

---

[1] *"The Book of the Bee: The Syriac Text Edited From the Manuscripts in London, Oxford, and Munich With an English Translation." By Ernest A. Wallis Budge, M.A. Oxford at the Clarendon Press. 1886. Chapters 38-39.* [2] *"Homilies on Matthew 6:1." John Chrysostom, Fourth Century.*

He also cites that John Chrysostom, from the fourth century, was also reading *Revelation of the Magi*, because he knew the Star was actually the same, of ancient origin. However, Chrysostom was also guilty of trying to justify his illiterate position to explain away the *Revelation of the Magi* which he was clearly aware. In fact, in his Homilies[2] on the matter, he expressed frustration that his misleading led some in his congregation to justify Astrology. It is odd he could not see he was the author of such when he demanded that the Kings came from Persia.

The footnote for this point offers another confirmation that scholars knew the Star appeared two years prior to the Wise Men arriving in Jerusalem. They knew this was not actually a Star, as we see them, but far brighter, which is an excerpt in concept from *Revelation of the Magi*. That further details another point, which also brings attention to the Philippines, as it says the Star appeared in the form of an eagle. That is the national symbol of the Philippines to this day and that eagle appears in prophecy. It is the largest eagle on Earth. Within the Star was the form of a young child, (which is also a direct quote from *Revelation of the Magi*). One can see attacks on this important information early in the corrupt church, proving that even most so-called "Early Church Fathers" were those who crept in unawares. He knew it was a "secret power" and not an actual Star. That was the Light of Messiah Himself which is from *Revelation of the Magi*. Knowing this makes it obvious why the Vatican hid this manuscript for so long.

*"Καὶ γὰρ πρὸ πολλοῦ χρόνου δοκεῖ μοι ὁ ἀδτὴρ φανῆται {Greek: Καὶ gàr prò pollou xrónou dokei moi o aothr fanhtai}. See Migne's edit., vol. vii, col. 76. '**Two years before Christ was born, a star appeared to the Magi;** they saw a star in the firmament of heaven which shone with **a light greater than that of any other star**. Within it was a maiden carrying a child with a crown upon his head.' Brit. Mus. Add. 25,875, fol. 40 a, col. 1. See Bezold, Die Schatzhöhle, p. 56. Another legend says that the star was in the **shape of an eagle having within it the form of a young child**, and above him the sign of the cross. Sandys, Christmas Carols, London, 1833, p. lxxxiii foll."[2]*

Chapter 39 of *The Book of the Bee* also cites the Cave of Treasures, where Adam placed the resources for the coming birth of Messiah. That proves to also originate in *Revelation of the Magi*. *The Book of the Bee* quotes that Adam handed the prophecy to Seth, who handed it down to the Magi over the ages. This was an ancient priesthood, just as in *Revelation of the Magi*. The Star's disappearance when they reached Jerusalem and reappearance soon after is also right out of *Revelation of the Magi*. Though the deviations are not credible, *The Book of the Bee*, in the 11th century, and John Chrysostom, 'early church father', in the 4th century, both quoted *Revelation of the Magi*. This is obviously suppressed knowledge because it does not fit the Catholic position, which is based on fiction.

The fact these were Kings, and their names were not Melchior, Caspar, and Balthazar, is well attested throughout history. However, *The Book of the Cave of Treasures,*[1] an occult corruption, (also not scripture), attempts the names of Three Kings. Again, they are Kings. That is another fairly early text attributed to Ephraim the Syrian, who lived in the fourth century *(306-373)*. Regardless of occult embellishment, this also quotes *Revelation of the Magi*, proving it was most certainly in circulation prior to the fourth century. Even the title and concept of the Cave of Treasures originates in *Revelation of the Magi*.

These Wise Men were, in fact, Kings and sons of Kings. This concept originates in *Revelation of the Magi*. It adds Persia as well, (in ignorance), but the Kings were from Persia, Sabha (Seba), and Sheba, confirming Psalm 72 is actual, valid geography and not fiction, as King David wrote the truth. Hormizdad is one of 24 names from *Revelation of the Magi*. The other two names are corruptions of other names, in the same regard. However, Sabha is a direct quote from *Revelation of the Magi*, and it is Seba. *The Cave of Treasures* further connects Perozadth as the King of Sheba, and it geographically locates Sheba East of Persia. That is amazing, and is quoting Psalm 72, (as well as *Revelation of the Magi*), but the name is not included in the *Book of Psalms*. We will test the 24 names. You will observe some are Filipino, some are Hebrew, and some lead to Ophir and his brothers, including Tarshish.

"[The names of the Magi.]
These are they who bore offerings to the King, kings, the sons of kings:--
*   1. HÔRMÎZDADH (Hormizd) of Mâkhôzdî (false change: Sanatruq was his father), king of Persia, who was called "King of Kings," and dwelt in Lower Âdhôrghîn.*
*   2. ÎZGARAD (Yazdegerd), the king of Sâbhâ. (Ahširaš son of Sahban)*
*   3. PERÔZÂDH, the king of Sheba, which is in the East." (Nasardîh son of Baladan)"*[1]

The name *Hormizd* appears first in *Revelation of the Magi*. *Makhozdi* is a false change, as his father was *Sanatruq*. He was not from Persia; the geography given points to far beyond Persia, which we are sure the author knew when he mentioned *Sheba*. *Sabha* is altered, from *Sahban* which is close. *Perozadh* is the King of Sheba in the Far East. Wow! Anyone who does not know geography well enough to know Africa is not East, should be disregarded. This is the Sheba from where the Queen of Sheba originated in the Philippines. This makes the association that *Nasardih* and *Baladan* were from Sheba, East of Persia. This should not be difficult.

---

[1]   *"The Book of the Cave of Treasures, A History of the Patriarchs and the Kings Their Successors from the Creation to the Crucifixion of Christ." Translated from The Syriac Text of the British Museum MS. ADD. 25875 By Sir E. A. Wallis Budge, Kt., M.A., Litt.D (Cambridge), M.A., D.Litt. (Oxford), D.Lit. (Durham), F.S.A. pp. 208-209. London Religious Tract Society. 1927.*

Other data cited, which originates in the ***Revelation of the Magi***: the Star was brighter than every other Star; it appeared in the East (not in Israel originally), and the Kings followed it to Jerusalem, where it disappeared for a short time, and then reappeared. The Star appeared at Messiah's birth, two years prior to the arrival of the Magi in Israel. It mentions that the son of the King of Sheba learned from a Rabbi, which is an illiterate insertion. The fact that they knew Sheba was involved in this proves they knew, as far back as in the fourth century, that Psalm 72 was a prophecy of Messiah; not of Solomon. This occult account, from ***The Cave of Treasures***, deviates in embellishment, which is not found in the ***Revelation of the Magi*** such as their being named Magi, due to their magician's clothing, which is utterly stupid to add. The text also forgets the two-year period, and claims the gifts were presented when Jesus *(Yahusha)* was eight days old. That is a very large conflict in their own writing. They also insert Nephilim nonsense, calling Messiah "giant of the world."

Also, noted in the translation by Sir Budge, the ***Fourth Book of Adam***[1] also defines these Magi as Three Kings, and repeats they are from Persia, Saba, and the East *(Sheba)* similar to ***The Book of the Cave of Treasures***. This concept is originally from ***Revelation of the Magi***, and has been obviously manipulated by spurious scribes. *Hor* is *Hormizd*, *Saba* is *Sahban*, and the Kings are 12 (not three), from the extreme East.

The original Ethiopic version of ***The Fourth Book of Adam and Eve***[1] is believed to have existed as early as the sixth century. That is not scripture, but the book recounts ***Revelation of the Magi***, with manipulations. It could be quoting ***The Cave of Treasures***, but if so, it is originally from ***Revelation of the Magi***, as it is still being used from the sixth century and beyond. *The Gospel of Matthew*, the *Book of Psalms*, and the *Book of Jeremiah* do not offer names of the Kings. *Hor*, *Saba*, and *King of the East* are all concepts from ***Revelation of the Magi***.

"In the Book of Adam (4th Book. 15) the kings are called Hor, king of Persia, Basantar, king of Saba, and Karsundas, king of the East."[1,2]

The information in ***Revelation of the Magi*** exposes scholars' unwillingness to learn, and consider just how wrong they have been for so many centuries. They are dishonest, whether they intend to be or not. We know Bible scholars personally, who are not bad men or women, and have no such intent of dishonesty, but someone needs to enlighten us with truth, if scholars will not. If you are reading this book, you are not likely in this category. However, even so, prove out everything we conclude for yourself and do not ever allow yourself to be deceived.

---

[1] *"Fourth Book of Adam and Eve."* [2] *Verified from "The book of Adam and Eve books 3 and 4." By Peter Thompson. University of Notre Dame.*

We will offer the evidence and draw conclusions, of which we are entitled, (unlike most scholars on this topic). Once you take those findings and test them even further, you as well will be qualified to render a conclusion, which level most scholars refuse to rise to on this topic. However, their consensus to remain stupid as a group on this subject is not a debate point. It is time they face the music for allowing the entire Christmas story to be defiled with fictional leaven, so that no one ever needed to believe the Bible account.

Next, we enter an arena of the extreme obvious. *Revelation of the Magi* is the account of origin for the Apostle Thomas' visit to India. India, in the ancient perspective defined on many maps, is not only the nation we call India today. It is vast in territory, sprawling from Afghanistan to the Malay Peninsula, including Indochina, sometimes even China, and most especially, the Indies, which includes the Philippines. There are Gnostic Gospels which use this account and lead to modern India in fiction. Thomas knew nothing of that land. He knew the Philippines (or ancient Ophir) was the Land of the Magi. Thomas intended to confirm what the Kings already knew, after Jesus *(Yahusha)* promised the Magi, twice.

Even some of the Northern Kingdom tribes migrated to the Philippines, according to Columbus, and Italian-Jewish scholar, Ferrisol, in the 15th and 16th centuries. We have covered that at length in *The Search for King Solomon's Treasure: The Lost Isles of Gold & the Garden of Eden* as well as *Garden of Eden Revealed: The Book of Maps.* Any Bible scholar who is not aware the Northern Kingdom never returned to Israel by the days of Jesus *(Yahusha)* has conducted no research on the topic. All were taken into Assyria and none returned, according to scripture.

Jesus *(Yahusha)* said He was specifically sent to reach the House of Israel, in which there were lost sheep, not in Judaea. When Messiah said He had other sheep that needed to be reached, He was specifically referring to the Northern Tribes of Israel, as some stayed in Assyria *(2Esd. 13)* and the remainder migrated to the Far East, to Ophir. Of all the destinations in the area referred to as India, Ancient Ophir, Sheba, and Tarshish, Philippines was at the top of the list. We knew this was the likely scenario, and now, we have evidence of this visit.

John 10:15-16 KJV
*As the Father knoweth me, even so know I the Father: and **I lay down my life for the sheep.** And other sheep I have, which are not of this fold: them also I must bring, and they shall hear my voice; and there shall be one fold, and one shepherd.*

Matthew 15:24 KJV
*But he answered and said, **I am not sent but unto the lost sheep of the house of Israel.***

Though the Apostle Thomas' expeditions are lost in the modern Bible Canon, there is record that he traveled to India. *Revelation of the Magi* defines his destination as the extreme East of the Earth, which geography charts as East of Persia, and modern India, to the famous Isles of Gold, where the Northern Lost Tribes are known to have migrated. King David told us of this migration in Psalm 72, as well as the Prophet Ezra *(2Esd. 13)*. In the account, Thomas arrived in the Isles of the Magi and a great revival broke forth. The lost sheep heard the voice of the Messiah in Thomas' teachings which affirmed their own. This is a lost historic account of New Testament communities ignored in scholarship. This is why they would prefer to keep this book suppressed. They have failed.

In the Gnostic Gospels, we find a continuation of geography for the Apostles, especially that of Thomas in *Acts of the Apostles In Asia: Judas Thomas Didi.* Many read the account and think he only went to mainland India but that is erroneous, even to the account. Indeed, this is a Gnostic writing and not scripture. However, in addition to India (regardless of how one would define that vast territory, historically), Thomas made it as far as the Far East, to an island inhabited by black men, and even to Japan from there. This account of the travels of Thomas originates in the *Revelation of the Magi* and not the other way around. One sentence in this text does not become the origin of a significant account of monumental geography. Indeed, this Gnostic manipulation inserts the occult often. but the geography does still serve as affirmation Thomas made it to the Philippines. Also, the name *Judas Thomas* appears first in *Revelation of the Magi* in the first century, before this writing attributed to Thomas from the second century. It would be backwards reasoning otherwise.

"Later Thomas was in India and also in an island inhabited by black men, and even in Japan where he made predictions about the future of religion in these countries." [1] *(p. 106)*
"Thomas passed some time in Judah, preaching the gospel, and then went into distant countries, inhabited by savage races, as Parthia, Media, Persia, Hyrcania, and came, at last, to India." [1] *(p. 107)*
"He made the largest number of converts in India. This immense territory he traversed in every direction, and established Christianity in it so firmly, that traces of it were found there in the 16th century, 1500 years after his death. Even in China, indubitable signs of it were discovered; he erected many churches, and placed Christian teachers in them, that the faith he had personally preached during his life might be preserved after his death." [1] *(p. 107)*
"The lot came out to Thomas to go to the country of India." [1] *(p. 107)*

Indeed, the story in this *Gospel of Thomas* differs greatly from *Revelation of the Magi.* The *Gospel of Thomas* is dated by most scholars to approximately the second century. However, the detail for the isles of the Far East are found in *Revelation of the Magi* as the origin of that claim and not the other way around. It does not cover modern India as *Revelation of the Magi* does, so the focus should be the Southeast

---

[1] *"The Gospels of Thomas With Acts of the Apostles In Asia." Full English Version. Filbluz Editions*

Asian isles. In this account, Thomas is taken as a slave into India, which is not even true. They attempt to match an Indian king named *Gundafore*, with a Magi named *Gudaphar*, who was not from India, and that name is Hebrew. However, India was not known in this Gnostic account as the land of the Three Kings, and that fails the vaildity test. It is similar but wordplay alone is not a theory. The Wise Men arrived in the first century B.C. and *The Gospel of Thomas* occurred after Messiah's ascension. The likelihood of Gudaphar being King still was not great, but far worse, he would have recognized Thomas and what he was preaching and embraced him.

The India-based portion of the story is a clear embellishment, likely all made up in a Gnostic haze. However, the geography of Thomas reaching the Southeast Asian isles vets with *Revelation of the Magi* as its origin. The full account exists in *Revelation of the Magi* and no detail is given in *Acts of the Apostles In Asia.*[1] Thomas was supposedly killed in modern India, which may still be true, but Ophir welcomed him with open arms, and that is the reason the largest multitude of new believers came from Asia. This remains to this day. The Philippines is surrounded by nations that have small percentages of Bible believers while it remains mostly so.

In the *Gospel of the Infancy of Jesus*[1] *(p. 3)* (attributed to Thomas erroneously, as it is written more than 1000 years later), the Magi account within this Gospel originates in *Revelation of the Magi.* Similar features include: the Star that appeared in the East, guiding them on their journey, the titles given as Kings and chief men, and their experience of revival when they return home. Certainly, this Gospel inserts occult concepts with the swaddling-cloth having magical powers. The Bible never needs such, and when an item is used, it is only a conduit for Yahuah's power.

This geography is affirmed in *The Acts of Philip and Miriam,* (another Gnostic account, not scripture), as it sends *"Thomas to India (p. 49)."*[2] Such area would include the Philippines in the perception of that era.

Ultimately, the origin of all these mentions is really the suppressed *Revelation of the Magi.* It is the more detailed account, which claims to have been written in the first century by the Magi themselves. No one has produced evidence that the Magi did not write this book, and that burden remains on them when the book tells you who wrote it and when. Then, even more so, it vets as accurate. We will explore this content throughout this book. Thomas may have made it to India, but his destination would have been Ophir, not mainland India. The following timeline organizes the thoughts in this chapter chronologically to better realize the precedence of *Revelation of the Magi.* It is not scripture, but it is credible history proving that *The Gospel of Matthew* has always offered an historic account and David's prophecy came to pass as he predicted and with the geography he knew.

---

[1] *"Gospel of the Infancy of Jesus." Acts of the Apostles In Asia. Full English Version. Filbluz Editions.*
[2] *"The Gospels of Thomas With Acts of the Apostles In Asia." Full English Version. Filbluz Editions.*

T I M E L I N E

150: Infancy Gospel X repeats several details from Revelation of the Magi. Acts of the Apostles uses geography from Revelation of the Magi.

198: Clement of Alexandria The Stromata uses the month and day of Jesus' birth from Revelation of the Magi.

SECOND century

300: John Chrysostom cites data from Revelation of the Magi.

350 or earlier: Syriac Holy Spirit in feminine form dates to 2nd-4th centuries.

350: The Book of the Cave of Treasures quotes Revelation of the Magi on details.

FOURTH century

450: Opus Imperfectum in Matthaeum repeats the same story verbatim in large part directly from Revelation of the Magi.

FIFTH century

500: Fourth Book of Adam and Eve uses elements from Revelation of the Magi.

550: Catholic fiction of Melchior, Balthasar, and Caspar fabricated.

SIXTH century

700: Theodorus bar Kōnī notes arrival month from Revelation of the Magi.

775: Chronicle of Zuqnin copied over existing Revelation of the Magi from an earlier text.

EIGHTH century

800 or so: relocated to a monastery in the Egyptian desert.

NINTH century

1200: The Book of the Bee quotes portions of Revelation of the Magi.

ELEVENTH century

1700's: G. S. Assemani transferred the document to the Roman Vatican Library where it remains.

MODERN centuries

1950: Finally, translated into Italian.

* All dates are approximations.

2010: Finally, translated into English.

Revelation of the Magi Precedence

Chapter 4:
Magi Is Not a Word From the Greek

The Birth of the Son
No Sorcerors Allowed!

One of the greatest revelations needed from *Revelation of the Magi (RotM)* is that the word Magi or Magos from the *Wise Kings* narrative does not originate in the Greek language. Greece is not East. The same could be said of Africa (which some scholars try to force), but for this to work, one must forget what direction both left and right are. Those are not theories. Yes, it is written in Greek in the New Testament (as the rest of the canonical books are), but is it Greek in origin? What if, instead, there was evidence that the word derives from its land and its language of nativity? It turns out, there is, thanks to this text. How many times have we all heard the Christmas sermon about how the Wise Men were not Kings? That is false, they were certainly Kings. 12 in all, there were more than three in number indeed, but three still has precedence, as you will find.

Then, even the highest of scholars takes us to the faulty assumption the Babylonian and/or Persian Magoi are injected by *The Gospel of Matthew.* They ignore that those Magoi were not even in power in the first century. They are still rebuked as satanic sorcerers in the same New Testament. One does not need to go to the Old Testament to learn how to read a word well defined in the New. They are changing the Bible when they do so, against its own interpretation itself.

They will make up fiction, supposing the sorcerers converted to the religion of Daniel. That is not ever a Bible account; it is poor assumption they cannot make. The fact that they have to manufacturer such a story to make their lie work should be evident. Certainly, Daniel was the head over the Biblical Wise Men, such as Shadrach, Meshach, and Abednego, but sorcerers were his satanic enemy. For a theologian to assume such a thing is nonsense. Daniel never became head of the magicians. He was head of the *Sophos*; the Wise Men.

Were the Magi Sorcerers?

Imagine the assertion that Yahuah informed very few of the birth of His son, and of those, the top of the list were satanic sorcerors, not even "worthy *(17:9)*" as Herod. It is obvious that the invitation list sounds skewed. Even the Pharisees were not notified, for the same reason no satanic sorcerer was. They were the ones who confused and reckoned the Magi as Magianism falsely *(17:2)* which fraudulent label only occurs one time in rebuke in *Revelation of the Magi* because it was not the origin of their name; Magi, which is not Greek. That title originated in their homeland in the Far East, and linguistics prove this fact to be accurate. However, now that we know the word Magi has no connection to this satanic cult from Babylon and Persia, but originates in their own land, we can fully discount that any scholar repeating that nonsense is not representing a Bible position, (intended or not).

Daniel's Wise Men Were NOT Magi!

The Apostle Matthew's use of the Greek word Magos (translated as Wise Men in Matthew 2:1, 2:7, and 2:16), is not the same as Daniel's enemies called the Magi. If that is considered church doctrine, it is so, untested. Anything any denomination espouses that it does not test remains suspect until proven. No one credible reading and summarizing ancient texts has concluded this strange new view.

Greek: μάγος: *Magos:*
a Magian, i.e. Oriental scientist; by implication, a magician -- sorcerer, wise man (G3097).

The reference to the *Book of Daniel's* Wise Men of Daniel 5:8, for instance, is not *Magos.* Daniel uses the Hebrew word *hakim,* which is a general term for those considered to hold knowledge above the regular folk. Taking that generality and assuming it into Matthew's Wise Men is illiterate. However, he rattles off others in a listing that separates them. The King's Wise Men that are described in the *Book of Daniel* were not the Magi described in the *Book of Matthew.* Even the era is very disconnected, as those Magi had no part in the New Testament except as enemies. One who supposedly converted to the Biblical faith would no longer be called a sorcerer. They would have to leave that satanic paradigm.

The Wise Men described in the *Book of Daniel,* however, are not *Magos* in Greek. According to the *Greek Septuagint* translation, the word is *sophos* meaning *wise;* not even *Magos.* It would not matter, however, if it was the same word; it most certainly is not the same concept in the *Book of Matthew.* Indeed, among those the King considered wise could definitely be sorcerers, however, they are still not called *Magos* by Daniel in the *Greek Septuagint.* They are still called *sophos,* instead, in Daniel 2:12, 13, 14, 18, 24, 27, and 48. Matthew's Gospel repeats that in 23:34, using *sophos* as well; referring to prophets, wise men and scribes. Daniel does not even call them *Magos.* To equate that term solely based on a misunderstanding of a different word is not scholarship.

Hebrew: חכים: *chakkîym: Wise Men (Aramaic origin) (H2445).*
Greek: σοφός: *sophós: Wise Men (G4680).*

Here is where the confusion sets in. The only other time the New Testament Greek uses this word *Magos,* outside of the four times in the *Gospel of Matthew,* for these Kings who brought gifts to the Messiah, is in the *Book of Acts.* That was written by Luke, not Matthew. In Acts 13:6, 8, Luke, the author of the *Book of Acts* rebukes a false prophet, identifying him with the term *Magos.* Somehow, scholars miss the term false, and then, attempt to placate an inept view that never belongs in any Bible discussion. Therefore, not only do scholars use the wrong term, but even the general term *Magos* or *Wise Men* as sorcerers from Persia and Babylon. Note, Babylon is not even on the list of the Three Kings even. This group of holy men honored their covenant relationship with Yahuah by bringing the Messiah gifts directly from the Estate of Adam, in their homeland. They should not be defined by one guy who was a false one (as scholars assume a false word use in the *Book of Daniel* that is not even there). If Daniel, did in fact convert sorcerers to his faith, they would never assume the title of magicians and sorcerers again. This was about 500 years later, when the Greeks already conquered Persia, and the Romans conquered the Greeks. Those sorcerers had no bearing on this account and the word, *Magi*, used in the *Book of Daniel*, is not associated whatsoever with the use in the *Book of Acts*, nor does it derive from the Greek language. The word is from the land of the nativity of the Kings.

One must first restore the geography of Psalm 72, as well as ***Revelation of the Magi***, and then, this is obvious. The wall of objections comes crashing to the ground. How could a scholar (such as the translator) recognize that this word originates in Southeast Asia, but does not bother to research the ancient royal class or the words for prayer' or silence in said languages? All three connotations, in the Philippines, derive from the word, *Magi*. "That is impossible!" they will say.

Indeed, we agree, it can only be possible if it is the truth. What is truly inconceivable is they remain illiterate, willingly, and many of those scholars will scorn and scoff at this evidence they never knew and still refuse to test it for validity. This research is further evidence that the academic and scholarly class slips on their racist glasses when reviewing maps and history hiding the Philippines.

Filipino Ancient Royal Class Known as Magi!

What if the Philippines actually had a documented social class of royals known as the *MAGI* in their native, ancient language? Of course, that would be impossible. No such thing could ever occur... unless... it does! Filipinos already know what we are conveying as there is an ancient royal classification known as the MAGInoo. This was the highest social order, which included what one would refer to as Kings and princes. Then, ***Revelation of the Magi*** tells us these were Kings, sons of Kings, and Wise Men. It is not difficult.

MAGInoo: Tagalog: *gentleman; gentlemanly; honorable.*[1]
maginoohin: *of gentlemanly habits or bearing.* **Root:** *ginoó: mister; sir; gentleman. The female counterpart to "ginoo" is "ginang."*[1] ***pagka-máginoó: Tagalog:*** *quality of being noble, worthy or stately.*[1]

---

[1]*Tagalog.com, Retrieved Oct. 2, 2024.*

This title for royalty in the Philippines preceded the Spanish arrival recorded in use in 1571 and 1690 among other references. Better yet, it was recorded in the first century by the Apostle Matthew, who used the Greek language to express a word that was not of Greek origin. He was translating Tagalog into Greek.

1571: Plasencia translates "Lord God" as Panginoon Dios, and one of the leaders who surrendered the Port of Manila in 1571 was **Maginoo** *Marlanaway.*[1]

1690: There are **three kinds and classes of people:** *the chiefs, whom the Visayans call* **dato** *and the Tagalogs* **maginoo;** *the timauas who are the ordinary common people, called* **maharlica** *among the Tagalogs; and the slaves, called* **oripuen** *by the Visayans and* **alipin** *by the Tagalogs.*[2]

1690: The penalty of death was never imposed by process of law, except when the murderer and his victim were common men and had no gold to satisfy the murder. In such a case, if the man's **dato or maginoo (for these are one and the same)** *did not kill him,* **the other chiefs did,** *spearing him after lashing him to a stake.*[2]

This also proves the *MAGInoo* were not a Muslim class (as some have attempted to claim), as it far predates the migrations of Muslims into the Philippines for more than a thousand years after *Revelation of the Magi* was written. Islam did not exist.

Filipino Word For "Prayer" Derives from Magi!

However, the scoffing academic would then ignorantly claim, "that is simply not enough." No, it is not, and that is not the end of this narrative. What about these two definitions of *prayer* and *silence?* Certainly, neither of those could be of Philippine origin. Scoff! Scoff! Snark! Oops! They both are! In Tagalog, the national Filipino language, the prefix *mag* is used in *magdasal,* meaning *to pray.* *MAG* and *MAGI* are the origin, the root words, with a plethora of combinations in linguistics, which identify even other traits of the ancient Magi Filipino. Wow!

mag+root: [affix/verb] to do something; to do an occupation; to go; to use something; to wear something; to do a reciprocal action; to be.[3]

MAGdasál: *Tagalog: to pray.*[3]

MAGa-ampo: *Ilonggo/Hiligaynon: to pray.* **managampo:** *Bisaya: ampo: to surrender.*[4]

---

[1] *William Henry Scott. Philippine Studies, Vol. 28, No. 2 (1980). p. 146.* [2] *The Philippine Islands: Explorations by Early Navigators, Descriptions of the Islands and their Peoples, their History and Records of the Catholic Missions, as related in contemporaneous Books and Manuscripts, showing the Political, Economic, Commercial and Religious Conditions of those Islands from their earliest relations with European Nations to the close of the Nineteenth Century. Edited and annotated by Emma Helen Blair and James Alexander Robertson, with historical introduction and additional notes by Edward Gaylord Bourne. Translated from the Originals. Vol. 40. Chapter 16.116. p. 85-86. 1690-1691. The Arthur H. Clark Company.* [3] *Tagalog.com, Retrieved Oct. 2, 2024.* [4] *Viewer who is a Local Native Speaker.*

Filipino Word For "Silence" Derives from Magi!

Then, there is the Filipino Ibanag word for *remain silent* which also begins with *MAGI*, and includes other associations as well. When we reached out to a close friend from Cagayan Province, for clarification, they immediately rattled off the word, which we were able to confirm in a credible, very rare Ibanag dictionary. Many scholars would require that because they disrespect an actual Ibanag to know their own language.

The Ibanag tribe originates in Northwest Luzon where the entrance to the Cagayan River is known in their local language as that of "many priests"–Aparri.[1] Notice, one of the names of the Magi according to **Revelation of the Magi** is Gudaphar which appears too similar to ignore. There is also an apparent association with the word Ophir *(A-U-P-I-R: אופיר: H211)*. Add the "ri *(רי: H7377)*" on the end of that word and it would render as "watering Ophir" which makes sense, as that is the longest river in the Philippines, originating in the gold mountains. Even the word Cagayan appears Hebrew in origin as *"chaggayah: חגיח: Feast of Yah, a Levite. Origin of name Chaggay or Haggai the prophet."*[2] Add the ending "yan" which is *"Yah's Grace"* [H2282, H2291, babynames.merchant.com#70864]. In Ancient Hebrew, this word reveals much as it is literally "Feasts of Yah" or "Feasts of Yah's Grace." Also, understand there is a *Cagayan* in all three of the Magi segments of the Philippines in Luzon *(Ophir)*, Visayas *(Sheba)*, and Mindanao *(Tarshish)*.

Of course, we are supposed to ignore such direct and simple associations and allow the so-called experts to continue to offer obtuse etymologies of these words in ignorance. We will not. Test these for yourself, because you will typically hear "Scoff! Scoff! Snicker!" from a group who lost the Land of Gold, lost the Garden of Eden, and lost the home of the Magi. They are proven to stupidly continue to cover up the history their paradigm willingly forgot in favor of their own captors. Then, they refuse to accept facts which they do not test for validity, when these facts resurface. This information is from a Vatican document which the "powers that be" have hidden for more than 1000 years. Scholars do not get to scoff without at least testing it for truth.

Below is the second definition of the Magi word origin for *silence*, exactly as it is accurately specified in **Revelation of the Magi.**

MAGImammo: Ibanag: remain silent, silence, restrain, peace.[3] *to be still; to stay home.*[4]
Word Associations: MAGIbannag: Ibanag: to rest.[4] *MAGImman: Ibanag: to stop.*[4] *MAGIdda: Ibanag: to lie down.*[4] *MAGIlawa: Ibanag: leaving the harvest for the corners for the poor.*[3]

---

[1] *"Aparri." Wikipedia. Retrieved Oct. 2023.* [2] *"Chaggiyah." Strong's Concordance #2282 and 2291. BibleStudyTools.com.* [3] *Local Ibanag Viewer. Usage confirmed with Glosbe.com, Retrieved Oct. 14, 2024.* [4] *"An Ibanag-English Dictionary." Zorayda Beltran Ibarbia. Texas A&M University. 1969.*

Magi Family of Tagalog Words:

Wait a minute! You mean the practice from the Bible of leaving the corners of the harvest for the poor somehow made it to the Philippines? Of course, it did, as did circumcision, and numerous other similar observances, which are not Catholic in origin, not pagan, and further prove the Magi of the Philippines were not just aware but practicing covenant believers. This is the land of covenant who knew the Messiah from His birth to their death, and passed down these stories through their generations. They experienced two New Testament revivals in the first century B.C. - A.D.. Magellan and those after him tried to kill this. They failed, and now we know these truths once again.

There are many other words in Tagalog that are preceded by *MAG* or *MAGI*, which carry definitions very similar to the story of the Magi from the Philippines. For those skeptics, keep reading as this truth becomes very firm. Of course, the most important is that which adheres to the ancient Filipino royal class of the MAGInoo, and the two definitions of *MAGI*, from ***Revelation of the Magi***, meaning: *to pray* and *silence*. What a trifecta as all three originate in Philippine languages. Wow!!! However, these other associations are secondary evidence, making this truly overwhelming.

MAGdalá: to bring; to carry; to deliver; to convey; to take to; to carry on.[1]
MAGmág: common sense; sense; judgment; practical sense; discernment.[1]
MAGising: to awaken.[1]
MAGIsá: to be alone; to do something alone; to be the only one; to be one.[1]
MAGIng: to become; to be.[1]
MAGIsíp: to think; to think of; to think intensely; to plan; to come up with (a plan); to devise (plan).[1]
MAGIbâ: to demolish; to collapse; to break down.[1]
MAGIpón: to save; to collect; to assemble; to accumulate; to raise.[1]
MAGIwan: to leave behind; to evacuate.[1]
MAGIngat: to be careful; to take care; to beware; to look out.[1]
MAGhanáp: to search; to seek; to look for.[1]
MAGbigáy: to give; to grant; to equip; to donate; to allow. to give out.[1]
MAG-ulat: to report.[1]
MAG-aral: to study; to learn.[1]
MAGInit: to heat something.[1]
MAGInat: to stretch oneself.[1]
MAGIwi: to take care of children.[1]
MAGalak: to rejoice.[1]
MAGaayos: ordain.[1]
MAGaang: light.[1]
MAGaari: possess; steward; inherit; shall possess; shall inherit.[1]
MAGara: nicely dressed.[1]
MAGIlas: dynamic.[1]

MAGImbak: to conserve; to hoard; to store; to store away.[1]
MAGaalas: receive.[1]
MAG-ulit: to renew the action; to repeat.[1]
MAGadya: preserve.[1]
MAG-uurong: to retreat; to move; to step back.[1]
MAGalang: polite; courteous.[1]
MAGaaral: learn to; they learn; student; learn.[1]
MAGaling: healed.[1]
MAG-upo: to sit down; to sit on.[1]
MAGpadala: send; to transmit.[1]
MAGIlaw: to light up.[1]
MAGanda: tbeautiful; pretty; good in appearance of quality; lovely; cute.[1]

However, we believe the connection here to be far more intense and revealing. History and archaeology align with these linguistics in a miraculous manner. It is difficult to dismiss this in any arena of logic.

Famous Filipino Necklace Found in Egypt Also Named Magi!

In a coffee table book, ***Ginto: History Wrought in Gold,***[2] published by the Central Bank of the Philippines *(Bangko Sentral ng Pilipinas)*, a finding was documented that really brings this understanding to light. After we covered this in our teaching series, Bangko Sentral removed the book, and even the CD from circulation. When we ordered a copy, they kept the money and never delivered it, telling us it was out of print. However, to their credit, years later, they did finally return the money and just recently, they have now uploaded a PDF file of the book for all to review. We appreciate this gesture. Sadly, we had to call them out, but at least they did right.

"Some of the non-Indian borrowed designs found only in their original sources and in the Philippine area suggest direct linkages with other cultural currents from the Indian Ocean. Among these are kamagi necklaces (Aldred 1978: 105) and penannular, barter rings which both show Egyptian influence (Aldred 1978: 20, 94). The earliest insular Southeast Asian products reached the Mediterranean through a port on the Arabian Gulf, which were transported overland to the headwaters of the Nile, then shipped down to Alexandria. Austronesian traders are also known to have reached Madagascar (Miller 1969; Taylor 1976), so the African connection is an established fact." – Ramon N. Villegas, Bangko Sentral[2]

First, what is a *KA-MAGI* necklace? It should be far more famous than it is. This is the necklace of the Philippines documented to be traded as far as Africa and the Mediterranean since ancient times, even before the first century. Whoa!

---

[1] *Tagalog.com, Retrieved Oct. 2, 2024.* [2] *"Ginto: History Wrought in Gold." By Ramon N. Villegas. Manila: Bangko Central ng Pilipinas. 2004. p. 45.*

Here is the link; we are printing this here in our book, publicly, so that if it is removed again, everyone reading will have it in their possession: *https://www.bsp.gov.ph/Media_And_Research/Publications/Ginto.pdf.*

We have well covered the ships of Philippine design of antiquity which are believed to have sailed all the way to Israel, even as early as 200 B.C. as well [Horridge [1]]. This *ka-MAGI* necklace, named for the Magi of the same land, made it to the Middle East and Africa as a matter of "established fact" just as the Three Kings and their group of Magi visited Messiah two years after His birth in Bethlehem. There is another corroborating source in academia for this history as well.

*"Apart from India and China, **Butuan is known to have had extensive trading connections with Arabia** and in all probability with Sumatra and Java. The locally produced gold necklaces comprising of dentate interlocking beads seem to have reached Egypt, later to be mistakenly identified by European collectors as Egyptian." –Laszlo Legeza, Arts of Asia* [2]

"Hellenistic trade beads of West Asiatic and Egyptian origins found in early burials in many places in the Philippines, prove that such early trade contacts, no matter how irregular, existed between the Philippine archipelago and West Asia by the first centuries of the first millennium A.D."
–Laszlo Legeza, Arts of Asia [2]

The Magi necklace mistaken as an Egyptian-designed ornament originated in the land of the Magi and is called by their name ka-MAGI. Wow! This rare gold design, name, and Magi origin is indisputably proven in historical accounts, by illustrations from the 1590's (right), in archaeological finds (such as the Surigao Treasure from the 1890's), and on physical display at the Ayala Museum in Makati City, Philippines. When we review the linguistical understanding of this word, *KA-MAGI*, it becomes a strong connection, which must be the case, in the land of the Three Kings, according to this Vatican manuscript. We have a match. Not only does this prove the Magi etymology in their land of origin, but even in trade. The unique jewelry traded by the Magi circulated in the same areas as they made their famous journey in the first century. In other words, there is also firm evidence the Magi did execute such a voyage with success in the first century, and long before. Trade goods bearing their name were left behind in the Middle East and Africa in the same era. There is no debate.

---

[1] *"The Austronesians: Historical and Comparative Perspectives." By Edited by Peter Bellwood, James J. Fox and Darrell Tryon. (Professor Adrian Horridge). A publication of the Department of Anthropology as part of the Comparative Austronesian Project, Research School of Pacific Studies. The Australian National University Canberra ACT Australia. 2006. p. 146.* [2] *"Tantric Elements in pre-Hispanic Philippines Gold Art," By Laszlo Legeza. Arts of Asia, July-Aug. 1988, pp.129, 131 and 137.*

1590 Illustrations of the Magi Generations

This is how the Magi actually appeared. Tagalog Maginoo couple wearing kaMAGI necklaces which were found in archeology in the Surigao Treasure. 1595 Boxer Codex. Lilly Library, Indiana University, Bloomington, Indiana (U.S.A.), Catalogue Record of the Boxer Codex. p. 119, 115, 23, 70, 123. C.R. Boxer. Public Domain.

*kaMAGI: a large necklace or collar made of gold; gold collar; gold necklace (**Root: MAGI**)
ka+root. ka: you (second person singular). term of address for elders and distant uncles or aunts.
Magi is a common word root in the Filipino language.*[1]

When we look at other native languages around the Philippines, one especially emerges as a strong match for magi. In the Waray language of Visayas and Mindanao, Philippines, they use the word *Maagi* appropriately fitting to the action of the Magi who passed by or dropped by Bethlehem to offer gifts to the Messiah.

MAaGI: Waray: will pass by. Will drop by (natural). Other forms: maagian, magigin.[2]
MiAGI: Bisayan: ago; last; passed; past; underwent.[3]
MAaGIan: Bisayan: passable.[3]
MAGawI: Bisayan: useful.[3]
MAGIhud: Kamayo Barbaro: go.[4]
maMAGI: Kamayo Davao: pass by.[4]

In other words, just as the Magi represent the entire archipelago of ancient Ophir, Sheba and Tarshish, they survive in origin in the prominent languages in Luzon, Visayas and Mindanao just as ***Revelation of the Magi*** documents. This, along with all the many verifiable truths in the document prove it to be valid. If we had the written history the Vatican trashed illegally and immorally, ***Revelation of the Magi*** would be there, and likely written in Ancient Hebrew, Baybayin, or similar. For an academic to claim no one can read it or treat it as credible (when it proves accurate on every level), is another stupid paradigm of those who lost the Magi in the first place. Who cares what they think nor how they scoff their way around these facts, sidestepping their own guilt.

Chinese Document Filipinos as Magi!

The Chinese were documenting the account all along. They went to the Philippines to trade with an island, likely Mindoro, which they called *MA-I* or *MA-YI*. Wait! You mean they were attempting to express *MAGI?* We find that likely.

"An edict of 972 indicates that Mindoro (Ma-i) was part of that trade: In the fourth year of the K'ai Pao period [972], a superintendent of maritime trade was set up in Kwangchow, and afterwards in Hangchow and Mingchow also a superintendent was appointed for all Arab, Achen, Java, Borneo, Ma-i, and Srivijaya barbarians, whose trade passed through there, they taking away gold, silver, strings of cash, lead, tin, many-colored silk, and porcelain..." –William Henry Scott[5]

---

[1] *Tagalog.com, Retrieved Oct. 2, 2024.* [2] *3NS Corpora Project Waray Dictionary.* [3] *Binisaya.com, Retrieved Oct. 2, 2024.* [4] *Kamayo Dictionary. http://kamayo-dictionary.blogspot.com.* [5] *"Filipinos In China Before 1500." By William Henry Scott. Asian Studies Journal. (Manila: De La Salle University China Studies Program, 1989), pp. 1 and 3.*

"The first Philippine tribute mission to China appears to have come from Butuan on 17 March 1001. Butuan (P'u-tuan) is described in the Sung Shih (Sung History) as a small country in the sea to the east of Champa, farther than Ma-i..." –William Henry Scott[5]

Mindoro is on the way to Butuan, and we vet that further in *The Search for King Solomon's Treasure: The Lost Isles of Gold & The Garden of Eden.* However, one of the most amazing facts about Mindoro or Ma-Yi, is the name of its indigenous tribes – the MAGI! Mindoro is historically famous for its skill in working with gold in fact.

Mangyan:
*Mangyan is the generic name for the eight indigenous groups found in Mindoro each with its own tribal name, language, and customs. The Mangyans were **once the only inhabitants of Mindoro.***[2]

Certainly, gold is very well affirmed in the Philippines; after a more than 3,000-year gold rush, it maintains the second largest, untapped gold reserves in the ground of any nation on Earth. Of course, the scoffer would then level an unresearched charge, claiming that frankincense only comes from Ethiopia, and myrrh from areas like Yemen. This has always been an extremely uninformed position. Those are not scholars.

𝒻rankincense and 𝒩yrrh in the 𝒫hilippines?

Jeremiah 6:20 KJV
*To what purpose cometh there to me **incense** (frankincense: lĕbownah: נובל) **from Sheba, and the sweet cane from a far country?** your burnt offerings are not acceptable, nor your sacrifices sweet unto me.*

First, the prophet Jeremiah defines Biblical frankincense as originating in a land that also has sugarcane. Ethiopia has no ancient application of native sugarcane until the sixteenth century. Therefore, though its incense is valuable and a fine substitute indeed, it is not the origin of Biblical frankincense. The Philippines has had frankincense and sugarcane since ancient times; even before King Solomon's era.

"Sugarcane has been cultivated by smallholder farmers since 16th century in Ethiopia and preceded the commercial production." –Hindawi Advances In Agriculture, 2018[3]

---

[1] *"Filipinos In China Before 1500." By William Henry Scott. Asian Studies Journal. (Manila: De La Salle University China Studies Program, 1989), pp. 1 and 3.* [2] *"Mangyans." Wikipedia. Retrieved Oct. 2025.* [3] *"Research Article: Sugarcane Landraces of Ethiopia: Germplasm Collection and Analysis of Regional Diversity and Distribution." Hindawi Advances In Agriculture, Aug. 14, 2018. Vol. 2018, Article ID 7920724, 18 pages.*

In addition, Chinese history records the Philippines trading wine made of sugarcane in 982 A.D. before both the Muslims and Spanish arrived, and such tradition continues today. Thus, it was already growing there natively. This fits the Bible, Ethiopia does not.

"The sugar industry of the Philippines has had a colorful and dramatic history. The industry started some two to four thousand years before the Christian era where vessels from the Celebes brought sugarcane cuttings to Mindanao. Eventually, these plants spread further north to the Visayan islands and Luzon." –Republic of the Philippines, Dept. of Agriculture [1]

But the Philippines does not have frankincense, right? Yes, it does. It is called "poor's man's frankincense" (due to not being blessed by illiterate Rabbis), it is cheaper. However, the science and history are there to affirm this.

"Manila elemi, from Canarium luzonicum, one of the best known and single largest source of the world's supply of elemi." [2]
Philippine frankincense and myrrh: Burseraceae family (same as frankincense and myrrh)
Gum Elemi (Manila Elemi) (soft): Canarium commune "From the Philippines. Elemi produces a bright lemony, woody fragrance with a hint of fennel, frankincense and grass. Elemi is a cousin to myrrh and frankincense (Boswellia carterii) and is often referred to as "the poor man's frankincense," as it is a bit easier on the pocket." [2]
Pili (Manila Elemi) (soft): Canarium genera, Canarium ovatum, Canarium luzonicum
From the Philippines. Cousin to Myrrh and Frankincense. [2]

"The elemi tree is related to frankincense, myrrh and opoponax, all belonging to the Burseraceae family. When lacerated, the bark yields a sharp, green, and pungent, white or yellow oleoresin. Elemi has properties and uses similar to Frankincense; ergo, also referred to as "Poor Man's Frankincense." France has been the largest single market, followed by Germany, and increasingly by Japan."
"Both Canarium luzonicum and C. ovatum are locally known as pili. The Manila elemi of commerce is derived from both species. There is a confusing sharing of common names and scientific names between Canarium ovatum (pili) and Canarium luzonicum (sahing)." –Dr. Stuart [2]

In fact, this variety of frankincense is also myrrh in the ancient perspective. How do we know this? Science has now tested both frankincense and myrrh found in ancient Egypt. It tests scientifically as elemi and not what we call these today. In

---

[1] *Sugar Regulatory Administration. Republic of the Philippines. Department of Agriculture. Retrieved Dec. 17, 2019.* [2] *a. "Young Living sees growing demand for essential oils." By Zsarlene B. Chua. Apr. 22, 2019. Business World. bworldonline.com. Confirmed by numerous distributor sites such as: theoildropper.com, essentialoilexchange.com, mountainroseherbs.com, bmvfragrances.com, butterflyexpress.com. b. "Reference Guide for Essential Oils." By Connie and Alan Higley. Abundant Health. Ninth Edition. Revised Oct. 2005. p. 66. c. "Canarium luzonicum. Manila Elemi." Stuart Xchange. Godofredo U. Stuart Jr., M.D. Updated June 2017.*

other words, the Philippine frankincense and myrrh from the pili tree qualify as both Biblical spices. Even when provided details such as this, scholarship has lost track of the elements, the language, and even history that affirms it. The academic sector and religious leaders seem to purposely hide the truth from the rest of the world. Even today, the Philippines dominates the elemi marketplace internationally. This has not even evolved in that sense but remains the valid paradigm.

"After the Middle Ages the resin from the Boswellia frereana tree, a Somalian variant (Maydi) of the genus that gives as frankincense, was referred to as "elemi." Its inclusion in Coptic incense (i.e. the incense used by the Coptic Christian church of Egypt), helped the confusion, as elemi is frequently a participant in incense blends." [1]

"Elemi's use in embalming, found in sarcophagi buried in ancient tombs has been celebrated through the ages. The ancient Egyptians championed elemi in the intricate embalming process..." [1]

These conclusions are explosive yet undeniable. There is no other way to view the account of the Magi. They did not originate in Persia, India, and Arabia. They were never named Melchior, Caspar, and Balthazar and there were more than three. They were never magicians and sorcerers but a holy Biblical priesthood. Their label was never Babylonian or Persian but originates in the land of their nativity in the Philippines, which proves to be fact.

The native languages of the Philippines include the royal class of Magi, the MAGInoo, exactly as it should to fit this narrative. They have the definitions of *MAGI,* as outlined in **Revelation of the Magi** as origin words in *MAGdasal* meaning "to pray" as well in *MAGIammo* for "be silent." Surely, there can be no argument against these very direct words as the origin of the word *MAGI,* as we are instructed.

Local, Spanish and Chinese History confirm Magi in the Philippines in the Mangyans of Ma-Yi in Mindoro. Even in trade, we can confirm the famous ka-MAGI necklace found as far as Africa and the Mediterranean originated from the Magi for which it was named from the Philippines. Just based on this chapter alone, it is time academia and scholarship adjust their views to include this text as an accurate account, and restore the ancient, Biblical Magi as holy priests from Ophir, Sheba, and Tarshish, Philippines.

We have only presented the linguistics of the word, and frankly, the evidence is already significant. However, as we enter the geography of **Revelation of the Magi,** which affirms Psalm 72, there is no more debate on this topic. Scholars would have to attempt such in ignorance and certainly some will. Our hope is that even a few scholars will awaken to the truth presented here, and take the time to prove it for themselves. We encourage everyone to do the same.

---

[1] *"Perfumery Material: Elemi." By Elena Vosnaki. Perfume Shrine. Dec. 18, 2012.*

*Historic fraud of the of the Magi in Catholic-generated art. The erroneous Magi of the wrong races the church knew was wrong. Above: Basilica of Sant'Apollinare Nuovo in **Ravenna, Italy:** The Three Wise Men" (named Balthasar, Melchior, and Gaspar). Detail from: "Mary and Child, surrounded by angels", mosaic of a Ravennate italian-byzantine workshop, completed within 526 A.D. by the so-called "Master of Sant'Apollinare." Wikimedia Commons. Public Domain.*

Did Ravenna, Italy know Where Adam Dwelt & the Far East existed?

"...these are kings, sons of Eastern kings, in the land of Shir, which is the outer part of the entire East of the world... at the Ocean, the great sea beyond the world... that place in which dwelt Adam..."
– RotM 2:4

650 Ravenna Map Knew the Extreme East Was the Islands of Paradise

Full Map on page 16.

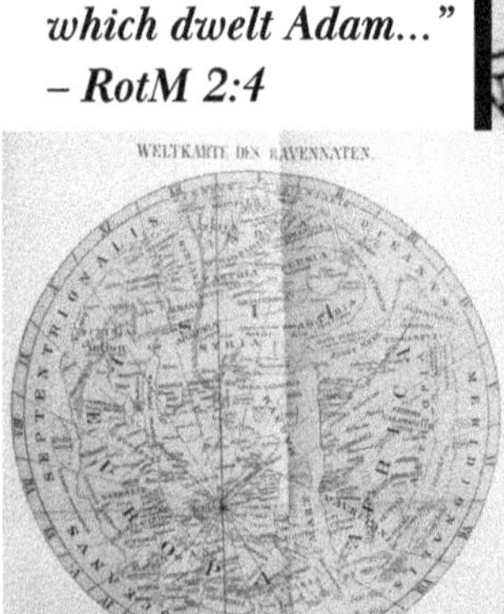

Chapter 5: Geography of the Land of Shir

*"RotM 1:2 An account of the revelations and the visions, which the kings, [sons of kings,] of the great East spoke, who were called **Magi**..."*

*"RotM 2:4 These are kings, sons of **Eastern kings**, in the land of **Shir**, which is the **outer part of the entire East of the world** inhabited by human beings, at the Ocean, the great sea beyond the world, east of the land of Nod, that place in which dwelt Adam, head and chief of all the families of the world."*

*"RotM 4:1 And those books of hidden mysteries were placed on the **Mountain of Victories in the east of Shir**, our country, in a cave, the **Cave of Treasures** of the Mysteries of the Life of Silence."*

Where is the "outer part of the entire East of the world?" The Catholic Church knew where it was when they created the mosaic art *(left)* in 527 A.D. in Ravenna, Italy. Not only did they have the precedence of the map of Cosmas in 550 *[p. 14]*, but the 650 Ravenna, Italy Map demonstrates they still knew this a century later. However, these lies continued all the way until the present time. The Catholic leaders knew, long before their fraud was perpetrated from maps, even until 196 B.C.. They knew in Ravenna, and hid ***Revelation of the Magi*** for more than 1000 years from the public eye, to cover up their maleficence and gross negligence.

Anyone who just answered "Persia is the extreme East of the world in that era," needs to turn in their scholar credentials. That is a ridiculous response, when ancient maps, geography, the Bible, and written history say otherwise. "Saudi Arabia" is an even more laughable response. India is also far from the ends of the Earth, though the Indies are part of the mindset of the ancients (though not associated in any sense with modern India). At that point in time, that was no mystery, as maps in the first century affirm the ancients well knew of the islands of Southeast Asia especially the Philippines.[2] Just as the New Testament Bible comes to us in the Greek language (in origin, largely), first century maps label these isles in Greek as Chryse *(Gold in Greek synonymous with Ophir in Hebrew)* and Argyre *(Silver in Greek synonymous with Tarshish in Hebrew)*. Not only was this Solomon's route and those after him for centuries, but the Greeks also inherited these directions from the Phoenician sailors they acquired into their empire, as well as from Tarshish's family as his father, Javan *(Yavan/Ionan)* was the founder of Greece.

For instance, in 196 B.C., some renditions of Eratosthenes' Map *[p. 84]* documented two islands Southeast of China in the South China Sea which would become known as the Isles of Gold and Silver. In 43 A.D., Pomponius Mela *[p. 85]*[2] indisputably defines two islands Southeast of China in the Philippines. Between 50-70 A.D., the

---

[2] *All maps in full color, high resolution in Garden of Eden Revealed: The Book of Maps. Schwab/ Zamoranos. 2024. www.OphirInstitute.com.*

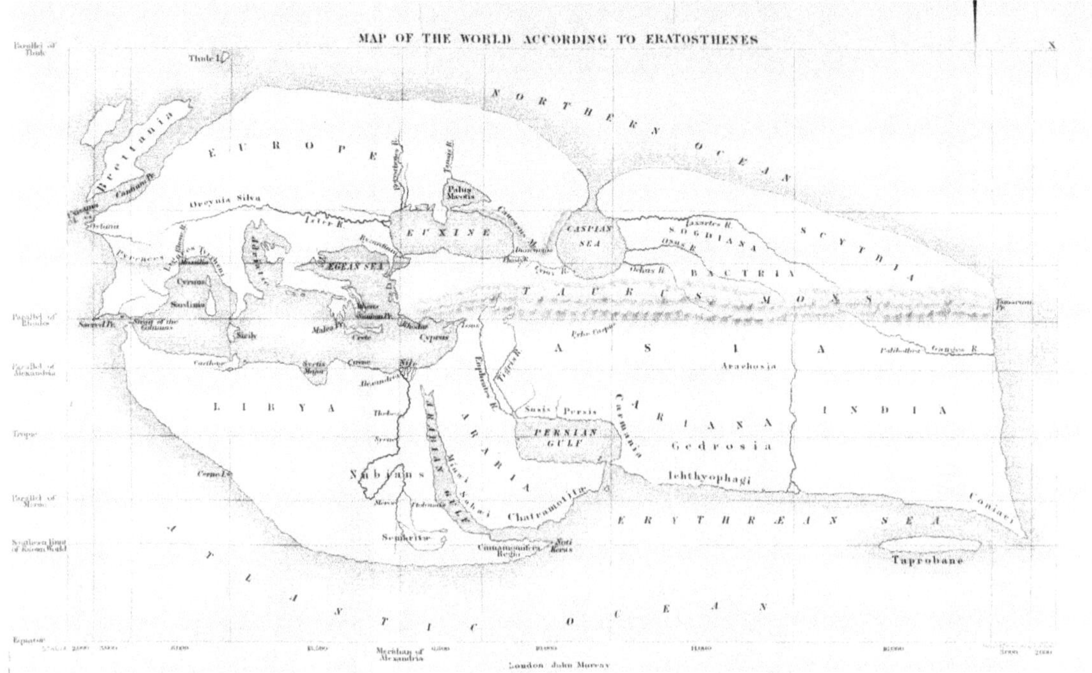

19th century reconstruction of Eratosthenes' map of the known world, c. 194 BC. Bunbury, E.H. (1811-1895), A History of Ancient Geography among the Greeks and Romans from the Earliest Ages till the Fall of the Roman Empire, page 667. London: John Murray, 1883. Wikimedia Commons. Public Domain.

Outer Part of the Entire East: Far East
At the Ocean: South China Sea
Great Sea Beyond the World: Pacific

2 ISLANDS SOUTHEAST OF THE SOUTH CHINA PENINSULA, TAMUS.

Coniaci is the Malay Peninsula. Tamus is Southeast China. The isles in between are called the Philippines today. Though not labeled, this is Chryse (Ophir) and Argyre (Tarshish). Anyone seizing on the Ganges (out of place here) is no scholar. The Indus River, though not labeled, is over where true India is. India on ancient labels is far more vast than modern India and included included both Indochina and the Indies at times, as well. The reason the Ganges was drawn flowing into the South China Sea towards the Philippines is because Josephus confused these directions, claiming the Ganges was the Pison River. This mapping adjusts for Josephus' erroneous concept in labeling, while drawing the Pison (Ganges River) flowing toward the land of the Garden of Eden in the Philippines where it should be. Taprobane is Sumatra, not Sri Lanka as Herodotus corrected for many. That mindset also ebbs and flows and must be determined by permanent positions one cannot move such as China, the Philippines, and the Malay Peninsula. Brent Landau, the translator, was obviously not thinking right when he guessed China was in the Pacific Ocean!

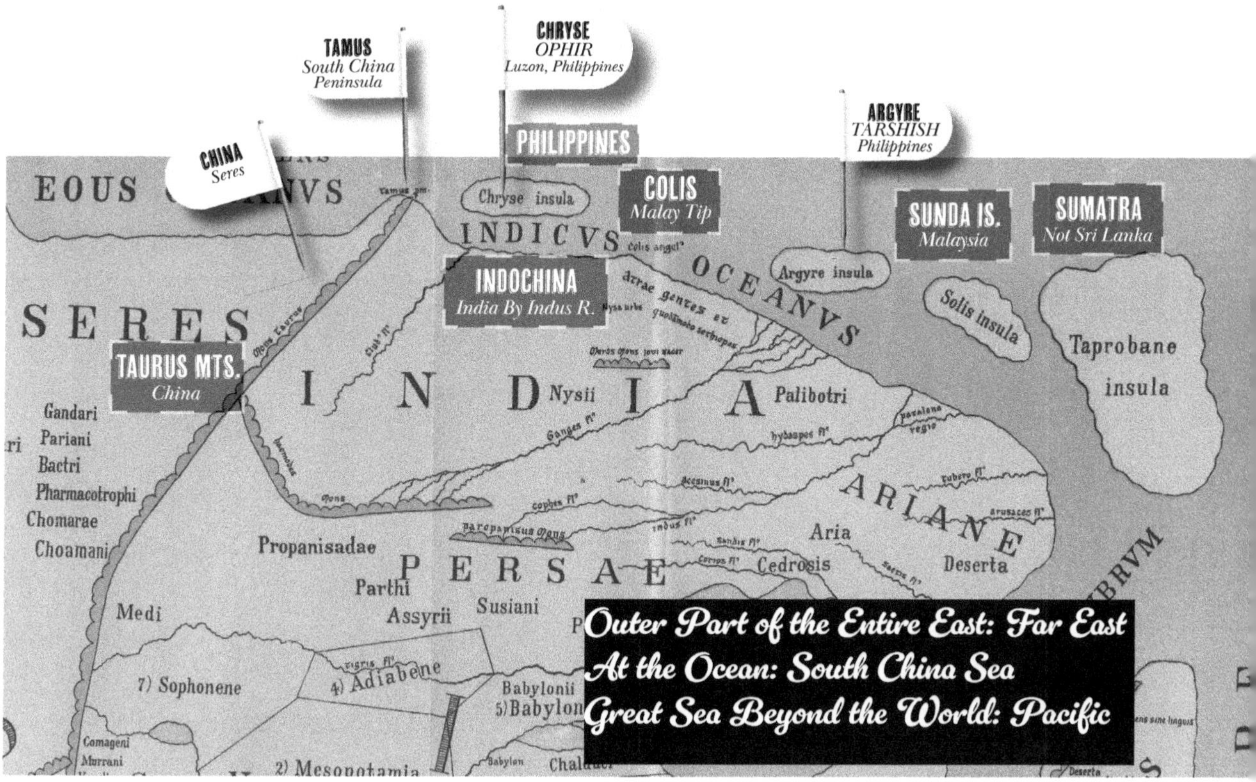

World Map of Pomponius Mela as reconstructed by K. Miller (1898). "Orbis habitabilis ad mentem Pomponii Melae", Mappaemundi, Heft VI. "Rekonstruierte Karten", Tafel 7. Dr. Konrad Miller. Wikimedia Commons. Public Domain.

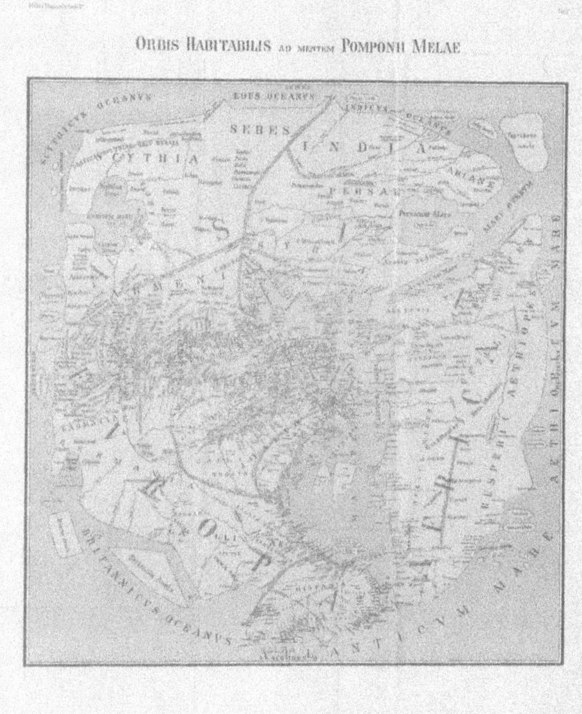

2 ISLANDS SOUTHEAST OF THE SOUTH CHINA PENINSULA, TAMUS.

Chryse (Ophir) is clear and indisputably Luzon Island, Philippines. Colis is the Malay Tip. Argyre is placed too far South in relation to the Ganges River, but this is reconciled by the Sunda Islands, as shown South of the Ganges, with Taprobane below. It is all out of position, but in relation to each other; Argyre is Mindanao. This is corrected as maps improve.

50 A.D.
GREEK MAP

ISLAND SOUTH AND EAST OF CHINA IN THE SOUTH CHINA SEA WHERE SUBSOLANUS IS PINPOINTED. TAPROBANE IS SUMATRA, NOT SRI LANKA HERE. UNDER THE VERY NORTH IS SOUTH OF THE TROPIC OF CANCER. THIS HAS ALWAYS BEEN THE PHILIPPINES!

ISLE OF GOLD
SOUTHEAST OF CHINA
PHILIPPINES

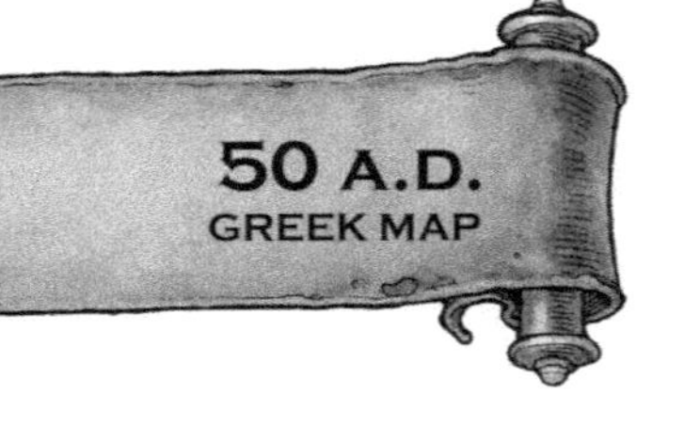

"The Periplus of the Erythraean Sea, Travel And Trade In The Indian Ocean By A Merchant Of The First Century." Translated from the greek and annotated by Wilfred H. Schoff, Secretary of the Commercial Museum, Philadelphia. Longmans, Green, And Co. New York. 1912. Section 63-64. Original housed at The British Museum (Add. MS 19391). Mapping By The God Culture. 2021.

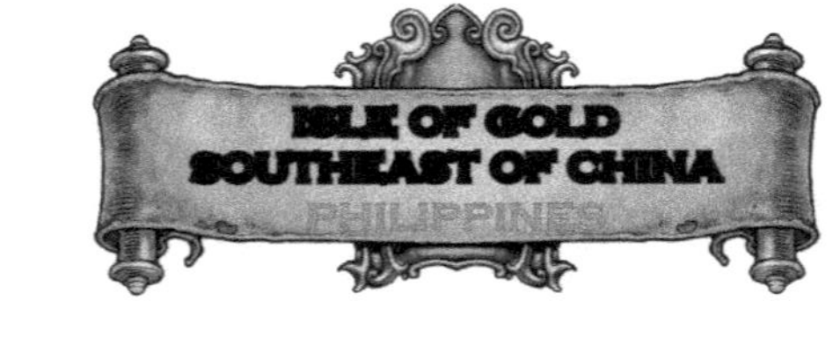

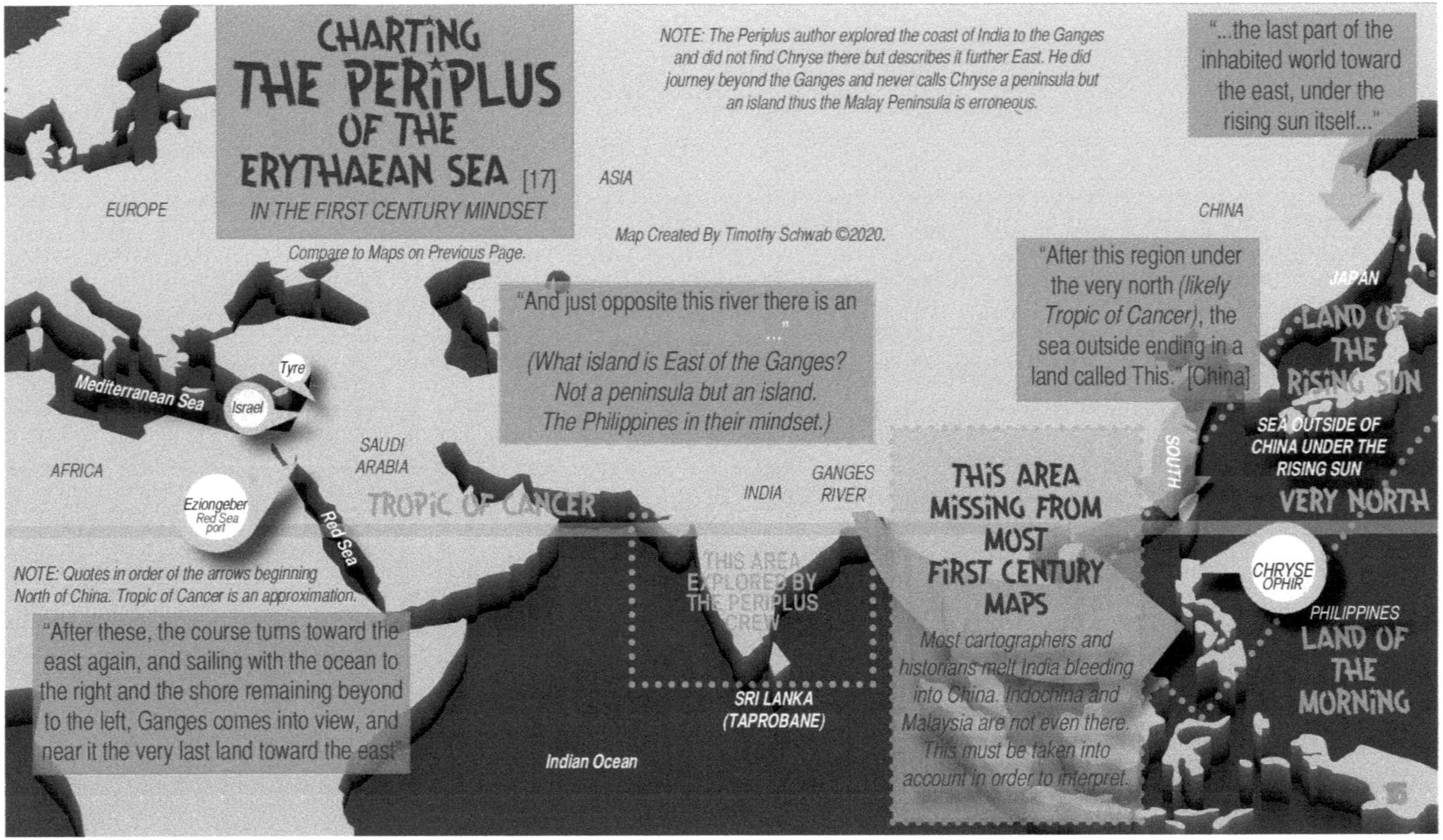

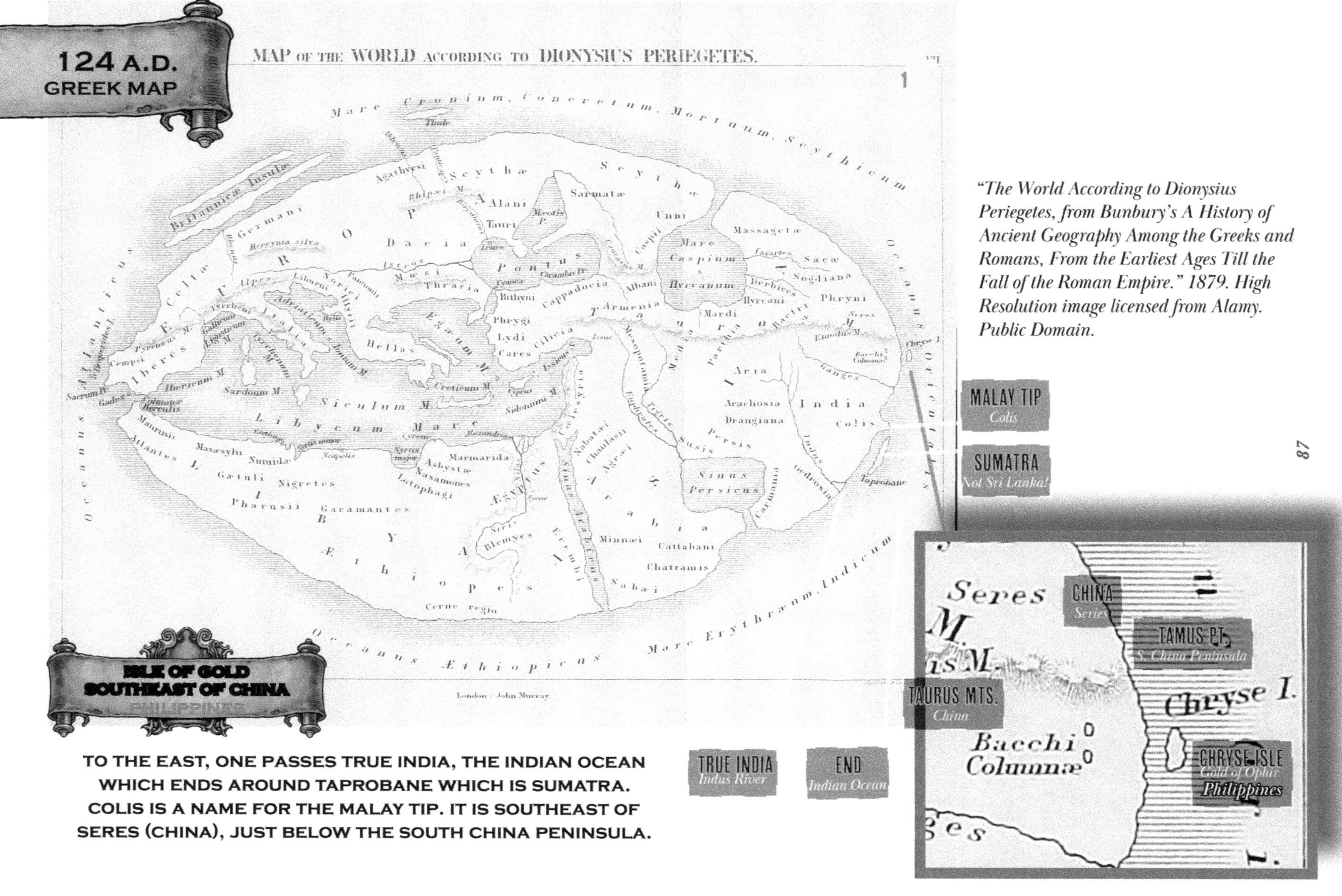

"*The World According to Dionysius Periegetes, from Bunbury's A History of Ancient Geography Among the Greeks and Romans, From the Earliest Ages Till the Fall of the Roman Empire.*" *1879. High Resolution image licensed from Alamy. Public Domain.*

TO THE EAST, ONE PASSES TRUE INDIA, THE INDIAN OCEAN WHICH ENDS AROUND TAPROBANE WHICH IS SUMATRA. COLIS IS A NAME FOR THE MALAY TIP. IT IS SOUTHEAST OF SERES (CHINA), JUST BELOW THE SOUTH CHINA PENINSULA.

ENOCH'S JOURNEY TO THE GARDEN OF EDEN

ANCIENT PERSPECTIVE

TREE OF KNOWLEDGE OF GOOD AND EVIL = LANZONES TREE OF THE PHILIPPINES

Remember, Enoch wrote this for us in the Last Days to understand because technology has afforded us a full perspective of this area from above as he did.

SEVEN ANCIENT MOUNTAINS OF EDEN

THE 7 MAJOR ISLANDS OF VISAYAS, WERE 7 LARGE MOUNTAINS PRIOR TO THE FLOOD. THEY ARE LOCATED ABOVE THE GARDEN OF EDEN.

Dudael, same as Duidain [6]. Raphael opened and cast Azazel into Gehenna next to Havilah, Philippines.

Apolaki Caldera, Benham Rise [23] "World's Largest Caldera" 10:4, 60:8.

BEFORE THE FLOOD: ISLANDS = MOUNTAINS

LUZON

VISAYAS
CEBU/SHEBA
MASBATE
SAMAR
ROMBLON
PANAY 1
2
3
4 LEYTE
CEBU
East of Garden
5 7 6
NEGROS
BOHOL
GARDEN OF EDEN

MINDANAO

NORTHEAST OF THE ERYTHRAEAN SEA (INDIAN OCEAN), BEYOND THE "MOUNTAINS OF FIRE" — GUNUNG GUNUNG API, INDONESIA. [34]

Where Enoch was taken from: East of the Garden where Adam was exiled and his righteous generations lived until the Flood, Havilah/Duidain/ Dudael. (Cf. 60:8, 10:4; Gen. 3:24; 2:11, Jub. 3:32).

WHAT IS NORTHEAST OF THE INDIAN OCEAN? THE GARDEN OF EDEN IN THE PHILIPPINES

These directions are affirmed by Jubilees and the Words of the Archangel Michael from the Dead Sea Scrolls.

"The Book of First Enoch: The Oldest Book In History." By Timothy Schwab, Anna Zamoranos. p. 123. Ophir Publishing. 2022. Methodology found in that full mapping.

GARDEN OF EDEN
SHEM'S SOUTHEAST BORDER

"The Book of Jubilees: The Torah Calendar." By Timothy Schwab, Anna Zamoranos. p. 82-89. Ophir Publishing. 2021.

Methodology found in that full mapping.

NOAH'S DIRECTIONS TO THE GARDEN OF EDEN FROM THE BOOK OF JUBILEES 8 & 9

THE OLDEST MAP OF THE WORLD

SHEM: **HAM:**   **JAPHETH:**

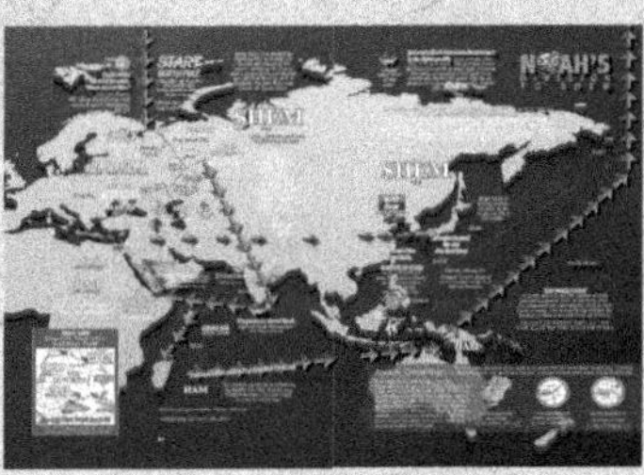

FULL MAPPING WITH DATA AT BOOKOFJUBILEES.ORG

A QUMRAN FRAGMENT: WORDS OF THE ARCHANGEL MICHAEL

"The Complete Dead Sea Scrolls In English." By Geza Vermes. P. 556. [22]

(4Q529,6Q23), FR. 1

Though not well preserved and a fragment, this Aramaic writing records the Archangel Michael as he appears to mention the building of evil Shinar at the time of the Tower of Babel. This is clearly a migration of the righteous away from there to the East, to the land of Gabriel, who is in the Garden of Eden. These 9 mountains, the land of silver (Tarshish) and gold (Ophir) and the Garden of Eden are a match to the modern Philippines. Though Vermes assumes this must be Zion or Sinai, we agree it is a holy mountain. It is the Mount of the East in the Garden of Eden, far away from Shinar. [See The Search For King Solomon's Treasure for Full Position].

Volcanoes.

Cf. 1 En. 24-25, 32. Same 7 mountains plus 2.

Cf. 1 En. 20:7. Gabriel is in charge of the Garden of Eden known as the Angel from the East. Rev. 7:2-3; Who stands in the presence of Yahuah which is the Garden's Holy of Holies. Luke 1:19.

Words of the book which Michael addressed to the angels... He said: I found there divisions of fire...
[and I saw there] **nine mountains**: two to the eas[t, and two to the west, and two to the north and two to the so] uth. **I saw there the angel Gabriel** . . .
like a vision. [Then] I showed him the vision. And he said to me:...
in the books of my Master, Yahuah of the world, it is written: Behold,... [between] the sons of Ham and the sons of Shem. And behold my Master, Yahuah of the

world... when they... the tear from... And behold **a city was built** to the name of my Master, [Yahuah of the world, and there] everything **that is evil** will be done before my Master, Yahuah [of the world]... And my Master, Yahuah of the world, will remember his creation... [and] my Master, Yahuah of the world, [will be] merciful to him and to him... the man will be in the **faraway province**... he, and he will say to him: Behold this... for me **silver and gold**... And he will say:... [and] the **righteous man**...

Only Shinar and the Tower of Babel fit this unification of the 3 sons of Noah building a city. They have been dispersed since.

This is not a place in the Middle East but a faraway province.

The land of silver (Tarshish) and gold (Ophir and Sheba).

Cf. Gen. 10:26-30. The Bible only records 1 migration at this time for the righteous and that is Ophir/Joktan.

"The Book of First Enoch: The Oldest Book In History." By Timothy Schwab, Anna Zamoranos. p. 124-125. Ophir Publishing. 2022. Methodology found in that full mapping.

1. MICHAEL LAYS OUT 9 MOUNTAINS WHERE GABRIEL ABIDES IN THE GARDEN OF EDEN. GABRIEL IS IN CHARGE OF THE GARDEN ACCORDING TO ENOCH.

2. HE DEFINES THE LAYOUT JUST AS ENOCH WITH 7 VISAYAS MOUNTAINS OF EDEN PLUS 2 - LUZON AND MINDANAO ADDED. ISLANDS BEFORE THE FLOOD WERE MOUNTAINS.

3. HE MENTIONS SHINAR AND A MIGRATION OF THE RIGHTEOUS TO A FARAWAY LAND OF SILVER AND GOLD.

THIS IS THE MIGRATION OF OPHIR, SHEBA, AND TARSHISH TO THE FAMOUS LAND OF SILVER AND GOLD WHICH WOULD BE NAMED AFTER THESE PATRIARCHS. THIS OCCURRED AT THE TIME OF BABEL AND THEY WENT TO SEPHAR (TREE OF LIFE IN THE GARDEN OF EDEN) AND THE MOUNT OF THE EAST (HOLY MOUNTAIN IN THE GARDEN OF EDEN). GEN. 10:26-30. THIS IS THE MODERN PHILIPPINES.

[See The Search For King Solomon's Treasure for Full Position].

Periplus of the Erythraean Sea *[p. 86]*[1] locates Chryse and Argyre in the Philippines Southeast of China. In 124 A.D., Dionysius the Tourist *[p. 87]*[1] anchors Chryse Southeast of China, directly below the Tropic of Cancer; meaning Southeast of South China, and South of Taiwan.

Prior to these maps, the *First Book of Enoch [p. 88]*[1] and the *Book of Jubilees [p. 89]*[1] provide ancient maps in the form of written directions, supported also by the Dead Sea Scroll fragment titled, "Words of the Archangel Michael" *[p. 90]*.[1] Joktan's sons migrated to the Philippines; their separation is also affirmed in an ancient manuscript which scholars oddly term, *Pseudo-Philo*, where twelve members of Joktan's family, especially, separate themselves as holy, rejecting all the Tower of Babel represented. Might that be the origin of the Magi order after the Flood?

These became the foundation of the entire T-O Map perspective for more than one thousand years, where the Catholic Church and the world largely knew of the location of Paradise in the Philippines, Southeast of China. Even Catholic maps demonstrate this. When one charts these out, they lead to the Garden of Eden in this exact placement that **Revelation of the Magi (RotM)** pinpoints the land of Shir, where they originated. This is the same.

In fact, in our publishing of **Garden of Eden Revealed: The Book of Maps,**[1] we review over 80 historic maps that lead to the Garden of Eden and Land of Gold in the Philippines over 6,000 years. Author Landau is unaware of much history on this matter and the ignorance of scholars does not rise to the level of hypothesis. We encourage everyone to read his footnotes in interpretation and judge them with the weight of the Bible, history, and georgraphy. He, as most scholars today, has little knowledge in this arena. Their opinion is impertinent.

When one is unaware of the dynamic of this archipelago, they confuse much. The details *"at the Ocean, the great sea beyond the world (RotM 2:4)"* are very obvious when one knows where this land abides. The South China Sea is the beginning of the ocean to the West of the Philippines. The Great Ocean, the Pacific, is to the East of this archipelago. That should not be so difficult for a scholar to conclude

---

[1] *All maps in full color, high resolution in Garden of Eden Revealed: The Book of Maps. Schwab/ Zamoranos. 2024. www.OphirInstitute.com.* [2] *Department of Archeology, University of Cape Town Rondebosch 7701. By Duncan Miller, Nirdev Desai & Julia Lee-Thorp. South Africa Archeology Society Doodwin Series 8, 91-99, 2000. University of the Witwatersrand, Johannesburg. p. 1-2.* [3] *"The Old Testament Pseudepigrapha, Vol. 2: Pseudo-Philo." Edited By James H. Charlesworth. Doubleday, New York. 1985. p. 311.* [4] *"Miners Shun Mineral Wealth of the Philippines." By Donald Greenlees. NY Times. May 14, 2008. Citing The Fraser Institute.* [5] *"Trillion – Dollar Philippine Economic Goldmine Emerging From Murky Pit." By Ralph Jennings. Forbes Magazine. Apr. 5, 2015.* [6] *"The death of gold in early Visayan societies: Ethnohistoric accounts and archaeological evidences." By Victor P. Estrella. Archaeological Studies Program. University of the Philippines Diliman. Aug. 15, 2014. p. 234. Citing Villegas, R. N. (2004). Ginto: history wrought in gold. Manila: Bangko Sentral ng Pilipinas. pp. 15-16.*

with even a simple reading. Landau concludes it is China, yet that requires him to misread his own translation, which he does many times in interpretation. It is very obvious the translation is not perfect, as the land of Nod is cited as being East of the land of Havilah, according to the *Book of Genesis*, where Adam and Eve lived all of their days after exile. It is a clear corruption in syntax.

However, the residence of Adam and Havah *(Eve)* is well secured in the Hebrew language, on ancient maps, and in history. Just because the Vatican ignores those facts, it does not change them. Their ignorance amounts to nothing. Adam and Havah *(Eve)* were exiled from the Garden of Eden back to the land of their Creation *(Jub. 3:27; Gen. 3:23)*. In Genesis 2:11, this land is called *Havilah,* which is named for *Havah (Eve)* varying her name to include her curse, from the judgement given in the Garden: labor/pain in childbirth. Havilah is the Land of Gold, known for its abundance, in which the Philippines is number one in all of history until the nineteenth century,[4,5] when South Africa had its first gold rush.

Even today, the Frasier Institute (who studies resources around the Earth), ranked the Philippines as number two in the world, for untapped gold deposits in the ground.[4,5] A report by Bangko Sentral, the Central Bank of the Philippines, characterized the Philippines as second in gold production per square km.[6]

It does not, however, have to produce gold in any ranking when it already has the most in the ground, except one other country who is very new to the gold business. That is the statistic that matters, not mining. For those from outlets (like Rappler), that appear hard of hearing, we will repeat the sources for the report we cite which are at the bottom of page 92. Please check at the bottom of page 92 for the correct root of those valid statistics. Go look at those before searching the wrong reports and claiming to be educated before you lie to the public again, Rappler.

This raises the query as to the location of Havilah, the land of Adam and Eve. Did the world know in ancient times where this was? First, the Garden of Eden and Havilah are fixed positions that cannot move. They are the same location, according to massive data, even in Revelation three times. In the Introduction and ***The Garden of Eden Revealed: The Book of Maps,***[1] there are a plethora of maps.

Giovanni Colonna was a Roman Catholic Cardinal who obviously knew where Havilah was, in the thirteenth century *[p. 95].*[1] The Catholic Cardinal mapped Evilath, the Latin form of Havilah, in the same land as the Garden of Eden. This is India, or really, Indochina in the Philippines. The Garden of Eden is anchored to the Pison River, among the five rivers of Eden, in the Far East, and never the Tigris River, (which is not even a word that is used in the entire modern Biblical Canon, in original Hebrew). Havilah is the Philippines.

As a second witness, in 1050, the Anglo-Saxon Map *[p. 94]*[1] identifies the very same location, with an area South of China labeled Evilath with those famous two islands just off the coast. Anyone educated on this paradigm knows that is Chryse *(Ophir)* and Argyre *(Tarshish).* Those not educated on this matter, scoff, from their

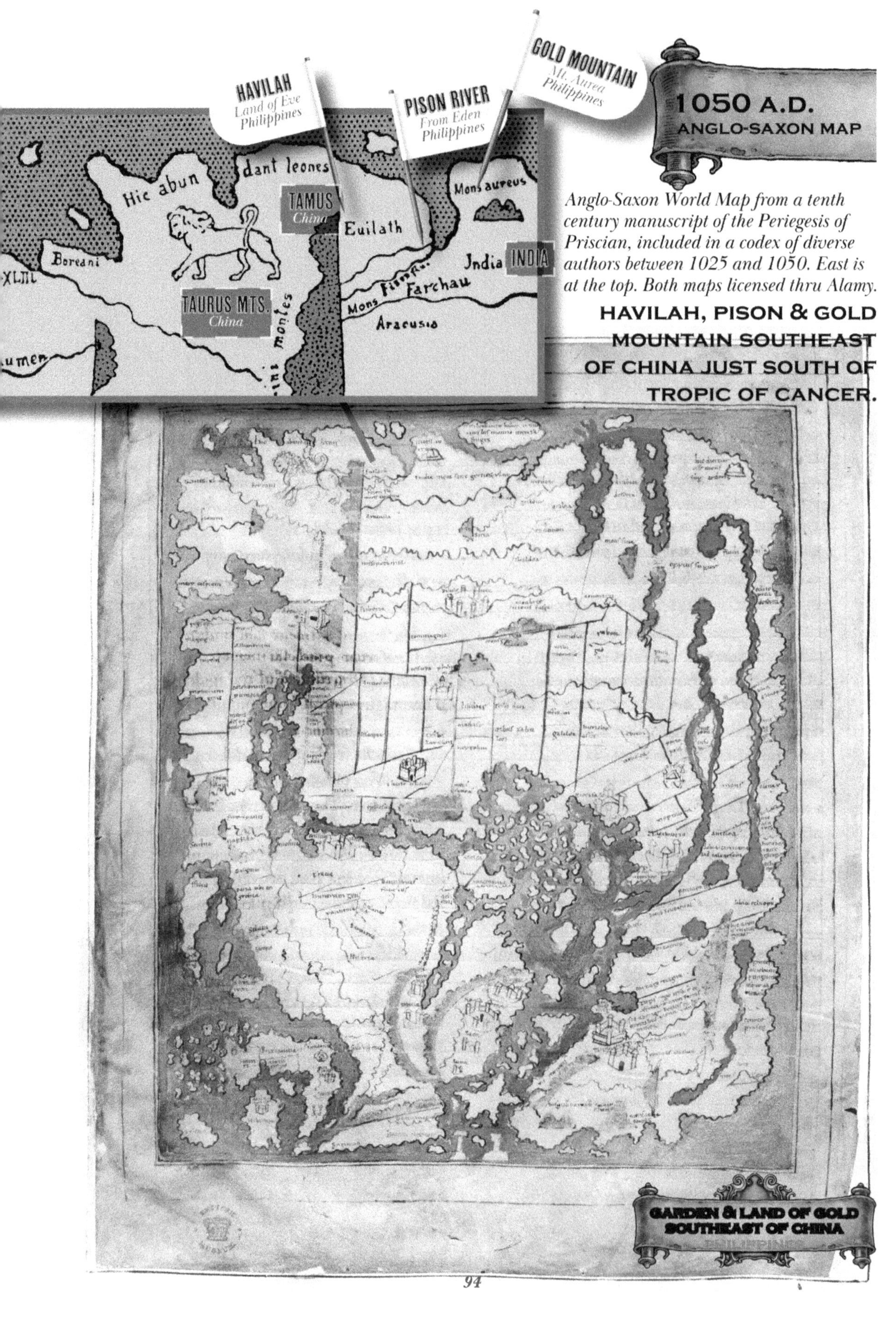

Anglo-Saxon World Map from a tenth century manuscript of the Periegesis of Priscian, included in a codex of diverse authors between 1025 and 1050. East is at the top. Both maps licensed thru Alamy.

HAVILAH, PISON & GOLD MOUNTAIN SOUTHEAST OF CHINA JUST SOUTH OF TROPIC OF CANCER.

1475 A.D.
COLONNA MAP

HAVILAH (EVILATH), THE GEN. 2 LAND OF EVE AND THE GARDEN OF EDEN IN THE PHILIPPINES EAST OF INDIA, NORTH OF TAPROBANE (SUMATRA OR BORNEO). OPHIR IS MARKED IN SAUDI ARABIA WHICH IS ANTIQUATED AS OPHIR NEVER LIVED THERE. IT IS HAVILAH, THE LAND OF GOLD.

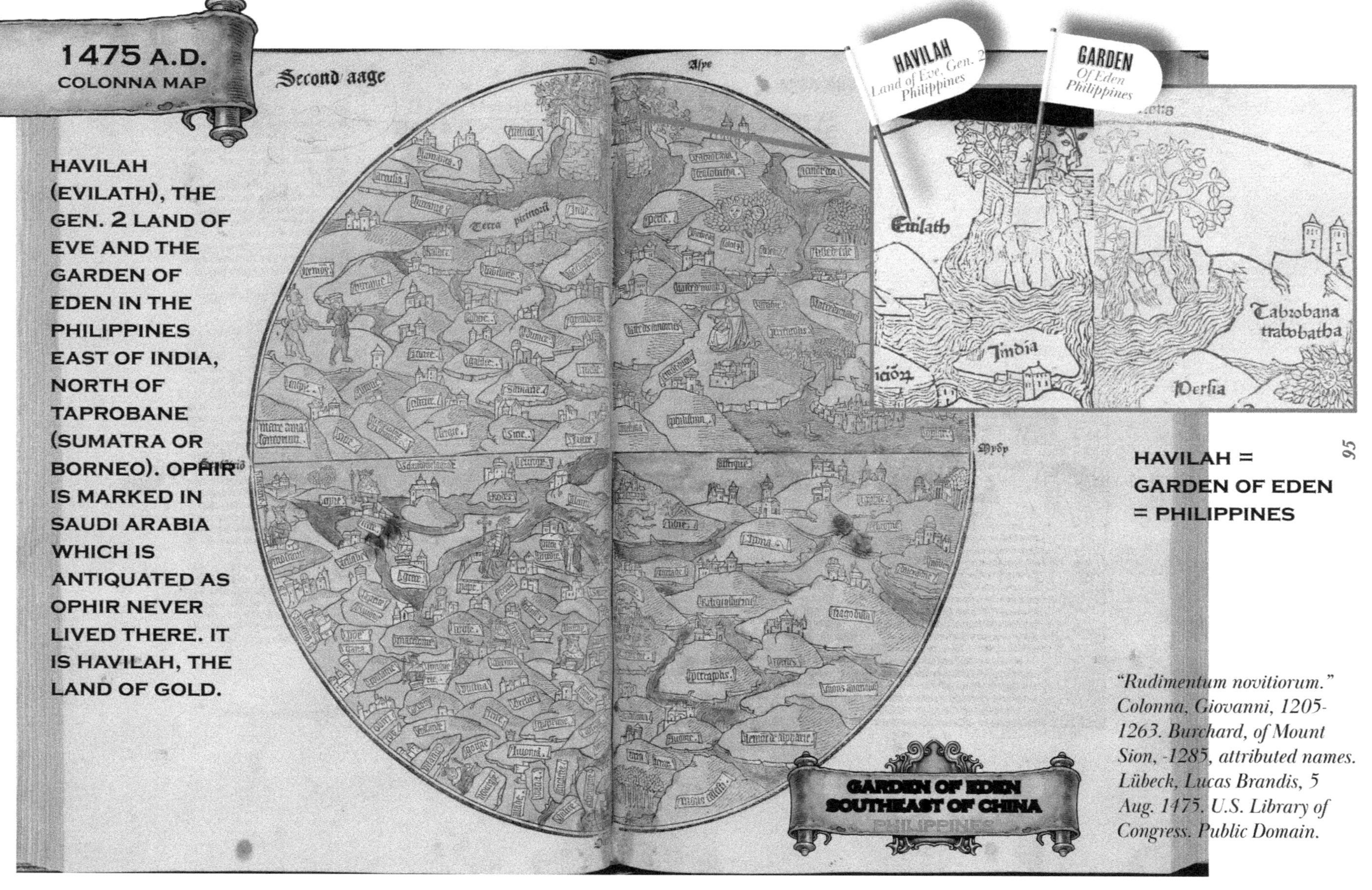

HAVILAH =
GARDEN OF EDEN
= PHILIPPINES

"Rudimentum novitiorum." Colonna, Giovanni, 1205-1263. Burchard, of Mount Sion, -1285, attributed names. Lübeck, Lucas Brandis, 5 Aug. 1475. U.S. Library of Congress. Public Domain.

95

position of ignorance. This map was published as a part of a Latin translation, *"Priscian's Periegesis"* which offers the directions from Dionysius Periegetes of Alexandria, whose map, in 124 A.D. *[p. 87][4]* demonstrates the same position for the Land of Gold: Chryse *(Ophir)* in the Philippines. That is almost a 1000-year track record of the geography of Dionysius still being used as credible and by the Catholic Church. This map has a date of 1025-1050, but the origin of the thought is 124 A.D. and Priscian continued that mindset even in the fifth to sixth century when he lived.

Moses continued to define this land of Havilah surrounded by the Pison River as the land of Pearl *(Gen. 2:11-12; bdellium is most definitively not an African resin from Ham's territory that was never named so in ancient times).* This becomes extremely easy when one steps in to settle scholarly debate on the meaning of the Hebrew word: bdellium. Indeed, a word in Genesis 2 cannot originate from any other language, regardless of how little scholars know. Jubilees defines Ancient, Biblical Hebrew *(not modern Yiddish-infused Hebrew)* as the original language which disappeared at the Tower of Babel from the Middle East, and was reinstituted when Yahuah taught Abraham how to read and speak it *(Jub. 12:25-26).* Their speculation to link it elsewhere is not linguistics, and is futile.

Bdellium is only used twice in the Biblical Canon, and since the second time in Numbers 11:7 defines manna as the color of bdellium. This precious resource is not an African resin (as is speculated erroneously, never mentioned as a Biblical spice in scripture at any time, and it would be mentioned if it were). African resin is blackish-brown in color, and not desirable to observe or to ingest (though it produces a terrific odor); not for food. It is option B, the white pearl. These kinds of simple narratives should not continue to flounder with no actual logic in academia, who should be able to reconcile such easily.

The largest pearl in history is 34 kg. from Palawan.[1] In fact, the 1492 Behaim Globe *[p. 21],[4]* the first globe map of the world commissioned by the King of Portugal, labels Palawan, Philippines as Thilis, the elusive Isle of Pearl, which science affirms. The Philippines ranks number one again and that cannot be coincidence.

The final resource from Havilah, in Genesis 2, is the onyx stone, which has historic precedence in Egypt.[2] What is called alabaster in the Bible (and to the ancients), proves to be onyx marble stone from Egyptian archaeology. That is the application of antiquity, not gypsum. Even according to the Romblon Tourism

---

[1] *"This $100 Million Pearl Is The Largest and Most Expensive in the World." By Roberta Naas. Forbes Magazine. Aug 23, 2016.* [2] *"Alabaster, Mineral." and "Marble, Rock." By Editors of Encyclopaedia Britannica. Encyclopaedia Britannica. Updated Jan. 24, 2018 and Jan. 24, 2020.* [3] *a. "Romblon: 8 Awesome Places You Should Visit in Romblon!" Our Awesome Planet. Sept. 7, 2016. 2. "The Romblon Marble." b. Ellaneto Tiger Marble Trader, Romblon. 2010. c. "Marvelous Marble" By Robert A. Evora. Manila Standard. Jan. 16, 2014.* [4] *All maps in full color, high resolution in Garden of Eden Revealed: The Book of Maps. Schwab/Zamoranos. 2024. www.OphirInstitute.com.*

Department, Romblon, Philippines is known to have the very strongest marble and onyx stone in the world.[3] This is no mystery, as Moses scientifically defined the Philippines as the land of Adam and Havah *(Eve)*. Anyone questioning the Rivers from Eden can review the comprehensive view presented in our published books, and in our *Rivers from Eden Series*, in video form.[4] These rivers were covered over by the Flood, and must be worldwide, according to all related Bible passages, where most scholars ignore the geography right there in the account. The Three Kings story is no different in their negligence. It is almost as if they do not wish to know; that fulfills the prophecy of Peter *(2Pet. 3)*.

Where Did Adam & His Righteous Generations Dwell?

Genesis 3:23-24 KJV
*Therefore the **LORD** God sent him forth from the garden of Eden, to till the ground from whence he was taken. So he drove out the man; and he placed at the **east of the garden** of Eden Cherubims, and a flaming sword which turned every way, to keep the way of the tree of life.*

Genesis provides amazing geography of a worldwide River System which watered the entire Earth, yet many Bible scholars are stuck in the Middle East, trying to study rivers that did not even exist before the Flood (according to Genesis 2:5), as they originate from rain, which did not occur yet at that time. Here again, Genesis anchors the Garden to the same land where Adam was exiled to Havilah, which is surrounded by the Pison River. That is never the Hiddekel, which is grossly misinterpreted as Tigris in fraud. Imagine, Bible scholars actually follow the Occult Creation Myth from the Nephilim of Mesopotamia, inserting it into Genesis, when it is not there.

Moses, as author of the *Book of Jubilees*, clarifies that Havilah/Elda is the land of Adam and Eve *(Havah)*, and he locates it just to the East of the Garden of Eden, which is the very "ground from whence he (Adam) was taken," meaning the Land of Creation. Can we read Genesis that way? When we examine the *Book of Jubilees*, it clarifies that is most certainly how we should all read Genesis.

Jubilees 3:32-35
*And on the new moon of the fourth month, **Adam and his wife went forth from the Garden of Eden**, and **they dwelt in the land of 'Eldâ, in the land of their creation**. And Adam **called the name of his wife Eve. 34 And they had no son till the first jubilee, and after this he knew her. 35 Now he tilled the land as he had been instructed in the Garden of Eden.***

All of these titles converge into one position on maps: the Philippines. This is why so many located the Garden in that region for the past 6,000 years. When ***Revelation of the Magi*** references Shir in the extreme East as the land of Adam and his righteous generations, this is not new. In fact, the Prophet Enoch had already provided that geography. We can observe this from a mapping of his directions of his travel into the Garden of Eden, to the land above it, and in other passages as well. He describes this same land by another title, Duidain, but by the same directions as Havilah in Genesis to the right of the Garden of Eden. He solidifies this was the residence of Adam and his righteous generations. Even Enoch was taken up from that land where he also lived. Cain, who was evil, left that land of the "presence of Yahuah" migrating further to the East *(Gen. 4:16)*. Indeed, ancient Havilah houses the Holy of Holies in the Garden of Eden *(Gen. 3:8; Jub. 8:19)*. Adam's righteous generations dwelled there all the way to Noah and his sons.

1 Enoch 60:8
But the male is named Behemoth, who occupied with his breast a waste wilderness named Duidain, on the east of the garden where the elect and righteous dwell, where my grandfather was taken up, the seventh from Adam, the first man whom Yahuah of Spirits created.

The Queen of Sheba from the Uttermost Parts of the Earth:

Matthew 12:42 KJV (Luke 11:31)
The queen of the south shall rise up in the judgment with this generation, and shall condemn it: for she came from the uttermost (πέρας: péras) parts of the earth to hear the wisdom of Solomon; and, behold, a greater than Solomon is here.

πέρας: *péras, per'-as; from the same as G4008; an extremity:—end, ut-(ter-)most participle (G4009).*

Regarding the extremities of the Earth, ***Revelation of the Magi*** affirms the geography of Jesus *(Yahusha)* who defines this land in Matthew 12:42 *(Luke 11:31)* as the land of Sheba where the Queen of Sheba came from. Though there is a Sheba from Ham's lineage, this Sheba must be Shem's progeny; Sheba, brother of Ophir, according to the passage that reads as a continuation of the expedition of Solomon's navy to fetch gold in Ophir. It was his navy who told the Queen during Solomon's Kingship, in her land called Sheba (named after her ancestor, the brother of Ophir).

It is dumbfounding when self-proclaimed Bible scholars adopt and share as truth the fraudulent legends from an occult-based writing, the *Kebra Nagast*, and accuse Solomon of having an affair and son with a goat lady. When they cannot even separate the different Shebas and follow simple geography, they are not educated enough to deserve our attention. Unfortunately, we are addressing Bible concordances, and most scholars (who prove illiterate on this topic when they travel in such stupid directions).

Finding the Land of Shir:

In the introduction of *Revelation of the Magi,* translator Brent Landau oddly refers to this land of Shir as "semi mythical" and in one footnote as "mythical." It is neither. This is because he never researched where it was and is unqualified to speculate. He cannot even seem to agree in his own footnotes. His translation appears unmanipulated, but his interpretation is unfortunately uneducated on this topic. There is nothing mythical about the land which we will prove has always existed and is even mapped for 6,000 years. Such terminology is deceiving, as it infers he draws conclusions to what he never researched. It is only myth to him because he does not have such knowledge. We find this inexcusable though routine in Bible scholarship.

If they do not understand it, it must be fiction. Perhaps this is their thinking: they possess a kind of godhood, which is mythical. However, having conducted this research for over a decade, we prove it to be the Land of Gold described in the Bible, which houses the Garden of Eden and is known as Ophir, Sheba and Tarshish in the Philippines. Even this word, *Shir,* is Hebrew in origin, and appears to be a direct characteristic and prophecy of the Philippines.

*shir: שיר: Masculine noun meaning **song** in much the same way as our English word. It's used for religious songs (Psalm 42:8, Nehemiah 12:46), triumphal songs (Judges 5:12), festive songs (Genesis 31:27), love songs (Song of Solomon 1:1), etc. Denominative verb: shir: שיר: to sing (Exodus 15:1, 1 Samuel 18:6, Isaiah 26:1). Feminine noun: שירה (shira), also meaning **song** (Exodus 15:1, Isaiah 5:1). This feminine noun seems to denote the more **odic song**.– Abarim Publications*

In Hebrew, the word *shir* is very revealing. It means *to sing* or *song* in Bible usage. Anyone familiar with the culture of the Philippines is aware that singing is deeply rooted in its DNA. This is really the mechanism that will lead to the fulfillment of Isaiah's prophecy of these famed isles at the end of the Earth who sing. Shir is a perfect connotation for the isles that sing at the ends of the Earth, precisely fitting the Magi geography from their first century writing, affirmed in Isaiah and Psalm.

Isaiah 42:10 KJV
*Sing (H7891: shîyr: שיר) unto the LORD a new song (H7891: shîyr: שיר), and his praise from the end of the earth, ye that go **down** to the sea, and all that is therein; **the isles, and the inhabitants thereof.***

Before locating Shir in the Philippines, one can further narrow this area down. ***Revelation of the Magi*** says, the *"**Mountain of Victories in the east of Shir, our country, in a cave, the Cave of Treasures**"* which is packed with clues that become evident. We will unpack those more in the next chapter. As this is the Land of the Garden of

Eden, it houses the Mount of the East which was the destination of Ophir and his brothers from Genesis 10:30.

Genesis 10:30 KJV
And their (Ophir and family) dwelling was from Mesha, as thou goest unto Sephar a mount of the east.

Sephar in Hebrew (ספר, *S-P-R*) is a reference to the Tree of Life in the Garden of Eden.[1] In Greek, it is rendered Sophir in the Greek Septuagint which replaces Ophir because the word is Sephar. Notice how close this etymology of Shir approaches as deriving from Sophir/Sephar. This is obvious as well.

"Alternative spellings of both variants... Opheir, Sophír, Sopheír and Souphír occur in the Septuagint..." (Σωφηρα) [2]

Mount of the East is not arbitrary, but one specific mountain in the Holy of Holies in the Garden of Eden within the Earth under the Philippines. Genesis 10:30 is a double reference to the Land over Paradise, known throughout 6,000 years of history and geography. Enoch offered incense there inside the Garden.

Jubilees 4:25-26
*"And he (Enoch) burnt the incense of the sanctuary, (even) sweet spices, acceptable before Yahuah on the Mount. For Yahuah hath four places on the earth, the **Garden of Eden, and the Mount of the East**, and this mountain on which thou art this day, Mount Sinai, and Mount Zion.."*

This was where Ophir, Sheba, and Havilah migrated on the ships of Tarshish around 2,200 B.C. Again, much Bible history and 6,000 years of maps affirm this *(See Introduction)*. We will cover why the mountain would be called Mountain of Victories in the next chapter. Its full title ***"Mountain of Victories in the East (4:1)"*** rings evident as the Mount of the East regardless. Somewhere near the top of the Mount of the East is the famous Cave of Treasures where Adam is said to have dwelled all of his days. This cave is where Adam put aside the very resources brought by the Kings: gold, frankincense, and myrrh. Adam's bones and those of his progeny were buried there (until Noah's flood), and precious scriptural writings were kept there. He even set this cave as a house of prayer, where the Magi, as a group of priests named for prayer, continued to meet monthly, even into the first century A.D., according to ***Revelation of the Magi. Prayer*** in Filipino languages is *MAGdasal*, in several forms of the word (such as the famous necklace of the MAGI, called *KA-MAGI*, found as far as Egypt in archeology). King David described Queens wearing the gold of Ophir *(Ps. 45:9)* in his time before Solomon, documenting this trade thousands of years ago. This gold is documented in ***The Book of the Cave of Treasures*** as well.

The Book of the Cave Of Treasures

*And Adam and Eve went down in . . . of spirit over the **mountains of Paradise**, and they found a cave in the top of the mountain, and they entered and hid themselves therein.*

*And Adam took from the skirts of the **mountain of Paradise (Mount of the East)**, gold, and myrrh, and frankincense, and **he placed them in the cave**, and he blessed the cave, and consecrated it that it might be the **house of prayer for himself and his sons**. And he called the cave "ME`ARATH GAZZE" (i.e. "CAVE OF TREASURES").*[3]

We find these Mountains of Paradise consistent with *1 Enoch* which identifies the Seven Mountains of Eden *[see p. 120]*[4] and the *Words of the Archangel Michael's* Nine Mountains of the East *[see p. 121].*[4] Though erased from modern textbooks, history affirms the Philippines had large ancient ships and trade routes as well.[2]

However, notice there is one specific Mountain of Paradise in which Adam found a cave and lived. This is the Cave of Treasures being referenced in **Revelation of the Magi.** That cave exists on the Mount of the East. Essentially, this ancient scroll links the Mount of the East in the Garden of Eden as the location where the Magi met and worshipped, as well as maintained as a storehouse for the Estate of Adam, identified as the Cave of Treasures. The Magi were the curators of this cave and its goods, a practice handed down from Adam and Seth. They would bring these giftings from the Estate of Adam to the Messiah after His birth, as predicted by David in Psalm 72 and long before Him, by Adam even. There is no mystery here.

*RotM 4:2 And **our fathers commanded us as they also received from their fathers**, and they said to us: "**Wait for the light** that shines forth to you **from the exalted East** of the majesty of the Father, the light that shines forth from on high **in the form of a star over the Mountain of Victories** and comes to rest upon a pillar of light **within the Cave of Treasures** [of] Hidden Mysteries. 4:3 And also **command your sons, and your sons their sons, until the mystery of the star** that shines forth from the exalted majesty **appears to your generations, a light like a star**, and giving light to the entire creation and **obscuring the light of the sun**, moon, and stars, and not one of them is seen or is able to stand in the presence of its light. 4:4 For **it is the great mystery of the Son of the exalted majesty, who is the voice of the Father**...*

---

[1] *"Sefirot." Wikipedia. "What You Need to Know about Kabbalah. Jerusalem: Gal Einai Institute." Rabbi Yitzchak Ginsburgh. 2006. Strong's Concordance #H5611.* [2] *"The Dispersal of Austronesian boat forms in the Indian Ocean." By Waruno Mahdi . Roger Blench & Matthew Spriggs (editors). Archaeology and Language III: Artefacts, languages and texts, One World Archaeology 34. pp. 144–179. London & New York: Routledge, 1999. p. 154.* [3] *"The Book of the Cave of Treasures." By Sir Ernest Alfred Wallis Budge. 2005. Cosimo, Inc., New York. Originally published by Religious Tract Society. 1927. p. 69.* [4] *All maps in full color, high resolution in Garden of Eden Revealed: The Book of Maps. Schwab/Zamoranos. 2024. www.OphirInstitute.com.*

Not only do we find a very specific prophecy here of the Star of the East, (which is never called the Star of Bethlehem in any scripture), but one can observe that this Star only appeared in the East, and it was not an actual star, or the sun, or the moon. It was not a planetary alignment of 2 days or less, which would need to have lasted for two years, changed course multiple times, and then stood still over the head of Jesus *(Yahusha)*. None of those random guesses have ever been logical.

How did the Magi know to watch for this appearance of Light, far greater than any luminary? They learned from their fathers who learned from their fathers. This was passed down as a practice and tradition for thousands of years, originating with Adam himself directing his righteous son, Seth. That instruction occurred in this same land where the Magi dwelled and met monthly to worship Yahuah in anticipation of the coming sign of the Messiah's birth. They were not magicians; they were holy men whose prophetic purpose was to worship and await this Light's coming. The Light was promised to appear over the Mount of the East in the Philippines and enter the cave there, where Adam once resided.

*RotM 6:1 Again, from the books that were in the Cave of Treasures of Hidden Mysteries: every word that our father **Adam**, the beginning of our great lineage, spoke with his son **Seth**, whom he had after the death of Abel, whom his brother Cain killed and over whom his father Adam mourned. 6:2 And Adam instructed Seth his son about [text missing], [and **about the revelation**] **of the light of the star and about its glory, because he [saw] it in the Garden of Eden** when it descended and came to rest **over the Tree of Life; and it illuminated the entire (garden) before Adam transgressed** against the commandment of the Father of heavenly majesty. 6:3 And **when he transgressed against** the commandment that (the Father) ordained for him, **the sight of the star was taken away from him**, and (it was also taken away from him) **because of the expulsion from Paradise.***

Adam is the source of this prophecy of the Star of the East, not Matthew, who is writing of the fulfillment of this event that King David also prophesied in Psalm 72, based on Adam's account. King David even quotes portions of Adam's account found in *1 Enoch*. Adam witnessed this Star in the Garden and knew of its presence as he lived in its glory. The Star or Light is the Son. Adam was removed from the Garden; the Light was not, necessarily. The geography of its position on Earth would remain in the Garden of Eden which is within the Earth below the Philippines, and it would leave the Garden to appear above the Mount of the East, just atop the Garden, in the first century B.C.

The land of Shir connects with Surigao and Siargao *(Shir-gaw)*, Philippines, right next to the Mount of the East, Camiguin Island, which we will vet further in the next chapter. It also matches the prophetic people who sing from the Philippines as the isles in the East at the ends of the Earth, with whom Isaiah was obsessed. There has never been a remote question in history as to where the ends or extremities of the East were located. Modern scholars displaying their ignorance does not change these well-recorded facts. It only exposes their miseducation.

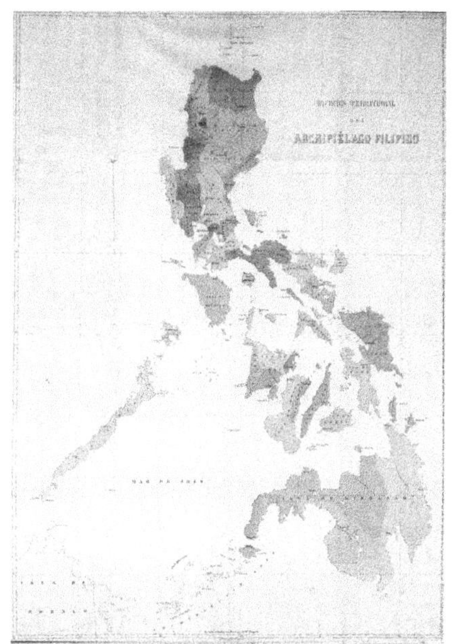

1880 Territorial map of the Philippines Philippine-Spanish Day Exhibit: Three Hundred Years of Philippine maps. Wikimedia Commons. Public Domain.

División territorial de la Isla de Mindanao en 5 Distritos. Año de 1880. Ficheiro:Philippine territorial map. Wikimedia Commons. Public Domain.

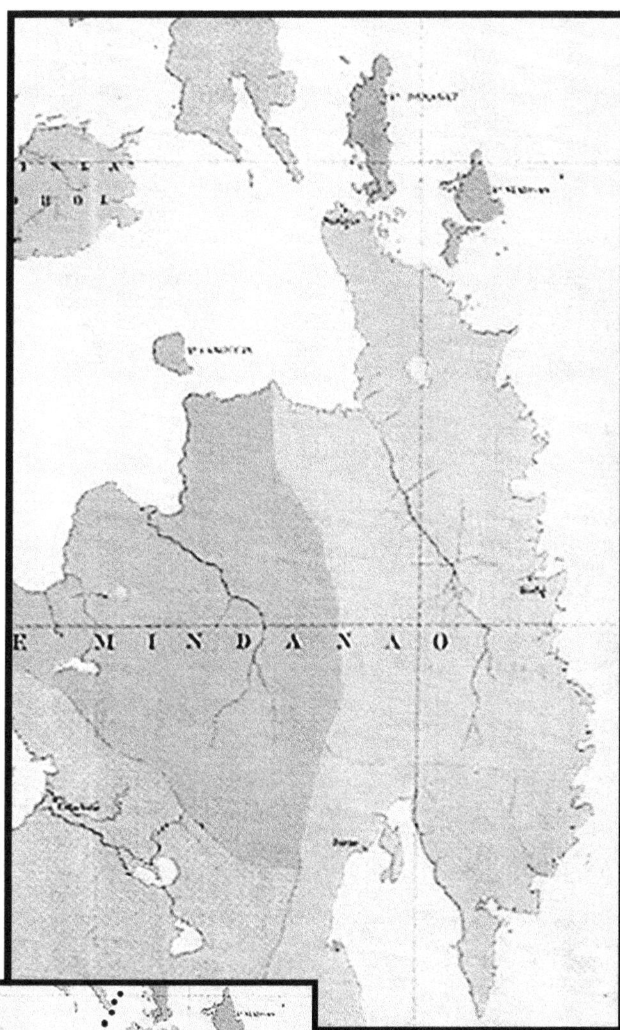

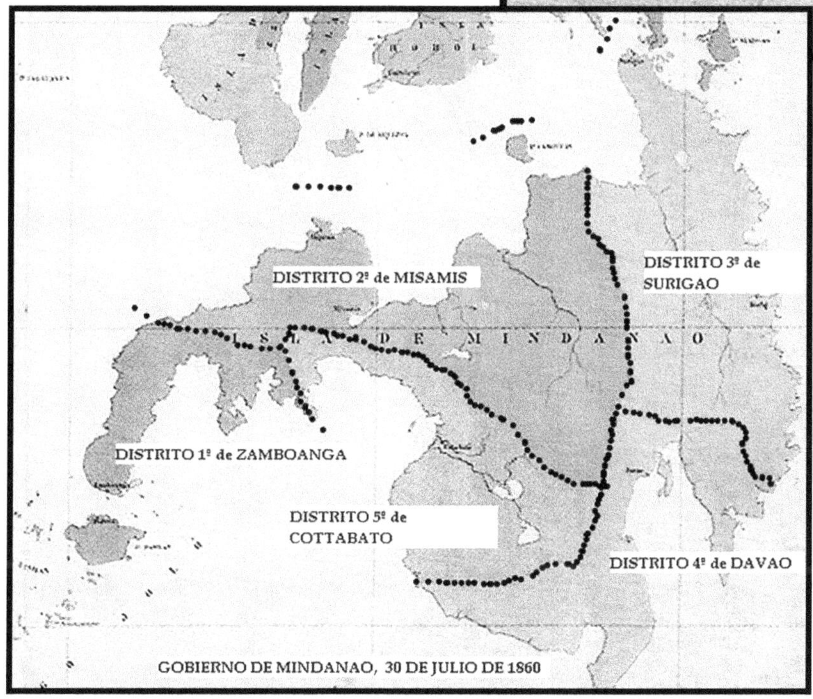

The island of Mindanao, eastern part. Image from a series of maps prepared by Filipino scientist Father Jose P. Algue and published by the United States Coast and Geodetic Survey. Manila Observatory. 1900. Atlas of the Philippine Islands., Washington [D.C.] : [U.S.] G.P.O. Smithsonian Institute. Public Domain.

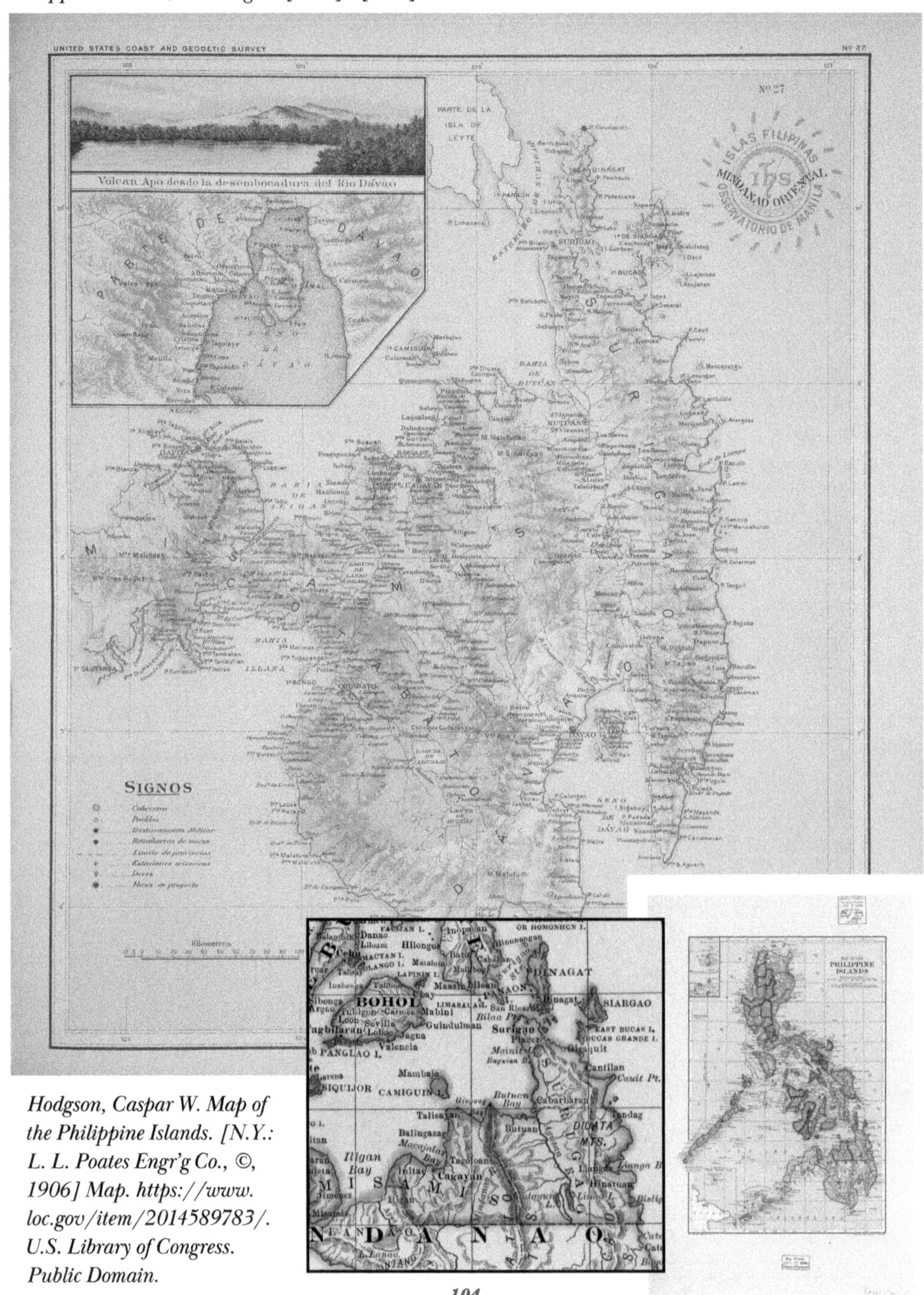

Hodgson, Caspar W. Map of the Philippine Islands. [N.Y.: L. L. Poates Engr'g Co., ©, 1906] Map. https://www.loc.gov/item/2014589783/. U.S. Library of Congress. Public Domain.

Map of the Philippine Islands published by Pedro Murillo Velarde in 1774. Wikimedia Commons. Public Domain.

Caraga is reminiscient of "Gaticara" from Pigafetta's Journal where Magellan set his destination to the land of gold. There could be a link there, but it is not necessary. In history, the province is labeled Surigao in whole, and it is right next to the Mount of the East, Camiguin Island.

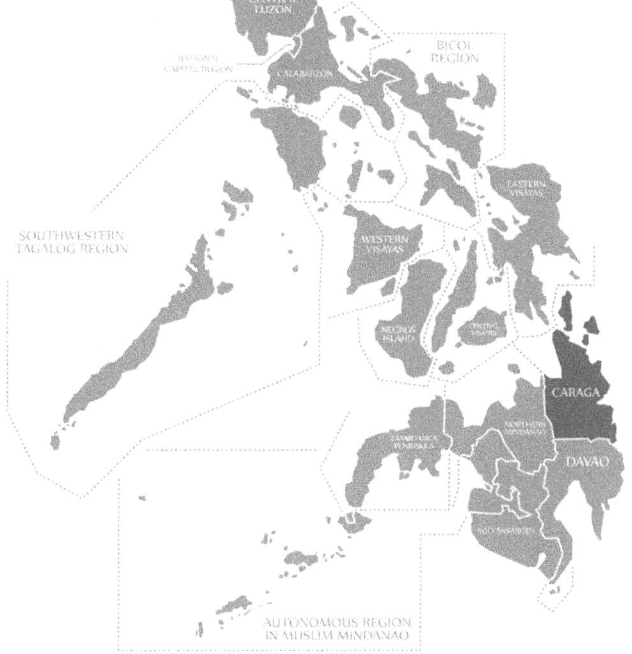

Adobestock.

Chapter 6:

Mountain of Victories, Cave of Treasures, & The Spring of Purification

*RotM 4:1 And those books of hidden mysteries were placed on the **Mountain of Victories in the east of Shir, our country,** in a cave, the **Cave of Treasures** of the **Mysteries of the Life of Silence.***
*4:2 And our fathers commanded us as they also received from their fathers, and they said to us: "Wait for the light that shines forth to you from the exalted East of the majesty of the Father, the light that shines forth from on high in the form of a star over the **Mountain of Victories** and comes to rest upon a pillar of light within the **Cave of Treasures [of] Hidden Mysteries.***

*RotM 4:7 Therefore, know that when this light from that majesty that has no end shines forth for you and will appear like a star to you so that you are able to see him: eagerly, with joy and love, and completely, with care, taking with you his own pure gifts, which were put in the **Cave of Treasures of Hidden Mysteries on the Mountain of Victories** by your fathers, go to where his light, the star, leads you.*

*RotM 5:2 And we went up to the Mountain of Victories, and when we were all assembled at the foothills of the mountain from each one's dwelling place, we **remained in one place for purification** on the twenty-fifth day of every month. 5:3 And we **bathed in a certain spring** that was **on the foothills of the mountain,** and it is **called "The Spring of Purification."***

*RotM 11:3 And each one came from his dwelling place **according to our ancient custom to ascend the Mountain of Victories** [text missing] **to wash in the Spring of Purification,** as we were accustomed. RotM 11:4And we saw [text missing] in the form of an ineffable pillar of light descending, and it came to rest above the water.*

*RotM 12:1 And when we **bathed in the Spring of Purification** with joy, and we **ascended the Mountain of Victories as we were accustomed,** and we went up and found that pillar of light in front of the cave, again a great fear came upon us.*

*RotM 14:9 And when all these things and others like them, of which there were many, (happened,) while **descending the Mountain of Victories,** we gave praise and repeated to each other everything that we saw and heard there.*

*RotM 17:4b And we came, rejoicing with our pure gifts, which were deposited by our fathers in the **Cave of Treasures of Hidden Mysteries on the Mountain of Victories.***

These quotes from ***Revelation of the Magi*** show iconic markers of the Magi in geography, and are not mysteries in ancient history. As we drill down further into this narrative, it only becomes more obvious the Magi lived and originated in the Philippines. Not only does the overall general geography match, even the specifics coalesce in ways that should not exist unless the narrative is true. Remember, the linguistic tie of the Magi is already proven fact.

The translation "victories" is erroneous in locating this mountain as they use the wrong language. This is the famous Mount of the East and only one option exists. We can identify this mountain in the Philippines with certainty and at its base, The Spring of Purification is there. Wow! The Cave of Treasures is located on the Mount of the East in credible texts as well as in *Revelation of the Magi (RoTM)*. In other words, these are all the same place. In this chapter, we will diseminate this data in a manner that anyone can understand. This is supported by credible history with precedence and this has been obscured only in the scholarly paradigm, which has chosen to exercise amnesia, forgetting the ancient record and acting as if it never existed. Their education proves very limited, and that is sad to see.

Mountain of Victories and the Mount of the East:

When *Revelation of the Magi* refers to the Mountain of Victories, it definitely connects it as the Mount of the East of *Genesis 10:30, Jubilees, First Enoch*, a Dead Sea Scroll titled *Words of the Archangel Michael*, and *The Cave of Treasures*, a text named for that very same cave of the Magi. All are affirmed as valid places. These tie to the land of the Garden of Eden as well as the land where Adam and Eve's righteous generations resided affirmed by the same texts cited above, and according to *Revelation of the Magi* which full title is *"Mountain of Victories in the East (4:1)"*. That is the Mount of the East. This vets with accurate Bible geography and 6,000 years of maps and history *(See Introduction)*.

Genesis 10:26-30 KJV
*And Joktan begat Almodad, and Sheleph, and Hazarmaveth, and Jerah, And Hadoram, and Uzal, and Diklah, And Obal, and Abimael, and **Sheba, And Ophir, and Havilah,** and Jobab: all these were the sons of Joktan. And **their dwelling was from Mesha, as thou goest unto Sephar a mount of the east.***

Eber, or Eberim (plural), is the origin of the designation "Hebrew" which includes a larger group than just Israel *(Jacob)*. There was no Israel before Jacob, and Abraham was not an Israelite, but part of a larger group from Eber=Hebrew. In addition to Abraham's ancestor, Peleg, Eber had another son, Joktan, who was also a Hebrew. He was not Israelite nor was Peleg, Isaac, or Eber. One would think scholars and even pastors would know this.

Israel was a defiled land before Abraham, since the fifth generation from Adam, as it was the origin of the Watchers and their Nephilim offspring. Enoch even defines that area as a place where he met the Watchers (who were evil), and he pronounced their coming judgement there, in Israel, in the territory of Dan. It is also the location of Mt. Hermon where they took the oath to sin. However, how many times have we heard the illiteracy from the modern pulpit that Israel was always the Holy Land. That is propaganda, not from the Bible, and it is a lie.

The reason we do not see much else about Jokton in this account, is due to his migration with his sons: Ophir, Sheba, and Havilah, to the Far East; to the isles that housed the Garden of Eden. That was known since Genesis 2 as the Land of Gold;

later it was named after the sons of Jokton, Ophir and Sheba especially. One of the Magi's fathers is also named Havilah *("Hawîlat" 2:3; Latinized form of Havilah)* for that matter, according to ***Revelation of the Magi.*** We also find linguistic connections to Ophir, Sheba, Tarshish, and about half of Ophir's brothers in these Magi names.

Havilah is the name of the land of Adam and Eve (from Genesis 2), where they were created, and were later exiled (from the Garden), returning to the same place of their origin *(Jub. 3:32)*. The land of their creation is known as the Philippines today. It is hard to believe a Bible scholar could not have recognized Havilah in its Latinized form, right there in these names, leading to a land very well documented, in scripture, especially. However, of the 24 names the book offers, Landau could only speculate on one of them. We will connect most of them in Chapter 8.

Genesis 10 describes a migration to the land of Sephar, a Hebrew reference to the Tree of Life which remains in the Garden of Eden, as it is referenced three times in the *Book of Revelation (Rev. 2:7, 22:2, 14)*. Those who speculate that the Garden was taken to "another plane of existence" have no education on the topic. That speculation originates in Kabbalah, not in the Bible. Revelation affirms it is still there and never moved. It affirms itself with a double marker; in the same way when it identifies the Mount of the East, which is not some mountain somewhere East of Israel. We are aware many Zionist scholars cannot read that simple direction, claiming the Garden is in Israel and yet, East of it at the same time? That is not logic. It is a Holy Mountain in the Garden of Eden on which Enoch sacrificed while in the Garden, yet, it protrudes from the interior of the Earth, where Adam made offerings, the day after his exile from the Garden. It is one of the four Holy Places of Yahuah on all of Earth.

Jubilees 4:22b-26
*...and **Enoch** testified against (them) all. And he was taken from amongst the children of men, and **we conducted him into the Garden of Eden** in majesty and honour, and behold there he writeth down the condemnation and judgment of the world, and all the wickedness of the children of men. And on account of it (God) brought the waters of the flood upon all the land of Eden; for there he was set as a sign and that he should testify against all the children of men, that he should recount all the deeds of the generations until the day of condemnation. **And he burnt the incense of the sanctuary,** (even) **sweet spices, acceptable before Yahuah on the Mount.** For **Yahuah hath four places on the earth, the Garden of Eden, and the Mount of the East,** and this mountain on which thou art this day, **Mount Sinai,** and **Mount Zion** (which) will be sanctified in the new creation for a sanctification of the earth;*

The Mount in the Garden is the Mount of the East where Enoch offered incense when he entered the Garden. This is the same as the *Mountain of Victories in the East* in this text *(RotM 4.1)*, even etymologically. However, Adam also burned offerings on this same mountain outside of the Garden of Eden after his exile. Therefore, it is both within the Earth where the Garden of Eden is enclosed and rises through the

Earth's crust into the sky as an island in the Philippines. We will identify this, along with the spring near it as well. Adam did not just know of the Cave of Treasures, it was his residence, and he is the one who first began to place aside the resources there for the Magi to present to the Messiah thousands of years later. It is truly laughable that some demand archaeology of cities built by Adam who never did so.

Jubilees 3:27
And on that day on which Adam went forth from the Garden, he offered as a sweet savour an offering, frankincense, galbanum, and stacte, and spices in the morning with the rising of the sun from the day when he covered his shame.

Cave Of Treasures
And Adam and Eve went down in . . . . of spirit over the mountains of Paradise, and they found a cave in the top of the mountain, and they entered and hid themselves therein.
And Adam took from the skirts of the mountain of Paradise, gold, and myrrh, and frankincense, and he placed them in the cave, and he blessed the cave, and consecrated it that it might be the house of prayer for himself and his sons. And he called the cave "ME`ARATH GAZZE" (i.e. "CAVE OF TREASURES"). [71]

The ***Revelation of the Magi*** book from the Vatican, translated into English, leaves no doubt regarding this prophecy of the Magi bringing gifts to Messiah after His birth. They were the ancient order in place, practicing since Seth, the son of Adam. They precede Abraham, as well as the Levites, as a priestly order with a specific purpose. Our Western view of the Bible truly fails on so many levels. This tradition was first prophecied by Adam, the Prophet Enoch, and then by King David, though scholars have attempted to explain it away in ignorance, as we have proved. The generations of the Magi continued to meet in the Cave of Treasures, from the antediluvian days before the Flood. The ancestors of the Magi would have been disconnected from practicing their traditions after the Flood, until the return of the lineage of Ophir, Sheba, and Tarshish (somewhere around 2200 B.C.). Part of the reason for their return was fulfilling their purpose as the Magi. These accounts cannot be disconnected and *Revelation of the Magi* only affirms them.

The gold is from the Land of Gold, and the Garden of Eden; the land of Adam, where he made his first oblation of gold, frankincense, and myrrh. The Queen of Sheba brought these exact donations to the Temple project, giving these same resources, as King Hiram, Solomon's Admiral, at the same time *(1Ki. 10)*. This is also the reason Solomon built a new port and navy, to travel the risky journey of such a great distance, for the resources which line the walls of the Garden of Eden in Yahuah's original Holy of Holies (which still survives). The Wise Men were following this custom as a Biblical covenant fulfillment of prophecy. This is actual Philippine history, from creation to 970 B.C., and forward into the first century, which all connect, and cannot be disassociated. It is profound, willing ignorance to claim the Philippines has no history until 1521.

*RotM 4:7b ...taking with you **his own pure gifts**, which were put in the Cave of Treasures of Hidden Mysteries on the Mountain of Victories by your fathers, go to where his light, the star, leads you.*
RotM 13:8 And again, take with you the treasure that was deposited in this cave by your fathers and [continue in joy] and worship the [text missing] I will be born like a human being.
*RotM 16:2 And we got ready with our whole encampment, and with our provisions, and with the **pure and holy gifts**, those that we brought out of the Cave of Treasures of Hidden Mysteries, in which they were [deposited] previously by our fathers...*
*RotM 17:4b And we came, rejoicing with **our pure gifts**, which were deposited by our fathers in the Cave of Treasures of Hidden Mysteries on the Mountain of Victories.*
RotM 27:6 And we offered him gifts that we took from the Cave of Treasures, which were deposited by our fathers from his own.

Their fathers (since the days of Adam and Seth), set aside treasures for the coming Son of Yahuah as the Savior of mankind. Though the cave would not be accessible from the Flood to the days of Ophir, Sheba and Tarshish (in their return), this prophecy survived for thousands of years. It should not be a surprise to a Bible scholar when Psalm 72:10-15 very clearly details Kings of these three regions would be the ones to execute this prophetic mission. Jesus *(Yahusha)* was not just a fulfillment of the covenant with Abraham, he was the embodiment of the prophesies since Adam, as evidenced prophetically in Genesis and Jubilees.

Genesis 3:15 KJV
*And I will put enmity between thee and the woman, and **between thy seed and her seed;** it shall bruise thy head, and thou shalt bruise his heel.*

Jubilees 16:26
*And he blessed his Creator who had created him in his generation, for He had created him according to His good pleasure; for **He knew and perceived that from him would arise the plant of righteousness for the eternal generations, and from him a holy seed, so that it should become like Him who had made all things.***

This should also not be strange to anyone as John also defines Messiah as the Light of Creation, quoting the *Book of Jubilees (John 1:1-5, 9, 14; Colossians 1:15-16; Hebrews 1:2-3)*. John does not stand alone on this doctrine, Paul and Hebrews affirm this but Jubilees is the origin of this concept as the first witness in all scripture. Indeed, it was the Light of Jesus *(Yahusha)* that was used to create all things. When ***Revelation of the Magi*** expounds on the details, it is well within Bible doctrine in doing so. We will cover that in full detail in the next chapter.

Additionally, the translation "Mountain of Victories in the East" from the Syriac/Aramaic language comes from the word "zaka." This demonstrates the shortcomings of the scholarly community. Rather than bother to consider that the Magi met on a famous mountain well connected in scripture and history named in Ancient Hebrew, this translator just left it with the assumption it can only be Aramaic or similar. This is the ancient mountain that represents one of only four

Holy Places that are set apart from the rest of the Earth.

If he only looked at the Hebrew definition of the word "zaka, זכך," it means *"clean (6x), clear (1x), pure (1x) (H2135)."* This is not the *Mountain of Victories in the East* (which is a poor translation); it is the *Mountain of Purification of the East.* That only fits one summit in all of history: the Mount of the East on which resides the Cave of Treasures atop the Garden of Eden. Adam purified himself the day after his exile on the Mount of the East and Enoch entered the Garden of Eden, making sacrifices on the same mountain within the Earth. This mountain stands alone and should never have been lost to the Bible paradigm of scholarship.

Bible Gold of the Garden of Eden, Ophir & Mount of the East:

1 Chronicles 29:4 KJV
*Even three thousand talents of gold, of the **gold of Ophir,** and seven thousand talents of refined silver, to **overlay the walls** of the houses withal:*

2 Chronicles 3:6-7 KJV
*Further, **he adorned the house** (Temple of Solomon) with precious stones; and the gold was gold from Parvaim. He also **overlaid the house** with gold—the beams, the thresholds and **its walls** and its doors; and he carved cherubim on the walls.*

The quote from the *Book of Chronicles* appears to be confused. That is how many scholars would view this. Instead, we see this as brilliance beyond measure. The walls of the Temple of Solomon were overlaid with gold from Ophir, no, I mean Parvaim. What is the difference? There is none. They are the same place. When we review these names in Hebrew, Parvaim/Sepharvaim is Sephar, which is also Ophir. Where is Sephar where Joktan and sons migrated? In the Orient, the Far East. This is the same location as Ophir and the Garden of Eden, especially since Sephar is a reference to the Tree of Life.

*Hebrew: **Parvaim:** Parvayim: פרוים: Oriental regions; Orient or eastern and is a general term for the east. Probably **Ophir.** Shortened form of **Cepharvayim** which occurs in the Syriac and Targum Jonathan for the "Sephar" of Genesis 10:30. Only used 1X.*[1]

In the Dead Sea Scrolls, we have confirmation of this concept. When Noah was born, his father, Lamech, wanted confirmation that his son was fully human, since he looked unique. Noah was perfectly created to carry the races' DNA through the Flood, in his lineage. However, Lamech's father, Methuselah, decided to visit his father, the Prophet Enoch. During this time, Enoch resided in the Garden of Eden. In this fragment below, that area of the Garden entrance is also known as Parwain or Parvaim. There actually is no "V" in Ancient Hebrew, so these are the same. Enoch would have exited the Garden as Methuselah would not be allowed inside.

Genesis Apocryphon Fragment. 1QapGen, 1Q20. Column II.
This fruit was planted by you and by no stranger or Watcher or Son of Heaven... [Why] is your countenance thus changed and dismayed, and why is your spirit thus distressed... I speak to you truthfully.' Then I, Lamech, ran to Methuselah my father, and I told him all these things. [And I asked him to go to Enoch] his father for he would surely learn all things from him. For he was beloved, and he shared the lot [of the angels], who taught him all things. And when Methuselah heard Enoch his father to learn all things truthfully from him... his will. **He went at once to Parwain and he found him there... [and] he said to Enoch his father, 'O my father, O my lord, to whom I...** *And I say to you, lest you be angry with me because I come here...*[2]

The other gold in the Bible very clearly associated with Tarshish and Ophir is Uphaz. This is mentioned by the Prophet Jeremiah, as affiliated with silver, originating in Tarshish, known today as Mindanao, Philippines, and the gold originating from Uphaz. Isn't the gold from Ophir? Yes, they are the same.

Jeremiah 10:9 KJV
Silver spread into plates is brought from Tarshish, and gold from Uphaz, *the work of the workman, and of the hands of the founder: blue and purple is their clothing: they are all the work of cunning men.*

Daniel had a vision next to the River from Eden known as the Hiddekel River in Genesis 2. It was never the Tigris (in any credible context), but the ancient River, East of Assyria, on the ocean floor. How scholars cannot figure out that the Tigris is the West border of Assyria by boundary, (therefore, not East of it), escapes us. Though inserted in fraud in many Bibles, the Tigris is never mentioned in the Hebrew scriptures. The Hiddekel is mentioned twice, and Daniel is in Persia at that point in the story. He is nowhere near the Tigris anyway. He is East of Assyria where the Hiddekel existed and remains on the bottom of the ocean.

Genesis 2:5 tells us the conditions of Earth's system, when the Hiddekel is mentioned; there was no rain on the Earth, but a mist came up from the ground to water it. Thus, the Tigris River never existed prior to the Flood, as its source is a lake basin, filled with rainfall. That is one of the most illiterate guesses we have ever seen. Bible scholars are leading their sheep to the occult doctrine of demons, and they don't even realize it. The source is the Sumerian Creation Myth, written by Nephilim, not the Bible. In the Bible, the Garden was planted in the Far East.

Notice the Messianic qualities in the next passage, of a being who has the feet of brass, eyes as lamps of fire, face as lightning, and a body as beryl. Wow! It appears this is the Archangel from the Garden of Eden. Some even say the Messiah, but the passage clearly defines an angelic principality who is held back in his coming by the

---

[1] *"Parvaim." Smith's Bible Dictionary, International Standard Bible Encyclopedia, ATS Bible Dictionary, Easton's Bible Dictionary, Strong's #H6516. BibleHub.com.* [2] *""The Complete Dead Sea Scrolls." By Geza Vermes, Penguin Classics. p. 481-482, Column II.*

prince demon of Persia. No demon can restrain Jesus *(Yahusha)*. Notice, Persia is in the way, just as with the Magi narrative.

Daniel 10:5 KJV
*Then I lifted up mine eyes, and looked, and behold a certain man clothed in linen, whose loins were girded with **fine gold of Uphaz**: His **body** also was like the **beryl**, and his **face** as the appearance of lightning, and his eyes as **lamps of fire**, and his arms and **his feet** like in colour to **polished brass**, and the voice of his words like the voice of a multitude.*

Uphaz is Ophir and that is the Garden location as well. We know this because Uphaz is the gold of the Pison River, which surrounds the whole land of Havilah, Philippines, which leads the Earth in the three resources of that region: gold, pearl, and the Onyx stone. The Archangel of the Garden is Gabriel, according to *1 Enoch* 20:7. He is the Angel of the East in Revelation 7:2. He appears in anointing just as Messiah does in Revelation 2:18, which is why his appearance is similar. In this vision, Gabriel is wearing the belt of fine gold from the Philippines, very similar to the one found in the Surigao Treasure in the 1980's. Do we actually have archeology of Daniel and we do not even know it?

Uphaz is the same word as *Ophir*, varied, to particularily refer to its gold. AU is the chemical symbol for gold which originates in AUpyr *(Ophir)*. For those incapable of connecting Aupyr as the origin of the Latin *Aurea*, Josephus did so.[1] Yes, Ophir is the origin of gold as it is *Aurea*, and that is never credibly a peninsula; but isles, that are not found in Malaysia or modern India. It is the area of the Indian isles which included the Philippines. *Uphaz* is also rendered improperly to Ancient Hebrew and when corrected reads *A-U-P-Z*. *Paz* is the Hebrew word for *gold*. That is literally "*gold, gold*" and a derivative of *Aupyr*, as these are the same land. *Uphaz* is definitively the gold of Ophir, which is the gold of the Land of the Garden of Eden, surrounded by the Pison river, which is key; not the Tigris. This is why this land has always been a part of the Biblical paradigm whether scholars know it today, or not. Their forgetfulness of Biblical facts is not scholarly, or a position.

UPHAZ: Hebrew: אופז*: 'Uwphaz: Fine Gold, gold of Phasis or Pison. Perhaps a corruption, Probably another name for* אופיר*: 'Owphiyr: Ophir.*[2]

---

[1] *Antiquities of the Jews – Book 8.6.4. Flavius Josephus.* [2] *"Uphaz." Hitchcock's Bible Names Dictionary, ATS Bible Dictionary, Easton's Bible Dictionary, International Standard Bible Encyclopedia, Strong's #H210, #H211. BibleHub.com.*

Garden of Eden, The Star of the Magi, & Mount of the East Location:

RotM 6:2 And Adam instructed Seth his son about [text missing], [and about the revelation] of the light of the star and about its glory, because he [saw] it in the Garden of Eden when it descended and came to rest over the Tree of Life; and it illuminated the entire (garden) before Adam transgressed against the commandment of the Father of heavenly majesty. 6:3 And when he transgressed against the commandment that (the Father) ordained for him, the sight of the star was taken away from him, and (it was also taken away from him) because of his expulsion from Paradise. And Adam our father mourned over (his) foolishness, that he was humbled from his greatness. 6:4 And he strongly warned his son Seth, and he taught him to walk in righteousness so that he might find mercy before the Father of majesty.

In affirmation, we find even more geographical markers in *Revelation of the Magi* which serve to confirm what we have already proven. In the portion with an account from Seth, which is completely scriptural, it was Adam who already foretold of the famous Star, predicted to appear at the birth of Messiah. Adam knew prophecy, and that is well attested in Jubilees, First Enoch and other texts. However, this identifies an association in location of the Star, which would appear to the Magi at the Cave of Treasures on the Mount of the East with the same Light that appeared in the Garden of Eden in this same location. Adam lost the ability to see the Light, so it would be reserved for the Magi. However, Adam knew of its prophetic return. This Star is not what we would term a *star*, but far brighter and greater in significance since Creation, even before stars were created.

Map to the Garden of Eden & Mount of the East in the Book of Jubilees:

In addition to 6,000 years of mapping *(See Introduction)*, there is far more detail provided in the historic Bible perspective to this Mount of the East translated as Mountain of Victories. The Mount of the East is documented in Genesis and Jubilees (as we have seen). However, it is also mapped in the *Book of Jubilees*, as the Garden of Eden is defined in the Far East on the southeastern border of Shem. In Chapters 8 and 9, Moses records the detail of Noah's Division of the Earth.

Moses tells us that Noah knew the Garden was East of India in the Far East at the end of Shem's Asia to the southeast. Then, when providing Ham's inheritance in territory, Noah expounds in definitive detail, as Ham progresses West across the Americas, crossing the Pacific all the way to the right *(or East)* of the Garden of Eden. That is a border of the East and the South, as the Garden is found just above and just to the West of it *(map on p. 118)*.

Noah defines a short distance from the Garden as being just North of the Southern border of Asia, between Shem and Ham, and then, he brilliantly preserves this for his descendents. He sets the border in southeast Asia at "all the mountains of fire."

In Indonesia, this remains a Javanese connotation as *Gunung Gunung Api*, which is the name of its 147 volcanoes. In English, this is "Mountains of Fire" exactly as Noah defined. He named those mountains.

In both directions for Shem and Ham, the Garden of Eden is just North of the border, placing it within the Earth, beneath the Sulu Sea of the Philippines. Having plotted these complete directions, described in two chapters, the location is not up for debate. Those who attempt to use these as directions typically have never charted them in order, and thus, lose themselves in the middle, not knowing where the directions were prior and after that plot point. Let us not refer to that as logic. The methodology behind this mapping and full grid is found in our book: ***The Book of Jubilees: The Torah Calendar***, which is even free in eBook at ***BookOfJubilees.org***, with a 52-week teaching series in support titled: ***Answers In Jubilees***.

Enoch's Seven Mountains of Eden:

In the *Book of 1 Enoch* (chapter 32), the Ancient Mountains of the East are referred to as the Mountains of Eden, essentially. As the Mount of the East resides within and protrudes out of the Garden of Eden, this is simple to comprehend; the same mountain as the Mount of the East, in modern Philippines. Enoch provides exact geography in his journey to the Garden of Righteousness, which is due Northeast of the exit of the Indian Ocean *(map on p. 120)*. That is the Philippines. Then, he offers amazing detail that these mountains above the Garden orient geographically, exactly as the seven major islands of Visayas. Prior to the Flood, islands were mountains.

He further defines the resources, which are a perfect relation to these same seven islands, including the alabaster. In ancient Egypt, alabaster found in archaeological digs tests as brown or yellow marble onyx stone.[1] It just so happens Romblon Island exists right where Enoch said it would be, and it is the world capital for the strongest onyx and marble stone on Earth.[2] This full position can be found in video form on The God Culture platforms including our app, and in ***The First Book of Enoch: The Oldest Book in History***, available free in eBook at ***FirstEnoch.org***. The Mount of the East should never have been lost in scholarship. It has been charted and located throughout thousands of years in the Philippines with consenting resources and markers which all align.

---

[1] *"Alabaster, Mineral." and "Marble, Rock." By Editors of Encyclopaedia Britannica. Encyclopaedia Britannica. Updated Jan. 24, 2018 and Jan. 24, 2020.* [2] *a. "ROMBLON: 8 Awesome Places You Should Visit in Romblon!" Our Awesome Planet. Sept. 7, 2016. b. "The Romblon Marble." Ellaneto Tiger Marble Trader, Romblon. 2010. c. "Marvelous Marble" By Robert A. Evora. Manila Standard. Jan. 16, 2014.* [3] *The Complete Dead Sea Scrolls in English. Revised Edition. By Geza Vermes. Penguin Books. London, NY. Revised 2004. Originally Published 1962. p. 556.*

Michael's Nine Mountains of the East:

Words of the Archangel Michael: (4Q529, 6Q23), fr. 1: [3]
Words of the book which Michael addressed to the angels... He said: I found there divisions of fire...
[and I saw there] **nine mountains: two to the eas[t, and two to the west, and two to the north**
and two to the so]uth. I saw there the angel Gabriel . . . like a vision. [Then] I showed him the
vision. And he said to me:... in the books of my Master, Yahuah of the world, it is written: Behold,...
[between] the sons of Ham and the sons of Shem. And behold my Master, Yahuah of the world...
when **they***... the tear from... And behold* **a city was built** *to the name of my Master, [Yahuah of the*
world, and there] **everything that is evil** *will be done before my Master, Yahuah [of the world]...*
And my Master, Yahuah of the world, will remember his creation... [and] my Master, Yahuah of the
world, [will be] merciful to him and to him... **the man will be in the faraway province***... he, and he*
will say to him: Behold this... **for me silver and gold***... And he will say:... [and] the* **righteous man***...*

The *Words of the Archangel Michael* is a fragment from the Dead Sea Scrolls. No
one has made a case for its induction into the modern Canon, but it has survived
for thousands of years, and was found among what is authenticated as Bible Canon.
Even as a secondary test of history and geography, this account vets accurate. We
know these Nine Mountains of the East are describing the area just above the
Garden of Eden, as that is where the Archangel Gabriel resides on Earth, according
to 1 Enoch 20:7 *(map on p. 121)*. We have ratified that is the modern Philippines and
these are the Mountains of the East. There is one within this region that is known
as The Mount of the East and we will investigate that.

When one assesses these, they are the seven mountains of Visayas or Eden (as
Enoch termed it), plus two others. This becomes very obvious when zooming out
on a map of the Philippines. Even though there are so many islands, the two which
would be added to the seven are clearly Luzon and Mindanao, to equal nine. This
is pretty easy, and the topography and mineral deposits of the positions coalesce.
The faraway province is the Philippines, where Ophir and his righteous Magi
brothers migrated prior to the fall of Babel. This is why linguists have connected
many words from Filipino languages as originating in Ancient Hebrew. The Mount
of the East is in the Philippines, Northeast of the Malay Peninsula and North of
Borneo, as well defined in these ancient texts.

Finding the Mount of the East in the Philippines:

The next logical progression after locating the Garden of Eden under the Sulu
Sea within the Earth, would be to find the Mount of the East. We believe we can
locate this as well, though it will not be quite as scientific as the previous. We did
map oil pockets, noting that where they are would not likely be the location of the
Garden, thus revealing a shape that leads to an island to the East and just North of

Shem's Division from Noah.

Asia.

From Jubilees 8

(See our publishing of the Book of Jubilees for full-sized, detailed color maps)

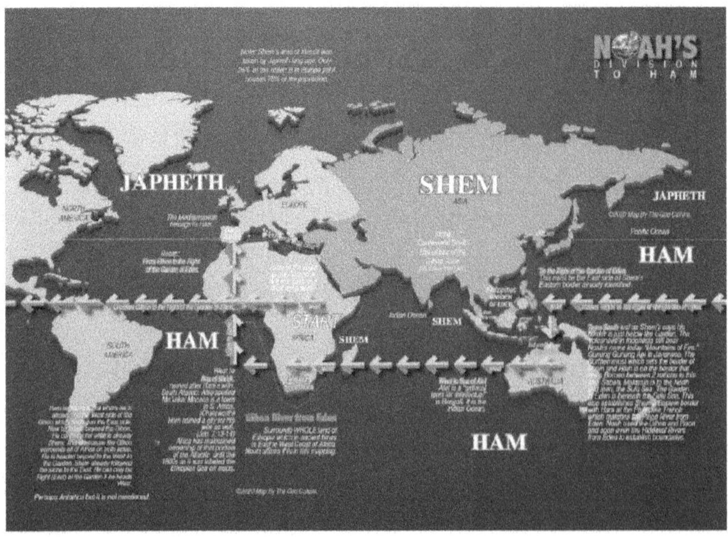

Ham's Division from Noah.

Southern Hemisphere except Asia..

From Jubilees 8

(See our publishing of the Book of Jubilees for full-sized, detailed color maps)

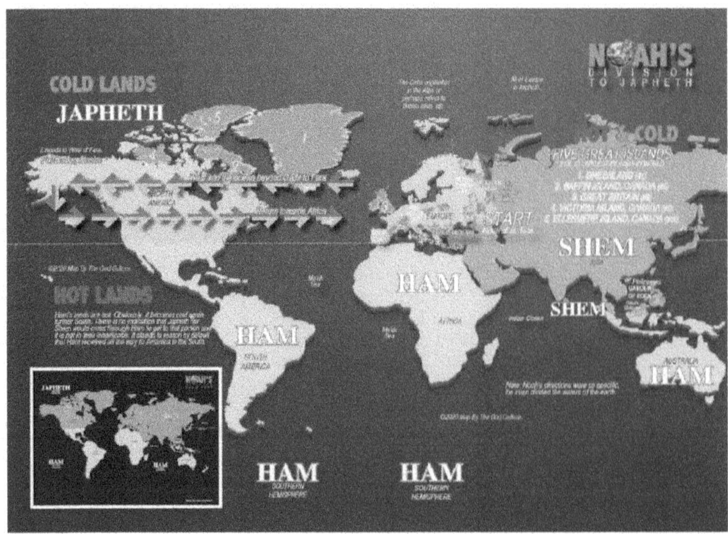

Japheth's Division from Noah.

Northern Hemisphere except Asia.

From Jubilees 8

(See our publishing of the Book of Jubilees for full-sized, detailed color maps)

NOAH'S DIRECTIONS TO THE GARDEN OF EDEN FROM THE BOOK OF JUBILEES

GARDEN OF EDEN
SHEM'S SOUTHEAST BORDER

MOUNTAINS OF FIRE
"Gunung Gunung Api" in Javanese
147 Volcanoes forming a natural geographic border between Shem and Ham in the Far East. [34]

GENESIS 3:24 KJV - EAST OF THE GARDEN
So he drove out the man; and he placed at the east of the garden of Eden Cherubims, and a flaming sword which turned every way, to keep the way of the tree of life.

TESTING THE RESOURCES OF HAVILAH [31][32]

GOLD
In all of history, the Philippines leads in gold mining since before 1000 B.C. and still remains #2 on earth in untapped gold reserves. There is no other land which competes. It is the ancient land of gold by historical record. [27]

PEARL
Bdellium is never a Biblical spice and all such spices are recorded in scripture. It is pearl. The Philippines has the largest pearls in all of history with no 2nd. [28]

*Puerto Princessa Pearl. 2006. 34 kg (75 lb.)

ONYX STONE
Ancient onyx especially in Egypt was known as alabaster used in ornamental construction. The Philippines has the strongest onyx and marble on earth in Romblon. [29]

MARINE LIFE

Marine life is the true measure for the Land of Creation as it was not wiped out by the Flood. The Epicenter of Marine Biodiversity on ALL of earth is the Philippines in the Sulu Sea. [30]

Tubbataha Reef in the Sulu Sea.

In resources, history, geography, science, language and the Bible, this is Ophir.
See "The Search for King Solomon's Treasure: The Lost Isles of Gold and the Garden of Eden" for Evidences.

GENESIS 2:11-12 KJV
The name of the first is Pison: that is it which compasseth the whole land of Havilah, where there is gold: And the gold of that land is good: there is bdellium and the onyx stone.

HAVILAH [31][32]
= GARDEN OF EDEN
= LAND OF CREATION
= OPHIR
= PHILIPPINES

JUBILEES 3:32
Adam and his wife went forth from the Garden of Eden, and they dwelt in the land of 'Elda, in the land of their creation.

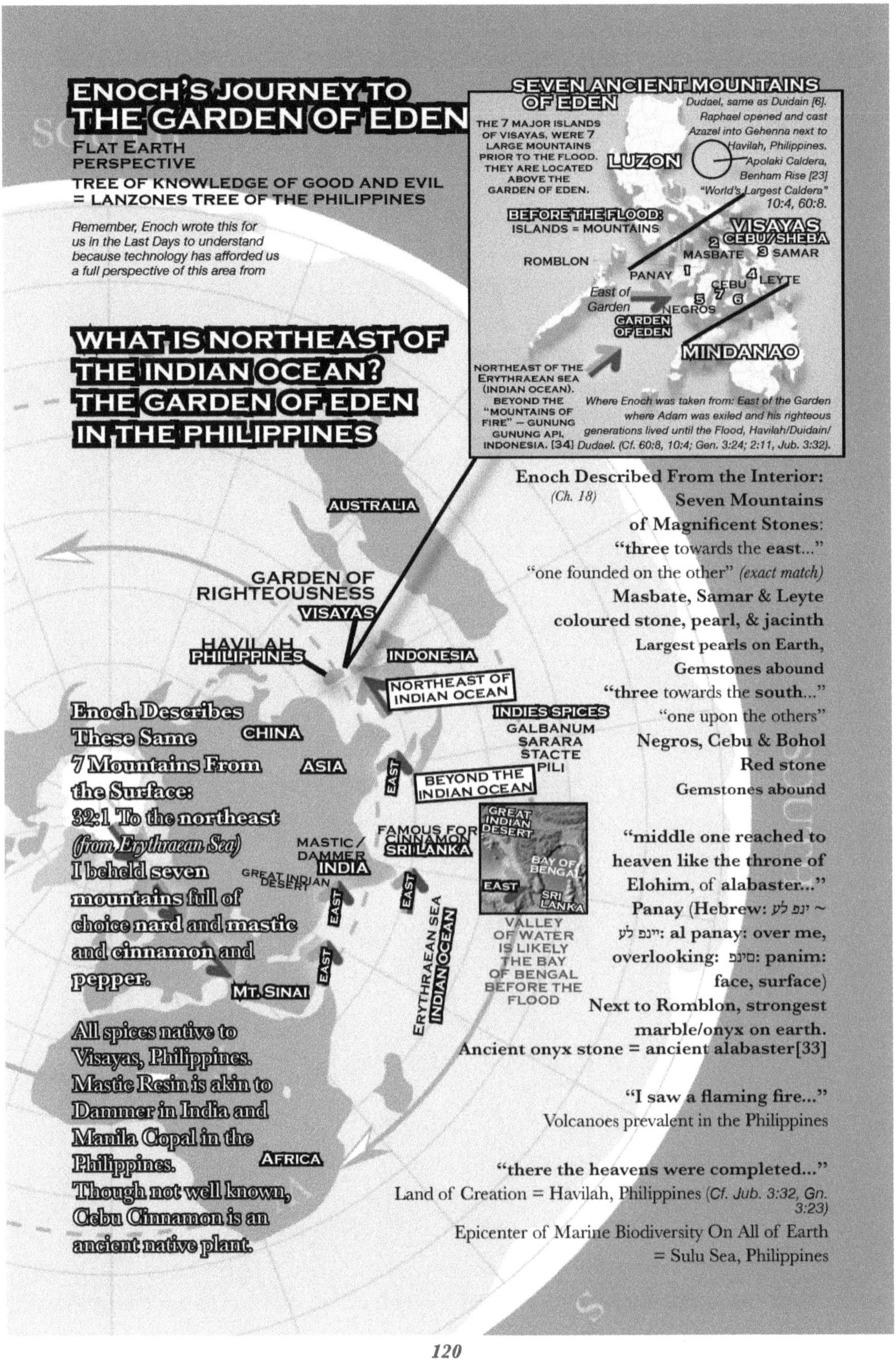
ENOCH'S JOURNEY TO
THE GARDEN OF EDEN
FLAT EARTH
PERSPECTIVE
TREE OF KNOWLEDGE OF GOOD AND EVIL
= LANZONES TREE OF THE PHILIPPINES
Remember, Enoch wrote this for
us in the Last Days to understand
because technology has afforded us
a full perspective of this area from
WHAT IS NORTHEAST OF
THE INDIAN OCEAN?
THE GARDEN OF EDEN
IN THE PHILIPPINES
SEVEN ANCIENT MOUNTAINS
OF EDEN
THE 7 MAJOR ISLANDS OF VISAYAS, WERE 7 LARGE MOUNTAINS PRIOR TO THE FLOOD. THEY ARE LOCATED ABOVE THE GARDEN OF EDEN.
Dudael, same as Duidain [6]. Raphael opened and cast Azazel into Gehenna next to Havilah, Philippines.
Apolaki Caldera, Benham Rise [23] "World's Largest Caldera" 10:4, 60:8.
LUZON
BEFORE THE FLOOD:
ISLANDS = MOUNTAINS
VISAYAS
CEBU/SHEBA
ROMBLON
2 MASBATE
3 SAMAR
PANAY 1
4 LEYTE
CEBU
5 7 6
East of Garden
NEGROS
GARDEN OF EDEN
MINDANAO
NORTHEAST OF THE ERYTHRAEAN SEA (INDIAN OCEAN). BEYOND THE "MOUNTAINS OF FIRE" — GUNUNG GUNUNG API, INDONESIA. [34]
Where Enoch was taken from: East of the Garden where Adam was exiled and his righteous generations lived until the Flood, Havilah/Duidain/ Dudael. (Cf. 60:8, 10:4; Gen. 3:24; 2:11, Jub. 3:32).
AUSTRALIA
GARDEN OF
RIGHTEOUSNESS
VISAYAS
HAVILAH
PHILIPPINES
INDONESIA
NORTHEAST OF
INDIAN OCEAN
INDIES SPICES
GALBANUM
SARARA
STACTE
PILI
CHINA
ASIA
EAST
BEYOND THE
INDIAN OCEAN
GREAT INDIAN DESERT
BAY OF BENGAL
EAST
SRI LANKA
FAMOUS FOR
CINNAMON
SRI LANKA
MASTIC/
DAMMER
INDIA
GREAT INDIAN DESERT
EAST
EAST
EAST
ERYTHRAEAN SEA
INDIAN OCEAN
VALLEY
OF WATER
IS LIKELY
THE BAY
OF BENGAL
BEFORE THE
FLOOD
MT. SINAI
AFRICA
Enoch Describes These Same 7 Mountains From the Surface:
32:1 To the northeast (from Erythraean Sea) I beheld seven mountains full of choice nard and mastic and cinnamon and pepper.
All spices native to Visayas, Philippines. Mastic Resin is akin to Dammer in India and Manila Copal in the Philippines. Though not well known, Cebu Cinnamon is an ancient native plant.
Enoch Described From the Interior:
(Ch. 18)
Seven Mountains of Magnificent Stones:
"three towards the east..."
"one founded on the other" (exact match)
Masbate, Samar & Leyte
coloured stone, pearl, & jacinth
Largest pearls on Earth,
Gemstones abound
"three towards the south..."
"one upon the others"
Negros, Cebu & Bohol
Red stone
Gemstones abound
"middle one reached to heaven like the throne of Elohim, of alabaster..."
Panay (Hebrew: ינפ לע ~ ינפ לע: al panay: over me, overlooking: םינפ: panim: face, surface)
Next to Romblon, strongest marble/onyx on earth.
Ancient onyx stone = ancient alabaster[33]
"I saw a flaming fire..."
Volcanoes prevalent in the Philippines
"there the heavens were completed..."
Land of Creation = Havilah, Philippines (Cf. Jub. 3:32, Gn. 3:23)
Epicenter of Marine Biodiversity On All of Earth = Sulu Sea, Philippines

1. MICHAEL LAYS OUT 9 MOUNTAINS WHERE GABRIEL ABIDES IN THE GARDEN OF EDEN. GABRIEL IS IN CHARGE OF THE GARDEN ACCORDING TO ENOCH.

2. HE DEFINES THE LAYOUT JUST AS ENOCH WITH 7 VISAYAS MOUNTAINS OF EDEN PLUS 2 - LUZON AND MINDANAO ADDED. ISLANDS BEFORE THE FLOOD WERE MOUNTAINS.

3. HE MENTIONS SHINAR AND A MIGRATION OF THE RIGHTEOUS TO A FARAWAY LAND OF SILVER AND GOLD.

THIS IS THE MIGRATION OF OPHIR, SHEBA, AND TARSHISH TO THE FAMOUS LAND OF SILVER AND GOLD WHICH WOULD BE NAMED AFTER THESE PATRIARCHS. THIS OCCURRED AT THE TIME OF BABEL AND THEY WENT TO SEPHAR (TREE OF LIFE IN THE GARDEN OF EDEN) AND THE MOUNT OF THE EAST (HOLY MOUNTAIN IN THE GARDEN OF EDEN). GEN. 10:26-30. THIS IS THE MODERN PHILIPPINES.

[See The Search For King Solomon's Treasure for Full Position].

Mindanao. This information is compelling and worthy of review. Once you test it, you may well come to the same conclusion. Let's review a different rendering of Enoch's sacrifice in the Garden of Eden.

Jubilees 4:25 (Rabi-Kohan Shalomim Y. Halahawi, Ph.D, N.H.T. Min.) And he (Enoch) burnt the incense of the sanctuary, (even) sweet spices acceptable before the Lord on the Mount Qater.[1]

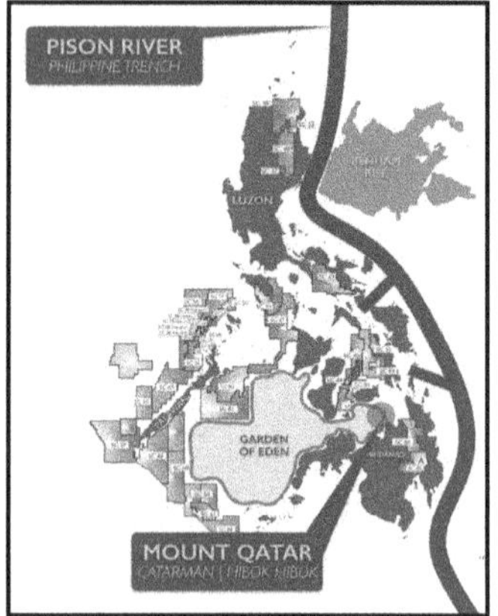

Mapping the Garden of Eden shape by the presence of oil pockets.

Rabi-Kohan Halahawi identifies the Mount of the East, mentioned in the *Book of Jubilees* by name, as Mount Qater/Qatar. Why would this be named such? Enoch made smoke sacrifices on this mountain as did Adam upon his exile. Also, in Kabbalah (in which the Rabbi may be involved), the highest rung of the Tree of Life is named Keter, which is the same word. We do not follow Kabbalah and reject it in every sense, but the Hebrew is still Hebrew and is useful in this case.

Hebrew: Qatar: קטר: *to make sacrifices of smoke, incense.*[1]

Again, after assessing oil pockets, this appears to open up and lead right to Camiguin Island, where the tallest summit would be Mt. Hibok Hibok. Could this be Mt. Qatar? Oddly, this is Hebrew, yet again, and not just any Hebrew, but that which bears a very appropriate meaning. This is not in just one name, but both designations of this mountain as it has an international name, Mt. CATARman.

Mt. Hibok Hibok (Hiboc-hiboc volcano):
Hebrew: hiboch!: היבוך! ~ היבוך!: *an imperative meaning (to a man) be embarrassed!*[2]

How can this possibly be the case? How can *Hibok (Hiboch)* be a direct and matching Hebrew word which essentially means "sorry" (specifically to a man, like Adam, for instance). In translation, this is *Mount Sorry! Sorry!* with exclaimation marks even, and in the Hebrew language, it is rendered: *Hiboch! Hiboch!* Was Adam not embarrassed when he made an atonement sacrifice on this very mountain, named for this event? Of course, this is impossible enough, until you consider there is a second international name for this same mountain: Mt. Catarman. Catar or Qatar? As in smoke sacrifices? As in the Mount of the East where Ophir migrated and where Adam and Enoch sacrificed?

---

[1] *""Mt. Qatar." "Developing and Establishing Effective Leadership for a Prosperous Edenic Hebrew Civilization. A Manual and Manifest for Laying the Foundations to the Eternal Kingdom of Yahwah." By Rabi-Kohan Shalomim Y. HaLevi, Ph. D, D. Div., O.R. Thrpst. S.A.C. 2004. p. 32.*
[2] *"Hiboch!" pealim.com #3963-lehiboch.*

Mt. Catarman (Mt. Hibok Hibok International Name):
Hebrew: Qatar: קטר*: to make sacrifices of smoke, incense.*[1]
Hebrew: Maan: מען*: purpose, intent.*[2,3]
Our Interpretation: Intended to Make Smoke Sacrifices

We are wading in absolutely improbable territory here. A mountain with two names that appear of Hebrew origin both in definition bridging Adam's first sacrifice of atonement. That is compelling.

Shir in the Philippines:

Also, we mention the antediluvian Mount of the East is not just the tallest summit, but the entire island of Camiguin. If you visit this area, you will find it is a true paradise, even for the ancients. On Camiguin you will find numerous freshwater springs, hot springs and even soda springs. It is rich in agriculture and very abundant in what may well be the Tree of the Knowledge of Good and Evil; the Lanzones tree. A sweeter variety of Lanzones (for which Camiguin is famous), bears such legend, as it was originally defined as *poison*, thus the word *Lason'* from the Tagalog dialect of the Philippines. Enoch defines this tree as having leaves like a carob tree and fruit that grows as bunches of grapes *(1En. 32)*.

Very close to Camiguin Island in Northern Mindanao, there is a large province known historically as Surigao with Siargao *(Shir-gaw)* Island as well. Maps have identified it as an ancient region with the name of *Shir*. Coincidence? The name originates in the local Waray language which is extremely revealing.

sirak: Waray: Sunlight, Sunshine. Other forms: sirahi, sirahan, siring. sirot, sirong, sirom.[4]
suri: Waray: To jest.

It is interesting that Surigao/Siargao *(Shir-gaw)* comes from the Waray word "sirak" meaning "sunlight or sunshine." Imagine this definition even leads to the Land of Light. This name translates to Greek, even in the apocryphal book: *Wisdom of Sirach/Ben Sira*, from the 1611 KJV. In Hebrew, that form is sirah *(*סרה*: Çirâh: withdrawing of a fountain, Gesenius' Hebrew-Chaldee Lexicon H5626)*. However, it also leads us to Shir from the prophecy of the Philippines in Isaiah 42:10 *(H7891: shîyr:* שיר*)* in this prophetic Land of Song.

In his margin notes regarding Shir, Landau notes the Gnostic Gospel from Nag Hammadi mentions a "Mount Shir" where Noah's ark rested. Horsefeathers!

---

[1] *"Qatar." Strong's Concordance #6999. BibleStudyTools.com.* [2] *Ma'an." Strong's Concordance #4616. BibleStudyTools.com.* [3] *"Mai: Maon or Main ." abarim-publications.com.* [4] *3NS Corpora Project Waray Dictionary.*

It would be truly illiterate to claim the Land of Shir is now a mountain in western Asia, and forget that is not the Far East or extreme East of the world, which is the one referred to in *Revelation of the Magi.* Why do supposed scholars even take such illiterate routes? Landau knew better. He also mentions, in the Epic of Gilgamesh, the Nephilim claim of their ark landing, which was not Noah (though he fails to realize that). It rested on Mt. Nasir. First, Nasir is not Shir and what terrible wordplay. Why even mention it. Once again, he is aware this Shir is in the extreme East (in *Revelation of the Magi*), and yet, Landau does not even recognize that Turkey, located on the Western border of Asia, is not the Far East in ANY paradigm, EVER! He simply grabbed ScholarScramble wordplay, and assumed it was an academic explanation (while us normal folk can call it what it is: a retarded and illogical guess).

Google Earth and Google Maps *(right)* actually capture this evidence, somehow. We have not been able to confirm why, but on Camiguin Island, Philippines, located on the tallest mountain, Mount Hibok Hibok, Google recognizes and labels it "Mount of the East." How is this posssible? Perhaps, because it is the truth. We have no idea who added this to Google Earth, but that is not data that can be manipulated easily. We know of no one else who has proved that mountain as the Biblical Mount of the East. This is affirmation we never expected, and some may scoff, but in the realm of research, this is worthy of note as logical testimony of endorsement we will explore.

Notice, Google identifies "Encloser of the Mount of the East" about midway up the side of Mt. Hibok Hibok. This is the actual image from Google Earth, and we have not altered it or even added marks. We just sized and cropped it to fit the space, and that's all. The word "encloser" is nothing to be excited about, as it is a box for volcanic gas monitoring (for study), according to U.S.G.S. However, why does Google call it "Mount of the East?" Clearly, this is a scientific label by the scientists who study the volcanic activity there. But again, why do scientists refer to this as "Mount of the East?" This is impossible.

We can certainly anticpate a skeptical opinion about this find. Perhaps it is on the East of Camiguin Island, except Mount Hibok Hibok is located on the Northwest portion of the island. Maybe it is on the East side of Hibok Hibok, which is labeled, except that is also not the case. The label is on the West side of the famous mountain. There is nothing East about it. Is the island on the East border of the Philippines? No. The identification, "Mount of the East", originates in these ancient manuscripts: *Genesis, Jubilees, 1 Enoch, Words of the Archangel Michael,* and *The Cave of Treasures.*

However, we also found a reference to Biblical Ophir, as *Mount Ophir*, in the writing, *Pseudo-Philo (26:11).* The origin of one of the special stones, representing the Tribes of Israel, affirming Exodus 28:18-19. Though not scripture (that we have tested, at this point), and a deceptive title (as it has no association with Philo

Google Earth Data Attribution per Fair Use Act: These maps includes data from: Maxar TechnologiesData SIO, NOAA, U.S. Navy, NGA, GEBCOTerraMetricsData LDEO-Columbia, NSF, NOAAAirbusImagery from the dates:12/14/2015–newerNote, some visible imagery has unknown date information.

whatsoever), this writing serves as another witness, and affirmation of what we already know and prove. The most important holy mountain in the Philippines is the Mount of the East, as we saw in multiple texts already. Sephar was the destination of Ophir and brothers. *Sephar* is expressed in Greek as *Sophir* in the Septuagint, and in **Revelation of the Magi,** appears to be *Shir* as well. Mount Sephar and Mount Ophir are the same place: the Mount of the East.

*"And the engraving of the **ninth stone was pierced-work from Mount Ophir**, and there was written "tribe of Gad," and it was like agate." –Pseudo-Phil 26:11*[1]

The Philippines is absolutely famous for the agate stone, recorded many times in Spanish history, and the Filipino bead trade of antiquity is documented far and wide, even all the way to Mediterranean countries. Note this reference to the stone being pierced, as a bead.

*"Some wear strings of precious stones—cornelians and **agates**; and other blue and white stones, which they esteem highly." –Antonio de Morga, 1609*[2]

As ancient Ophir's resources were already ending up in the Middle East and Africa before Solomon ever built a navy *(Ps. 45:9; Job 22:24, 28:16),* it is no surprise this popular stone from the Philippines was used in Israel. It was from Mount Ophir, just like the gold and temple resources were. Agate is technically known as chalcedony, a classification of quartz. Today, they are mining chalcedony in the area of Shir *(Surigao/Siargao/Shir-gaw)* in the Caraga region, among other mining operations in Luzon and Palawan.[2]

Mount Ophir is a reference to the Philippines, indisputably. No, the British rebranding Gunung Ledang in Malaysia in 1801 is called *fraud,* as the Malays rejected that claim. Even their tourism department maintains their true, ancient name still. Ophir is an island, never a peninsula in any credible reference (which includes Ptolemy, who attempted to redefine something he could not). Magellan corrected Ptolemy and others on that as well, which scholars should know.

This land of resources is really equated in a similar story, rendering this land of precious stones as Havilah, which should not shock anyone, as both Ophir and Havilah reference the same Isles of Gold, since the mention in Genesis 2. Both **Pseudo-Philo** and the **Chronicles of Jerahmeel** employ *Havilah* as the source of precious stones (that cannot be valued). This is affirmed in the writings of Job, Psalms, and Genesis. **Chronicles of Jerahmeel** defines it as *Havilah,* which has bdellium and onyx

---

[1] *"The Old Testament Pseudepigrapha, Vol. 2: Pseudo-Philo." Edited By James H. Charlesworth. Doubleday, New York. 1985. p. 311.* [2] *De Morga, Antonio. History of the Philippine islands: From their discovery by Magellan in 1521 to the beginning of the XVII Century; with description of Japan, China and adjacent countries. Translated by Blair and Robertson. Ohio: The Arthur and Clark Company. 1907.* [3] *Mindat.org. Rosario-Bunawan District, Caraga Region By Co-O Mine. Kolb, J. & Hagemann, St. (2009): Mineralium Deposita 44, 795-815.* [4] *"Chronicles of Jerahmeel." By M. Gaster. Oriental translation fund, London. 1899.*

stones, also like the description in Genesis 2. This is the Land of the Garden of Eden, (not the one from Ham), and it is in the Philippines, as is *Mount Ophir*. These accounts expose that the Amorites were able to get a hold of resources (which they likely stole, if true). Regardless of the actual historicity of the accounts in these books, where did the writers get this geography? The occult does not lead to Havilah, Philippines, it suppresses it, as the Pope does.

"The precious stones they brought from Havilah, where the bdellium and the onyx are found. These were the stones used by the Amorites for their idols." – Jerahmeel 57:14 [4]

"Those precious stones, among which were crystal and prase, were brought from the land of Havilah; and they had a pierced style. And one of them was cut on the top, and another like spotted chrysoprase shone in its cutting as if it revealed the water of the deep lying beneath it. And these are the precious stones that the Amorites had in their sanctuaries, the value of which cannot be estimated..." –Pseudo-Philo 25:11 [1]

Pseudo-Philo again describes more of a bead, as it is pierced. He uses crystal, which is quartz, essentially. They are mining quartz in so many places in the Philippines (according to mindat.org, which lists the mining companies and their locations for this resource), that if one has to ask, they have never conducted an ounce of research. However, as he mentions *prase* with it, that narrows this down. That is the same as the agate or chalcedony, which is currently being extracted in the Caraga Region/Ancient Shir of the Philippines.

In fact, notice the variety of *prase* listed as *CHRYSoprase/chrysoprasus*, which is green in color. Would that name's origin not be the famous Isle of Chryse (χρυσός: *gold in Greek*) which is Ophir? Wow!!! Even Wikipedia knows that nativity in language. Indeed, though rare, *Chrysoprase*, in modern times, is mined in many countries, none of which have ancient mining history as the Philippines, which also has a green-colored quartz. No one tested chemical signatures in ancient times to differentiate terms that are more defined today. Where the ***Chronicles of Jerahmeel*** first identified agate comes from Mount Ophir, later clarifies that Mount Ophir is Havilah, as they are equated. *Jerahmeel* resolves that is the ancient Havilah of Genesis 2. It is the Philippines.

Spring of Purification on Camiguin Island, Philippines:

As ***Revelation of the Magi*** documents, the Magi purified themselves in a spring, before scaling the sacred mountain, to reach the Cave of Treasures. This well fits Mount Hibok Hibok. To the Southeast of the volcano, we find Sa-ay Cold Spring with Katibawasan Falls nearby. Talk about a tie to the Magi. In Hebrew, David uses šay, שׁי (H7862), three times in Psalm meaning *"gift, presents."*

The area just south of there is called called *Magting*. That title is possibly some remnant of the *Magi*, linguistically. As we uncover these meanings, it is *manservant* in Bisayan, which certainly pertains to the manner in which the Magi are described.

Magtiting: Bisayan: manservant.[2]
Magtiting: Tagalog: get together.[1] *matingnán: Tagalog: to be able to look at something.*[1]

In Tagalog, it bears the definition, *"to be able to look at something"*, and *"get together"*. Is this NOT where the Magi gathered in the beginning of each month, according to ***Revelation of the Magi?*** Wow! Are they not known for observing the Star? Additionally, another coincidence is a label, *"View of Eden"* next to it. All these locations are within a region called *Soro Soro*, which appears to be a reference to a medicinal plant, yielding anti-human coronavirus, anti-cancer, anti-HIV, anti-inflammatory, anti-diabetic properties, according to Dr. Stuart.[3] Did the Magi plant that in this area, perhaps? One can only speculate.

To the Southwest of the mountain is Tuasan Falls with Sto. Nino Cold Spring nearby which name is new. Worship of the child Jesus is not Biblical; He grew up. The form in which He should be worshipped is His glorified one, which cannot be depicted through artwork. This statue brought by Magellan in 1521 (with the original still housed in Cebu), is recognizable in archaeology as a Greek god of Wealth (Ploutus), in child form, over 400 years before Messiah's birth. His image is an exact match; it includes his mother as well. She happens to be the likeness of what locals call Mama Mary. The same image of her was also used in worship of the Harlot of Babylon, centuries earlier *(Semiramis).* Pigafetta's Journal never says Filipinos accepted that idol as the King of Cebu. A Hindu leader from Sumatra (who was in Philippines leadership) accepted and promoted the idolatry; he was not Filipino in ancestry. The Magi would have rejected any such form of worship, which explains why the Catholic Church had to crush the Philippines, even eliminating anything historical.

Camiguin also has an area named Bura, at the base of Hibok Hibok's west side, where Bura Soda Spring is located. This is incredible! In Waray, this Soda Spring seems to be amply defined as bura, meaning "bubble." In Tagalog, *bura* means "marks left behind by an erasure," which is similar to the Hebrew definition. Of course, that could be a positive connotation as purification is an erasure of our sins. Is this a reference to a history of the Magi which would be erased by the conquerors of this land? In Hebrew, this really takes a direction that is almost unbelievable. When one consumes or cleans out, is this not a designation of purification? In fact,

---

[1] *Tagalog.com, Retrieved Oct. 2, 2024.* [2] *Binisaya.com, Retrieved Oct. 2, 2024.* [3] *"Soro Soro." Godofredo U. Stuart Jr., M.D. StuartXchange.* [4] *3NS Corpora Project Waray Dictionary.* [5] *"Baara." Abarim Publications.* [6] *"Beyond the volcanoes: a brief guide to Camiguin." By Henrylito D. Tacio. GMA News. Published January 12, 2013.*

in this definition, is it purification by the stripes, or wounds taken on by our Savior? Could this be "The Spring of Purification" of *Revelation of the Magi?* That is likely. Wow! This is far too much "coincidence" to ignore.

*burá: **Tagalog:** erasure marks.* [1]
*burá: **Waray:** bubble.* [4]
*bara: בערה: **to consume** or **to clean out.** rare word for fire, consumer or that which consumes. Baara wife of a Benjaminite (1 Chr. 8:8). The name Baara comes from the verb בער (ba'ar), meaning either **to kindle** or, rather unkindly, to be stupid (referring to cattle), or even **to remove evil from the land.** [5] **chabburah:** הבורה: blueness, bruise, hurt, stripe, wound; Or chabburah {khab-boo-raw'}; or chaburah {khab-oo-raw'}; from chabar; properly, bound (with stripes), i.e. A weal (or black-and-blue mark itself) -- blueness, bruise, hurt, stripe, wound. (Strong's Exhaustive Concordance, H2250).*

In fact, Camiguin is extremely distinctive on all of Earth. There are more volcanoes per square kilometer there than on any other island in the world.

"With seven volcanoes, it has earned the distinction of having the most number of those formations per square kilometer than any other island on earth." [6]

As this continuation in deeper research is mostly a linguistic journey, we know the Mount of the East, the Garden of Eden and the Land of Gold exist and are not fiction. No speculation is needed for such conclusion. It has always been the region we call the Philippines throughout all of history. This is the same as the Mountain of Victories in the East and Land of Shir in the extreme East in *Revelation of the Magi.* It contains the Cave of Treasures with the Spring of Purification at its base as it should. There are two strong options for that spring, even in surviving names. The origin of the word Magi in Filipino languages is definitive as well. These data points reflect what massive history affirms. The geography of Psalm 72 proves accurate as the origin of the Magi from Matthew 2. Our text serves to combine these scriptures in understanding, bringing explosive revelation that cannot be effectively challenged. This is too overwhelming.

We can find affirmation in history and other texts that may not be Bible, but are conveying the same data confirming the ancient understanding. What becomes extremely clear is that the Vatican is not telling the truth here. At best, they lost it, and ignorance is no excuse for forgetting the location of the Garden of Eden, Land of Gold, and origin of the Magi. They had *Revelation of the Magi* for 1,200 years, even refusing to release it to the public in a known language. That pattern is undeniable from a church that burned translators at the stake for doing so in history. One does not get to conquer most of the world stealing resources, land, and histories and not be made accountable for such satanic behavior. It is time we all realize this and take a stand for the truth.

*RotM 21:9 And again, I have made known to you, your fathers,
and even to that ancient race of yours, your freedom, because you
are from the race of light."*

*"RotM 21:10 ...I clothed myself in your form, that by it I might
bring to an end and destroy all those who afflict you and your
captors."*

*"And I shall set you free with love, and with truth, with pure
water, and the birth of the Holy Spirit..."*

Confirmed in Matthew 12:42; Luke 11:31

Chapter 7: The Prophecy of Messiah's Star

When visiting the Philippines during their Christmas season (which is really three or more months), one will not find the Christmas Tree at the heart of the celebration. Instead, the parol Star is the centerpiece of decorations. This is not a Catholic practice, nor is this the little star atop a tree. No, this is a giant Star displayed inside and out of many houses. They light them up, but they stand alone as a singular element not needing all the other trappings of Christmas. Why is the Philippines so set on a Star at the forefront of its observance? No other really does. This is simple to surmise when one knows this is the very land of the Magi who saw the Star in the Eastern sky, in the Philippines which account we will test.

In fact, one must wonder why the Philippines has the longest celebration on Earth for Messiah's birth. That, also, is not Catholic. They begin their season in September and end with the birth of Messiah three months later. The culmination is Three Kings' Day or Epiphany. Sure, the Catholic Church injected the occult Christmas at the wrong time of year, with the wrong Magi, and the wrong Jesus *(Yahusha)*. They add even occult elements far from scripture in embellishment.

In our chapter titled When Was Jesus Born? *(10)*, we will lay out the timeline Luke especially preserves for Messiah's birth on the Bible Feast of Shavuot in June, nowhere near December. His death and resurrection were during the Feast of Unleavened Bread. The logical reason for the precedence of three months is this Feast cycle. Jesus *(Yahusha)* was put to death on the First Day of Unleavened Bread in Abib *(March-April)*. He was born on Shavuot in June *(See Chapter 10)*. That is a long celebration in which He embedded Himself in the Biblical Feasts. This practice can never pass away, and does not in any scripture. Even Paul kept these Feasts in the New Testament which he preached as well.

In the Magi Isles, the Catholic Church (the captor who conquered them), obviously took the three-month observance and moved it to the occult Christmas (formerly known as Saturnalia), the birth of His enemy and the sun god of many names (such as Mithra). Should we not be greeting: "Merry Mithras" instead? Though corrupted today, we can see the base elements of this practice in the Spring Feast cycle. Even the conqueror could not root out the deep knowledge in the DNA of the Filipino, who are the Magi. The Philippines will soon see a release from that satanic power. The practice of including a giant Star on the birthday of Jesus *(Yahusha)* should be expected in the Isles of the Three Kings.

However, what do we know of this Star in prophecy? For starters, Matthew's book is not the only account of the Magi. When Matthew quotes the Book of Numbers, the Book of Psalms, and the Prophet Jeremiah, it is shameful that a Bible scholar would dare claim it stands alone and therefore must be dismissed as theology, nor history. This is the view of one who does not believe, and is disconnecting elements to attack, rather than reconciling the facts which link sufficiently.

The first prophecy in the modern Bible Canon of a Star representing the coming Messiah literally is in Torah written by Moses. Most pastors quote this but forget it is the account of the Magi (in part). It is not the only such account.

Numbers 24:15-17 KJV
So he took up his oracle and said:
*"The utterance of **Balaam the son of Beor**,*
And the utterance of the man whose eyes are opened;
The utterance of him who hears the words of God,
And has the knowledge of the Most High,
Who sees the vision of the Almighty,
Who falls down, with eyes wide open:
*"I see **Him**, but not now;*
*I behold **Him**, but not near;*
*A **Star** shall come out of Jacob;*
*A **Scepter** shall rise out of Israel,*
And batter the brow of Moab,
And destroy all the sons of tumult.

How many times have we heard from the pulpit, in Christmas stories, and seasonal songs that there was a Star of Bethlehem at Messiah's birth? The Bible never mentions a Star of Bethlehem even once. This Star appeared in the Far East and led the Magi to Bethlehem, where it rested, two years later, but still, it is NOT the Star of Bethlehem. No narrative ever points to a Star that even appeared in Bethlehem but one that was only seen in the East. Herod's astrologers (and even the Pharisees) did not see the Star. It was not a constellation or movement of planets or anything similar, as it appeared for two years in the sky and it moved changing directions at least three times. That is not a star in any understanding we have of the way they move, including one that only occurs every several thousand years (if such thing actually exists). So, what is this?

First, in the prophecy of Balaam, the "Him" here is firmly the Messiah to come. We are not unaware of any scholar that would debate that. Balaam can see Him prophetically in the future, not in his time and he beholds him far away from himself as a Star, literally. We know Jesus *(Yahusha)* descended from Jacob/Israel from the Tribe of Judah, as prophecy specifies many times. We also know the "scepter" is a well-known reference to that of Messiah in prophecy. However, how can Jesus *(Yahusha)* be a Star? Is that scripture? It certainly is not Gnostic and any scholar claiming such is illiterate of massive Bible references.

We know He will come in the form of a Star, as this Star comes out of the bloodline of Jacob; a man in human form as a Star, literally. This is affirmed in *Testament of Judah* 24 in interpretation.[1] Numbers is actually quoting that text, which also identifies Messiah not only as the Star of Jacob, but as the "Sun of Righteousness."

Jacob and Israel are never represented by a Star in any other fashion. The so-called "Star of David" is a fictionalization of scripture to insert the occult. If Jews were genuinely His people, they would have to embrace Jesus *(Yahusha)* period. He is the only Star of David. The Bible rebukes their star in worship, which does not represent the Messiah, as the star of Chiun or Remphan *(Amos 5:26; Acts 7:43).*

The six points are satanic in symbology from the ancient Mystery religions especially (Ishtar/Semiramis/Baphomet). It is two pyramids—one pointing up and the other down. That is the ancient satanic moto "As above, so below" equating Yahuah and satan. You will find that particular religion, in origin and leadership, to be the very ones who are trying to steal the identity of Israel as Revelation 2:9 and 3:9 warned. They are also attempting to abduct the origin of the Magi as their roots of Kabbalah and Persian Zoroastrianism promote the wrong Magi. They are the conquerors (or at least, embedded within). No one should expect these liars to present valid historic interpretation, and especially not accurate Biblical exegesis. Yet, many scholars defer to these deceivers.

The Star is not a constellation, nor a planetary alignment, nor would we even investigate "fake space." His Star outshined them all, according to ***Revelation of the Magi (RoTM),*** and that is affirmed many ways in scripture. This should not be foreign to any Bible believer. Jesus *(Yahusha)* is the fulfillment of this prophecy, and no other can be. This is NOT occult, nor Gnostic.

Testament of Judah 24 Charlesworth (RH Charles 4:20)[1]

*"And after this there shall **arise for you a Star from Jacob** in peace: And a man shall arise **from my posterity like the Sun of righteousness**, walking with the sons of men in gentleness and righteousness, and **in him will be found no sin**. And the heavens will be opened upon him to pour out the spirit of grace on you. And you shall be sons in truth and you will walk in his first and final degrees. This is the Shoot of God Most High, this is the fountain for the life of all humanity. Then he will illumine the scepter of my kingdom, and from your root will arise the Shoot, and through it will arise the rod of righteousness for the nations, to judge and to save all that call on the Lord.*

Notes: A mosaic of eschatological expectations based on Num 24:17, Mal 4:2, Ps. 45:4 (in LXX) and Isa 53:9. CD 7:11-20. For the star, TLevi 18:3.[1]

Indeed, the Prophet Malachi certainly knew this. In fact, it appears he was reading Testament of Judah as he quotes this term "Sun of Righteousness."

Malachi 4:2 KJV

*But unto you that fear my name shall the **Sun of righteousness** arise with healing in his wings; and ye shall go forth, and grow up as calves of the stall.*

Additionally, this same account of Balaam's prophecy of the coming Star being the Messiah Himself was found in the Dead Sea Scrolls in 4Q175 *[Vermes, p. 527-528]* as well as the War Scroll 11:6 *[Vermes, p. 176].*

---

[1] *"Testaments of the Twelve Patriarchs: Judah 24:1-2." Edited By James H. Charlesworth. The Old Testament Pseudepigrapha: Apocalyptic Literature & Testaments. p. 801.*

Oracle of Balaam son of Beor. Oracle of the man whose eye is penetrating.
Oracle of him who has heard the words of God, who knows the wisdom of the Most High and sees the vision of the Almighty, who falls and his eyes are opened. **I see him but not now. I behold him but not near. A star shall come out of Jacob** *and a* **sceptre shall rise out of Israel;** *he shall crush the temples of Moab and destroy all the children of Seth (Num. 45:15-17).*[1]

This is also confirmed in ***The Testament of Levi.***[2] Jesus *(Yahusha)* is called a "new priest" through whom all the words of Yahuah will be revealed. His Star rose in Heaven, and Heaven opened, exactly as ***Revelation of the Magi*** witnessed first-hand. This Light overwhelms all luminaries and shines forth like the sun. The Messiah originated in the "Temple of Glory" which one would assume is Heaven. However, that is far more likely the Garden of Eden as ***Revelation of the Magi*** attests. He rested over the waters (as ***Revelation of the Magi*** affirms in observation, as well as His speech to the Magi). As the Magi and believers around the world followed Jesus *(Yahusha),* Israel was diminished in ignorance *(Ez. 16:27-30; Gal. 3:14; Rom. 11:25).* That remains true to this day. As He has the keys to death and Hades *(Rev. 1:18),* the Inner Earth, including the Garden of Eden, He will open the Garden of Eden, giving us access to the Tree of Life *(Rev. 2:7, 22:2, 14).* That is abundant in scripture.

Testament of Levi: 18:3, Charlesworth (RH Charles 5:13)[2]
And the **Lord will raise up a new priest, to whom all the words of the Lord will be revealed,** *he shall effect the judgement of truth over the earth for many days, and* **his STAR shall rise in heaven like a king, kindling the light of knowledge, as day is illumined by the sun.** *And he* **shall be extolled by the whole inhabited world.** *This one* **will shine forth like the sun** *in the earth, he shall take away all darkness from under heaven, and there shall be peace in all the earth. The heavens shall greatly rejoice in His days, and the earth shall be glad; the clouds will be filled with joy, and the knowledge of the Lord will be poured out on the earth like the water of the seas. And the angels of the glory of the Lord's presence will be made glad by him.* **The heavens will be opened, and from the temple of glory, sanctification will come upon him,** *with a* **fatherly voice,** *as from Abraham to Isaac, and the* **glory of the Most High shall burst forth upon him.** *And the spirit of understanding and sanctification shall* **rest upon him in the water.** *For he shall give the majesty of the Lord to those who are his sons in truth forever. And in his priesthood, the nations shall be multiplied in knowledge on the earth; and* **they shall be illumined by the grace of the Lord, but Israel shall be diminished by her ignorance and darkened by her grief. In his priesthood, sins shall cease, and lawless men shall rest from their evil deeds.** *And he shall* **open the gates of paradise,** *he shall remove the sword that has threatened since Adam, and he will grant to* **the saints to eat of the tree of life.** *The spirit of holiness shall be upon them, and Beliar*

---

[1] *"Testimonia or Messianic Anthology: 4Q175: 9-13" The Complete Dead Sea Scrolls in English. By Geza Vermes. Penguin Books. 1962. Revised Edition 2004. p. 135. p. 527-528.* [2] *"Testaments of the Twelve Patriarchs: Levi 18:3." Edited By James H. Charlesworth. The Old Testament Pseudepigrapha: Apocalyptic Literature & Testaments. p. 794.*

shall be bound by him. And he shall grant to his children the authority to trample on wicked spirits. And the Lord will rejoice in his children; he will be well pleased by his beloved ones forever. Then Abraham, Isaac, and Jacob will rejoice, and all the saints shall be clothed in righteousness.

*Notes: **The image of the STAR builds on Numbers 24:17** the motif also appears in **CD 7:18** where there is a differentiation between the **STAR, who is the interpreter of the law, and the scepter, who is the Messiah of Israel,** and a kingly figure (CD 7:19-20) In **1QPsJ 9-13** the **STAR** is an eschatological figure presumably the king, and is distinguished from Levi (1QPs J 14-18) The Num 24 passage is also referred to in **1QM 9:6** [Vermes, War Scroll 11:6, p. 176] **4QPBless 5:27** [4Q175]).[1] see TJud 24:1.[2]*

He received the scepter of Judah as He was from Judah and that scepter remains in His hand until the Day of Judgment. That, too, should not be bizarre to a Christian who reads the Bible. When one peruses a map, where is the *Brow of Moab?* Look at a map; Moab equates to the Southeast region of the Dead Sea. Bethlehem (where numerous prophesies declare Messiah would be born), is right there, at the eyebrow in position, Northwest of the Dead Sea. For those who try to even move ancient Bethlehem, this brilliantly preserves Bethlehem where it is known to exist today. They really do attack every angle, and yet, we can all sift through the nonsense and understand these details because the Bible is a masterpiece, retaining knowledge in ways scoffers cannot even figure out fortunately.

Balaam is a prophet from a town synonymous to the Biblical Carchemish, which is about 400 miles North of Moab *(modern Jordan)* on the border of Turkey and Syria. For those supposed scholars who claim one must be in Mesopotamia in order to live on the Euphrates River, which begins in Turkey, let us not pretend they have any grasp on geography. However, if in fact they were right, (though they seem oblivious to geography), it would only further disprove the Wise Men coming from Arabia or Babylon. The setting of this story is both Carchemish (on the way to Moab), and in Moab itself. This geography is located around the same longitude in the Middle East.

Map showing states around Israel & Judah. The Kingdoms around Israel & Judah are shaded differently: Phoenicia, Aram Damascus, Amon, Moab, Edom, and Philistia. The map shows the region in the 9th century BCE. Wikimedia Commons. Public Domain.

The previous research is relevant because Balaam tells us he beheld Messiah as a Star, nowhere near the Middle East. His prophecy aligns with the following witnesses: the *Gospel of Matthew*, the geography in King David's Psalm 72, the Prophet Malachi, the Prophet Jeremiah, as well as ***Revelation of the Magi***. Balaam identifies in prophecy this future Star would literally be the Messiah and it would appear far away from Israel, just as Matthew and the ***Revelation of the Magi*** specify; in the East, not Israel. Psalm 72 has the same distinction when one knows where David's territories exist. Considering these other texts, Balaam's prophecy comes to life and vets as accurate. The ancients knew this.

However, would one not be considered crazy to reference Jesus *(Yahusha)* as a Star as Moses did in Numbers? That's Torah! Anyone that would say so is no Bible scholar. We anticipate their ridicule and if you hear such, you know they are not Bible believers. Jesus *(Yahusha)* Himself confirms He is the Star, and the Scepter belongs with Him in the *Book of Revelation*, multiple times. He said that He is the Bright and Morning Star. If a Bible scholar debates that, they do not know Him in a basic sense from scripture.

Revelation 22:16 KJV
*"I, Jesus, have sent My angel to testify to you these things in the churches. I am the Root and the Offspring of David, **the Bright and Morning Star.**"*

Revelation 22:25-28 KJV (To Thyatira)
*"But hold fast what you have till I come. "And he who overcomes, and keeps My works until the end, to him I will give power over the nations— He shall **rule them with a rod of iron;** They shall be dashed to pieces like the potter's vessels'— as I also have received from My Father; "**and I will give him the morning star.***

Peter also invokes this same concept of Jesus *(Yahusha)* as the "morning star in our hearts." We are aware that the *NIV* (along with other translations from the corrupt group of Westcott and Hort manuscripts) attempt to insert Lucifer/Satan as the morning star and that is unfounded and frankly, satanic in nature.

2 Peter 1:19 KJV
*And so we have the prophetic word confirmed, which you do well to heed as a light that shines in a dark place, until the day dawns and the **morning star rises in your hearts;***

We initially deduced this Star from the East (which traveled), had to be an angel, because no constellation or celestial event could ever fit the passage. The Star moved, stopped, and changed direction for two years. That is no event which "space" has ever seen. It is a miracle of epic proportion. However, this was no angel. It was Messiah Himself, showing up as Light, while born in the flesh on the other side of the world. Can He do this? Well, the Bible says He can, and He is "the Light of the World." In fact, this is how He could exist in Heaven and the Garden of Eden at the same time. We all recite that, but do we understand the magnitude of that declaration from the lips of Jesus *(Yahusha)* Himself.

John 8:12 KJV
*Then Jesus spoke to them again, saying, "I am the **light of the world**. He who follows Me shall not walk in darkness, but have the **light of life.**"*

John 9:5 KJV
*"As long as I am in the world, **I am the light of the world.**"*

He is also the Light of Life. What could that even mean? It is not symbology; it is a concept that is exact to the Creation account as He was and is the Light that creates. Sound peculiar? Tell the Apostles John and Paul, as well as Moses. Go argue with them because we did not proclaim this position, they did. For a theologian to brand them "eccentric" is an oxymoron. If a so-called Early Church Father lost this information, then we already know they and their paradigm are those who crept in unawares *(Jude 1:4)*, not that of the ekklesia of Messiah. This is a challenge for seminaries. They must agree with the Bible or their positions are worthless.

John 1:1- KJV
*In the beginning was the **Word**, and the **Word** was with God, and the **Word was God. The same was in the beginning with God. All things were made by him; and without him was not any thing made** that was made. In him was life; and the life was **the light of men. And the light shineth in darkness;** and the darkness comprehended it not. There was a man sent from God, whose name was John. The same came for a witness, to bear witness of the Light, that all men through him might believe. He was not that Light, but was **sent to bear witness of that Light. That was the true Light, which lighteth every man** that cometh into the world.*

John 1:14 KJV
*And **the Word was made flesh, and dwelt among us, (and we beheld his glory,** the glory as of the only begotten of the Father,) full of grace and truth.*

Colossians 1:13-17 KJV
*Who hath delivered us from the power of darkness, and hath **translated us into the kingdom of his dear Son: In whom we have redemption through his blood,** even **the forgiveness of sins: Who is the image of the invisible God, the firstborn of every creature: For by him were all things created, that are in heaven, and that are in earth, visible and invisible,** whether they be thrones, or dominions, or principalities, or powers: **all things were created by him, and for him: And he is before all things, and by him all things consist. And he is the head of the body, the church: who is the beginning, the firstborn from the dead; that in all things he might have the preeminence. For it pleased the Father that in him should all fulness dwell;***

Genesis 1:3 KJV
*And God said, **Let there be light: and there was light.***

Philippians 2:5-6 KJV
*Let this mind be in you, which was also in **Christ Jesus: Who, being in the form of God, thought it not robbery to be equal with God:***

Jesus *(Yahusha)* was the Light of Creation and His Light was and is part of Elohim's Creation. It is incredible to read the many commentaries that try to deny that Jesus *(Yahusha)* is Elohim. They fail to read the Hebrew word Elohim, which is plural, not singular. This is the Father and the Son Creating together, according to John and Paul. Perhaps a modern scholar thinks they are above the writers of scripture as they try to render interpretation that cannot be assumed. Did not the Prophet Isaiah tell us that the Messiah was the mighty Elohim? Indeed, he did.

Isaiah 9:6 KJV
*For **unto us a child is born, unto us a son is given:** and the government shall be upon his shoulder: and **his name shall be called Wonderful, Counsellor, The mighty God** (El: אל, H410), **The everlasting Father** ('âb: אב, root of Abba, H1), **The Prince of Peace.***

The Son is prophesied as El, as part of Elohim. This is because the Hebrew word even in Genesis 1 is Elohim *(אלהים: ĕlôhîym, H430; plural of H433, אלוה: el-o'-ah)* plural, not singular. The Son was there and created, according to John 1 as well. Many teach a doctrine called Trinity, which is not a Biblical word. However, the Father, Son and Holy Spirit were indeed all present at Creation. That is indisputable. We are given the roles of the Father and Son as Creators. The Holy Spirit is not equated as such but certainly was there. Angels are not Creators in any sense and were not included in the Creation account as doing anything but rejoicing at the wonders of the Creations of the Father and Son. Any doctrine that leads to angels falling before Creation (before they were even Created), is not Biblical. They did not exist until the First Day of Creation *(Jub. 2)*.

We also know that Jesus *(Yahusha)* would be called *The Everlasting Abba,* which scholars have missed. Why? He is the Son and part of the Elohim of Creation. Though the Father is always the head, Jesus *(Yahusha)* is part of that duo called Elohim. Many equate the Holy Spirit there as well to form a doctrine, named with a word not even in the Bible. That is a huge debate today and really, it is just a polarized ball of nonsense. What matters is the roles of the Father, the Son, and the Holy Spirit as they are certainly three operating together.

It does not really matter if one understands the role of the Holy Spirit, who is not a Creator but the Helper, Teacher, and Comforter *(John 14:26; 1 John 2:27)*, and the Revelator *(John 16:12-24)*. He reveals things to us, comforts us, teaches us and helps us (according to scripture), among other attributes, but none include Creating.

He can even heal or raise the dead *(Rom. 8:11)* and He did hover over the waters in Genesis 1, but that says nothing of Him Creating. Where is the Holy Spirit ever called Abba, or even Elohim for that matter in any scripture? It is not there.

We observe further detail of the Son being predicted from the earliest passage in Genesis 3:15, Jubilees, and 1 Enoch. Moses and Abraham well knew the Messiah already existed in spirit since Creation in which He participated. Otherwise, a scholar would characterize John 1 and Colossians 1 as strange doctrine. It is the ancient dogma. Anything against that is another Gospel, which Paul and the Apostles never preached *(2Cor. 11:4; Gal. 1:6-12)*. We will continue to highlight this.

Genesis 3:15 KJV
*And I will put enmity between thee and the woman, and **between thy seed and her seed; it shall bruise thy head, and thou shalt bruise his heel.***

Jubilees 16:26
*And he (Abraham) blessed his Creator who had created him in his generation, for He had created him according to His good pleasure; for He knew and perceived that **from him would arise the plant of righteousness for the eternal generations, and from him a holy seed**, so that it should **become like Him who had made all things.***

Jubilees 21:24 (Abraham to Isaac)
*And He will bless thee in all thy deeds, And will **raise up from thee the plant of righteousness** through **all the earth**, throughout **all generations** of the earth, And my name and thy name will not be forgotten under heaven for ever.*

It is amazing how many inept scholars attempt to insert the nation of Israel (in illiterate assumption), in the *Book of Jubilees*, as the "plant of righteousness through all the earth, throughout all generations." One could not be more uninformed and incapable of reading. Only the Messiah fulfills that and 16:26 even calls this seed a Creator. Thus, the choice is only one: the Son.

Now that we have established the Light of this East Star is the Messiah Himself, we know that ***Revelation of the Magi*** does not present new nor strange doctrine. However, what does Matthew actually say of this Star? It defines this is not an actual star, not an angel, and not a scientific event. It is amazing what we learn when reading the Bible, as a believer reconciling with valid texts and other passages, as opposed to many scholars who begin with scoffing. Before Matthew, scripture well knew Messiah would appear in the form of a Star, as well as in the flesh at His birth.

Matthew 2:2 KJV
*Saying, Where is he that is born King of the Jews? for **we have seen his star in the east,** and are come to worship him.*

The Magi observed "His Star," not that of an angel, nor that of a constellation, but His actual Star, from His own Light. No other light could match His. This will become very evident in *Revelation of the Magi* which details this narrative. We are aware some scholars would already have an issue with Messiah actually being the Light He said He was. Let us all test their words with scripture as they fail. When they enter Jerusalem, the Wise Kings approached King Herod to find out where in Israel the Messiah was born. Herod did not know. He and his astronomers did not see the Star in Israel because it appeared in the Far East. There is no such thing as a Star of Bethlehem in scripture and it was in the East at His birth to alert the praying, holy Magi; a Biblical priesthood since Seth. It was not in Israel until the Wise Men visited as they followed it there from the East.

Herod then asks when the Star appeared; which he would have known if it appeared in Israel. Even if he missed it, his astrologers and the Pharisees would not have. However, the brightness of this Star could not be missed by anyone, if it were to appear there in the manner suggested by practically every scholar out there in ignorance. It did not and it is truly shocking that so many seminaries cannot seem to read this. The reason the Magi visited Herod was to get directions to the birthplace. They followed the Star, and it clearly disappeared for a time. This was supposed to happen. They tell Herod of the timing of the Star, two years earlier, which we know, because Matthew 2:16 describes Herod's calculation of two years, in his decree to kill children. This number was solely based on the timing given him by the Wise Men.

The star reappears; it is the same one that had appeared in the Far East. The Wise Men followed it to Israel, and traveled almost two years with it at sea. That cannot be a planetary alignment. They rejoice, demonstrating it disappeared and reappeared, according to Matthew's Gospel, which will soon be confirmed. That same Star moves from Jerusalem to Bethlehem, leading to the exact location of Messiah's birth. That rules out any such "space event" at any time. No Star can do that. Jesus *(Yahusha)* was a toddler at that time, but still waited for His Wise Kings to bring their gifts from the Estate of Adam, as was prophesied. He knew this since the days of Adam as well.

Matthew 2:7 KJV
*Then Herod, when he had privily called the wise men, enquired of them diligently **what time the star appeared**.*

Matthew 2:9-10 KJV
*When they had heard the king, they departed; and, lo, **the star, which they saw in the east, went before them, till it came and stood over where the young child was. When they saw the star, they rejoiced** with exceeding great joy.*

Enter *Revelation of the Magi* from the Vatican Library, translated into English and published in 2010 by Brent Landau. Notice how this text explains Matthew and brings clarity to this entire account. That is what inspired documents do and when they do, they prove to be inspired. One does not have to add this to the Canon, but we should all be aware of the information in geography and all the many holes in Matthew get filled in. We then, find that knowledge some would call "new" in error, when it is the ancient record affirmed by Jeremiah, David, Enoch, and Matthew (among others). This account exists far beyond just the *Gospel of Matthew*, and that very statement is grossly uninformed, and always has been. *Revelation of the Magi*, written by the Magi of the Philippines, tells us exactly what scripture always has.

RotM 4:2 And our fathers commanded us as they also received from their fathers, and they said to us: "Wait for the light that shines forth to you from the exalted East of the majesty of the Father, the light that shines forth from on high in the form of a star over the Mountain of Victories and comes to rest upon a pillar of light within the Cave of Treasures [of] Hidden Mysteries.

The Light of Jesus' *(Yahusha's)* Star was prophesied in Numbers as His Light; the Apostle Matthew affirms that along with many other sources. *Revelation of the Magi* has confirmed this concept in detail, as this Light is the very Light of the Father through His emissary the Son. The Son always points to the Father He affirmed multiple times in His words *(John 10:29-30, 6:38, 8:42, 12:49, etc.)*. The Light shines forth not as a star, but in the form of a star. It appears over the Mount of the East and becomes a pillar of Light, like what we see in the Exodus as well *(Ex. 13:21)*. That pillar enters the Cave of Treasures on the Mount of the East penetrating the abode of Adam from his nativity. Understand Jesus *(Yahusha)* is also the fulfillment of the most ancient of prophesies, not just those to Abraham. He fulfills Genesis and Jubilees, but also, 1 Enoch greatly details His attributes of literally being the Light of the World. That has never been an analogy. He literally is says scripture if one believes it.

In the first century, there was a written book/scroll from Seth. Perhaps Enoch was his scribe, as he was the first among men to write anything, period *(Jub. 4:17)*. No human document precedes the Prophet Enoch, the seventh from Adam's righteous seed, in any written form in all of history. That has always been the Bible paradigm. No Nephilim rock can change that scribal tradition, through which texts have been copied for thousands of years.

Where is this text from Seth? This is very likely a reference to the writings of 1 Enoch, in which righteous Enoch covers the account of Cain, Abel, Seth, and mentions the commandments from Adam. Though Enoch does not mention a Star appearing in the East, he does define the Son, in Heaven, in spirit form, before the Flood. He prophesied in great detail of His coming, including His death and ascension *(1En. 89-90)*. From the very first chapter, Enoch begins with a description of the Messiah as the Light. In fact, verse 9 is repeated, quoted, and directly attributed by Jude to the Prophet Enoch's words written in his book. We are aware of scholars who play stupid, claiming this must refer to some other book Enoch wrote (that we do not possess, when it is a direct quote with attribution).

1 Enoch 1:8-9
*And **light shall appear unto them**, [And **He will make peace with them**]. And behold! **He cometh** with ten thousands of [**His**] **holy ones to execute judgment upon all**.*

Jesus *(Yahusha)* is the greatest Light in all of scripture and history. This was true in spirit form at Creation and continues to be genuine. His Light filled the Garden of Eden when Adam was there. When He came in the flesh, this Light was not seen by most but it still remained as part of His being. Enoch prophesies about the End Times, and still, He is the Light. He is also the Light of Salvation (as ***Revelation of the Magi*** attests) as well as grace and peace. These are all nativity narratives as well, in connotation, which we know. Jesus *(Yahusha)* appears as Light again on the Day of Judgment. In fact, when the *Book of Revelation* details how the sun, moon, and stars disappear, and no mention of their recreation exists, it also is speaking of our being in the full presence of the Light of Jesus *(Yahusha)* in which we will need no other luminaries. The intensity of His Light is well attested.

1 Enoch 5:7-9
*"And all the... shall rejoice, And there shall be forgiveness of sins, And every mercy and peace and forbearance: **There shall be salvation unto them, a goodly light**. And for all of you sinners there shall be no salvation, But on you all shall abide a curse. **But for the elect there shall be light and grace and peace**, And they shall inherit the earth.*

1 Enoch 38:2
*And when **the Righteous One shall appear** before the eyes of the righteous, whose elect works hang upon Yahuah of Spirits, **And light shall appear** to the righteous and the elect who dwell on the earth.*

Enoch also affirms John 1, Jubilees 16, etc. in declaring the Son as the Light of the World *(Gentiles/Goyim/Nations)*, and since before the Creation of the world. There is nothing weird about this long-standing Bible exegesis.

1 Enoch 48:4-6
*He shall be a staff to the righteous whereon to stay themselves and not fall. And **he shall be the light of the Gentiles**, And the hope of those who are troubled of heart. **All who dwell on earth shall fall down and worship before him**, And will praise and bless and celebrate with song Yahuah of Spirits. **And for this reason hath he been chosen and hidden before Him, before the creation of the world and for evermore**.*

There is the language David quoted in Psalm 72:10-15 from *1 Enoch*, regarding the Messiah, before whom all kings will bow down, and the whole earth will worship.

Yet again, Catholic heresy (which claims Psalm 72 is about Solomon) was always inept. David was also quoting *1 Enoch* from the knowledge given to Seth by Adam. There is nothing strange about that, and if Adam did not give Seth this knowledge, he would have been negligent. Messiah shall be the Light, yet again.

This concept, presented by Enoch, is also the origin of Jesus' *(Yahusha's)* words, in John 8:12 as we all know He is the Light of the World, indeed. These concepts agree; and they are the ancient view of scripture. For Seth's book is found in *1 Enoch*, in large portion. We do not need to search for a hidden book, Enoch was likely his scribe and included his words there. He was first to write, not Seth.

This tradition was passed down since Adam, to the righteous generations (which included the Magi), from their migration, originating in Eastern Iran *(Persia)* to the Philippines *(Ophir)* around 2,200 B.C. or so *(See Introduction)*. In fact, Josephus documents the origin of the label "Chaldeans" were Peleg and Joktan, who lived in Eastern Iran.[1] They were not sorcerers. However, Joktan left the region, completely removed to the Far East, and he did so as a holy patriarch. He is the origin of the Magi after the Flood as they returned to ancient Havilah. However, Peleg's descendants migrated to the West, into Ur, where Abraham was born. Those were indeed idol worshippers, and the origin of ungodly Chaldeans, known as sorcerers.

Joktan's descendants became known as the praying, righteous, silent, royal Magi *(Maginoo/Magdasal/Magiammo)*. They kept the covenant in the Philippines *(Ophir, Sheba, Tarshish)*. Joktan was a righteous ancestor, and to confuse him with the imposters hailing from Ur of the Chaldees is illiterate. In the first century, B.C., Abraham/Abram was holy, even as a young child, and he restored the relationship with Yahuah in the Middle East, followed by his son Isaac and grandson, Jacob.

Abraham was not the ONLY righteous man on Earth. He moved from Ur to the land of Canaan, which became Israel, centuries later. Notice, that it was still a defiled land, even at the point of Joshua's entry into the Promised Land. Israel never flushed out all Nephilim giant tribes, or occupied ALL the land promised to Arphaxad renewed in Abraham. It remained so unholy that Yahuah exiled them from the land, not to return until the Last Days. They will do so in peace, not as a murderous, warlike people (as modern Israel's government has proven to be). ***Revelation of the Magi*** also documents this historic track of this sect of holy priests.

RotM 4:3 And also command your sons, and your sons their sons, until the mystery of the star that shines forth from the exalted majesty appears to your generations, a light like a star, and giving light to the entire creation and obscuring the light of the sun, moon, and stars, and not one of them is seen or is able to stand in the presence of its light. 4:4 For it is the great mystery of the Son of the exalted majesty, who is the voice of the Father; the offspring of his hidden thought; the light of the ray of his glory; the will and image of his hiddenness; 4:5 the all-engendering word of his thought; source of life never-failing from his spring; the all-governing word according to the will of the one

---

[1] *"Antiquities of the Jews." Josephus, Flavius. 93 A.D. Book 1, Section 143.*

who sent it; an image that has no form or likeness among any things that exist. 4:6 This one, by whose power and word all the worlds were set in order and established, is the Son of perfect mercy, is the ray of light of the glory of the Father of ineffable majesty. 4:7 Therefore, know that when this light from that majesty that has no end shines forth for you and will appear like a star to you so that you are able to see him: eagerly, with joy and love, and completely, with care, taking with you his own pure gifts, which were put in the Cave of Treasures of Hidden Mysteries on the Mountain of Victories by your fathers, go to where his light, the star, leads you.

The sun, moon and stars are not this miraculous Light which outshines them all. That is because this is the Light of the World, Jesus *(Yahusha)*. This is very consistent with scripture. Scholars may call this a Gnostic concept, but in doing so, they become foreigners to scripture. The Light is like a Star, but is not an actual star which cannot do what this Light does. In fact, stars would not even be seen in the presence of this Light. That doesn't happen in a planetary alignment (which fails miserably). No angel has this much Light, either. The great mystery of the Son of the exalted majesty is direct language from *1 Enoch*. When Enoch speaks of the mystery in such a way (in Chapter 103), he defines the events of the Day of Judgment, in which Jesus *(Yahusha)* is the Great One, executing final judgment of sinners (which the *Book of Revelation* also quotes). This is not the Father, but the voice of the Father. That is the Son who is the Word *(John 1:1, 14; Rev. 19:13)*.

Revelation of the Magi expresses it well: *"This one, by whose power and word all the worlds were set in order and established, is the Son of perfect mercy."* This One is the Son, not the Father. *Revelation of the Magi* knows He was a Creator with Yahuah. By the Son's power and Word, were all the worlds created. That is consistent with the whole of scripture as we have demonstrated. Indeed, it is His Light which appears like a Star; but is not an actual Star. His Light led the Magi to the place of His birth. The Magi knew this and awaited the arrival of Messiah for thousands of years. This is the ancient practice of the truly righteous, hidden by Popes and Pharisees.

The *Gospel of Matthew* 2:9 says, *"...lo, the star, which they saw in the East, went before them...."* Matthew says the Star moved, and the Wise Men followed it. For those who claim the Magi did not follow the Star, please learn how to read. Skeptical scoffers may try to split the movement, and claim it was only from Jerusalem to Bethlehem. They saw the Star in the Far East, and followed it on a journey that culminated in Jerusalem. Think much, scholars?

When song writers mention this concept, they are certain, because they CAN be. This Star was followed for two years, in different directions, and that whole line of thought is based on the position of the *"..seat of the scornful..."* (Psalm 1).

The pattern and tradition of the Magi is well-established in *Revelation of the Magi,* consistent with the Apostle Matthew's account, and all that we read about their ministry. When scoffers think they are evil magicians, no wonder they forget they are righteous priests with a holy mission. It is criminal to lose that beautiful understanding. They passed this down to their sons and their sons' sons, documenting they had this prophecy in written form in the Cave of Treasures. Yes, the ancient Philippines kept scripture. So, where is it, Vatican? Again, we have demonstrated this through the ancient manuscripts of: Numbers, Psalms, Jeremiah, 1 Enoch, and numerous others that record this coming encounter, not just the *Book of Matthew*. Also, the terms *mysteries* and *revelations* are Biblical language, not specifically Gnostic. This is a Biblically based account and its doctrine vets as accurate. Many scholars' writings do not.

*RotM 4:10 Also, take care and **command your sons**. And if the **coming of the light of the star** does not happen in your days, **also have your sons tell it to their sons, until** the mysteries and revelations shall **come to pass that are written about his coming."***

Timing of the Magi Worship Fits Scripture:

*RotM 5:2 And we went up to the Mountain of Victories, and when we were all assembled **at the foothills of the mountain** from each one's dwelling place, we remained in one place for purification on the twenty-fifth day of every month. 5:3 And when we **bathed** in a certain spring that was **on the foothills of the mountain**, and it is called "The Spring of Purification."*
*5:6 And when it **became the first of the month**, we ascended and went to the **top of the mountain** and **stood before the mouth of the Cave of Treasures** of Hidden Mysteries.*
*5:8 On **the third of the month we entered the cave up to the treasures**, the treasures that were prepared as the star's own [gifts] and for the **adoration of that light that we awaited**.*

The Magi met at the base of the Mount of the East on the twenty-fifth of every month. Remember, the date on the Biblical Calendar has no connection whatsoever to Pagan Christmas, which would be ridiculous. Christmas, as in the birth of Christ, did not even occur on the 25th of the month, on the Hebrew calendar. They purified themselves until the first of the month when they would scale the mountain approaching the entrance of the cave. Five to six days of purification would be due to their entering the Cave of Treasures sanctified, especially if Messiah's presence of His light would someday be there.

This purification ritual is similar to the ordinances given at Sinai, when Moses told the people to purify themselves before entering the Presence (this was also carried out by the High Priest) and it is Biblical *(Ex. 19:10-15)*. Today, we do not sacrifice animals anymore *(Heb. 10)* because Jesus *(Yahusha)* is our sacrifice. However, we continue to sanctify ourselves and others with the truth of the Word *(John 17:17)*. Yes, Old Testament concepts remain in the New. The power of the full presence of Jesus' *(Yahusha's)* Light is unbearable for those not purified. This entire time, the Magi were preparing for the first day of the month, which is a worship pattern (established by Noah) in origin. That is Biblical. King David observed this as well *(1Sam. 20:5; חדש: ḥōḏeš: H2320)*.

We challenge everyone to conduct a word study on the mistranslated phrase "new moon." This is fraud, which we have proven in our videos on the topic. The word, in original language, is not "moon" even once, in scripture. It is always a reference to the new month or first day of the month in every application. In the days of David, they were still keeping that tradition with a monthly Feast on the first of each month. The new moon cycle is never a Biblical way to determine a month as it is 29.5 days and therefore, arrives ten days too soon *(rebuked in Jubilees 6:36)*. In Chapter 72, Enoch teaches the course of the sun over its 364-day cycle beginning with the sun, on a daily basis, not the moon. The new moon is never the Bible calendar, but that of Babylon. When they inserted it into our Bibles, in fraud, they exposed themselves as Mystery Babylon.

Why would the Magi wait for three days to enter the Cave of Treasures on the third of the month? One could attempt a connection to the three days and nights Messiah would die and resurrect, but there is nothing there to suggest that. The precedence would be fine but more likely, this is the same as the Sinai account. The people had to be purified for three days before even seeing the presence of Yahuah *(Ex. 19:11)*. They did not even enter it. This timeline vets as scriptural and demonstrates a group committed to the Covenant. This changes everything we thought we knew about the ancient Filipino culture.

The Queen of Sheba also upheld an engagement with Covenant in similar ways, as the aged convention that truly commenced with Seth. The gifts also define this. No, it is not the Abrahamic covenant, as Abraham did not exist yet. This priestly class of nobles *(Maginoo)* in the Philippines would fulfill the antediluvian prophesy that no other could.

Again, this ritual would continue for thousands of years, as it was passed from father to son. They took this seriously as their ministry and they were devoted, just as Levites were. They better be, if Yahuah was going to inform them of the birth of His Son in the flesh. It is ludicrous to insert sorcerers into the account of Matthew, in gross negligence.

Revelation of the Magi continues to refer to Jesus' *(Yahusha's)* Light as a Star, in the passage below. We will study this further.

*RotM 5:10 And if it should chance that one of us should pass away, we would **raise up his son or one of the sons of his family [in his place,]** as when we succeeded our fathers, until the time of the coming of the star has been fulfilled.*

Revelation of the Magi references a prophecy from Seth, son of Adam, regarding this Star's arrival at Messiah's birth. We demonstrated these elements are found in *1 Enoch (1En. 1:8-9, 5:7-9, 38:2, 48:4-6, 103, 104:12)* where Enoch declares the mystery of the Light as the Salvation of the World. We do not need to look for a book written by Seth, necessarily, though some elements in *Revelation of the Magi* are not contained in the *Book of 1 Enoch* (such as this passage). Adam knew this Star and its Light because it is the same Light that illuminated the Garden of Eden. There is no sun in the Garden so that makes sense as it was the Son instead, the Light of the World. It is also the same Light that will illuminate the entire world, according to the prophecy contained in the *Book of Revelation* after the luminaries disappear *(Rev. 7:16; Isa. 60:19-20).* The sight of the Star was taken away from Adam upon exile. Adam was the one removed, and likely, Jesus *(Yahusha)* remained in the Garden while also in Heaven. He can be in two or more places at once, especially as Light.

RotM 6:2 And Adam instructed Seth his son about [text missing], [and about the revelation] of the light of the star and about its glory, because he [saw] it in the Garden of Eden when it descended and came to rest over the Tree of Life; and it illuminated the entire (garden) before Adam transgressed against the commandment of the Father of heavenly majesty. 6:3 And when he transgressed against the commandment that (the Father) ordained for him, the sight of the star was taken away from him,

The Star Appears:

RotM 11:1 Then, when the time and fulfillment of what was written in the books happened, concerning the revelation of the light of the hidden star, we were indeed thought worthy for it to come in our days and to receive it with joy, as we were commanded by our fathers and as we ourselves read in the books. 11:2 And each of us saw wondrous and diverse visions that were never before seen by us, but their mysteries were in these books that we were reading. 11:3 And each one came from his dwelling place according to our ancient custom to ascend the Mountain of Victories [text missing] to wash in the Spring of Purification, as we were accustomed. 11:4 And we saw [text missing] in the form of an ineffable pillar of light descending, and it came to rest above the water.

When the time came for this Light, well described and detailed, as Jesus *(Yahusha),* who is the Bright and Morning Star, the Magi once again purified themselves and ascended the Mount of the East. They saw the Light appear over the water first (which is affirmation of scripture we covered). This means they are on a mountain that overlooks the water, and Mt. Hibok Hibok again fits this. They saw the Light, not as a star, but as a pillar of Light consistent with Torah, employing the word "ineffable." That is something too great for words to express. The Rabbis place that tag on the name of YHWH (as meaning it cannot be pronounced), yet the Hebrew Tanach notes this name over 6,800 times. It is pronounced many of those (even by Abraham), and by Yahuah Himself. That is not Bible. Messiah's Light is.

RotM 11:5 And we were afraid and shook when we saw it. And we cannot speak about the brilliance of the star of light, since its radiance was many times greater than the sun, and the sun could not stand out before the light of its rays. 11:6 And just like the moon looks in the daytime in the days of Nisan, when the sun rises and it is absorbed in its light, so also did the sun seem to us when the star rose over us. 11:7 And the light of the star, which surpassed the sun, appeared to us ourselves and the sons of our mysteries, but it did not appear to anyone else, because they were removed from its mysteries and its coming. And we rejoiced, and glorified, and gave unmeasured thanks to the Father of heavenly majesty that it appeared in our days and we were thought worthy to see it.

This Light, shining many times greater than the sun, is no planetary alignment. It is not seen by anyone else but the Magi, meaning it is not literally a star in the sky. Here, it is compared to the days of Nisan (or April) which is the hottest month of the Philippines pinpointing the location where this occurred in yet another manner. However, Landau admits in his footnote regarding Nisan: the word used is the word for Springtime, not specific to the month of Nisan. As this turns out to be the very birthdate of Messiah, it already narrows it down; between April and June. It was never December. That will be affirmed, and we will test it in Chapter 10.

RotM 12:1 And when we bathed in the Spring of Purification with joy, and we ascended the Mountain of Victories as we were accustomed, and we went up and found that pillar of light in front of the cave, again a great fear came upon us. 12:2 And [we knelt] upon our knees, and we stretched out our hands according to our ancient custom, and we praised in silence the vision of its wonders. 12:3 And again, we saw that heaven had been opened like a great gate and men of glory carrying the star of light upon their hands. And they descended and stood upon the pillar of light, and the entire mountain was filled by its light, which cannot be uttered by the mouth of humanity. RotM 12:4 And (something) like the hand of a smallperson drew near in our eyes from the pillar and the star, at which we could not look, and it comforted us. And we saw the star enter the Cave of Treasures of Hidden Mysteries, and the cave shone beyond measure.
12:5 And a humble and kind voice made itself heard by us, which called out and said to us: "Enter inside without doubt, in love, and see a great and amazing vision." And we were encouraged and comforted by the message of the voice. 12:6 And we entered, being afraid, and we bowed our knees at the mouth of the cave because of the very abundance of the light. 12:7 And when we rose at its command, we lifted our eyes and saw that light, which is unspeakable by the mouth of human beings.

The Light was so powerful, they could not look upon it, and even struggled to stand. Jesus *(Yahusha)* emerged from His Light, and revealed Himself in the form of a child. He was not born in the Philippines; he was born on the other side of the world at the same time. He is Elohim and yes, He can do so. At least in spirit form, He chose to visit the Magi of the Philippines before anyone else. The significance and sanctity of their ministry is not something a modern scholar can call into question. This concept of the ineffable Light of Messiah is predicted in *1 Enoch*.

1 Enoch 58:5-6 (Origin of 1 John 2:8 and Isaiah 60:19-20)
And after this it shall be said to the holy in heaven that they should seek out the secrets of righteousness, the heritage of faith: For it has become bright as the sun upon earth. And the darkness is past. And there shall be a light that never endeth, And to a limit (lit. 'number') of days they shall not come, for the darkness shall first have been destroyed, [And the light established before Yahuah of Spirits] And the light of uprightness established for ever before Yahuah of Spirits.

Who is the heritage of our faith? Jesus *(Yahusha)* is the founder (or author and finisher) of our faith *(Heb. 12:2)* and He is the same yesterday, today and forever *(Heb. 13:8)*. For Him, yesterday was Creation, as His Light was established then and forever. He has become bright as the sun upon Earth and His Light never ends. ***Revelation of the Magi*** is espousing good theology here.

*RotM 13:1 And when it had concentrated itself, **it appeared to us in the bodily form of a small and humble human**, and he said to us: "**Peace to you, sons of my hidden mysteries.**" And again, we were astonished by the vision, and he said to us: "Do not doubt the vision that you have seen, that there has appeared to you that **ineffable light** of the voice of the hidden Father of heavenly majesty. 13:2 And again, (do not doubt that) it appeared to you to concentrate **its light in its rays**, or that it appeared to you in **the form of a small, humble, and unworthy human**, because indeed, **the inhabitants of the world cannot bear to see the glory of the only Son of the Father** of majesty, unless it appeared for them **in the form of their world**. 13:3 And again, other signs shall appear in it, which are hidden and (would be) shameful for the heavenly majesty, for the sake of the redemption of the lives of human beings, because **my Father has loved them that they should not perish** by the error in which they have persisted. 13:4 And again, **I will perfect the love of the Father**, even unto the death of a cross. For the sake of **their salvation I will descend to raise them up with me** in love and indivisible peace if **they shall believe in me without doubt**, and **give thanks**, and **glorify through me the Father** of that glorious majesty **who sent me for their salvation**. 13:5 And I have loved them that they may not perish by the error in which they have persisted. And therefore, since I have appeared to them in the fullness of all the times, they have no excuse for their offenses **unless they repent and believe in me**. 13:6 And also you, everything that you were commanded by your fathers, and everything that you learned from the **mysteries of the books that you have read**, do, since behold, **the hidden mysteries of the light of the star** that you have been waiting to see, behold, **he himself** has (now) told you about himself as you are able to hear. 13:7 And you will believe without doubt, seeing in me **signs of many forms**. 13:8 And again, **take with you the treasure that was deposited in this cave by your fathers** and [continue in joy] and **worship** the [text missing] **I will be born like a human being**. 13:9 And again, **worship me there** [text missing]: even now, as **I am speaking with you I am also there**. Because my Gospel has been proclaimed by angels, **I am both there and with the majesty of my Father**. 13:10 And **I am everywhere, because I am a ray of light whose light has shone in this world from the majesty of my Father**, who has sent me to fulfill everything that was spoken about me in the entire world and in every land by **unspeakable mysteries**, and to accomplish the **commandment of my glorious Father**, who by the **prophets preached about me** to the contentious house, **in the same way as for you, as befits your faith**, it was revealed to you about me. 13:11 And **I am going up with you and am a guide for you on the entire journey that you are traveling, seeing signs, glorious wonders, and great victories upon the entire earth**. And you will see the completion of all the mysteries in Jerusalem, and everything that was spoken with you will come true for you. 13:12 And again, you will see signs of **humility**, even a lowly and weak form, such that **people will act boldly against me**, and they will desire to do that which they plotted in **deceit against me**, and they will not be able to have [their goal] take place. 13:13 But **all that they do will be for their killing and their destruction, and the will of the Father shall be fulfilled for the sake of the salvation** of the life of the whole world."*

Messiah appeared in human-like form, and explained to the Magi that He will be born in the flesh, into the world, near Jerusalem, Israel. It was time for them to execute their mission; to travel, and they brought their offerings in covenant. These items from the Estate of Adam were the same as those the Queen of Sheba brought to the Temple, which housed the presence of Yahuah. This covenant is thousands of years old and precedes even Israel and the Flood. Jesus *(Yahusha)* is very clear that He said that He is from the Father. He said that He is the promised Messiah who has come in the flesh to save mankind.

What an honor for these Filipino men to live with the humility and to be blessed, as one of the few on Earth to be notified of the birth of the Son of Yahuah. This was not a chance meeting, however. It was their calling, from the days of the most ancient of times. It does not get more Biblical than that. Only a racist, colonial, Zionist view would suppress this and attempt to hide what the ancient Filipino represented in the kingdom. In all, He speaks with humility, continuing to represent the Father as the most important, as He does throughout His earthly ministry. Essentially, these are the beginning elements of the New Testament, first revealed to Ophir, Philippines. Before any disciple was chosen, they were. In fact, twelve of them would go to make offering to Him.

Jesus *(Yahusha)* told the Magi that He would be their guide on the journey, not a star of any other kind; especially not a constellation or planetary alignment. The message of salvation was given to the Magi first. They were the first "twelve disciples." Salvation is a message throughout the Old Testament as well, but in the New Testament age, this is the first account. Wow!!! He affirmed these priests had writings in their Cave of Treasures. Either the Catholic Church destroyed these very original documents, or they hid them in the Vatican along with this later translation. Either way, they were responsible for losing the Magi record, and they continue to ignore even this translation, pushing the erroneous tale of Melchior, Balthazar, and Caspar.

RotM 14:2 And we took that entire treasure that was deposited in the cave, letters having been sealed in which it was placed. And we descended from the mountain, glorifying the mysteries of the revelations of the light of the star that appeared to us. 14:3 And each of us was speaking about the revelations and visions that had appeared to him in the Cave of Treasures of Hidden Mysteries, but our visions did not resemble each other, and all the wonders of many forms that appeared to us. 14:4 There is one of us saying, "I saw a light in which there were many images that were amazing." And there is one saying, "I saw an infant who had unspeakable forms." 14:5 And there is one saying, "I saw a youth who did not have a form in this world." And there is one saying, "I saw a human being who was humble, unsightly in appearance, and poor." 14:6 And there is one saying, "I saw a cross and a person of light who hung upon it, taking away the sins of the entire world." And there is one saying, "I saw that he went down to Sheol with force and all the dead rose and worshiped him." 14:7 And there is one saying, "I saw that he ascended in glory, and he opened the graves, and he raised up the dead, while they are crying out and saying: 'Holy is our king and holy is his descent to us! Because of our sins he humbled himself to save us.'" 14:8 And there is one saying, "I saw him ascending to the heavenly height, and angels opening the gates of heaven before him. And clouds of seraphs and angels are taking him upon the palms of their hands, and the Paraclete Spirit taking a diadem ad a crown and making victory shine before him, and all the hosts praising and singing the honor of his humility, which prevailed in the whole struggle of error and death.

These honored men who lived holy lives in covenant, then took the accumulated treasure from the Cave of Treasures (that amassed since the days of Adam), and offered them to the Savior of mankind. This was no small amount. The boxes, depicted in artwork, pale in comparison, to this treasury from the Estate of Adam. As Jesus *(Yahusha)* completed His visitation, He showed Himself in different stages of His life to come. The Magi literally saw His ministry, His hanging on the tree, His awakening the dead spirits of the righteous sleeping within the Inner Earth or Sheol, and even His ascension into Heaven long before it ever happened. This is one of the most beautiful accounts one could ever absorb.

Modern scientists claim we are stardust; they do not know what they are saying. We are indeed all created with the Light of Messiah, the very Light that appeared to the Magi. Stardust itself has no creative powers, and no one has ever observed a star creating in any sense. No life comes from a star and no star has ever spawned life in any observation at any time. However, Jesus *(Yahusha)* was the Light of Creation and through His Light we have life. That is not just an account from ***Revelation of the Magi*** as we have observed.

How do we know the Magi were a truly holy lot? In fact, the Magi are on record as keeping the Feasts; so is Adam. The Magi did not change that to celebrate Christmas, which we know, in foundation, is Saturnalia in Catholic history; even according to Tertullian in 155 A.D. He appears to lament such replacement. He admits the Catholic Church had lost the Biblical devotion (even that early on, totally disconnected). Tertullian shared that Christians (meaning Catholics), were no example of solemnity (adherence to their own Bible). Saturnalia has always included gift-giving, to honor Zeus, who is their gift-giver. Sports and banquets distracted everyone just as with Christmas today. The occult feasts of January also included Epiphany, or Three Kings' Day, and is celebrated at the absolutely wrong time of year, with the wrong center of celebration. These pagan holidays also included figurines, just as we see today in the corrupted nativity creche' and Christmas Tree decorations. The Christmas Tree is outright and directly rebuked in Jeremiah 10.

*"By us who are strangers to Sabbaths, and new moons, and festivals, once acceptable to God, the Saturnalia, the feasts of January, the Brumalia, and Matronalia, are now frequented; gifts are carried to and fro, new year's day presents are made with din, and sports and banquets are celebrated with uproar; oh, how much more faithful are the heathen to their religion, who take special care to **adopt no solemnity from the Christians.**" –Tertullian, 155 A.D.*[1]

Saturnalia is a debauchery day of pure evil that has been transformed in the public relations arena in modern centuries as Christ's Mass, and shortened to Christmas. Protestants continue the corrupt tradition, embellishing their revelry

---

[1] *"Tertullian, De Idolatria." c. 14, Vol. I, p. 682., 155 A.D.*

in USA megachurches, with million-dollar productions that represent only lies. The people think they are celebrating the birth of Messiah, but it is at the wrong time of year, with the wrong Savior at the forefront (usually accompanied by Santa, Rudolph, and Frosty leading camels toward the front of the sanctuary, where a baby in a fake manger awaits their worship, and a wealthy pastor awaits their money). Adam warned of that practice in prophecy. Let none of us attempt to justify such occult behavior as supposedly including the Messiah who does not participate.

*RotM 9:2 And [text missing] of the majesty, but **at the end times of that generation** they will again be [**rebelling,**] and they will not be afraid of my foolishness and of the judgment that I have. Instead, they shall be headstrong and shall **speak blasphemy** unto the heavenly majesty. 9:3 And they will say many things, and shall also make **painted idols and graven images,** and shall serve **the sun and the moon,** and they shall **speak words of blasphemy.** 9:4 And all these things that are among them from the deceits of my treacherous deceiver, because he will offer the **love of his fraud and his deceit filled with poison** to each of the generations that will be after me. 9:5 And he will [show] and make them desire the **empty praises of great riches, pride, clothes, property, fornication, boastfulness, injustice, greed,** and various possessions. 9:6 And he will appear to them **like a lover or a friend and entice them.** And again, with **reveling, drunkenness, impure, and defiled feasts,** which are an illusion [of his] empty [**apparitions,**] and again, with **possessions of sorted excess,** he will take hold of them with **fraudulent affection,** which is **not virtuous,** just as also to me through Eve.*

Adam declared that the generations of the End Times will defile the sacred Feasts; he was keeping them, and so did the Magi. Adam did not observe them all, but the Magi went to Israel in the days of Solomon and well knew Torah (according to ***Revelation of the Magi,*** which frequently quotes Torah). They were a priesthood of Covenant which they derived from Adam and Seth. This is a Biblical relationship, and yes, there were those on Earth some would even term "Gentiles *(goyim)*" who were in covenant relationship with Yahuah: other sheep in the Far East *(John 10:16)*. They would have to be so, to be worthy of the news of the birth of Yahuah's Son. Anyone inserting evil sorcerers into that narrative, is telling an occult tale; shame on them.

For Herod, the Pharisees and the Priests of Zoroastrianism were all not deemed "worthy *(17:2)*" to be notified of the Messiah's birth, because of their "blindness." That should be common sense. However, in ***Revelation of the Magi,*** Jesus *(Yahusha)* Himself promised the Magi (when they arrive at Jerusalem), this:

RotM 19:6 And together, you will be witnesses for me in the land of the East together with my disciples, those who are chosen by me to preach the Gospel.

The Magi knew the Light of the World before disciples were even chosen. Their twelve holy men precede the others in Israel. They knew the Light of the World, even before the shepherds. No scripture ever says the shepherds had to be the very first witnesses. Such debate is based on a faulty foundation, and is playing games with definitions as well. This is what Pharisees do. They add leaven to the Word, expanding it, making it read like fiction, and defilimg it, as they have for more than 2,000 years. It is no surprise we find this in the Catholic Church, and flowing into Protestant Churches as well.

Martin Luther was wrong, with close friends in high places. He was a hypocrite; which is defined as an actor, just like his ancestors, the Pharisees. He was not planning to protest the Catholic Church whatsoever, but was a spurious scribe with an agenda. Luther should have tore it down and rebuilt it on the foundation of the solid rock, Jesus *(Yahusha)*. He began in a good direction, in true Jesuit deceptive style, but to continue within the borders of Catholicism is to be ignorant of history, and especially Biblical exegesis. Instead of being burned at the stake, or tortured and beheaded for his "protest of 95 theses" he was given a slap on the wrist, then sent to live in a castle and translate the Bible into German. His lingering symbol of a red cross on a white rose is occult, reeking of Rosicrucianism. Luther complained about the *Book of Revelation*, and even omitted it from his first translation, claiming it was "neither apostolic nor prophetic.... Christ is not taught or known in it" (*Book of Revelation*, Wikipedia.org). Lutherans and Episcopals today even call themselves "light Catholics" as there is not much difference in theology. They are dead churches, created by the Pope and Rosicrucians *(satanists)*, to provide a solution to the problem the corrupt Catholic Church created themselves.

As additional verification, ***The Testaments of the Twelve Patriarchs*** also affirm that Jesus *(Yahusha)* would come in the form of a Star. This was never a mystery to the true Biblical paradigm. We already saw this in The Testaments of Judah and Levi. However, the Testament of Benjamin also includes the prophecy of this Star.

Testament of Benjamin 9:1-3 (Charlesworth) [1]
*"From **the words of Enoch** the Righteous tell you that you will be sexually promiscuous like the promiscuity of the Sodomites and will perish, with few exceptions. You shall resume your actions with loose women, and the kingdom of the Lord will not be among you, for he will take it away forthwith. But in your allotted place will be the temple of God, and the latter temple will exceed the former in glory (Hag 2:9). The twelve tribes shall be gathered there and all the nations, until such time as the Most High shall send forth his salvation through the ministration of the unique prophet.[b] [He shall enter the first temple, and there the Lord will be abused and will be raised up on wood. And the temple curtain shall be torn, and the spirit of God will move on to all the nations as a fire is poured out.*[1]

---

[1] *"Testaments of the Twelve Patriarchs: Benjamin 9:1-3." With Footnote 9b. Edited By James H. Charlesworth. The Old Testament Pseudepigrapha: Apocalyptic Literature & Testaments. p. 827.*

We all know the Second Temple in no way exceeded the First (in glory, in any sense). The Ark of the Covenant was not there as it was in the First. This is a reference to New Jerusalem, which is not a concept ever associated with the land we call Israel today. That is poor assumption. New Jerusalem will exceed the First Temple by far, as it will come down from Heaven over the Garden of Eden and the Tree of Life which will be the Holy of Holies within it. No longer will mankind need a box for Yahuah's presence. In our new bodies and a condition without sin, we will be able to live in His full presence for the first time since Adam in the Garden of Eden; it remains the Holy of Holies within the Earth under the modern Philippines.

In 1 Enoch 89-90, the Prophet Enoch describes this process when New Jerusalem comes down in location. It specifically says the First Temple is folded up (in his vision), and taken to the South of Israel (which is the Indian Ocean). Then, after the Day of Judgment, New Jerusalem will descend from above, onto the Earth, encompassing an entire continent, in size, of approximately 2,000 km cubed *(Rev. 21:16, 12,000 stadia long, wide, and high)*. It does not enter modern Israel but will be positioned to the South of it, in the Indian Ocean where the former was placed. There will be no more sea then, as the ancient Rivers from Eden will be restored *(Rev. 21:1)*. It must come down over the Philippines where the Garden and Tree of Life exist. The holy city will extend past India, to the West; perhaps over a large portion of the area we now call the Indian Ocean. All the sheep were never in the First nor Second Temple. They will be in New Jerusalem, which is also noted to be far larger here.

1 Enoch 90:28-29
*And I stood up to see till **they folded up that old house; and carried off all the pillars, and all the beams and ornaments of the house** were at the same time **folded up** with it, and they carried it off and laid it in a place in the south of the land. And I saw till Yahuah of the sheep brought a new house greater and loftier than that first, and set it up in the place of the first which had been folded up: all its pillars were new, and its ornaments were new and larger than those of the first, the old one which He had taken away, and all the sheep were within it.*

Prior to the Second Coming of Jesus *(Yahusha)*, the twelve tribes will be gathered in the land of the Latter Times where New Jerusalem comes down in the end. That is not modern Israel. The unique prophet is Messiah, as only He can administer salvation. This sets the prophetic conditions for the Revelation 12 event; the travailing woman who is always Israel in prophecy, never the spotless, virgin bride. Representing all twelve tribes, she appears in Heaven to offer a First Fruit offering which is the 144,000. They are children who sing and do not war. The innumerable multitude of the blood-stained martyrs are the ones who join the war in the end.

The woman is protected by Havilah, land of Havah *(Eve)* named for her travail in childbirth, even. That is the nativity of the Magi who will protect Israel and believers in these Last Days. It is the land of the sun, even its origin according to

Enoch. The moon is at its feet as the largest moon cult historically is Islam, whose Allah is the Moon God, Hubal, of Mecca, and of course, the crescent moon and star symbol. The twelve stars in her crown are the circle of twelve islands, called the Babuyan Islands, or in their local language, the burning isles/stars. That is also representative of the twelve Magi, the very children of the Light according to Messiah, who brought offerings to the Son. That designation is also used in the Dead Sea Scrolls about twenty times; the Levites call themselves the "sons of light" and it appears in the prophecy of John the Baptist as such as well *(Luke 1:79)*.

The Testament of Benjamin warps back to the First Temple where Jesus *(Yahusha)* entered it and was indeed rejected, found guilty wrongly, and abused, as prophesied. This is Benjamin writing, about 2,000 years prior. Fragments of *The Testament of the Twelve Patriarchs* were found in the Dead Sea Scrolls dating prior to Messiah's arrival. This is incredibly accurate prophecy. He was placed on the stake *(cross)* of wood as predicted. The veil of the Temple was rent, and the Holy Spirit came to us. That is a benchmark in testing that one cannot dispute. When prophecy is this accurate, the text is inspired. We will release this book in publishing soon, as well.

However, in his edition of *The Testament of Benjamin*, James H. Charlesworth realized incredible revelation here. In his footnote, he wisely connects this passage in Benjamin to the prophesied Star of Messiah from Numbers 24:17 we covered. He also ties that to the Damascus Document of the Dead Sea Scrolls. This Star being the Messiah is not a mystery in the slightest. This is a massive amount of substantiation in scripture. If it were not the Messiah Himself as this Star, it would be wrong. In other words, for any scholar to call that "Gnostic" or strange in any sense is evidence they do not know scripture.

Footnote b. The expectation of the eschatological prophet builds on Deut 18:15 and figures importantly at Qumran: 1QS9.10-11; lQS^{a}2.11-12. Possibly the star, mentioned in CD 7.15-20 (which is based on Num 24:17) is the One Who Teaches Rightly (1QS 1.11), forerunner of the unique prophet of the endtime. The prophet is directly mentioned in PssJosh 5-8 (= 4QTestim [Vermes, p. 527]) in a passage which leads into a declaration about the star. The text from Num 24 is quoted in Stephen's sermon (Acts 7:37), where it is taken to refer to Jesus as the eschatological prophet.[1]

On top of all the other references we have covered, this is a strong chain of evidence in affirmation. If only scholars would spend more time in that type of reconciliation instead of what they call "textual criticism," in destruction and confusion, we would all know much more than we do. We have covered multiple writings in the Dead Sea Scrolls where this community documents their being exiled by the Hasmoneans and Pharisees into the Wilderness of Judaea. There they

---

[1] *"Testaments of the Twelve Patriarchs: Benjamin 9:1-3." With Footnote 9b. Edited By James H. Charlesworth. The Old Testament Pseudepigrapha: Apocalyptic Literature & Testaments. p. 827.*

prepared the way for Messiah, fulfilling Isaiah 40:3. John the Baptist, from this Temple priesthood family of Zadok/Aaron/Levi operated there and baptized Jesus *(Yahusha)* in Qumran, which is Bethabara. They kept Biblical statutes and Canon at this location, a record which no place else in history bears.

They refer to that community as Damascus, not to be confused with the one in the North, which was no longer Israel at that time. They were also fulfilling prophecy in doing so, as the *Book of Amos* 5 already prophesied the true Levites would be exiled and replaced, as did Daniel 8 and Psalm 83. Of course, today we have an entire scholarly community who lost track of that enemy and assumes they are in fact, the Tribes of Israel, when they are the synagogue of satan who say they are Yahudim and are not, but do lie *(Rev. 2:9, 3:9).*

I will exile the tabernacle of your king and the bases of your statues from my tent to Damascus (Amos 5:26-7). The Books of the Law are the tabernacle of the king; as God said, I will raise up the tabernacle of David which is fallen (Amos ix, 11). The king is the congregation; and the bases of the statues are the Books of the Prophets whose sayings Israel despised. **The star is the Interpreter of the Law who shall come to Damascus; as it is written, A star shall come forth out of Jacob and a sceptre shall rise out of Israel (Num. 24:17). The sceptre is the Prince of the whole congregation, and when he comes he shall smite all the children of Seth (Num. 24:17).** [1]

Just as with ***Revelation of the Magi,*** notice the mention of the children of Seth. Jesus *(Yahusha)* is the "Interpreter of the Law" and the Star Himself exactly as our text affirms. Anyone looking for this Star to be anything but Messiah, is not following the Bible. Only the Magi were shown this Star, and it did not appear in Israel until the Magi arrived almost two years after the birth of Messiah.

Finally, we have the witness of ***Ben Sira/Wisdom of Sirach*** 50 which we have seen no one understand to date. He tells the story of what appears to be a High Priest named *Simon* who is the son of Onias *(Latin)/* Uzziah *(Hebrew).* This is one of the most misconstrued translations in history. *Simon/Simeon* in Hebrew derives from: שמע: *shama'* [2] meaning, *listen.* *Uzziah* means *power of Yah [*עזז *('azaz)* יה *(yah)].* [3] These are not names. This appears fraudulent, and is trying to hide Messiah. Instead, the passage should begin as, *Listen, the High Priest, the son of the power of Yah.*

We are expected to believe that Sirach heralded the patriarchs in Chapter 49, contrasting them as far greater than Zerrubabel and Yahusha, the son of Yosedec, who led the rebuilding of the Temple. Then, Sirach begins another chapter, progressing backwards to a High Priest who simply spruced up the Temple further. Clearly, this is a symbolic prophecy of the coming Messiah, not any priest who lived in any era otherwise. In the previous chapter, Sirach just finished clarifying that

---

[1] *"The Damascus Document. CD 7.15-20." The Complete Dead Sea Scrolls in English. By Geza Vermes. Penguin Books. 1962. Revised Edition 2004. p. 135.* [2] *"The Name Simon." Abarim Publications.* [3] *"Uzziah." Abarim Publications.*

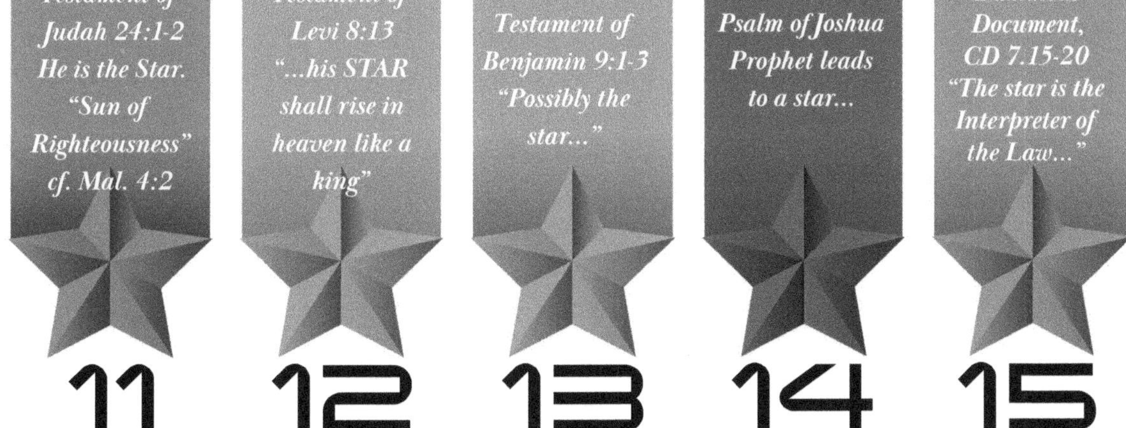

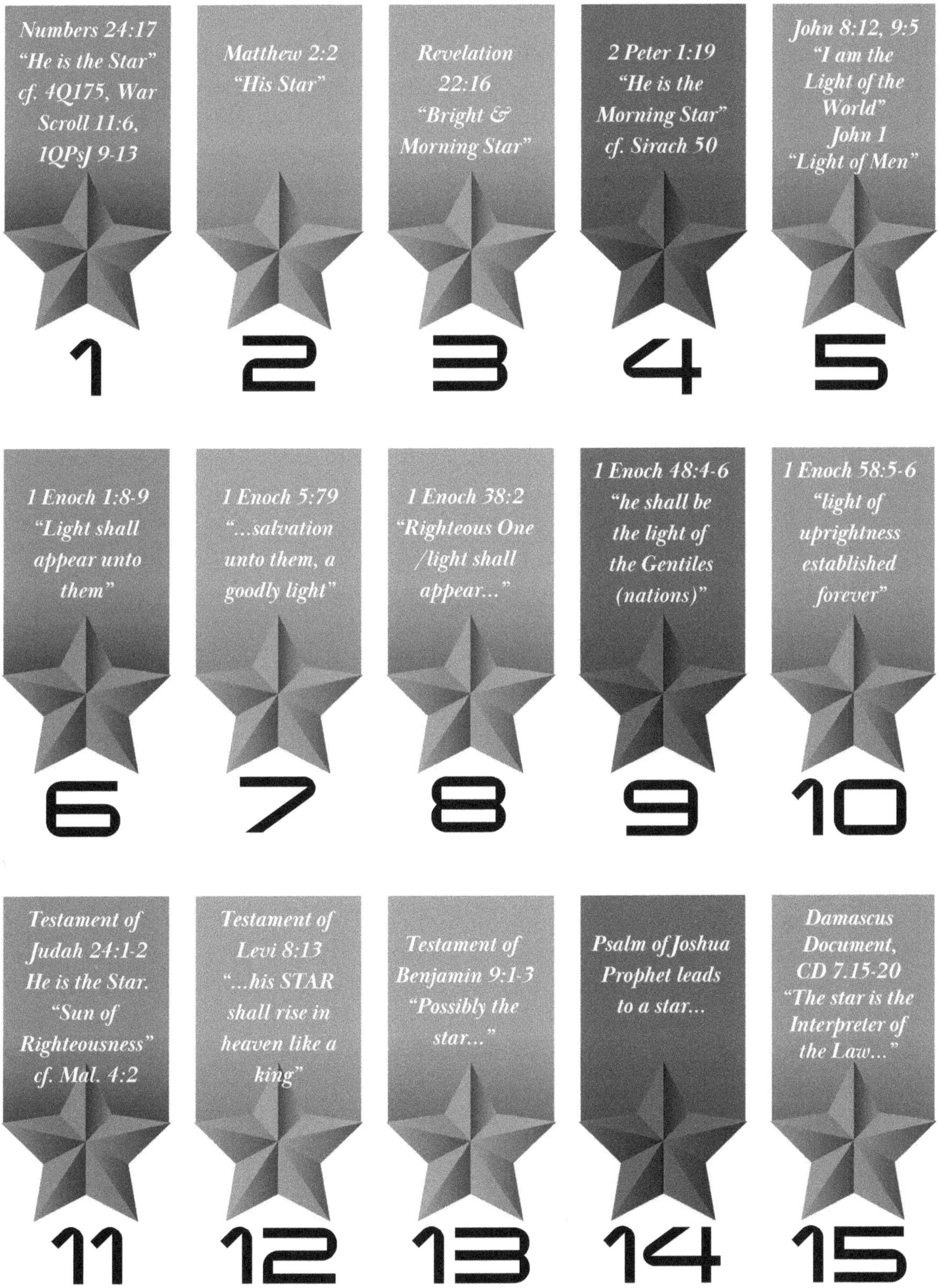

Jesus (Yahusha) Himself Was the Star

A BIBLE CONCEPT AFFIRMED IN REVELATION OF THE MAGI. THIS IS NOT GNOSTIC!

there is no comparison to the Prophets: Enoch, Joseph, Shem, Seth, and Adam. It would make no sense for him to then praise another far lesser High Priest undeservingly. Instead, he is ramping up to the greatest High Priest of them all: Jesus *(Yahusha)*. Josephus did not know our Savior and never represented Him as a High Priest. He was a Pharisee who hated the Savior, and does not interpret Sirach.

We know this because Sirach likens this character to the "Morning Star." We know who that is. There is little to debate. The wall of the Temple was raised to double the height, which is not historic, but a future foreshadowing of New Jerusalem which Jesus *(Yahusha)* builds. The water is far too much for any normal man to have created a sea. That is the future. This High Priest is honored as the "Morning Star," "as the moon at the full," and "as a rainbow giving light." All of that would be ridiculous in context if this were an actual historic High Priest whom none could fit any of these descriptions. It invokes Spring, just as the month of flowers, in which the Magi entered Jerusalem. Also, there is the frankincense tree in the Summer, which was brought to Messiah at the end of Spring. This is somewhere else, not Israel, fitting the Far East where His Star appeared and the spice originates. Other resources such as gold and precious stones are also fitting to the narrative of the Magi isles of Ophir.

This man named *Simon* has Messianic qualities such as: *"When he put on the robe of honor, and was clothed with the perfection of glory, when he went up to the holy altar, he made the garment of holiness honorable (11)."* There is no way any High Priest ever matches that description other than Messiah, who became our High Priest indeed *(Heb. 4:14)*. When it comes to the wine, this man pours out the "blood of the grape" at the "foot of the altar." All the people on the Earth immediately bow down and worship Yahuah. That has not happened and will not until the Day of Judgment. This is a Messianic prophesy likely corrupted in translations as the words simply mean what they mean and are not names. It is affirmation once again of the Morning Star.

Here, we have over fifteen mentions from scripture that Jesus *(Yahusha)* is literally the Star, some with very specific reference to the Star appearing at His birth. He was and is that Star. No one needs to look at Stellarium software as His Star will not show there. Planetary alignments and other such cannot be used to identify His birth as they are impertinent. Whenever the fictional event of the satanic god, Jupiter, entering the womb of the occult goddess, Venus, is injected by a Bible scholar, suggesting that has anything to do with scripture, run away. They are not providing Bible exegesis, but occult babble. Those false gods and goddesses are never a part of Bible interpretation. In fact, we have gone so far in research as to prove every mention in English of a constellation in the Bible is erroneous to the Hebrew language, which has no concept of constellations, space, or the universe. Yahuah does not identify His Stars by fallen angels and Nephilim. The association has always been the worst in scholarship. Test this for yourself.

Chapter 8: The Real Names of the Magi

The Three Magi, an illustration from the reproductions of Herrad of Landsberg's Hortus deliciarum by Christian Moritz Engelhardt, 1818. Wikimedia Commons. Public Domain. This is propaganda, not history nor art. The Magi were twelve, not from Persia, and did not look Jewish (as these do). Their names are on record before this fraudulent fairy tale was fabricated by the Catholic Church.

Language Dictionaries used in this Chapter:
[1] *Tagalog.com, Retrieved Oct. 2, 2024.* [2] *Binisaya.com, Retrieved Oct. 2, 2024.* [3] *Arta, Another Philippine Negrito Language." Lawrence A. Reid. Oceanic Linguistics. Vol. 28, No. 1, A Special Issue on Western Austronesian Languages (Summer, 1989), pp. 47-74 (28 pages). University of Hawai'i Press.* [4] *"The Last Language on Earth: Linguistic Utopianism in the Philippines." Piers Kelly. Oxford University Press. Glossary. 2022.* [5] *3NS Corpora Project Waray Dictionary.* [6] *Ilocano-Ingles Diksionaryo" By Dr. Santiago Reolalas.* [7] *Hiligaynon Dictionary." By Cecile L. Motus. University of Hawaii Press. 1971.* [8] *"An Ibanag-English Dictionary." Zorayda Beltran Ibarbia. Texas A&M University. 1969.*

*"RotM 2:3 The names of the wise men and kings were called as follows: **Zaharwandad** son of **Artaban**; **Hôrmizd** son of **Sanatruq**; **Auštazp** son of **Gudaphar**; **Aršak** son of **Mihruq**; **Zarwand** son of **Wadwad**; **Arîhô** son of **Kosrau**; **Artahšišat** son of **Hawîlat**; **Aštanbôzan** son of **Šîîšrawan**; **Mihruq** son of **Humam**; **Ahširaš** son of **Sahban**; **Nasardîh** son of **Baladan**; **Merôdak** son of **Bîl**. 2:4 These are kings, sons of Eastern kings, in the land of Shir..."*

In researching these names of the twelve Wise Men of the Philippines of which some were Kings, sons of Kings and others Wise Men, it would be negligent to fail to at least attempt to connect some of these to the Filipino languages in origin. The geography is truly indisputable, and now, let us see if the linguistics are as well. We are not only given the twelve, but also the names of their fathers, for a total of twenty-four. This also serves to preserve in part how ancient Filipinos were named before the Spanish invasion and confusion. Many have pondered that.

It should stand to reason some may have been corrupted through translation, or what appears to be transliteration instead. At least eight of them strongly appear to be from direct Tagalog, and other native words of the Philippines. Even better, we can identify names that include Ophir, Sheba, Havilah, Tarshish, and even Sephar as well as at least six of Ophir's thirteen brothers in these names. This really becomes a grand slam.

In this search, we simply used dictionaries from multiple Filipino languages which search anyone can easily reproduce. Some of these names certainly appear Filipino in origin. Indeed, we observe many Spanish names today in the Philippines which would not affect the ancient names, but when direct Tagalog words are used in some of these, it is difficult to dismiss. Also, it would be even more negligent to ignore the Hebrew connection. Joktan was Hebrew, and spoke this language when he left Iran, prior to the destruction of the Tower of Babel. Thus, even in mixture, it would be expected to find Hebrew elements as well.

This is research no one seems to have ever conducted, but with the proper geography, we at least know we are looking in the right place. This really fulfills a leg of affirmation as well as it can in any language. For those who would say some of these could be other languages, they should first test the geography, which they have not, or they would not attempt such an illiterate point. The purpose of this exercise is not to promise definitive relation, but to test an association that should exist, at least for some. Once again, we have a match with even direct names.

Let us begin with the strongest matches for Filipino languages. These are truly impossible, yet they appear to coalesce. Notice that some even have a form with the prefix *MAG*. Could that be the same as the origin word for *MAGI* in their native language from which the word Magi derives, not Greek?

We have reviewed King David's prophecy in Psalm 72, which lists at least two Kings from Tarshish, two from Ophir and two from Sheba. So, we know there were more than six Kings in total. Of course, they would not have to all be Kings beyond that either. Here we have Kings, sons of Kings (which would be princes), and Wise Men still, even though the Greek word and English translation do not actually apply. The origin is what matters.

All of these Magi would certainly be *Maginoo*, Filipino royals as Kings and sons of Kings, men of *magdasal (prayer in Tagalog)* and *magiammo (silent in Ibanag, which tie seems impossible, yet there it is)*. Are we "storytelling" or presenting the facts? You know better. The Greek is impertinent in determining whom these are, and a list has always been available, but hidden by the Vatican who failed to translate this document for more than 1,000 years. It was in their care leaving it a mystery, even though Psalm 72 has never actually been so. They would assail Biblical geography, as if it were not there, with occult inferences, perpetrating the kind of evil that Jesus *(Yahusha)* warned about many times, as leaven. Again, the precedence of three still makes perfect sense as Luzon *(Ophir)*, Visayas *(Sheba)*, and Mindanao *(Tarshish)* remain today as a region of three. Three leaders, thus, three Kings are appropriate in context, and they were Kings.

Strong Matches to Filipino Languages:

Wadwad: (Exact Filipino word match)
wadwad: Ilokano: in disarray; scattered; crumpled; rumpled; wrinkled; mussed.[1]
wadwad: Ilokano: much blessing. Gen. 22:16 uses "wadwad" in the 1996 printing of the Ilokano Bible Version by the Philippine Bible Society.
wadwad: Bisayan: till, toil.[2]

Humam: (Exact Filipino word match)
humamon: Tagalog: to dare; to **challenge**; *to confront; to meet defiantly Related word with Mag prefix: maghamón: to challenge; to put up a fight.*[1]
human: Bisayan: done, after, finish.[2]

Sanatruq: (Exact Filipino word match) (Sîtârûk / Santarôk according to The Book of the Bee)
sana: Tagalog: hopefully; hope; wish; hopefully; should; i hope; if only; only. Prefix Mag: magsanay: to train; to practice; to exercise.[1]
san: Tagalog: shortened and informal form of "saan" = "where."[1]
si: Tagalog: a word placed before a proper noun (singular).[1]
tarók: Tagalog: measuring depth; the act of measuring how deep something is; depth measurement; fathoming; sounding; plumbing.[1]
tarók: Bisayan: erect.[2] *arrow point (Davao local).*

Note: This name is manipulated by the translator to attempt Persian connection when he already disproved such. A Persian King in 200 A.D. is impertinent and this is forced. This is far more likely Filipino words from the native land of the Magi which was not Persia. You can see the form in The Book of the Bee which still includes the Tagalog and Bisayan **tarók** *directly rather than the corrupted* "**truq.**"

Sahban: *(Exact Filipino word match)* (*Sâbhâ according to The Book of the Cave of Treasures*)
saban: Bisayan: propeller (Davao local).
sahab: Tagalog: heat that is **steaming off**; *vapor; steam; fumes.*[1]
sahà: Tagalog: banana tree skin/sheath.[1]
sahí': Hiligaynon: special, distinct, distinguished.[7]
ban: Tagalog: wheel.[1]
bána: Hiligaynon: husband.[7]
sabihan: to tell something to someone; to give notice to someone; to admonish someone.[1]
sab-an: Waray: tell[5]
sabang: Waray: Mouth of the river.[5]

Baladan: *(Exact Filipino word match)*
bala: Tagalog: threat; warning; bullet; ammunition.[1]
addan: Arta Negrito: stairway, ladder.[2]
adan: Adam in Tagalog, Bisayan, Ilokano, etc.[1, 2]

Artaban: *(Exact Filipino word match)*
Arta: name of the Negrito tribe in **Quirino Province, Philippines.**[3]
Artá: Tagalog: 1. a suffix used to form nouns and adjectives with a feminine gender.
2. an interjection expressing doubt or a pause in speech.; aha!; uh-oh!; oops!; hm![1]
ban: Tagalog: wheel.[1]

Arîhô: *(Close Filipino word match)*
arihán: Tagalog: the desire to **compete** *with others in fields like dressing, knowledge, wealth, and similar areas; competition; rivalry; one-upmanship.*[1]
arihán: Bisayan: come here.[2]

Îryâhô in the Book of the Bee:
irayá: Tagalog: upland; upward area; a place situated above or at a higher position; highland; elevated area; upper area.[1]
yahód: Tagalog: scrubbing hard; vigorous scrubbing; scrub; scour.[1]
Note: *There is a volcano considered sacred to the locals in the very North of the Philippines in Batanes called Mt. Iraya. It is known as "mother overlooking her children" or cloud cover signifies the death of an elder.*[9] *Also, in Mindoro, there is a tribe of Iraya Mangyans*[10] *who seem to bear this name and Magi in the land the Chinese termed "Ma-Yi."*

---

[9] *"Mount Iraya." Wikipedia.* [10] *"Iraya Mangyan." Wikipedia. Both Retrieved Oct. 2025.*

Merôdak: (likely Filipino origin) (Merôdâch in the Book of the Bee)
meron: Tagalog: to have; has; possesses. exists; there are; there is.[1]
dako: Tagalog: direction; part; region; spot; around; around (+time).[1]
miron: Bisayan: beggar, moocher, scrounger.[2]
dako: Bisayan: big, great, large.[2]
miridu: Eskaya: husband.[4]
merkado: Waray: marketplace. Other: **merkadohan, markado, marusdak, murado, murasak.**[5]
Note: This is likely another corruption to lead to the Persian god Marduk. There is no Persian connection as this translator proves. The name cannot be Marduk.

Ancient Name of the Philippines Directly Referenced:

From Genesis 10:25-30, we find there is one named Havilah, who is brother of Ophir and Sheba, the sons of Joktan from Shem, not Ham. He is named after the land to which he and his brothers would return, where Adam and Eve once dwelled. They were displaced in the Flood, and this was their return to their homeland. Scholars confuse the one from Ham as well, even assuming everyone named Havilah or Sheba in the Bible must live in the same land land (which is inept). The word Havilah is not actually accurate to Ancient Hebrew, which had no "V" until the 1500's or so, when it was infused from what we now call Yiddish, originating in the Russian Steppes. That is not Bible Hebrew and should not be used to render words in concordances in ignorance. This is *Hawilah* really in Ancient Hebrew.

In Latin, the translation becomes *Evilat* or *Evilath*, even on maps we have covered in ancient times [such as two we already explored (see Chapter 5)]. The word is still *Hawilah*, regardless in origin. However, if one were to Latinize *Hawilah* as *Hawilat*, it is the very name of this particular Magi. *Hawilah* should actually be rendered *Hawilat*, appropriately, and it is that exact Latin form; easy to connect. *Hawah (Eve)* was named at the same time the land now called the Philippines was named by Adam, just after the Garden exile, as *Hawilah. Hawah (Eve)* did not have a name in the Garden. *Hawilah* is still *Hawah (Eve)* in name, altered to the definition of her curse of labor pain in childbirth. This is a concrete tie to the land of Adam *(soil, dirt)* and *Hawah (Eve, mother of all living, life-giving)* in the Philippines.

Hawîlat; (Clearly Latinized Form of Hebrew Havilah, Philippines)
Havilah: Hebrew: חוילה: *Eden through which flowed the river Pison (H2341).*
Note: Evilat(h) in Latin typically. "W" is the accurate way to render Ancient Hebrew. Is this the Hebrew word Hawilah which is the Philippines in every designation as the land of Adam and Eve and Garden of Eden? (See Introduction)

חוילה: *havilah: that suffers pain; that brings forth, circle.*[1]

Genesis 3:20 KJV
*And **Adam** called his wife's name **Eve**; because she was the mother of all living.*

חוה: **hawah:** *life-giver; Chavvah (or Eve), the first woman:—Eve. [42] Latin form: Eva.*[2]

Possible Matches to Filipino Languages:

Some of these do not appear to directly connect on the surface until one digs deeper. However, understand that the translation we have in English originates in the Syriac and Latin versions. The likelihood of corruptions occurring is guaranteed, in at least some cases. This is why we include these names from other books at times, to assess such. This is not uncommon in translation, and Landau executed a reliable translation regardless. However, he was unaware of what land he found and needed foundation by which to establish context. We will assist.

Artahšišat: (Obvious corruption of Tarshish)
Arta: *name of the Negrito tribe in Quirino Province, Philippines.*[3]
Artá: *Tagalog: 1. a suffix used to form nouns and adjectives with a feminine gender.*
2. an interjection expressing doubt or a pause in speech.; aha!; uh-oh!; oops!; hm![1]
sisáp: *Tagalog: sycophantic; overly ingratiating or obsequious; suck-up; flatterer; toady; bootlicker.*[1] ***sisante:*** *Tagalog: dismissal; deposing.*[1]

Ahširaš: (From Seba: *King of Sâbhâ/Seba according to The Book of the Cave of Treasures*)
ahas: *Tagalog: snake; serpent.*[1] *a treacherous person.*
irás: *Tagalog: anxious; uneasy.*[1]
sirâ: *Tagalog: 1 broken; damaged; ruined; defective; destroyed; not working; worn-out 2 crazy.*[1] *Other forms: makasirà. siraan, masirà.* **sirâ:** *Ibanag: fish.*
Note: Sabah, Malaysia is historically territory of the Philippines. Saba is Seba of Psalm 72.

Aštanbôzan: (Ashtôn `âbôdân in the Book of the Bee)
astá: *Tagalog: posture; demeanor; action; act; acting; aspect; how a person carries oneself.*[1]
astangí: *Tagalog: a type of fragrant smoke; incense; perfumed smoke; fragrant fume.*[1]
bosolan: *Tagalog: a **rafter** in the roof; a structural beam that supports the roof.; rafter; beam; roof beam.*[1]
basolan: *Ilokano: sin (local Ilokano rendering).*
boloson: *Ilokano: release a fish (local Ilokano rendering).*
Continued...

---

[1] *"Havilah." Hitchcock's Dictionary of Bible Names from BibleHub.org and KingJamesBibleDictionary.com, Strong's Concordance #H2341. Blue Letter Bible.* [2] *"Eve - Havah." Strong's Concordance #H2332. Blue Letter Bible.*

aatubangon: **Waray:** *will confront and deal with or accept a difficult or unpleasant task, fact, or situation; will be confronting and dealing with or accepting a difficult or unpleasant task, fact, or situation.*
kabód: **Tagalog:** *a method of mining by digging a well that is dived into by miners; shaft mining; well digging.*[1]

Aršak: *(Arshakh in the Book of the Bee)*

asák: **Tagalog:** *excessively following trends or fashion; trendy; fashion-forward; fashionista; stylish.*[1]
arasaw: **Ilokano:** *water used in rinsing rice.*[6] Ilokano Local
siak: **Ilokano:** *me (pronounced shak).*

Auštazp: *(Possibly Filipino)* *(Gûshnâsâph/Gushnasp in the Book of the Bee)*

astá: **Tagalog:** *posture; demeanor; action; act; acting; aspect; how a person carries oneself.*[1]
sapà: **Tagalog:** *stream; brook; creek; river.*[1]

Alternative: Gûshnâsâph: *(Likely Hebrew)*

gustuhín: **Tagalog:** *to like something.*[1] **Forms: magustuhán and kagustuhan.**[1]
nasa: **Tagalog:** *in; at; on; located at; contained. aspiration; desire.*[1]

gush: גוש: **Hebrew:** *a clod, lump. (H1487).*
nāšā': נשא: **Hebrew:** *to beguile, deceive (H5377). to lift, bear, take, carry (H5375, H5376).*
'aph: אף: **Hebrew:** *nostril, nose, face. anger. (H639).*

Bîl *(Beldarân in the Book of the Bee)*

bili: **Bisayan:** *value, worth.*[2]
bilís: **Tagalog:** *speed; quickness; fast.*[1]
bilik: **Eskaya:** *beautiful.*[4]
bilog: **Ilokano:** *a boat travel on the water.*[6]
bilag: **Ibanag:** *sun; sunshine.*[7] *bilao:* **Ibanag:** *flat basket.*[7] *bilang:* **Ibanag:** *count; number.*[7]

Alternative: Beldarânin:

baldá: **Tagalog:** *having a disability or impairment in the body; disability; impairment; handicap; infirmity.*[1]
praníng: **Tagalog:** *paranoid; crazy; cuckoo (considered a newer word).*[1]
ani: **Tagalog:** *harvest; crop; product. ani + ligature 'ng' =* **aning.**[1]

bel: בל: **Hebrew:** *"lord," a chief Babylonian deity (H1087).*
dar: דר: **Hebrew:** *pearl, mother of pearl (H1858).*
ani: עני: **Hebrew:** *poor, afflicted, humble, wretched (H6041).*

Nasardîh: (Likely Hebrew from early Genesis in the Philippines)

nāšā': Hebrew: נשא*: to beguile, deceive (H5377). to lift, bear, take, carry (H5375, H5376).*

nasar: Hebrew: נצר*: to guard, in a good sense (to protect, maintain, obey, etc.) or a bad one (to conceal, etc.) (H5341). to hold aloof, i.e. (intransitively) abstain (from food and drink, from impurity, and even from divine worship. (H5144).*

râdâh: Hebrew: to rule, have dominion, dominate, tread down as in Gen. 1:26 (H7287).

dîy: Hebrew/Aramaic: who, which, that (particle of relation). that of, which belongs to, that (mark of genitive). that, because (conjunction) (H1768).

nasa: Tagalog: in; at; on; located at; contained. aspiration; desire.[1]
Rendered with Magi in beginning: magnasa: to want; to desire.[1]
rodilyo: Tagalog: in jewelry, a metal tool used for designing; rolling pin; roller.[1]
naasar: Ilokano: roasted.[6]

Alternative: Sardâlâh in the Book of the Bee
sarì: Tagalog: kind; species; genus.[1]
dalahin: Tagalog: load.[1]

The Book of the Cave of Treasures renders Nasardih as "PERÔZÂDH, the king of Sheba, which is in the East." Sheba in the East can never be Africa. Certainly, scholars should know Africa is not East of Bethlehem. This is the Sheba of the Queen of Sheba from the Far East. The forgotten Sheba from Genesis 10:25-30 in Shem's lineage that is brother of Ophir. In researching this name, it also could originate in Tagalog.

pero: Tagalog: [conjunction] but.
sadyâ: Tagalog: purpose; intention; aim; intent; errand; mission; act of getting something made-to-order.

PERÔZÂDH could also originate in the Biblical paradigm of Hebrew and Greek. Either language proves close.

paraz or perez: Hebrew: פרז*: to separate, i.e. Decide; a chieftain -- village (H6518).*
paras: פרץ*: to break through (Abarim Publications).*
"Here at Abarim Publications we suspect that our nouns חןפα *(pera) and pero may have a Semitic origin, specifically the verb* פרר *(parar), to split and make more, expand or multiply, or the related verb* פרה *(para), to bear fruit or be fruitful." –Abarim Publications*
adah: עדה*: to pass by or to ornament (Abarim Publications).*

שדה*: (sadeh), meaning open field or pasture land (Genesis 29:2) or home of wild beasts (Genesis 4:8, Jeremiah 14:5). Abarim Publications*

Gudaphar: (Likely Hebrew referencing the Land of Creation, Philippines and the Actual Family of Aupir/Ophir)
gud: Hebrew: גוד*: to invade, attack (H1464).*
aphar: Hebrew: עפר*: dry earth, dust as in Gen. 2:7 in the land of Creation (H6083).*

dapâ: Tagalog: lying face down, lying on one's stomach, letting down on the ground, lying prostrate.[1]
gadapa: Tagalog: already kneeling or bowing down. (Local Filipino)
gulada: Eskaya: shoe, slipper.[4]

Some scholars (such as Landau in his introduction) try to connect this name as a king of India. That is the only name he even attempted to research, as he never studied this out, yet rendered interpretation without basis (which is nonsensical). The problem with the name confusion here occurs when they try to connect the Apostle Thomas visiting an Indian King with a similar name as one of the Magi (but not quite), in *Acts of Thomas*. However, this *Gudaphar* is named in Hebrew (and is obviously not Indian). He was a Magi, who visited Messiah at his birth, and was likely dead by the time Thomas visited the land of Shir, Philippines. That King did not hire Thomas as a slave, which is a ridiculous thought, when he would have welcomed the Apostle with open arms. That is not logic nor a position in any form. However, in the next section, we will go deeper into this.

Mihruq: (Likely Eskaya) (Mîhârôk in Book of the Bee)
muruki: Eskaya: was carried on the head.[4]
mirikilyu: Eskaya: doctor.[4]
miridu: Eskaya: husband.[4]
mahirap: Tagalog: poor (financially). difficult; hard to do; complex; laborious; cumbersome; arduous. poor person.[1]
maraque: Ibanag: bad; harmful; undesirable.[8]

mi: Hebrew: מי*: who? (H4310)*
rûwach: Hebrew: רוח*: Spirit or spirit (232x), wind (92x), breath (27x), side (6x), mind (5x), blast (4x), vain (2x), air (1x), anger (1x), cool (1x), courage (1x), miscellaneous (6x) (H7307).*

Alternative: Mîhârôk
mihit: Tagalog: a dislike or aversion towards what is not desired or liked; dislike; aversion; antipathy.[1]
miyâ: Tagalog: kitten; young cat; baby cat.[1]
arók: Tagalog: depth gauge; understanding.[1]

Zarwand:

sarwag and *isarwag:* **Deep Ilokano:** *throwing the net to the ocean to catch fish.* [Local Ilokano]

sariwà: **Tagalog:** *fresh; crisp; new; recent.*[1]

nido: **Tagalog:** *edible bird's nest.*[1]

sawardit: **Eskaya:** *examination.*[4]

zâhar: **Hebrew:** זהר: *to gleam; figuratively, to enlighten (by caution):—admonish, shine, teach, (give) warn(-ing) (H2094).*

Kosrau: **(Likely Hebrew)** *(Kesro/Khusrau in the Book of the Bee)*

kôs: **Hebrew:** כוס: *a cup (as a container), often figuratively, a lot (as if a potion); also some unclean bird, probably an owl (perhaps from the cup-like cavity of its eye):—cup, (small) owl (H3563).*

râ'âh, raw-aw': **Hebrew:** ראה: *see (879x), look (104x), behold (83x), shew (68x), appear (66x), consider (22x), seer (12x), spy (6x), respect (5x), perceive (5x), provide (4x), regard (4x), enjoy (4x), lo (3x), foreseeth (2x), heed (2x), miscellaneous (74x).*

Note: This is another transliteration likely stretched to try to fit a Persian king named Khosrau from around 530 A.D. which is impertinent, yet some attempt such connection. This is an exact fit to the Hebrew meaning of a prophetic container which is the Cave of Treasures containing the Estate of Adam which would be brought by the Magi as well as the cave which the light of Jesus (Yahusha) was contained. There are also Filipino possibilities as well.

kostilyas: **Tagalog:** *rib (body part); ribs; rib bone.*[1]

kasariwaán: **Tagalog:** *freshness; youth.* **Other:** *kasinsariwà.*[1]

kasarián: **Tagalog:** *gender; sex (e.g., boy / girl / male / female); kind; species; genus.*[1]

kasiraán: **Tagalog:** *corruption; destruction.*[1]

sirà: **Tagalog:** *damage; tear; defect; flaw.*[1]

kusà: **Tagalog:** *automatically; voluntary; voluntarily; deliberate; by itself; on one's own initiative.*[1]

raw: **Tagalog:** *it is said; according to another person.*[1]

raún: **Tagalog:** *leaf.*[1]

araw: **Tagalog:** *day, sun.*[1]

kasar: **Ilokano:** *wedding.*[6]

kúsinero: **Tagalog:** *cook; chef.*[1]

raún: **Tagalog:** *leaf.*[1]

Šîîšrawan: *(Shîshrônin the Book of the Bee)*

susì: **Tagalog:** *key.*[1]

arawán: **Tagalog:** *on a daily basis; daily.*[1]

raw: **Tagalog:** *it is said; according to another person.*[1]

shishshîy: šiššî: **Hebrew:** ששי: *sixth (H8345).* **Sisera: Hebrew:** סיסרא: *Hebrew name (H5516).*

Awan: **Ancient Hebrew:** און: *first daughter of Adam (Jubilees 4:1).*

Zaharwandad: (Likely Derivative of Ophir's brother)

zâhar: Hebrew: זהר: to gleam; figuratively, to enlighten (by caution):–admonish, shine, teach, (give) warn(-ing) (H2094).

sahà: Tagalog: banana tree skin/sheath.[1]

raw: Tagalog: it is said; according to another person.[1]

andadór: Tagalog: baby-walker.[1]

andadasi: Tagalog: coffee senna; a shrub (cassia occidentalis) with yellow flowers and flat seed pods, native to tropical America; also known as stinking weed or styptic weed.; stinking weed; styptic weed.[1]

sawardit: Eskaya: examination.[4]

Hôrmizd: (Hor in Book of Adam; Hôrmîzdâd in the Book of the Bee)

hirám: Tagalog: borrowed. Name of Solomon's admiral who went to Ophir for gold.[1]

isadsád: Tagalog: to beach something; to cause something to run aground.[1]

isá-dalawá: Tagalog: one or two.[1]

Note: Hormizd is a direct Persian name for the god Ahura Mazda. This appears to be a stretch to fit the Catholic legend which fails. This is not a translation but a transliteration from the original language into Syriac, into Latin and finally translated into English. It is doubtful this is Persian.

In the **Book of Adam**, this name is simply "Hor." Of course, it is then is assumed to be Persian. However, any Bible scholar that does not know Aaron, the brother of Moses died on Mt. Hor is illiterate. "Har" is also the general word for mountain in Hebrew and the Mount of the East is the center of the Magi's worship gathering. Again, this appears to be a corruption easily reconciled.

The name Hor is the same as the noun רה (har), meaning mountain. In fact, the phrase "Mount Hor" employs twice the same word: רהה רה (har hahar). –Abarim Publications

After conducting a study of these names, we can confidently conclude at least nine of them derive from languages of the Philippines, not including the direct designation of Havilah. Are some of these affiliated with Ophir, Sheba, Tarshish, and Sephar as well? That would affirm that the Wise Kings of Matthew 2 and Psalm 72 were from the Philippines indeed. In assessing the others, we find what appears definitive Hebrew, which is exactly what one would expect in the Philippines. Ancient Ophir connected to Israel before there was an Israel, as Hebrews from Eber. Even Josephus admits that the term Hebrew was never a term reserved for only Israelites. Abraham was not an Israelite, as the nation did not even exist yet until Jacob was named so. Josephus characterizes that all the lineage of Eber are Hebrews, as the word Hebrew is actually Eberim, the plural form of Eber.

*"...and his son was **Heber**; from whom they originally called the Jews Hebrews."*
– "The Antiquities of the Jews 1.6:4." Flavius Josephus.

These Hebrews from Joktan continued to serve Yahuah (at least in this small sect), and this is exactly what would be found in their own writings, if the Vatican did not destroy or hide them. Vatican historians, such as Padre Chirino, define all the Filipinos he encountered to be literate; reading and writing in their own language. They were reading something. Where is it Vatican? You were in charge, which was your own desire, to conquer.

The same paradigm that lost this information, then scoffs, demanding one produce an original copy. They reject works like ***Revelation of the Magi***, not because they prove them invalid, but because they are too uneducated to understand Psalm 72 has always provided this geography, which is affirmed in Matthew 2. They dismantle the story and reassemble it without the instruction manual; throwing it away, because we are supposed to believe them over what the Bible clearly says. That is their satanic Doctrine of Infallibility, in fact. We proved that position without this new find from the Vatican archives. The notion that we should throw out David's geography, because they can't read, and don't believe the Bible is the position of satanists. When they behave in such a manner, they deserve the label.

As the test deepens, one must address the elephant in the room here. If, in fact, these names are from the Land of Gold, known as Ophir, Sheba and Tarshish and the Garden of Eden, then there should be at least remnants of some of these patriarchs in their names. If there were not, it would not disprove the obvious geography, but this is the next logical step in testing, which is what we are conducting here. It turns out this is in fact the case, as we can find residual elements of the names Ophir, Sheba, Tarshish, and even Ophir's brother Havilah, who is named after that very land of Adam and Eve, all within the names of the Magi. That is impossible unless there is such connection. Then, we can take the names of Ophir's brothers who migrated to the Philippines with him, and see if we can find some remnants of their names as well.

Remnants of the Name Ophir in the Names of the Magi:

Even in tradition, Filipinos are known to give themselves a high five exclaiming "aphir." The Magi, *Gud-APHAR* is most likely a form of Ophir which is never actually spelled *O-P-H-I-R* in Ancient Hebrew. The Bible Ophir is actually *A-U-P-R* or *A-U-P-I(Y)-R*.

Ophir: אופר: *Aupr:* אופיר: *Aupi(y)r: Ophir, the name of a son of Joktan, and of a gold region in the East:—Ophir (H211).*

This name survives within the name *Gudaphar* which is not an Indian king, and this makes perfect sense.

Gudaphar: (Likely Hebrew referencing the Land of Creation, Philippines)
gud: Hebrew: גוד: *to invade, attack (H1464).*
aphar: Hebrew: עפר: *dry earth, dust as in Gen. 2:7 in the land of Creation (H6083).*

Remnants of the Name Sheba in the Names of the Magi:

The name *Sheba* is one of the most misunderstood names we have found, as scholars fail to even include *Sheba* from Joktan (as they only erroneously assume he must be the one from Ham, which is illiterate). They even admit *Saba* is an appropriate way to express *Sheba* (and we agree). It does not lead to Yemen, however. Imagine, the Magi named Sahban is literally *Sheba* or *Seba* in name. Wow!

שבא: *Sh^ebâ, S-B-A; Sheba, the name of three early progenitors of tribes and of an Ethiopian district:–Sheba, Sabeans. (Note: this definition in Strong's is false propaganda and oblivious that there are indeed two Shebas in Gen. 10, not three and one is not from Ham and would have no place in Africa in any sense. That is illiterate and does not belong in any Bible concordance. The second Seba is brother of Ophir from Shem and migrated to the Far East to the Garden of Eden land in Gen. 10:25-30.)*

Sahban: (Exact Filipino word match)
saban: Bisayan: propeller (Davao local).
sahab: Tagalog: heat that is steaming off; vapor; steam; fumes.[1]
sahà: Tagalog: banana tree skin/sheath.[1]
sahí': Hiligaynon: special, distinct, distinguished.[7]
ban: Tagalog: wheel.[1]
bána: Hiligaynon: husband.[7]
sabihan: to tell something to someone; to give notice to someone; to admonish someone.[1]
sab-an: Waray: tell[5]
sabang: Waray: Mouth of the river.[5]

The son of this King is called *King of Sâbhâ*, according to ***The Book of the Cave of Treasures***. This is *Sheba* and *Seba* and very close to Sabah, Malaysia which is part of the Philippines historically. *Seba* means territory of *Sheba* in Psalm 72. ***The Book of Adam*** lists this name as *Basantar, King of Saba*. That confirms King David's geography from Psalm 72 indisputably.

The Book of the Cave of Treasures lists Nasardih as "*PEROZADH, the King of Sheba, which is in the East.*" That is not Ham's Africa. This is a direct tie to *Sheba* or *Seba* in these names. It is time to forego complacent scholarship that has never researched this adequately and test this complete narrative logically.

Remnants of the Name Tarshish in the Names of the Magi:

Tarshish (תרשיש: *T-R-S-I-S: taršîš*) was son of *Javan* (יון: *Yawan: or the Greek Ioanan*), father of Greece, whose ships were used to bring Ophir, Sheba and Havilah to the Philippines. Clearly, Tarshish received property in Ancient Havilah as payment for his risk and service. One can observe all the elements of the word *Tarshish*, in the Magi named *Artahsisat*, with even the same linguistic accents on the two s's. The King of Spain hired explorers to travel to *Tarshish* and Ophir together in Southeast Asia. Spain was never *Tarshish*. That is stupid.

Artahšišat: (Artahshesht in the Book of the Bee)
Arta: name of the Negrito tribe in Quirino Province, Philippines.[3]
Artá: **Tagalog:** 1. a suffix used to form nouns and adjectives with a feminine gender.
2. an interjection expressing doubt or a pause in speech.; aha!; uh-oh!; oops!; hm![1]
sisáp: **Tagalog:** sycophantic; overly ingratiating or obsequious; suck-up; flatterer; toady; bootlicker.[1]
sisante: **Tagalog:** dismissal; deposing.[1]

With these elements in mind, we can confidently conclude that Psalm 72's geography of the Kings of Tarshish, Sheba and Ophir was accurate all along. It is the location of the origin of the Magi, once and for all, thanks to **Revelation of the Magi**. It was never a scholarly position to ignore it. It was always literal geography leading to the Philippines.

Remnants of the Names of Ophir's Other Brothers:

Another route that would make sense would be to explore some of Ophir's other brothers existing within these Magi names as well. They all migrated with Joktan, Ophir, Sheba and Havilah in Genesis 10:30. As there are thirteen sons in total, we already established *Havilah*, as the Latinized form of the name. It is there, as well as Ophir and Sheba. *Tarshish* is not in their family, but his famous ships carried the brothers to ancient Havilah, in which he received a portion (obviously as payment for services). However, can this possibly be yet more evidence of the connection between the Magi, the Land of Gold and Garden of Eden?

Almwadad, Brother of Ophir:

Ophir's oldest brother is *Almodad* in the KJV. Though close, that is not quite accurate to Ancient Hebrew. The ו is really a *W*, making the more accurate spelling *Almwadad*. This is Hebrew in Genesis 10, not any other language.

אלמודד: *A-L-M-W-D-D: probably of foreign derivation Almodad, a son of Joktan:—Almodad. (Almwadad reflected accurately)*

When we match this more appropriate rendering to the names of the Magi, we have a mixed word that appears to have the name Almwadad within.

Zaharwandad:

zâhar: Hebrew: זהר*: to gleam; figuratively, to enlighten (by caution):—admonish, shine, teach, (give) warn(-ing) (H486).*

This etymology in Hebrew appears directly, Wandad, from Almwadad, and he is a teacher (or similar role). Perhaps the shine refers to the very Star that appeared, and he and his generations taught the Prophecy of the Star. This could not be a more appropriate name for a Magi. The similarities to this word, as *Wadwad*, one of the other Magi (the name derives from the Filipino languages), is also potentially synergistic.

The name *Zarwand* also appears to be a shortened form of *Zaharwandad*. These names lead to at least two other names on the list, that originate through Ophir's brother.

Obal, Brother of Ophir:

עובל*:* '*Ôwbâl, o-bawl'; of foreign derivation; Obal, a son of Joktan:—Obal (H5745).*

The Hebrew letter *Ayin*, "ע," is silent, thus this is rendered *O-B-L, U-B-L,* or *W-B-L* in Ancient Hebrew pronunciation. Though it is a very short name, and some will object (without basis), this appears to be the name of *Bil,* from the Magi list of names. Once again, modern concordances ignorantly show a word that is clearly Hebrew in origin, as "of foreign derivation". These are not linguists. They do not know geography and go to the wrong lands to conduct wordplay in ScholarScrabble. Their notion of *Obal* ever living in or near Saudi Arabia is baseless, and thus, they begin from the wrong foundation from multiple tracks. This could also even be a corruption of *Yobab,* Ophir's youngest brother, who migrated to the Philippines with the family.

Bîl:

bili: Bisayan: value, worth.[2]
bilís: Tagalog: speed; quickness; fast.[1]
bilik: Eskaya: beautiful.[4]
bilog: Ilokano: a boat travel on the water.[6]

One can go deeper in this journey though connections are not as firmly grounded. However, possibilities exist in etymology for other brothers of Ophir who migrated to the Philippines and are the origin of the Magi. Anyone uncomfortable beyond the point at which we already arrived can advance to the next chapter.

Hazarmaveth, Brother of Ophir:

חצרמות: *H-Ts-R-M-U-T ḥăṣarmāvet̲: from H2691 and H4194; village of death; Chatsarmaveth, a place in Arabia:–Hazarmaveth (H2700). Court of death.*

The concordances render the origin of this word in two words.

חצר: *H-Ts-R: châtsêr, khaw-tsare'; (masculine and feminine); from H2690 in its original sense; a yard (as inclosed by a fence); also a hamlet (as similarly surrounded with walls):– court, tower, village.*
Note: This is a rendering in Yiddish, not Ancient Hebrew. H-Ts-R is not kasar which would lead one to the Russian Steppes peoples erroneously.

This word *Hatsar* derives from the root חצר: **ḥāṣar** *(H-Ts-R still)* which is actually the same word and should be the same definition in Ancient Hebrew. This word means: *to sound a trumpet*, as in worship; this is what Levite trumpeters did before the Ark of the Covenant *(see 1 Chron. 15:24)*. The Magi were priests as well. The corrupt Masoretic Text (from which most English translations of the Bible originate) added vowel points and changed words that are the exact same in structure, but different in definition. That is nonsense that needs to be rooted out of Bible scholarship. It is a strong delusion indeed.

The other root word, according to concordances, is: מות: *M-W-T* or *M-U-T* meaning *death (H4194)."*

Could this actually be a reference to the Garden of Eden in which the Hebrew word, *gan*, actually means *enclosure*, as well as *garden?* Again, as a corrupt form, *Hormizd* could well be *H-T-R-M-U-T*, the fifth son of Joktan and brother of Ophir. If in transliteration, for instance, the final *T* is actually *Tsad* instead of *Tet*, that would explain the *Z-D* sound on the end as well. We cannot prove this, but it is worthy of consideration especially in lieu of all else.

Hôrmizd: (Hor in Book of Adam)
hirám: Tagalog: borrowed. Name of Solomon's admiral who went to Ophir for gold.[1]
isadsád: Tagalog: to beach something; to cause something to run aground.[1]
isá-dalawá: Tagalog: one or two.[1]

Sheleph/Selep, Brother of Ophir:

We cannot directly connect *Sheleph*, other than to speculate that perhaps *Austazp* is a corrupt form. *AU* is for *Auphir*, which is the origin of the chemical symbol for gold as it is the origin of the Latin word *Aurea*. *Stazp* is essentially a corrupt form of *S-L-P*, which is *Sheleph* (שלף: H8026). We cannot prove this any further, but even still, one cannot rule out that in its original form, this also may be a match.

Possibilities also exist for Ophir's other brother *Uzal*, within this word, but not solidly. Again, this is not primary evidence nor a position, but testing.

Auštazp: (Possibly Filipino)
astá: Tagalog: posture; demeanor; action; act; acting; aspect; how a person carries oneself.[1]
sapà: Tagalog: stream; brook; creek; river.[1]

Diklah, Brother of Ophir:

Diklah is another word that appears corrupted, and leans into Mesopotamian origins (in ignorance). One thing we know for sure is no concordance should ever assume *Diklah* or his brothers ever lived in or near Saudi Arabia. Of course, these same supposed experts in linguistics fail the test of geography and then claim a Hebrew word of Hebrew origin from Genesis 10 must be "foreign." Also, the word, in Ancient Hebrew, had no vowel points and the letters we have are *D-K-L-H*. This may well be found in the name of the Magi, *Merodak*, which is clearly a corrupted form attempting to stretch the etymology to Persia (which fails, even according to translator Landau, in his own words). Would this be better in derivation from *Meron-Dako?*

דקלה: Diqlâh, dik-law'; of foreign origin; Diklah, a region of Arabia:—Diklah. (H1853).

Merôdak: (likely Filipino origin)
meron: Tagalog: to have; has; possesses. exists; there are; there is.[1]
dako: Tagalog: direction; part; region; spot; around; around (+time).[1]
miron: Bisayan: beggar, moocher, scrounger.[2]
dako: Bisayan: big, great, large.[2]
miridu: Eskaya: husband.[4]
merkado: Waray: marketplace.[5]
Other: merkadohan, markado, marusdak, murado, murasak.[5]

We do not find *Jerah* (which is erroneous) among the rest of these names. His is the actual Hebrew word for *moon, Yerah (ירח)*, which is never rendered with a J. This added letter never existed in the Hebrew language until about 1500 A.D.. *Hadoram, Uzal,* and *Abimael* also appear to have no connections to these Kings, at least in name.

Finally, we see no connection to *Jobab* directly in these names either. However, *Yobab (no "J"),* is very curious as etymologically one must wonder if this leads to Job writing in the days when they lived in a land named for his brother *Uzal* as *UZ.* Perhaps in time research will bear this out.

However, the fact that we can find direct associations to Ophir, Sheba, and

Havilah from Joktan as well as Tarshish is impressive especially in lieu of the firm linguistic origin of the word *Magi* from the Tagalog royalty: *Maginoo*. Additionally, the Filipino words for *prayer* and *silence* originate in the *Mag/Magi* word family, just as **Revelation of the Magi** specifies must be the case. However, *Jobab* has a tradition that may tie with derivatives of his daughters' names possibly existing in the Magi.

Jobab, Son of Joktan in the East:

Though it is not scripture, the **Book of Jasher** also possesses a very odd claim in geography. It says Levi and Issachar went all the way to the East to get wives from the daughters of *Jobab*, the youngest brother of Ophir. That would be called the Philippines today.

Jasher 45:5 (Jasher is Not Scripture)
"And Levi and Issachar went to the land of the east, and they took unto themselves for wives the daughters of Jobab the son of Yoktan, the son of Eber; and Jobab the son of Yoktan had two daughters; the name of the elder was Adinah, and the name of the younger was Aridah."

The daughters bear Hebrew names it appears which would make the most sense. *Adinah*'s root, linguistically, is Eden. Imagine that in the Land of the Garden of Eden. Wow!!! *Aridah* is defined *as one who is freed*. Logically, this fits as Ophir and brothers were essentially freed from Shinar's grasp when they relocated to the Philippines. In Tagalog, one can even see what the true, ancient root of the word for *sibling, ading* might be, as these are famous sisters. We cannot hold to *The Book of Jasher* as absolute truth (as it contains occult concepts), but the Garden of Eden and Land of Gold in the Philippines is the opposite. It is the occult and controllers of world governments who do not want this connection to be made. When such dynamic occurs, one knows it must be the truth unedited.

Adinah: Hebrew: עדינא*: pleasant, luxurious. Root* עדן *('eden; A-D-N).*
Aridah: Hebrew: ארידתא*: Aridatha: very free one, lion's law.*

In making name associations from the Magi, *Nasardîh* rings similar as containing the name of *Aridah* within. In assessing *Adinah*, *Baladan* may well include her name. We cannot connect these firmly, but the similarities are interesting. Perhaps Jobab is there in these names similar to his daughters. We cannot vouch for this new **Book of Jasher** (which cannot be the ancient one mentioned in the books of Joshua and Samuel). However, one must wonder where this geography derived, as it certainly affirms **Revelation of the Magi,** and really, all of scripture on this point. We do find affirmation for the concept of Peleg's lineage taking wives from among the daughters of Joktan in Pseudo Philo 4:10[1] and Chronicles of Jerahmeel 27:5.[2] Resources from **Mount Ophir** being used in Israel, prior to Solomon, are also referenced in *Pseudo-Philo* 26:11.[1]

Remnants of Sephar in the Names of the Magi:

Another probable relation here is the word *Sephar* (ספר) from Genesis 10:30. This is the land to which Ophir and brothers migrated. It is a reference to the Tree of Life in the Garden of Eden. Notice, the name *Zahar-wadad* could actually be *Sephar*, as half of the word, with the other half being Ophir's eldest brother, *Almwadad* (אלמודד), who resided in *Sephar/Sophir/Shir*. Also, is the land of *Shir* actually a corrupt form of *Sephar*, as well? One must wonder whether *Arsak*, the Magi, is a corrupted/shortened form of *Arphaksad*, the ancestor of Joktan and Peleg.

The Magi commenced in Ophir, Sheba, and Tarshish, which is already outlined in Psalm 72. This is the isles of the Far East known today as the Philippines. As far as linguistics are concerned, many Filipino words can be connected to Ancient Hebrew. Even their ancient alphabet, *abakada*, begins with the letter **Abba**, and ends with the letter **Yah**. Wow!!! That nation is beginning to awaken, recognizing their physical and spiritual enemies, and it will rise up in the Last Days. No one can subvert the prophesies of Jesus *(Yahusha)* in Matthew 12:42 *(Luke 11:31)*, Isaiah in 60:9, nor Ezekiel in 38:13. As the Philippines learns its true history, even from the Bible, revival is eminent. Keep your eyes on the Isles of the Magi as they return to the world scene, restoring the worship of the Creator.

In that relationship, the Magi did not desire a shrine with their bones. They are not to be venerated as gods, and they would not wish to have a day set aside for themselves, when they were all about the worship of the Messiah for thousands of years. They would offer the opposite in practice. They were the men of silence and prayer who rocked the world with their actions. No, they were not monks in any sense. No shrine is necessary.

These holy men would never take away from funding the Messiah's ministry and celebrating His birth. The Bible is about Him, and anything that detracts from Him becomes an idol/obstacle to true worship, in spirit and in truth. May we all discover the relationship with our Savior that these Wise Kings once had, long before colonialism, and restore it. The following chart will serve to recap these names into categories and percentages.

---

[1] *"The Old Testament Pseudepigrapha, Vol. 2: Pseudo-Philo." Edited By James H. Charlesworth. Doubleday, New York. 1985. p. 308, 311.* [2] *"Chronicles of Jerahmeel." By M. Gaster. Oriental translation fund, London. 1899.*

Wadwad (Tagalog, Bisayan, Ilokano)
Artaban (Arta, Tagalog)
Humam (Tagalog, Bisayan)
Santarôk (Tagalog, Bisayan)
Baladan (Arta, Tagalog)
Arîhô/ Îryâhô (Bisayan, Tagalog)
Mihruq (Eskaya, Ibanag, Tagalog) [twice]
Overlapping:
Merôdak (Waray, Eskaya, Tagalog, Bisayan)
Sahban (Hiligaynon, Bisayan, Tagalog, Waray)
Ahširaš (Tagalog)

Based on the data compiled in this chapter.

Unknown:
Šûšrawan
Aršak
Aštanbôzan
Kosrau

Shir: Sophir *(Greek):* **Sephar** *(Hebrew):*
Philippines: *Surigao/Siargao (Shir-gaw)*

Even Jobab & Daughters in the East

Hawîlat (Havilah)
Gudaphar (Aupir/Ophir)
Sahban (Sheba)
Zaharwandad (Almwadad)
Zarwand (Almwadad)
Artahšišat (Tarshish)
Bîl (Obal)
Ahširaš (King of Saba/Seba)
Nasardîh (King of Sheba)
Merôdak (Diklah)
Hôrmizd/Hor (Hasarmavet)
Auštazp (Sheleph)

Apostle Thomas Arrives:

AdobeStock.

Prophecy of Messiah Comes to Pass:
"RotM 19:6 And together, you will be witnesses for me in the land of the East together WITH MY DISCIPLES, those who are chosen by me to preach the Gospel."

"RotM 21:5 And again, you have been deemed worthy to be witnesses for me in the East WITH MY DISCIPLES, who were chosen by me before the world came to be."

"…I shall send to you some of my chosen ones who have been chosen by me for your land. And they shall speak and witness the truth with you that it may be your seal with one accord."

FIRST CENTURY REVIVAL IN THE PHILIPPINES
A LOST HISTORY RESTORED

RotM 29:1 When, again, Judas Thomas went down there (the land of the Magi) by the will of our Lord when he sent him, again the faith increased all the more in those who heard, through the many mighty works and signs that Judas Thomas, the apostle of our Lord, was doing there. 29:2 And when the nobles (Maginoo: Magi) had heard that Judas had gone there, as the light that appeared to them had said, they gathered together and went to him to meet with him in prayer and faith. And they saluted Judas with complete love, rejoicing in our Lord. 29:3 And Judas also greatly rejoiced with them, and while they were with him for (several) days, they related to Judas how they were deemed worthy to receive from the first day this gift of light of the world, and about their ascent to him at Bethlehem and everything that was spoken with them, and about the revelations and visions that they saw there in the cave, and about their descent, how he, in his light, accompanied their entire encampment with many visions and revelations. 29:4 And when Judas the Apostle recognized that the gift of our Lord had overflowed upon them, he also related to them about our savior while all the brethren were gathered together as one, and about the mighty works, and healing, and wonders, which he did in the very sight of his apostles, and about the forms of his images, and about his astounding appearances, about which we are not able to narrate, since he was always appearing to us so that we were amazed by him, and we stood in the outpouring and in the doubt of mind, since no one had ever appeared in such a way in the days of the world.

Indeed, many have heard that tradition tells us the Apostle Thomas made it as far as India, where he was killed. We believe that is a later manipulation of this original account. Of all places on Earth for the Apostles to visit, the land of the Magi would have been first on the list, especially since Jesus *(Yahusha)* promised. Some of the Lost Ten Tribes of the Northern Kingdom are said to have been there. The connection between Ophir and Israel is familial and allied, so they would have been welcomed. The Northern Kingdom had no other allies in that era except Babylon, after they released them from captivity. That is it. Even the Southern Kingdom was not allied with the North, at that time, and still remains so to this day. This division will continue until the Latter Days, according to much prophecy.

Again, we are not submitting **Revelation of the Magi (RotM)** for induction into Bible Canon, but as it vets accurate, we will treat it as a valid history. The Catholic and Protestant Churches have accepted far less documented texts that violate their own criteria in a double standard. We simply ignore their false paradigms when testing. Now that we know the geography and linguistics of this document are accurate, this account has no less affinity to scripture.

Revelation of the Magi calls the Magi *the nobles,* and we know *noble* originates in their land of nativity in the Philippines. The *MAGInoo*, the ancient royal/noble class of the Philippines were the Magi. Imagine, Catholic Colonialism came and conquered the land of the Three Kings, trying to cover up that they stole the gold, of Ophir and resources of the very land of Creation, which houses the Garden of Eden and Holy of Holies. You will notice they did not, as Solomon, trade for this gold but stole it; plundering, raping, killing, and destroying the Land of Creation. That is not an existence of a Biblical ekklesia in any sense. To know history, is to not be Catholic despite the control lines planted that claim the opposite.

The Magi address the visions and revelations they saw in the Star, which was the Messiah Himself, not an angel and certainly never an astrological nor astronomical anomaly. The *Gospel of Matthew* says no different on that but discounts that insertion as illogical. They saw the Messiah in different forms, meaning at different ages of His life, prophetically. Thomas heard this and affirmed their visions as accurate, sharing the actual life of Jesus *(Yahusha)*. Please don't tell us there are scholars who do not believe people of the Bible, especially holy men, known to serve Yahuah for many generations, receive heavenly visions. Anyone of that mindset is no Bible believer, as there are many accounts of visions among the prophets and apostles.

Even Paul saw the physical manifestation of the Light of Jesus *(Yahusha)* on the road to Damascus in this same age *(Acts 9)*. The voice of the Son came from that Light exactly as ***Revelation of the Magi*** recounts in their experiences. The others with Paul did not see Jesus *(Yahusha)*, exactly as the Magi describe in their account that no one else saw Him *(Acts 9:7)*. Once again, that tests as scriptural in concept. Those who scoff demonstrate they are not Bible believers. This account continues with a vision of Jesus *(Yahusha)* to Ananias *(Acts 9:10)*. If a scholar does not believe He operates through visions and revelation in these senses, they are not Bible scholars.

RotM 29:5 And when all the brethren heard what Judas related to them, they all glorified with one voice the Lord of heavenly majesty through his Son, the will of perfect salvation. And they sought from Judas, the apostle of our Lord, to make them partakers with him in the seal of our Lord. 29:6 And Judas said: "My brothers, I also rejoice, because it is for this gift that I was sent in salvation (Yahusha), since everyone who believes in salvation (Yahusha) and with love receives the seal of my Lord Jesus Christ in truth, the Enemy does not rule over."

Revelation of the Magi reads similar to the *Book of Acts*. It occurs in that era and has elements of scripture regardless of whether one votes it as Bible Canon (which is not needed for proof of validity). There is history and geography in ***Revelation of the Magi*** that proves historic. Anyone that believes we ignore all of history and only rely on the Bible, has never actually tested the Bible, which vets as accurate because of such history. We prove this all the time, and this account is very similar in that regard. Before Jesus *(Yahusha)* chose any disciples or Apostles, the Filipinos of Ancient Ophir, Sheba, and Tarshish were chosen as His vessels. They not only brought Him wealth of the world from their Land of Gold and the Garden of Eden, but they also witnessed to their fellow inhabitants as disciples. This final account sparks a great revival, much like we read about in the *Book of Acts*. Here, they wish to be partakers with the Apostle Thomas and the other Apostles in salvation and they go out and share it with everyone.

What is very clear in this passage is the name of Yahusha is used and the translator left it as "salvation" which is the same word. One does not believe in "salvation," they believe in Jesus *(Yahusha)* which meaning is "salvation." Thomas was not sent in the name of "salvation" but in the name of Jesus *(Yahusha)* which indeed means "salvation." That is an error a translator should not make but this one did.

The Apostle Thomas then broke into song, accurately terming Jesus *(Yahusha)* as the *"mystery of salvation (30:2)," "hidden mystery (30:3)," "birth of salvation (30:6, 9),"* and *"firstborn (30:7)."* These are very scriptural in basis, and everything Thomas said and did fits the Biblical paradigm, just as all the Magi said and did coalesce, as well. When one goes to the Gnostic accounts of Thomas, that is the opposite. They focus on the light of Kabbalah in an esoteric fashion. That is never Jesus *(Yahusha)*. As they are known to copy and manipulate, it is very obvious **Revelation of the Magi** is the origin of their accounts they changed to lead to the occult (as Gnostics do). Their manipulation proves **Revelation of the Magi** is the origin, which is not corrupt.

Thomas prayed that their bodies would become the temple of Yah, His temple *(30:9)*, adhering to scripture *(1 Cor. 6:19-20)*. As Thomas continued, he proceeded to baptize the Magi, in the name of the Father, Son, and Holy Spirit *(31:1)*. Once again, that is Bible in origin from the Gospels *(Matt. 28:19)*.

At that time, Jesus *(Yahusha)* appeared in the form of a child saying *"Peace be with you, sons of all my mysteries. And behold, now all the visions and revelations that you saw from the first day have been accomplished in your birth (31:1)."* Then, He appeared in the form of a young man, and He took a loaf of bread, broke it, and passed it around *(31:2)*. This is never referred to in scripture as as The Eucharist (which Landau injects in error), nor was it the seven sacraments of the Catholic Church (whose origin is from the occult). It was not the two sacraments pushed by "light Catholic" churches, Lutheran and Episcopalian, either. Jesus *(Yahusha)* returned to Heaven, from whence he came, consistent with all scripture *(31:3)*.

The account ends with a great revival like that of Acts, but this time, in the Philippines in the first century, beginning with the Magi. The Catholic Church did not bring Jesus *(Yahusha)*. He came Himself; the Magi brought Him, and so did the Apostle Thomas. Oops! These all outrank the Pope in scripture, regardless of his claim! They also precede the existence of the Catholic Church, which was not a continuation of the Biblical ekklesia, but those who *crept in unawares (Jude 1:4)*. They changed the Bible, and they hid accounts like **Revelation of the Magi.**

***RotM 31:9** And while they were delighted greatly in thanksgiving, and prayer, and visions of our Lord, a multitude of brethren were added to the faith day by day.*

Thomas also understood the Light of the World was Jesus *(Yahusha)* and proclaimed that the Magi and all those with them were to share the Gospel and the Light of Jesus *(Yahusha)* to the entire world, quoting Messiah's words in the Great Commission. We all know this. No, Thomas did not have to wait for the New Testament to be written to remember those words. Anyone saying so is no scholar. How could anyone think the Magi met Messiah as a toddler, having His Light appear to them, and they just forgot about it after that. Of course they would partake in the Bible ekklesia.

RotM 31:10 And Judas said to them: "Therefore, my brethren, let us fulfill the commandment of our Lord, who said to us: 'Go out into the entire world and preach my Gospel (Mark 16:15).' So, my brethren, be you also preachers of the Word like us, because you have also received the gift of our Lord. Also go out to every place and preach the gift of our light and of our savior generously to everyone."

The Magi took up the banner of disciples and went forth into *"every place,"* preaching *"in perfect love about the coming of our Lord Jesus Christ (32:1)."* They performed *"mighty works and healings in the name of our Lord."* This was done through the Holy Spirit who was *"poured out on them."* The Holy Spirit is the Teacher after all. They preached salvation by the *"perfect Light"* of the World, Jesus *(Yahusha)*, not in an occult manner, but according to the doctrine of the Bible, since the time of Genesis 1:2, that they well understood.

Two Revivals in the Philippines: First Century B.C. - A.D.

Not only was there revival when the Apostle Thomas arrived in ancient Ophir, there was a great revival prior to that in the Philippines. Before there were disciples and Apostles in the New Testament, a spiritual surge already began in the land of the Three Kings. Historically speaking, (though many falsely claim there is no history of the Philippines prior to Magellan in 1521), there were two great revivals in this Land of the Magi in the first century B.C. to A.D. Of course, all written history by Filipinos was discarded by the Spanish Catholics with the Pope's blessing. This document preserved by the Vatican was originally written by Filipinos, in fact. It survives! The Papacy did not want the world to know they conquered the already Biblical Land of the Magi. Oops! This is why the Vatican left this document uninterpreted for 1,200 years.

RotM 14:9 And when all these things and others like them, of which there were many, (happened,) while descending the Mountain of Victories, we gave praise and repeated to each other everything that we saw and heard there. And we were in great rejoicing and great exultation that we were thought worthy to see this complete gift of salvation for which all the kings, and righteous ones, and prophets, and powerful ones prayed, and hoped, and waited, that they might see this sight. But they did not see it...

The incubation period for a great revival began in the hearts of the Magi. They shared this with their families and others who would come together upon their return and experience a great awakening. This awakening is about to erupt again.

1. The Maginoo's Return from Bethlehem

*RotM 27:1 And when we journeyed on all (our stages) with his glorious signs until we **came to our borders**, and all **our families, children, and a multitude of the people of our land** came out to meet us. And when they heard that we had come, they met us with great joy and received us, rejoicing, and exulting, and glorifying. And they marveled at our appearance and the health of our entire encampment. And when we went to them, they assembled and came before us. And we began to speak and narrate for them **about how our ascent took place**, and **about the astounding visions that accompanied us**, and **about our entrance into Jerusalem**, and **about everything that was spoken with us**, and **about our journeying to Bethlehem**, and **about the glorious visions and revelations of the Father** of heavenly majesty, which **appeared to us in the cave: a great light and wondrous appearances in the bodily form of a humble human being, and about his light of the star, which went before us as a glorious guide.**

*RotM 27:6 And we offered him gifts that we took from the Cave of Treasures, which were **deposited by our fathers from his own**. And we **worshipped him, the Lord of worship,** and **he opened his splendid and glorious mouth and spoke [salvation] with us** as we were able and sufficient to hear it, and this way **he planted the word of salvation in us.** 27:7 And he **spoke and revealed** to us concerning **the place of salvation** and concerning **the heavenly kingdom of the Father** of majesty, the Lord of all, **who sent him for the healing of the worlds, to cure their sickness, because they could not be healed by one of the ancient prophets, but only through the will of the Son** of perfect mercy. 27:8 And **he dismissed us to come to our land in peace...**

As the people heard this message, they rejoiced. They even ate of the provisions of the Magi from their journey, which replenished before their eyes. This miracle led to many seeing visions of the Messiah just as the Magi did prior. They saw him in the different stages of his life as a child, an adult, on the cross, and ascending.

*RotM 28:5 And they came and heard from them the new and glorious teaching, and the mysteries, and the revelations, and everything that was spoken with them from that first day that they went out from their land until they came back in joy. And again, **day by day, revelations, and visions, and all kinds of powerful manifestations were increased for them. And the faith increased with the love of the testimony of our Lord Jesus Christ, by the mighty works which he did through them,** that **offspring of light who appeared to them** until **he accomplished** the will of the one who sent him in everything and was taken up with glory to that heavenly light, his first abode. **And the faith of salvation (Yahusha) increased in the land of the East in those who heard.**

Note: translator Landau forgot that the name of Jesus Christ occurs before the Thomas account and the Magi most certainly knew the name and used it.

2. The Apostle Thomas Arrives, Nationwide Revival Explodes

However, this story does not end here. The final revival is coming to the Philippines and the world, and this one will never end. We have entered the Last Days, when the Final Empire is rising to power right now. This is the day when Yahuah said He will pour out His Spirit on all flesh. Just as the Apostles and the Magi, whose experience cannot be separated, we will dream dreams and see visions once again. The days of the Acts of the Apostles have returned.

Joel 2:28-29 KJV
And it shall come to pass afterward, that I will pour out my spirit upon all flesh; and your sons and your daughters shall prophesy, your old men shall dream dreams, your young men shall see visions: And also upon the servants and upon the handmaids in those days will I pour out my spirit.

Jesus *(Yahusha)* declared this in prophecy very specifically regarding these native Isles of the Magi, that turns out to be the very Land of Gold; Ophir, Sheba, and Tarshish. This is the location of the Garden of Eden and Holy of Holies on Earth since Creation, not the temporary one in Israel. As this region has connected in history and geography for 6,000 years, as we have documented, it is also the most significant land in the Bible, period.

Modern Israel is called "spiritual Sodom and Egypt" in Revelation 11 and is where the Harlot of Babylon has risen to power. The Antichrist will declare he is God there, and the final world capital will be established there. This is because its Mass Aliyah from 1948-1952 is an exact match to the powers of Gog of Magog *(Ez. 38)* who attack the land of Israel, seizing it. The Prince Demon Gog's seat of power (according to the *Book of Jubilees* 8-9, when mapped), is actually Western and Central Europe, or the Colonial Powers, as well as the Roman Catholic Church. The same conquered the Land of the Magi. Gog is from Magog *(region of Russia)* in origin but that is not his seat of power *(Tubal and Meshech)*. Though Magog will ally and even be destroyed with the British Isles, it is not the seat. It was the British Empire who seized Palestine and gave it to one man, Lord Rothschild, in the 1917 Balfour Declaration. It is Gog OF Magog, not two powers (as many have misread). They are supposed to fit Isaiah 11 for the supposed return which has not happened, but they fail Isaiah's prophecy in geography by more than 70%. If one gets a "30% or less" score on a test, it would be an "F" no matter the curve. Modern Israel is a resintitution of the Pharisees (who migrated into the Russian Steppes), who were never Hebrews, generally. Scholars have lost track of the physical enemy.

Matthew 12:42 KJV (Luke 11:31)
The queen of the south shall rise up in the judgment with this generation, and shall condemn it: for she came from the uttermost parts of the earth to hear the wisdom of Solomon; and, behold, a greater than Solomon is here.

To this day, Cebu and Iloilo in Visayas carry this same nomenclature of "Queen of the South." That is no surprise. It is a direct reference to the Queen of Sheba, who originated in the Philippines. The Magi knew this. Thomas knew this. So did the Pope, which is why the Catholic Church hid this and continues to assail that nation from within. The Bible paradigm was well aware of the significance of this Land of the Magi all along, until scholars forgot it, about a century ago. However, the position of Pope began attacking this nation early, as he knew they will rise against him. It is time for the Philippines to restore its identity in Him. How does this occur? First, any revival begins with repentance.

We must humble ourselves and make Him first. We pray, seek His very face in pressing into His presence, and turn from our sin. To turn away, is to repent. Go in the opposite direction. This comes with a promise that He will hear, forgive and heal this land. Isn't it time for Ancient Ophir to be healed? As we turn in repentance, He will pour out His Spirit, and release understanding in the days of increasing knowledge that Daniel predicted *(Dan. 12:4)*. Those days are upon us now.

2 Chronicles 7:14 KJV
If my people, which are called by my name, shall humble themselves, and pray, and seek my face, and turn from their wicked ways; then will I hear from heaven, and will forgive their sin, and will heal their land.

Proverbs 1:23 KJV
Turn you at my reproof: behold, I will pour out my spirit unto you, I will make known my words unto you.

Is the Apostle Thomas Episode No Longer a Magi Account?

False criteria have been installed (in the halls of stupid scholarship), to impede any awakening amongst the learned. Well, that is not very educated, is it? In the case of the ***Revelation of the Magi***, the translator does this himself, trying to limit how anyone would view what is clearly very plain English. It makes him appear as if he cannot read. The paradigm places constraints on interpretation, so as to not allow one to even render an accurate understanding. That is what happens, and is accepted in the scholarly community, and this is why no consensus is needed by that group. Their peer reviews alone are daunting to a young graduate scholar, and without a positive review, one is shunned and mocked by seasoned scholars, and denied publishing access by scholarly review. When they concede to be ignorant, that does not equate to a debate point. Landau writes of the Apostle Thomas section in his footnotes:

"Not only does it seem superfluous from a narrative point of view, but it also has a number of literary features that do not fit very well with what has come before. First, the Thomas episode is narrated in the third person, whereas the rest of the Revelation of the Magi is narrated by the Magi themselves, in the first person."

Is it unnecessary for the Magi to record the Apostle Thomas' coming to their native land? Who would even agree with such dunderhead positions? If Thomas came to your home and you were part of a group who had written an account that actually predicts such to happen twice *(19:6, 21:5)*, then one would be negligent. Imagine him thinking he and other scholars have the right as gods to overrule the intent of an author, based on the supposition that they are not allowed to write an historic account as a group. That is not scholarship, it is stupid. Landau claims the writers were not allowed to include an Apostle visiting their region, in a New Testament encounter. This purposely sets up the test for failure. Of course, it cannot meet such false criteria. Nothing could, which is the point in corrupt scholarship. Landau, then, admits his own test is false.

"Although such shifts in the perspective of the narrator are not unheard of in ancient Christian writings, this shift is especially abrupt and unexplained within the narrative."

The only ones demanding such an explanation are Landau and other scholars, in a paradigm of ineptitude, protecting their fraud from being exposed. Who reads like this? Who tries to dismantle a text that proves accurate to scripture because of questions they admit are not even valid? Landau knows this practice happens with scripture other times when he states it is "not unheard of." Essentially, he just said he had no point to begin with. He is merely placating the arena of scholarship (which is utterly illiterate on this topic). We see this with Moses, whose final words appear written by someone else *(Deut. 34)* as well as Psalms; likely written in part by Solomon, King David's son. Then, there is the known practice of using scribes.

"Second, the Thomas episode contains a striking change in terminology as compared with the first-person section of the Revelation of the Magi. One of the most distinctive features of the first-person section is its complete avoidance of the proper name "Jesus Christ," to refer to the divine being whom the Magi encounter. Yet as careful as the author is to forgo this name and other obvious Christian terminology, the Thomas section is not at all concerned to avoid the name "Jesus Christ," using it almost twenty times!" – Brent Landau, translator

Landau just admitted he does not know that "Jesus Christ" is not the proper name of Messiah. The letter "J" cannot be rendered in Ancient Greek, Hebrew, Aramaic, or Latin. In fact, even Old French, Old German, and Old English had no "J" either until the Renaissance, when Ashkenazi (fake Jews) from the Russian

Steppes brought a language they infused into Biblical Hebrew and Greek. One cannot even say the name "Jesus" in either of these ancient languages. It always begins with a "*Y*." This is hypocritic double speak, especially when we realize that Landau erred in translating the Syriac/Latin word for *salvation* into English. It is the very name of *Yahusha* which means *salvation*. Even the writer uses it properly in the section concerning Apostle Thomas, but this word appears throughout the text. In other words, this is a lie, which is what textual criticism breeds; the translators are so determined to scoff, which is what they do, even with Biblical Canonical texts. They will make up debate points in ignorance. This is not even a point, it is untrue.

For a supposed Bible scholar and linguist to not know that "Jesus Christ" is not the name of our Messiah, and is not proper, is already evidence that he has no right to attempt an interpretation; he has no foundation in understanding. His translation is solid. His interpretation is useless. Furthermore, he cannot even read his own translation; the "Thomas episode" begins in Chapter 29, but the name "Jesus Christ" is used in the section prior to that. Landau does not actually explain this in his margin notes effectively, because it is nonsense.

"RotM 28:6a And the faith increased with the love of the testimony of our Lord Jesus Christ..."

The section ends with Yahusha's Hebrew name, even in the last line of 28:7 before the Thomas episode. No, it is not the corrupt form he seeks, but why would a Bible scholar look for such? How could he not notice he translated the Syriac/ Latin form of the name of Yahusha as "salvation" (which is the meaning), but how would he miss that is the name of Messiah? It is the faith of Yahusha which increased. Has he ever read the New Testament?

"RotM 28:7 And the faith of salvation (Yahusha!) increased in the land of the East in those who heard. Because of these reasons (two), I believe that the Thomas episode was a later addition to Revelation of the Magi."

From these two fallacious reasons (which are lies), Landau deduces that the section of **Revelation of the Magi** which introduces the Apostle Thomas is somehow a "later account" (by this he means "corrupted"). He repeats the word "tampering," which he has no right to conclude. That is fraud. Landau lied, and seems incapable of logic concerning this. In his own translation, Messiah says, two times, that He will send His disciples to the East to join with them in one accord *(19:6, 21:5)*. Thomas went to the East (with others, of course), and that is a natural progression for this account that belongs in this text.

He continues with a conclusion that the author of **Revelation of the Magi** must have "used written sources" from the New Testament to which he should not have had access. They, as the Apostles, met Jesus *(Yahusha)* personally; both in the cave, before their journey, and in Bethlehem. He spoke to them both times. The Apostles arrived, but Landau cannot figure out how the Magi would know this information from the New Testament. The translator is not thinking clearly. Jesus *(Yahusha)* did not write down His words yet, the Apostles remembered them, vividly recounting what they heard when they wrote. He also spoke directly to the Magi in the same manner, even about salvation. An inferred foundation of the Magi being "not so bright or committed" seems to be a necessity, in order for the reader to believe Landau's premise. That appears racist and inept. It is time we restore this full narrative to its rightful place as Philippine history. That is where this belongs. One cannot separate ancient Ophir and its practices in association and cooperation with Israel from the Bible.

Chapter 10: When Was Jesus (Yahusha) Born?

Jesus (Yahusha) was born in late Spring in Israel. There was no snow as that is the opposite time of year. The Catholic Church isn't even close, and they know it. AdobeStock.

Would it not sound extreme and brazen for a group to declare they know the actual birthdate of the Messiah? With the language from scholarship, one would indeed think this impossible. However, follow this research and test it for yourself. If nothing else, many will find this compelling. We will begin with the year of our Savior's birth and advance to the month, including the exact day. Can we really do this? It is incredible that we have never reviewed anything coherent about this from modern scholars. It appears the paradigm has collapsed into a hole of blackness on this topic, and from what we are finding, there is no good reason for that.

The Year:

Luke 2:1-4 KJV
*And it came to pass in those days, that there went out **a decree from Caesar Augustus,** that all the world should be taxed. (**And this taxing was first made when Cyrenius was governor of Syria.**) And all went to be taxed, every one into his own city. And Joseph also went up from Galilee, out of the city of Nazareth, into Judaea, unto the city of David, which is **called Bethlehem;** (because he was of the house and lineage of David:)*

We all know Joseph took Mary (who was with child), to Bethlehem, due to the census decree from Caesar Augustus. She did not ride on a donkey all that way as Joseph was not mad at her trying to punish her. That is never a part of any Bible story but more unnecessary embellishment. When was this in terms of years?

When Was the "Empire-Wide" Census of Cyrenius?

This is fairly easy as Emperors did not take a census often. Notice, this is not a local census but an Empire-wide one and anyone going to Josephus the Pharisee for confusion (he writes of a later local audit in 6 A.D.), is simply following the blind leading the blind. That is impossible already and they know it. Pharisees have never been motivated for us to know the actual birthdate. The writer of Wikipedia and other scholars conflict this detail, adding more confusion, which does not exist in this narrative. A census was usually executed at the transfer of power, for the new king or emperor to have a full accounting for his kingdom. Those attempting to move Herod's death (even to fit a bad theory), fail to realize there is no such audit in 1 B.C., or anywhere near it. This is far better documented than many lead us to believe.

First, what was this title of Cyrenius (Quirinius)? Who takes a census? NOT a Governor! In the KJV, this remains in parentheses, meaning the translators were unsure of the exact title. For one to assume this role for a Governor (when the translator spelled out that title was questionable, and needed further testing) is not scholarship. Cyrenius was a Consul, the leadership role with accounting responsibility, who executes a census. He BECAME a governor following the census. In the Greek, the official bore the same title as Pontius Pilate (who also was never a Governor).

ἡγεμονεύω: *hēgemoneúō: be governor (2x). to be leader, to lead the way. to rule, command. of a province, to be governor of a province. said of a proconsul, of a procurator (G2230).*

This title is general for leader, not necessarily Governor. It is used in this same form only one other time for Pilate, who was never Governor. Even in its other forms, it is still a general term for leader. In Luke 3:1, the Governors of a Tetrarchy *(a group of four leaders)* are listed. The ones that are true Governors are called Tetrarchs; Pilate is listed with them as a leader without the same title of Governor/Tetrarch. He would be mentioned as a Tetrarch if he were an actual Governor. This Herod is not Herod the Great, but his son as well.

Luke 3:1 KJV
*Now in the fifteenth year of the reign of Tiberius Caesar, **Pontius Pilate being governor** (**ἡγεμονεύω**: hēgemoneúō) of Judaea, and **Herod being tetrarch** (**τετραρχέω**: tetrarchéō) of Galilee, and his brother **Philip tetrarch** (**τετραρχέω**: tetrarchéō) of Ituraea and of the region of Trachonitis, and **Lysanias the tetrarch** (**τετραρχέω**: tetrarchéō) of Abilene*
ἡγεμονεύω: *hēgemoneúō: ...said of a proconsul, Luke 2:2; of a procurator, Luke 3:1.*[1]

Josephus addressed Pilate as "procurator of Judea."[2] Regardless, a procurator is more of a treasurer or Consul of sort but not a Governor. Certainly, both men had power, but the title matters, as that is what is used inaccurately to claim Luke erred. He did not. Indeed, in smaller provinces these positions had larger responsibilities. There is nothing wrong with the Governor title, if one is not going to then call the Biblical Author, Luke, a liar. Scholars would have to be able to read to understand Luke. Luke never called Cyrenius nor Pilate a Governor. That is poor translation.

Quirinius was Consul of Syria, according to Tacitus, who wrote this around 116 A.D. Quirinius started his position in 12 B.C., and ended about 4 B.C.. The Consul position executed a census, not the Governor, necessarily. Because Quirinius does not become Governor until about 6 A.D. (far too late for the timeline), this must be the period in which Jesus *(Yahusha)* was born. Some scholars assume the second term was ruled by his son, which does not matter, even if it was his second term

---

[1] *Excerpt from Thayer's Greek Lexicon. G2230.* [2] *Josephus. Antiquities of the Jews 18.3.1.*
[3] *Cornelius Tacitus, The Annals 3.48. Complete Works of Tacitus. Alfred John Church. William Jackson Brodribb. Sara Bryant. edited for Perseus. New York. : Random House, Inc. Random House, Inc. reprinted 1942.* [4] *The Oxford Classical Dictionary (3 ed.). Edited by: Simon Hornblower and Antony Spawforth.* [5] *BibleVerseStudy.com.* [6] *Translation into English from: "The Deeds of the Divine Augustus (AD 13-14)." P. A. Brunt & J. M. Moore, Oxford, 1969.*

(but as Governor, or similar this time). If Messiah was born in 6 A.D., all timelines would be misleading, especially those concerning the Emperor (anyone considering that possibility did not test anything to do with this issue). Scholars tend to ignore that Quirinius Sr. was Consul of Syria previous to his Governorship, and that Consul both holds a census and fits the timeline. That is dishonest.

*"About the same time he requested the Senate to let the death of **Sulpicius Quirinus** be celebrated with a public funeral. With the old patrician family of the Sulpicii this Quirinus, who was born in the town of Lanuvium, was quite unconnected. An indefatigable soldier, he had by his zealous services **won the consulship under the Divine Augustus**, and subsequently the honours of a triumph for having stormed some fortresses of the Homonadenses in Cilicia."*[3]

"Sulpicius Quirinius, Publius: Consul 12 BC, a novus homo from Lanuvium (on his career cf. Tacitus Annales 3.48)."[4]

"From 12 BC to 4 BC, Titius, Saturninus and Varus took turns managing Syria's 'domestic' affairs while Quirinius was in charge of Syria's 'external' affairs, not just the war effort against the Homonadenses, since Luke mentions him "governing Syria" (Luke 2:2) at the time of this census in Judea, which was adjacent to and being managed from Syria."[5]

There is only one option for an Empire-wide census under Caeser Augustus that could fit the Biblical time frame, and the *Gospels of Matthew* and *Luke* did not err. It is documented to 8 B.C., in terms of the release of the results. The census would be conducted the year prior in 9 B.C. Gaius Sentinus Saturninus was Governor of Syria at that time, which is no conflict, as Quirinius was Consul under him, and he would be the one to execute a census anyway. Luke never calls him governor.

*"As consul for the fifth time [29 BC] note by order of the people and the Senate I increased the number of the patricians. Three times I revised the roll of the Senate. **In my sixth consulship [28 BC], with Marcus Agrippa as my colleague, I made a census** of the people. I performed the lustrum after an interval of forty-one years. In this lustration 4,063,000 Roman citizens were entered on the census roll. **A second time, in the consulship of Gaius Censorinus and Gaius Asinius, [8 BCE.] I** again performed the lustrum alone, with the consular imperium. In this lustrum 4,233,000 Roman citizens were entered on the census roll. **A third time, with the consular imperium, and with my son Tiberius Caesar as my colleague, [14 AD] I** performed the lustrum in the consulship of Sextus Pompeius and Sextus Apuleius. In this lustrum 4,937,000 Roman citizens were entered on the census roll."*[6]

This is not just Roman record; it is written in stone by Augustus himself or his scribe in his own autobiography. There were only three total censuses to choose from, according to the words of Augustus. Anyone calling themselves an academic or scholar who is not aware of this is speaking in ignorance. The first census in which Augustus participated was the transfer of power to his administration. That was about 28 B.C. as it would be accomplished before he took power in 27 B.C. That

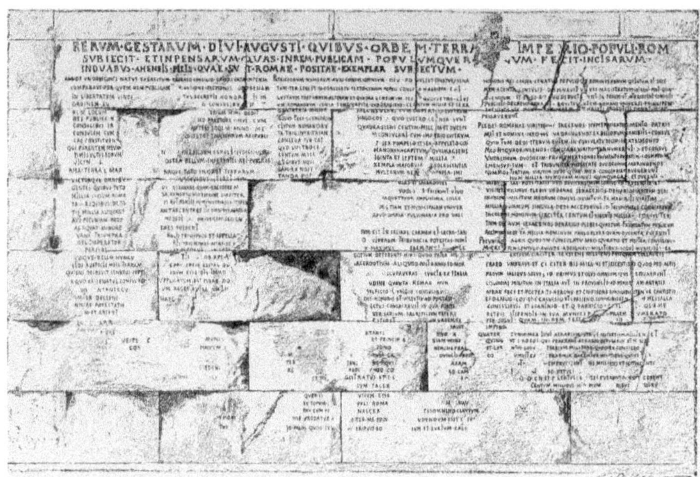

Drawing of the Res Gestae Divi Augusti inscription from "History of Rome and the Roman people, from its origin to the establishment of the Christian empire." By Victor Duruy. London. Contributing Library: Robarts - University of Toronto. Digitizing Sponsor: University of Toronto. Wikimedia Commons. Fair Use Act. Public Domain.

one is obviously not the birth of Jesus *(Yahusha)* as it is not special but customary, and if it were, all timelines would be ridiculously wrong. Neither Luke nor Matthew identifies that one for sure.

The third census was performed in 14 A.D. for the transfer of power to his son Tiberius. That one is far too late, not special, and all corresponding timelines would fail. Academics who seize on either of those are not scholars. The *Gospels of Matthew* and *Luke* rule it out as well. Let us not blame them for the shortcomings of dunderheads.

By process of elimination, using very simple logic of which a scholar should be capable, there is only one census that could even fit. It was a special census, whose results were released in 8 B.C.. Bible scholars know the early birth date of Jesus *(Yahusha)* destroys their unbased theories. Rather than embracing facts, they lie, spinning the narrative. It is not a difficult concept; the year of Jesus' *(Yahusha's)* birth must be 9 B.C., as the census begins.

Only males were generally counted in a Roman census, and this is reflected in the total population figure. The number of four million citizens remains consistent; all Empire-wide. The 8 B.C. date is the Census of Quirinius who was Consol of Syria with Judea under his jurisdiction at that time. His census must be part of the larger one, without question, according to Luke's Gospel. Luke preserved this with a double affirmation right there in the text. Anyone attempting to go in either direction would fail. They must assess both criteria and reconcile them to get the correct answer assuming that is their aim.

An Egyptian papyri, titled Oxyrhychus Papyri, affirms this year as well. As a large population center under Rome's control, Egypt conducted a local census every fourteen years. This pattern began around 10-9 B.C. consistent with Augustus' Empire-wide census.

---

[1]   *Augustan Egypt: The Creation of a Roman Province." Studies in Classics, v. 13. Livia Capponi. First Published 2005. Routledge. New York.*

Luke 3:23 tells us, "Jesus himself began to be about thirty years of age (KJV)." We are aware that scholars claim Messiah was EXACTLY thirty years old in this verse, when Luke worded it as a "ballpark" estimate. No verse in scripture says He was crucified at the satanic, occult number "33" years of age. Even Bible Commentaries, such as Jamieson-Fausset-Brown claim He "...was about thirty years of age when He began (His ministry)...makes better Greek, and is probably the true sense...".[5] He did not just turn 30-years-old which is no way to read that.

When Did Herod the Great Die?

Even one of our favorite scholars, the late Dr. Michael Heiser, tried to move the timeline for the birth year of Messiah by moving the death of Herod the Great. The problem is, no matter what gymnastics are applied, that cannot be done. Herod died in 4 B.C. and Messiah had to be born two years prior to that, at least. Any date for the birth after 6 B.C. fails every test immediately. The Wise Men came and met Herod first in Jerusalem. Therefore, Herod could not be dead prior to this, period. To say so is to claim the Bible is wrong. Josephus defines this with precision and without question. We will address how they selectively manipulate his words.

ToposText Version: 4 B.C.:[1]

§ 1.665 So Herod, having survived the slaughter of his son five days, died, having reigned thirty-four years since he had caused Antigonus to be slain, and obtained his kingdom; but thirty-seven years since he had been made king by the Romans... Event Date: -4 GR (B.C. or B.C.E.)[1]

Harvard Version: 4 B.C.:[2]

Margin: "Accession and promises of Archelaus 4 b.c."

"The necessity under which Archelaus found himself of undertaking a journey to Rome was the signal for fresh disturbances. After keeping seven days' mourning for his father and providing the usual funeral banquet for the populace on a sumptuous scale..."[2]

However, the Rabbis (who really have no right to discuss the Messiah, whom they put to death), agitate the story, and stupid scholars adhere. They enter "Pharisee Storytelling Mode," claiming that Herod died in 1 B.C.. Why? They actually try to use Josephus. They claim Josephus was vague. His declaring 4 B.C. is evidently

---

[1] *Josephus, Of the War, 1.665 (ToposText Web Version 3.0. Aik Aterini Laskaridis Foundation. Josephus, The Jewish War, The Works of Flavius Josephus, translated by William Whiston (1667-17520, Auburn and Buffalo. John E. Beardsley. 1895, a text in the public domain, digitized by the Perseus Project)* [2] *Josephus, Of the War, 2.2.1, Josephus. The Jewish War, Volume I: Book 2. Translated by H. St. J. Thackeray. Loeb Classical Library 203. Cambridge, MA: Harvard University Press, 1927.* [3] *"Antigonus." Jewish Virtual Library. Died 37 B.C. Retrieved Oct. 2025.* [4] *"Antigonus Mattathias." Jewish Encyclopedia. Died 37 B.C. By Louis Ginzberg. Retrieved Oct. 2025.* [5] *Jamieson-Fausset-Brown Bible Commentary on Luke 3:23.*

vague to them. Really? So, they parse out fragments the same way they bastardize scripture, and claim that Josephus said something about a lunar eclipse, then, Herod died and then, it was Passover. They'll ignore he gave the year.

For instance, the former Hasmonean ruler, Antigonus, was beheaded at Herod's order around 37 B.C., according to the Jewish Encyclopedia and Jewish Virtual Library.[3,4] Josephus just wrote: "*...having reigned thirty-four years since he had caused Antigonus to be slain.*" It appears some struggle with simple math. In 14.16.2 & 3 of Antiquities of the Jews,[1] Josephus dates this event at 37 B.C. Where exactly is the debate? There is none. Sure, one can argue a year off potentially, though the year 37 B.C. would count, as he ruled that year, too. Certainly, that would not justify three years in order to get to Herod's death as 1 B.C. This places Herod's death at 4 B.C. period. The Magi came before that. Oops! These are not scholars. They are trying to force an astronomical alignment that could not even match the account anyway. So, they commit fraud and change history, which cannot be done successfully. This is fully exposed in *Revelation of the Magi (RotM)*.

Then, we have the succession, as the kingship was not vacant for long. *The Book of Matthew* discussed that, as Joseph did not take the family from Egypt back to Nazareth until after Herod died. Therefore, there is even a period when they were in Egypt, awaiting Herod's death, and the assumption of 1 B.C. becomes ridiculous. Remember, the Wise Men do not show up for two more years. We know that Herod's successor, Archelaus, was removed from his position in his tenth year in 7 A.D. according to Josephus.[2] Don't forget there is no year 0, so that places the beginning of his reign at 4 B.C. For those that struggle with that math, let us go deeper into Josephus' writing; he is more specific. Archelaus also sailed for Rome after his father's death in 4 B.C., and was accused by his brother of pretending to shed false tears for his father's death; all in 4 B.C., according to Josephus.[3]

Josephus left no wiggle room here. Herod died in 4 B.C.. If he died in 1 B.C., and the Magi came then, that was two years after Jesus' *(Yahusha's)* birth, placing it in 3 B.C., when no planetary alignment occurred. They do not realize they are attempting to move Herod's death to 2 A.D., instead. Jesus *(Yahusha)* then would not be in his thirties at time of death. He was, in our timeline. We understand, scholars have no problem assuming both Luke and Matthew erred, because THEY must know better. They do not.

To move Herod's death, they would also have to move Antigonus' death and reign. They would have to rewrite history for Archelaus' start and removal. Herod's death would be moved into the previous Hebew year, in order to justify the eclipse occurring near Passover (months before). This is all completely illiterate.

Herod died in 4 B.C. and that is not debatable. Stellarium software does not know when Messiah's Star appeared, because He did not appear "in space." He

---

[1] *Josephus, Ant. 14.16.2-3.* [2] *Josephus, Antiq., 17.13.2.* [3] *Josephus, Antiq., 17.9.3-5.*

appeared on the Mount of the East and in the Cave of Treasures. He moved, changing directions multiple times, which no star can execute. *Revelation of the Magi* tells us His Star was brighter than the sun, moon, and stars. In other words, it was not what we would define as a star. The entire train of thought that discussed Jupiter and Venus in this text is occult Astrology, forbidden in scripture. Yahuah does not ever speak of such blasphemy.

When Did the Eclipse Before Passover Occur?

You know it is a Pharisee tactic when a group forgets that Josephus directly pinpointed the year, 4 B.C., as Herod's death (in several ways), but instead, pretends he did not. They try to reform the entire narrative based on vague details in leaven, going backwards. They will recite fragments as they do with scripture in order to change it, saying that Josephus mentioned an eclipse, Herod died, and then they celebrated Passover. The notion is already based on a lie, but we will address that.

In 4 B.C., according to NASA, there was a lunar eclipse about two weeks before Passover on March 23 at 21:17:09. That is an exact match, and this supposed vague language is concrete affirmation Herod died in 4 B.C. However, when one peruses the year, academics lie to fit Stellarium software's projection of a planetary alignment (that is never even in the narrative), this becomes laughable as an assertion. In 1 B.C., NASA catalogues the lunar eclipse on January 20th at 14:48:33. That is about three months before Passover and into the previous Hebrew year even. That is illiterate. The date remains 4 B.C. for the death of Herod the Great. No one has ever challenged that successfully. Enough babble.

The Month and Day:

RotM 17:1 "And when we arrived in the region of Jerusalem, in the month of flowers..."

In *Revelation of the Magi*, the Magi arrive in Jerusalem in the "month of flowers." Wildflowers in Israel are really in season from late January through late April. However, this merely says they arrived in Jerusalem at that time. When we reconcile this with another passage in our text, we find this to be late April. They would see Herod and tarry, awaiting the reappearance of the Star, which guided them, before heading to Bethlehem. In other words, this would be after the Feasts of Passover, of Unleavened Bread, and of the First Fruit Offering, when they arrived in Jerusalem. That means neither of those Feast dates would apply to the birth of Messiah.

---

[1] *Catalogue of Lunar Eclipses: -0099 to 0000 (100 BCE to 1 BCE)." N.A.S.A. eclipse.gsfc.nasa. gov/LEcat5/LE-0099-0000.html.*

Indeed, Passover and Unleavened Bread are embedded in His death and resurrection, but not His birth. This portion is even affirmed and quoted in Theodore bar Konai's *Mimra 7.17* in the eight century. Late April is also cited as the birth of Messiah by Clement of Alexandria in the second century, quoting *Revelation of the Magi*, but confusing the birthdate. Clement used the month of arrival, and assumed it to be the birth month (which is not the case). His date reconciles on the Roman calendar to about April 20-21 according to Landau. Again, that would be well after Passover. In the year Herod died, and he would have to be alive for this, he would be dead before Passover thus; he did not die that year.

A famous Messianic Rabbi claims that "lambing season" is the sign of the birth, yet he fails to tell the truth. Lambs are born over a five-month period in Israel, not specifically at Passover (even to this day). That information tells us nothing about the birth date, of which he has obviously no knowledge. That Rabbi follows Talmudic nonsense over what is observed scientifically. We see such embellishment in ignorance from Rabbis on a regular basis, as they are Pharisees.

However, *Revelation of the Magi* specifies when they arrived, not precisely the birth month of Messiah (though it does narrow it down). The manuscript will confirm Luke preserved the birthdate, which will fall within the timeline set forth.

RotM 11:6 *"And just like the moon looks in the daytime in the **days of Nisan**, when the sun rises and it is absorbed in its light, so also did the sun seem to us when the star rose over us."*

This translation is actually not necessarily "Nisan." Landau admits in this footnote: *"However, the phrase "in the days of Nisan" can also be translated idiomatically as "in springtime."* So, if we take these two references and overlap them for understanding in true reconciliation, we know that the month of flowers for wildflowers is really months; from late January to late April. This is the arrival date of the Magi into Jerusalem, not Messiah's birth. Again, Clement of Alexandria placed that event around April 20-21. This was Springtime, which occurs from mid-March to mid-June. Therefore, if the Magi arrived in late April as specified, they met with Herod while they waited for the Star to reappear. The timing for the birth is somewhere in the Springtime, after that. In other words, this really narrows it down to about a six-week period, from May to mid-June for the birth. Does that coalesce with scripture?

The answer is absolutely and indisputably, yes. The *Book of Jubilees* is the textbook of the Temple, with dates and details not found in Genesis. As a second witness, Jubilees affirms Genesis numerous times. The God Culture has published "Little Genesis,", with a complete Torah test executed, at *BookofJubilees.org*. It is quoted by Biblical authors, including John, Paul, the Apostles, and especially the Messiah Himself, on numerous occasions. They used the *Book of Jubilees* as Torah, especially for its calendar. Jesus *(Yahusha)* followed the covenant, not the Passover Lamb, who had no covenant in these terms. He was born by the covenant, following the

Patriarch Isaac's timeline. It is hard to believe that scholars have not researched this. They'll criticize Luke with dabbling their toe into the waters without reconciling.

Jubilees 16:12-13 [Isaac's Conception: Sixth Hebrew Month, 15th Day: September]
And in the middle of the sixth month Yahuah visited Sarah and did unto her as He had spoken, and she conceived. And she bare a son in the third month, and in the middle of the month, at the time of which Yahuah had spoken to Abraham, on the festival of the first-fruits of the harvest, Isaac was born.

The Feast of Weeks and First-Fruits of the Harvest is not the First Fruit Offering, which is not the harvest festival. Shavuot is that festival, which is why there is a counting in scripture of 50 days from the initial offering of Abib 26 to the actual feast. These are not dates that move in scripture, ever, and they have nothing to do with the barley harvest in modern Israel. Shavuot is always on the 15th day of the third Hebrew month, which is about the first week in June on our Roman calendar. That is when Jesus *(Yahusha)* was born. Wow!!!

This precedence continued in date for Israel in the days of the Exodus. Moses first went up Mt. Sinai on Shavuot, the 15th day of the Third Hebrew month. Yahuah proposed covenant with Israel, and it was ratified that day. Then, Moses went back up after that to receive part of Torah for 40 days *(Jub. 1:1-3)*. Shavuot is one day, never the 40 days the Rabbis claim represent the giving of Torah. Though close, they have lost the meaning of Shavuot which is about Covenant Renewal. It always has been, as it is the ancient Feast even kept by Noah, who waited for about two weeks to exit the ark and renew covenant on the 15th day of the Third Hebrew month *(Jub. 6:16-18)*. This is the same Feast kept by Abraham in which Yahuah

promised a son on that day and it is on Shavuot, that Sarah conceived, and Mary conceived, as it should be *(Jub. 16:12-13)*.

This is covenant; Bible scholars have lost that. It became disconnected because the modern church (and even the Pharisees of the first century) ignore the Temple textbook: *Book of Jubilees*. Even simply using it to affirm details is a valid use for a document, whose copy was found in about 150 B.C. in the Dead Sea Scrolls. We test this thoroughly and draw a deeper conclusion based on the evidence. Read our eBook free at *BookOfJubilees.org*.

The *Book of Luke* could not be more accurate and specific regarding this month. He comes right out and directly tells us that the Angel Gabriel visited Mary (which is when she conceived by the Holy Spirit), in the sixth Hebrew month, the same as Sarah. This was not a process that Gabriel started, for he said she would be pregnant, and she was. When an archangel says so, it is true, and it does not tarry. Could this really be that simple? We will assess. Scholars get involved and confuse this claiming it should read, yet it does not, as the sixth month of Elizabeth's pregnancy. No, it reads the sixth Hebrew month. What they miss is Elizabeth was six months pregnant in the sixth Hebrew month, which this really affirms.

Luke 1:26-28 KJV [Jesus' (Yahusha's) Conception: Sixth Hebrew Month: September]
*And **in the sixth month the angel Gabriel was sent from God unto a city of Galilee**, named **Nazareth**, To **a virgin espoused to a man whose name was Joseph, of the house of David**; and the virgin's name was **Mary**. And the angel came in unto her, and said, Hail, **thou that art highly favoured, the Lord is with thee: blessed art thou among women**.*

Luke 1:39-40 KJV [Mary Visits Elizabeth]
*And **Mary arose in those days, and went into the hill country with haste**, into a city of Juda; And entered **into the house of Zacharias, and saluted Elisabeth**.*

We know this for certain because Mary followed Sarah in covenant. We also know Mary arose "in those days" "with haste" to visit Elizabeth, meaning this is all in the same period. She went to the hill country of Judaea, which is a journey of about 80-100 miles *(130-160 km, Logos Bible Software)*. This was about a 3-to-7-day expedition to the hill county, and later from Judaea to her home. Mary stayed there for *"about three months (Luke 1:56)."* She stayed for John's circumcision on the eighth day *(Luke 1:59)* for a total of about four months. It is about that time (at the end of the Roman year, or beginning of the next) that Augustus decreed a special census, about the fifth month of Mary's pregnancy.

This led to the Spring Feast celebrations, in which Mary and Joseph did not likely travel to Bethlehem, as it was Mary's seventh month in term. That would place us in the timeline at around April on the Roman calendar. This fits the scripture in Luke 2:4-5, as Mary and Joseph left for Bethlehem when she was "great with child." Indeed, eight months pregnant is great. The travel to Bethlehem was about a 5-7-day journey *(93 miles/150 km, Logos Bible Software).* That would place them entering Bethlehem still in the eighth month of Mary's term. This all leads to a birth matching Sarah's delivery of Isaac on the 15th of the Third Hebrew month.

Scholars are accurate to place these accounts together, but they read them very poorly. The date was selected by Yahuah through Gabriel to match the conception of Isaac in the sixth Hebrew month on the 15th day. Why? Nine months later is Shavuot, the Day of Covenant Renewal; the month leads to the exact day. So, Isaac and Jesus *(Yahusha)* were conceived in the sixth Hebrew month in September on our calendar today. One must reconcile that each year, but that does not lead to a birth in December, does it? Sure, miracles happen in the Bible and it takes credit for them when they do. This is never catalogued as such. This is Messiah's calendar in which He would entrench Himself into the Bible Feasts. The Vatican knows little of these feasts it has abandoned from its inception, since 155 A.D., demonstrating it is not His ekklesia but those who "crept in unawares *(Jude 1:4).*"

Jesus *(Yahusha)* entered Jerusalem in the days leading up to His execution, which was specifically selected by this same covenant in dates *(Luke 19:28-40).* This occurred on the 10th of Abib when the Passover Lamb is also selected entering Jerusalem *(John 12).* That selection is not a covenant with the Passover Lamb but based on the one with Israel's people since Moses. He would be captured on Passover as the passage is clear He "ate" the Passover with the twelve *(Luke 22:13-23)* and would be put to death the next day on the First Day of Unleavened Bread. Passover ends at sunrise and is only a nighttime event. He was not crucified at night as the sun was out, in order to be darkened. Unleavened Bread's seven days begin with Passover.

What he is doing, however, is matching the timeline of Isaac once again. Isaac's sacrifice also took place on the First Day of Unleavened Bread, Abib 15. In the *Book of Jubilees,* this could not be clearer. On the 12th of Abib, satan challenges Abraham's faithfulness much like Job *(Jub. 17:15).* Abraham leaves on a journey for three days *(Jub. 18:3).* After three days, it is Abib 15 on the First Day of Unleavened Bread, and that is when he builds an altar to sacrifice Isaac *(Jub. 18:3-13).* That was also during the daytime which Jesus' *(Yahusha's)* timeline also concurs in the death and resurrection. He was following Isaac, never the Passover Lamb or any random pattern. This is clear-cut and perfect, requiring no speculation, no astrology, no faulty science that could not fit anyway, etc. The record has always been there.

He would then, raise from the dead on the Third Day, which was still the weekly Sabbath, during the seven days of Unleavened Bread. His calendar is Isaac's and they both were embedded in the Feast cycle (which cannot be ignored). Before sunrise, on a Roman "Sunday" is still the Saturday "Sabbath" on the Biblical calendar. We cover that in full with charts in *REST: The Case For Sabbath* free in eBook at *RestSabbath.org.*

The *Gospel of Luke* tells us that Mary was indeed, a virgin. His account does not involve relations, but the planting of a seed by the Holy Spirit. Mary is only to be respected. The Latin word *venerate* is not appropriate here, as it originates from a word that means *to worship*. Replacing the term, and saying that *we do NOT worship her, but meaning we worship her* is not exactly a statement one would wish to be caught making. We cannot pray to Mary (which is the same thing as asking her/ praying to her, to pray for us). If one does pray to her, and receives an answer, that answer comes directly from a demonic entity (as described in the Bible). We pray/ ask the Son to pray for us, as He is always our mediator *(1 Tim. 2:5; Heb. 8:6, 9:15, 12:24)* in scripture and the only way, truth, and life *(John 14:6)*.

Finally, Heaven has no Queen in any scripture anywhere especially Revelation where John describes the throne room in Heaven in detail and absent is any mention of a queen. There was a goddess who claimed to be the "Queen of Heaven" but Jeremiah rebuked her five times as essentially the Harlot of Babylon *(Jer. 7:18, 44:17-19, 25)*. When a church takes an opposite position on these basics, telling us to pray to, worship, and treat this holy woman as the Harlot of Babylon (replacing the Son of Yahuah), they are not representing the Bible. They are attacking the deity of Messiah just as they have done in suppressing this narrative. Even the "Mother of God" designation is somewhat factual, as she certainly birthed and raised Him. However, that is also an ancient designation of the same Harlot of Babylon. Mary would be disgusted to be misrepresented in such a way and yet, that is one of the base doctrines of Catholicism. That is exactly the kind of theology the Isles of the Magi will reject according to multiple prophesies *(Matt. 12:42, Luke 11:31, Is. 60:9; Ez. 38:13)*. So, the Bible never calls her "Queen of Heaven," nor "Mother of God"; those are lies as well. This is not vague in scripture; it is the occult being melted into that church just as they have done with the Magi.

We can test this further by figuring out when John the Baptist was conceived, which would lead us to Jesus' *(Yahusha's)* conception six months later.

Luke 1:5-9 KJV
*There was **in the days of Herod, the king of Judaea**, a certain priest named **Zacharias, of the course of Abia: and his wife was of the daughters of Aaron**, and her name was **Elisabeth**. And they were **both righteous** before God, **walking in all the commandments and ordinances** of the Lord **blameless. And they had no child**, because that **Elisabeth was barren**, and they both were now **well stricken in years. And it came to pass, that while he executed the priest's office before God in the order of his course, According to the custom of the priest's office**, his lot was to burn incense when he went into the temple of the Lord.*

John was the son of a priest of Abia *(Abijah)*, one of the twenty-four priestly families who served on a circuit in the Temple two or three times a year on their own, and then, on Feast Days as well with others. Through his mother, he was also a son of Zadok, the very Temple leadership since King Solomon built the First Temple. Zacharias was serving on his priestly cycle (which narrows this down to twice a year, typically). We know that the year of the birth of Jesus *(Yahusha)* was 9 B.C. Therefore, we can assess when Abia's family would serve in the Temple that year, roughly. Why? John will be conceived following this service. This matters.

Notice, Luke says this course was preserved and followed, even in the first century B.C. Any scholar claiming that impossible may struggle keeping track themselves, but these priests did not. Some wonder whether Zacharias served at the Jerusalem Temple or the place in Qumran/Bethabara where the actual Temple Priest leadership were exiled. That is a good question, and this account does not specify.

Luke 1:23-26 KJV
*And it came to pass, that, as soon as the days of his ministration were accomplished, he departed to his own house. And after those days his wife Elisabeth conceived, and hid herself five months, saying, Thus hath the Lord dealt with me in the days wherein he looked on me, to take away my reproach among men. **And in the sixth month the angel Gabriel was sent from God unto** a city of Galilee, named **Nazareth**...*

Immediately following this time stamp of the course of Abia, Elizabeth conceived John. She was pregnant for 5 months and then, in the sixth month (which is both the sixth month of her pregnancy and the sixth Hebrew month). Gabriel visited Mary in Nazareth and she conceived by the Holy Spirit. Scholars are correct these tie together (as verse 26 begins with "And"). The possible definitions for the conjunction, "De" in Greek, is "and, but, now, moreover," according to Strong's Concordance. This word in Greek can be translated as "but" which also fits in both concepts, which are the same. It is the sixth Hebrew month. This will vet as truth.

Luke 1:35-38 KJV
*And the **angel answered and said unto her, The Holy Ghost shall come upon thee, and the power of the Highest shall overshadow thee:** therefore also that holy thing which shall be born of thee shall be called the Son of God. And, behold, **thy cousin Elisabeth**, she hath also conceived a son in her old age: and **this is the sixth month with her**, who was called barren. For with God nothing shall be impossible. And Mary said, Behold the handmaid of the Lord; **be it unto me according to thy word.** And **the angel departed from her.***

The Holy Spirit is the source of conception here without any marital relations. Anyone inserting an angelic incursion is not following any scripture, and representing the Messiah as a Nephilim. That is awful. Mary was truly a virgin as prophecy said she would be. She said, "...go ahead and do it," and it was done.

There is no debate that Mary conceived in the sixth Hebrew month; which was also the sixth month of Elizabeth's pregnancy. An Archangel and the Holy Spirit are not powerless. This was immediate. Mary knew that Elizabeth was six months pregnant (when she saw her, in the sixth Hebrew month). It occurred in the month of September, in the Roman calendar. Please do the math regarding this issue; it places the birth of Messiah in 9 B.C., in the Roman month of June.

We refer to a wise gentleman named Kurt Simmons, whose live website contains the full calendar detailing this information at *Dec25th.info.* If you have difficulty accessing it, please email us at *thegodculture@gmail.com.* As we have now proven the appropriate year of Messiah's conception (10 B.C.) as well as His birth (9 B.C.), we merely need to locate the eighth priestly course: Abia.

Having tested this calendar on multiple points, it appears very close to accurate. Perhaps it could be a week off, or so, but it is close enough to determine the month (which is all we need to affirm). We already know Jesus *(Yahusha)* would follow the timeline of Isaac, the son of covenant who was born on Shavuot in the third Hebrew month on the 15th day. Of course, given the wrong year, Simmons attempts to make December 25th work. Though that conclusion is wrong on every level, his math is solid. He just picked the wrong year to test. John the Baptist was conceived in January, 10 B.C., approximately. This affirms the conception of both Mary and Sarah (wife of Abraham) in the sixth Hebrew month, and Messiah's birth in the third Hebrew month. Again, we have those dates from Jubilees to arrive at the day.

Paul affirms that this was the appointed time for Messiah's birth; not a random event. In Hebrew that is mo'edim (מועד) which is the Bible Feasts. Paul told us all along Jesus *(Yahusha)* was in fact, born on a Feast Day. There are only seven feasts per year, and the Feast of Shavuot is a match.

Galatians 4:1-5 KJV
*Now I say, That the heir, as long as he is a child, differeth nothing from a servant, though he be lord of all; But is **under tutors and governors until the time appointed of the father.** Even so we, when we were children, were in bondage under the elements of the world: **But when the fulness of the time was come, God sent forth his Son, made of a woman, made under the law,** To redeem them that were under the law, that we might receive the adoption of sons.*

Paul knew this timing (which every Biblical scholar should know). It seems this knowledge was lost and forgotten. It originates in the promise from Yahuah to Abraham on Shavuot, the appointed time in which Abraham was promised a son on a Feast Day. It turns out that promise came into being on a Feast Day, just as it did with Jesus *(Yahusha)* on Shavuot, the fifteenth day of the third Hebrew month.

Genesis 18:14 KJV
*Is any thing too hard for the LORD? **At the time appointed I will return unto thee, according to the time of life, and Sarah shall have a son.***

mô'ēḏ: מועד: an appointment, i.e. a fixed time or season; specifically, a festival; conventionally a year; by implication, an assembly (as convened for a definite purpose); technically the congregation; by extension, the place of meeting; also a signal (as appointed beforehand):—appointed (sign, time), (place of, solemn) assembly, congregation, (set, solemn) feast, (appointed, due) season, solemn(-ity), synagogue, (set) time (appointed) (H4150).

---

[1] *Reconciliation of Priestly Courses. By Kurt Simmons. Dec25th.info.*

There are a large number of those seeking truth who use this same information, and are led to the Feast of Tabernacles, focusing on one Bible verse that says Messiah tabernacled with us. Without any other relevant data and testing, that does not even rise to the level of speculation. Even the purpose of Tabernacles is a future event in which we receive new bodies and enter New Jerusalem as our permanent abode. That will be fulfilled after the Day of Judgment and has no association with the birth of our Savior.

Others assume His birth aligns with the Feast of Passover, but this feast concerns His death and resurrection; even His crucifixion occurs the day after Passover, not on it. Pharisees have put obstacles in place, using modern Rabbis and Bible Scholars to hide the true date of His conception and His birth. They don't want us to discover these facts, and never have. They do not embrace them; instead leading churches to the occult, satanic holidays; in replacement of the holy days of Yah.

When we understand that Shavuot is the Day of Covenant Renewal, there is little left to discuss on the day in which Messiah would come in the flesh. This meaning has been lost by the Rabbis *(Pharisees)* as well as the church in modern times. They have the wrong date, after a famous, early Rabbi rambled publicly about a wrong date for the Feast of Shavuot; Sivan 6 (it is actually the 15th, formerly public knowledge in the early church). Scholars do not understand the value of learning these holy Feasts, because seminaries teach nothing but contempt for them.

Many theologians rail on keeping the Biblical Feasts, yet they keep impotent, pagan occult replacements, while still attempting to celebrate His birth and death. These events have always occurred on Feast Days. They will claim these have passed away yet, several of the Feasts are foreshadowing of future events that have not occurred. They will redefine English words like "shadow," forgetting that if Heaven casts a shadow that includes the Feasts, the only way they can pass away, is if Heaven passes *(Heb. 8:5, 9:23-28; Col. 2:17)*. That has not happened. The Feast (the shadow), must remain.

Jubilees 6:21-22 (Meaning of Shavuot)
*For it is the feast of weeks and the feast of first-fruits: this feast is twofold and of a **double nature**: according to what is written and engraven concerning it celebrate it. For I have written **in the book of the first law**, in that which I have written for thee, that thou shouldst celebrate it **in its season, one day in the year**, and I explained to thee its sacrifices that the children of Israel should remember and should celebrate it **throughout their generations in this month, one day in every year**.*

Jesus *(Yahusha)* was born on the Feast Day of Shavuot, just as Isaac was. ***Revelation of the Magi*** proves a further affirmation of this timeline, aligning with an accurate interpretation of that of Clement of Alexandria. All the details of Luke and Matthew's Gospels completely agree and align, as they should. Modern scholars have no clue because they do not reconcile, they attack from the seat of the scornful. Prove all things for yourself *(1 Th. 5:21)*.

A New Day Dawns... At Sunrise!

Messiah rose before dawn (sunrise) still on the Sabbath (Saturday). This means the Biblical day began at sunrise not sundown. The dark hours of the morning were still Sabbath (Saturday) until the sun dawned. He rose on Sabbath which is only Saturday. At dawn it was the 1st Day.

Matt. 28:1, Mark 16:1-2, John 20:1

Evening is Still the Same Day!

Only the Pharisees' Lunar Calendar begins at sundown. Mary's did not. Joseph of Arimathea was a Pharisee on the Lunar Calendar. He placed the body in the tomb before his Sabbath observance. However, Mary would not anoint the body at that same hour on Sabbath because she was already observing the Bible Sabbath instead since sunrise.

Luke 23:54-56, Mark 15:42-43

Evening is Still the Same Day!

Later that day, when the first day began and the 7th day ended at sunrise, the evening was still the 1st day not a new day. If this were a Lunar Calendar, the day would have to change at sundown which would have made it the 2nd day but it did not according to the Bible.

John 20:19: After Sundown, it was still the 1st day.

Charting the Four Gospel Accounts. Details in Rest: The Case For Sabbath at RestSabbath.org.

7th Day
Sabbath
SUNRISE
1st day
Dawn

7th Day
Sabbath
SUNSET
Still 7th Day
Sabbath

Dawn
1st Day
SUNSET
Still **1st day**
Evening

First Day of Unleavened Bread: One of the 3 Most Important Feasts Requiring a Pilgrimage.

First Hebrew Month

Abib

Good Friday is Not Biblical! They can't count!

DIED ON FEAST SABBATH

Joseph of Arimathea On Pharisee Sabbath Not Bible One!

Jub. 17-18
John 20:1, 19

MIRRORS DATES OF ISAAC'S SACRIFICE

1 DAY IN GRAVE

---

6 am-6am	*6 am-6am*	*6 am-6am*
14	**15**	**16**
Tuesday	*Wednesday*	*Thursday*
Passover Evening	**ULB Feast Sabbath**	**ULB Feast**
		Mary Waited for Sabbath to End
Messiah Captured After Passover Meal	*9 am* Crucified *3 pm* Died *6pm* Tomb (Pharisee Sabbath)	*6 am* Anointed w/ Spices Counting Begins

Mary already keeping Sabbath before Dark   *1 Day, 1 Night*

LORD OF THE SABBATH

Mark 2:28
Matt. 12:8
Luke 6:5

AFFIRMED IN HIS DEATH & RESURRECTION

The Bible's Brilliant Accuracy Preserves the Start of the Biblical Day at Sunrise!

Messiah is attached to the Biblical Calendar and no one can change it. Forgetting the Sabbath is forgetting His Sacrifice and Resurrection!

Sabbath cannot pass away! He has restored it forever! The Bible is set on a Solar Calendar NOT a Lunar one!

He said He would rise after 3 Days & 3 Nights. That is exactly what happened. The 4th night did NOT complete, and is not counted. Enough scholarly gnat-straining accusing our Savior as a liar!

Mary waited to purchase spices on the 3rd Day, because Sabbath ended at sunrise. One does not buy or sell on Sabbath. Messiah had already risen!
Matt. 28:1

the GOD culture

Easter Sunday is Not Biblical! Sabbath is NEVER Sunday! The Roman Calendar is not the Biblical One!

ROSE ON WEEKLY SABBATH

2 DAYS IN GRAVE

3 DAYS IN GRAVE

EMPTY TOMB

6 am-6am
17
Friday
ULB Feast
In Tomb

6 am-6am
18
Saturday
Weekly Sabbath
Rose Just Before Sunrise at End of Sabbath

6 am-6am
19
Sunday
ULB Feast
Rose Before 1st Bible Day Began Before Sunrise Starts First Day

2 Days, 2 Nights

3 Days, 3 Nights

Chapter 11:
The Names of the Father & Son
In Revelation of the Magi

*Who was Jesus (Yahusha) in **Revelation of the Magi**?*
For those who will study the answer, all His attributes vet with scripture.
This stock image is not accurate (as Messiah was not white, nor was David,
Solomon, or Adam). Any photos from the Catholic or Protestant Church that
propogate a white Hebrew, are generally erroneous. This, too, comes from a
colonial, racist mentality, not from any actual history; especially not the Bible.
AdobeStock.

There is no doubt the scholarly tone of indifference will inject itself, regarding the ***Revelation of the Magi (RotM)***, not found in our modern Canon. Scholars will act as if they are gods, claiming a counsel of man-inspired scripture, when it was evil men who removed numerous manuscripts from what we now call the Bible. They agitated the narrative, even in 382 A.D., when Jerome the Catholic hid away pertinent books, calling them "apocrypha." Just as is done in abortion wordplay, in which a fetus is "merely the Latin for baby," scholars lay accusation of any non-canon text, "that is apocrypha."

It is rather simple to discern this term in English, rather than in Greek. It simply means "hidden away;" from the Greek "apo kryptein." It is not anything sinister, as implied. Why aren't scholars honest when they use such a term, and call it what it is? Even the 1611 KJV included the apocryphal/hidden books. Not all test as scripture, but most do, if one conducts testing without agendas. Why did Jerome think he was deified, and thus could change inspired Bible Canon? Why would any Catholic Counsel believe themselves to be more elevated than Temple Priests, who already determined Bible Canon for over 2000 years prior? Jacob and Moses decided these books belonged in holy writing volumes, no matter what language, and this did not change, as of the first century. We have that time capsule found in archaeology in Qumran/Bethabara where the Temple Priests were exiled.

However, let us conduct some testing of ***Revelation of the Magi.*** Is the story valid? We have already found the references to Jesus *(Yahusha)* as the Light of the World are indeed scripture. Whether any church doctrine applies such scripture is impertinent. The historicity of the existence of ***Revelation of the Magi*** is fairly close to the time of authorship in the second century. That is very good for such an ancient text. In this chapter, we will vet this further as well, cataloguing its affinity to the Old and New Testaments. When a writing aligns with Biblical Books, it proves to be written by one who is a Believer in Messiah, at least. Occult liars do not follow the Bible, they change it infusing their doctrines just as the Catholic Church has with this account and many others.

Let us commence with names of the Father and Son in ***Revelation of the Magi.*** Is the criticism founded that the text does not employ these? Our translator has demonstrated little knowledge on this topic. The results of this test are incredible.

The Son's Name in Revelation of the Magi:

One of the most inept criticisms by Brent Landau, translator of ***Revelation of the Magi,*** is his accusation of the text not mentioning the name of *Jesus.* It is hard to believe that a Bible scholar does not know that *Jesus* cannot even be rendered as a word in Ancient Hebrew, Greek, Aramaic, nor Latin. These languages did not contain the letter "J' until the 1500's, and the New Testament does not actually use that name either. It appears he never bothered to look up the Hebrew name of *Yahusha* which means "Yah is salvation." So, if we wish to find whether *Yahusha* was invoked in the text, we would simply look for the word "salvation." Such a word study proves that the name of *Yahusha* is there several times in context. This author translated the name into English, forgetting that is what His name is.

In fact, in some instances, the text is very clearly invoking the actual name of *Yahusha,* who is *salvation,* as if we are to believe in "salvation," which is erroneous in application. We are to believe in *Yahusha,* who is *salvation.* That is His name. Has Landau read the New Testament, or even his own translation? Landau translated the name "Jesus Christ" several times; once before the section involving the Apostle Thomas. It is not the only place where *Jesus Christ* is mentioned. Landau disassociates with that section invalidly, (which is ridiculous), as it is a necessary piece for the manuscript to be complete.

*RotM 29:6 And Judas said: "My brothers, I also rejoice, because it is for this **gift that I was sent in salvation** (Yahusha!), since everyone who believes in salvation and with love receives the seal of my Lord Jesus Christ in truth, the Enemy does not rule over."*

When the Apostle Thomas visited the Philippines on his mission there, he absolutely and indisputably spoke the name of *Yahusha.* Anyone can see the obvious where Thomas said: "I was sent in *Yahusha*" which is not accurate to say He was "sent in *salvation.*" Landau says "he who believes in *salvation.*" Even Satan believes in *salvation,* trembles, and knows it is fact. We are to believe in the Son, as scripture specifies. There is only one way to salvation, through the Son. Landau also translates it improperly when the Magi receive the seal of "my Lord Jesus Christ." This should read *Yahusha Messiah.* Even though this is Syriac, translated to Latin, then to English, Landau knew it was *Jesus,* but could not recognize *Yahusha's* name. The majority of Bible Scholars and most church-goers will not recognize this important dynamic of the text.

Yahusha means *salvation,* but His name is right there in the text, translated to English, forgotten in Hebrew, and close in Greek. It is His name, regardless of transliteration. Was *salvation* born, or was *Yahusha* born? An educated translator should have known this. The below descriptions would read so much better as the mystery, light, birth, child, gift, voice of *Yahusha.* There are too many to ignore.

*RotM 31:2 Behold the consummation and sealing of **your birth of salvation** (Yahusha!).*
*18:4b ...in which the **mystery and light of salvation** (Yahusha!) was born.*
Song of Thomas 30:2-9:
*...and you renew the body with the **birth of salvation** (Yahusha!).*
*...And may you **perfectly sanctify** them with the **birth of salvation** (Yahusha!).*
*23:1 ... and to **bring forth the child of salvation** of the eternal word,*
*23:2b ...**the great gift of salvation** that by your child was given to all the worlds.*
*23:3 ...**the treasure of salvation**... This **great gift and light of salvation**...*
*25:1 ...**of the voice of salvation**.*

It is also very clear that the new disciples (after the Apostle Thomas preached) were the disciples of the word of *Yahusha*, not the translated "salvation."

RotM 31:8 And all the new disciples of the word of salvation answered...

Does it make sense that faith of *salvation* increased in the land of the East, or that the faith of *Yahusha* increased in those who heard? That seems self-explanatory and indisputable to anyone not brainwashed by academia in such manner.

RotM 28:6 And the faith of salvation increased in the land of the East in those who heard.

One would think a New Testament Bible scholar would be aware there are no "commandments of salvation" in scripture. One who is saved indeed follows the commandments but following commandments is not *salvation*. Yet, he transitioned this word into English, making a mockery of himself. These are the commandments of *Yahusha*.

RotM 22:1a And when we received from him the commandments of salvation,

One could certainly say *salvation* is a blessing and at times, this works, but sometimes, it is clearly the name of *Yahusha*. In these instances, the translation is fine (as *salvation* fits), but *Yahusha* is the Savior invoked. It is only through Him. *Yahusha* is the treasure of *salvation*; or should this read, "salvation is the treasure of Yahusha?" *Salvation* is His name, but He is the one who set forth such. Though it could be fine, does *salvation* judge or is that *Yahusha*? Regardless, to claim His name is not here is unfounded.

RotM 4:9 And you will offer him your gifts, and you shall receive from him the blessing of salvation...
13:4 For the sake of their salvation... who sent me for their salvation.
13:13 ...will of the Father shall be fulfilled for the sake of the salvation of the life of the whole world.
15:1b ...behold, you are amazed, is (only) one drop of salvation from the house of [majesty]
15:7 ...for the salvation of human beings so that they would not perish.
18:7 And we opened our hidden treasures, and they being sealed, we took them and came near the treasure of salvation, who is sealed with heavenly majesty. 18:8 And we brought forth our treasures before him, who is the treasure of salvation, that we might receive them from him in the kingdom by many-fold before his own judgment seat of salvation.
Song of Thomas 30:2-9: O mystery of salvation... by grace for salvation...
20:4 And yours is the place of salvation, which you will give to your chosen ones.
23:4 ...he has been sent by his majesty for the salvation and redemption of every human being.
25:2 And because of you, Eve and her offspring will have hope and salvation...

When ***Revelation of the Magi*** speaks of the complete gift of *salvation* as something they and the patriarchs might see as a sight, that is clearly identifying the physical Messiah in the flesh, not just a concept. It reads very disjointed the way it is translated as opposed to what believers know to be true.

*RotM 14:10 And we were in great rejoicing and great exultation that we were thought worthy to see this complete **gift of salvation** for which all the kings, and righteous ones, and prophets, and powerful ones prayed, and hoped, and waited, that they might see this sight. But they did not see it because it was not then the time of the coming of the star of light, giving perfect salvation to its believers.*

The same element exists in this sentence which invokes *Yahusha* as the one who knows the Father. No one else does. He is The Word but the word of *Yahusha* is also a better translation here, in our opinion.

*RotM 15:2 And no one knows the Father except **the voice bringing forth the word of salvation**...*

Does *salvation* itself have a will? It only does in one context, when it is *Yahusha* and the word is exactly that. This is *Yahusha*, period.

*RotM 21:12b "Amen! **The will of complete salvation**, joy and peace to all the worlds!"*

Indeed, *Yahusha* spoke *salvation* but He planted the Word of *Yahusha* in the place of *Yahusha* really. Regardless, what we know is *Yahusha* is the topic here and to claim the passage does not invoke Him because a translator flubbed the context is inexcusable.

*RotM 27:6 And we worshiped him, **the Lord of worship**, and he opened his splendid and glorious mouth and **spoke [salvation]** with us as we were able and sufficient to hear it, and in this way **he planted the word of salvation in us**. 27:7 And he spoke and revealed to us concerning **the place of salvation**...*

In the portion of ***Revelation of the Magi***, the Apostle Thomas mentions "Jesus Christ" in the English translation almost twenty times. Landau assumes the name of Messiah is not mentioned (as he states), and then admits it is mentioned, at the same time. The notion is an oxymoron. He attempts a way of discounting what is right in front of his eyes which is called witchcraft. Understand that is "Isho M'shiha" in Aramaic, which should be the Syriac rendering he translated from or similar. In English, that would be rendered as "Yahusha Messiah" accurately (not "Jesus Christ," which is never an appropriate name for *Yahusha*). That is His name, *Yahusha*, meaning *salvation* (almost twenty more times). It is also used before this section, which Landau fails to notice. The point is invalid.

Landau attempts to disconnect the portion which includes the Apostle Thomas as written by someone else, and not the same story. Scholars are known to make excuses in similar fashion, when they have illiterate assumptions set in false paradigms. No wonder Bible Scholars are oblivious to ancient Bible geography. They are lacking on this topic, as proven numerous times. They will claim that the Magi could not write a manuscript over a period of a century, with more than one author. That is never a problem for the Bible paradigm (as we see this often in the canonical text). Landau admits this, and then ignores it, to draw an erroneous conclusion he has not earned the right to infer.

In the prophecy of the Magi, regarding the Star that appeared, they are told they would be visited by an Apostle. They are given the Great Commission. However, pandering to a brood of hypocrites, to separate the natural continuation of the account (in fulfillment of its prophecy), is the worst scholarship imaginable. Landau has no evidence (not even data) by which to draw such conclusions, and claims we should ignore the chapters involving Thomas. However, that portion agrees with historical documents, and is certainly the natural progression to complete this account. It is Jesus *(Yahusha)* who promised to send His disciples to the Philippines twice *(RotM 19:6, 21:5)*.

Abba in Revelation of the Magi:

Magellan's historian, Pigafetta, chronicled in his journal that Filipinos in the sixteenth century were still worshipping *Abba.* He was authorized by the King of Spain to record this and he did with obvious accuracy. There is no other true eyewitness account of Magellan's landing and experiences in the Philippines. Anyone that says otherwise, is not honest. When asked by Magellan about their God and their worship, this is what Filipinos answered according to the official Spanish government record.

*"Then he asked whether they were Moors or Gentiles, and in what they believed. **They answered that they did not perform any other adoration, but only joined their hands, looking up to heaven, and that they called their God, Aba.** Hearing this, the captain was very joyful, on seeing that, the first king raised his hands to the sky and said that he wished it were possible for him to be able to show the affection which he felt towards him." –Antonio Pigafetta*[1]

In other words, their answer to Magellan was to quote scripture. Oops! They knew Jesus *(Yahusha)* firsthand, having experienced His light and presence in their own Cave of Treasures first. Then, they followed His Light in the form of a Star to

---

[1] *"The First Voyage Round the World by Antonio Pigafetta." 1522. translated by Lord Stanley of Alderley. pp. 82, 103 and 104.*

Bethlehem where He was birthed two years earlier. He spoke to them on both occasions. No, He was not in Egypt until after the Magi came, according to the *Gospel of Matthew*.

We all know whom *Abba* is. It is a designation from the lips of the Son in the Garden of Gethsemane and Paul repeats the title twice. This is no enigma. The Magi knew this title and used it before Jesus *(Yahusha)* was born. Then, they repeated it 1,500 years later to Magellan. The sheer gravity of this is overwhelming. One can begin to understand why it has has been covered up.

Abba: **Αββα***: "The Father, My Father"* [1]

Mark 14:36 KJV
*And he said, Abba (**Αββα**), Father, all things are possible unto thee; take away this cup from me: nevertheless not what I will, but what thou wilt.*

Romans 8:15 KJV
*For ye have not received the spirit of bondage again to fear; but ye have received the Spirit of adoption, whereby we cry, Abba (**Αββα**), Father.*

Galatians 4:6 KJV
*And because ye are sons, God hath sent forth the Spirit of his Son into your hearts, crying, **Abba** (**Αββα**), Father.*

Therefore, not only does ***Revelation of the Magi*** invoke the name of *Yahusha*, but it also explains how the Magi learned His title for the Father from the Messiah directly. Anyone attempting to claim *Abba* has Muslim origins has never bothered to research the matter. Allah has 99 names. Even Allah is not a name but a title meaning "Chief God." Missing from this list of 99 names is the word *Abba*, which is never used (in such an abundant list), for their God. One could certainly infer their god is not *Abba Yahuah*, but regardless, they do not call Allah by the title of *Abba*.

Revelation of the Magi refers to Yahuah as "The Father" many times. That is *Abba* in Syriac/Aramaic just as it is in our Bibles. The Magi call Him *Abba* and so does Jesus *(Yahusha)* about 57 times of which about half are spoken by Messiah Himself. In fact, it is the principal manner in which Yahuah is expressed throughout the text, which is the origin of the same religion/relationship of the Filipino in 1521. Magellan met the Magi (or at least their people), as that title of *Maginoo* still existed in his age, and they still worshipped the same *Abba*. No wonder the Pope had to wipe out local history. Landau should have connected this.

---

[1] *"FactChecker: Does 'Abba' Mean 'Daddy'?" By Glenn T. Stanton, Focus On The Family. The Gospel Coalition. May 13, 2013.* [2] *" MarYA = YHWH." TheAramaicScriptures.co*

*"Holy and glorious Father (**Αββα**):" [1X] RotM 1:3.*
*"Father (**Αββα**) of All:" [1X] RotM 2:2.*
*"The Father (**Αββα**):" [27X] RotM 3:5, 4:2, 4:4, 4:6, 6:3, 13:4 (twice),* 13:13,* 15:2 (3 times), 15:4, 15:6, 19:7,* 20:4,* 21:3,* 21:6,* 21:8 (twice),* 21:10 (twice),* 21:11,* 23:3, 25:3,* 25:4,* 31:1.*
*"Father (**Αββα**) of (heavenly) majesty:" [16X] RotM 5:7, 6:2, 6:4, 10:9, 11:7, 13:1,* 13:2,* 15:3, 15:4, 15:5, 19:1, 19:7,* 19:9,* 21:6,* 27:3, 27:7.**
*"My Father (**Αββα**):" [10X] RotM 13:3,* 13:9,* 13:10 (twice),* 19:7,* 21:5,** 21:7,* 21:8 (twice),*25:4.**
*"His Father (**Αββα**):" [1X] RotM 24:2 (Mary).*
*"Exalted Father (**Αββα**):" [1X] RotM 31:5 (Thomas).*
** Messiah speaking Abba.*

We do not find *Abba* as a new term in the New Testament as it was already used by the Magi before Messiah was born. Messiah uses the term "Abba" on numerous occasion, in conversation with the Magi. Mary used "Abba" when speaking with the Magi. Both Thomas and Paul knew and used "Abba" in writing. When Filipinos were explaining their Biblical relationship to Magellan, they were identifying the practices of this very text in continuation of the Magi's embracing Jesus *(Yahusha)*, including the direct New Testament messages from the Apostle Thomas. How could this be lost today? Imagine, a New Testament community of ekklesia scholars know nothing about.

YHWH in Revelation of the Magi:

YHWH is used over 6000 times in the original Hebrew Old Testament, yet they deceptively translate it as the lesser title "Lord," replacing His name; hiding it. Landau is no different; one cannot ignore that he stepped all over the name of *Yahuah*. Abraham and the patriarchs spoke the name *Yahuah*, as Yahuah spoke His own name to them.

Landau took the Syriac word for "Lord," MārYā, and translated it as "Lord" which would seem appropriate, but such practice has never been. This is the Syriac expression of the Tetragramaton, YHWH, used in the Aramaic Peshitta Old Testament. That would have been easy to confirm, but in his paradigm, they remain uneducated on this restoration to the original Bible texts. In fact, some Aramaic versions even render this name in the New Testament when quoting the Old.

In the Aramaic Peshitta Old Testament, every place where the Tetragramaton or, YHWH is written/spoken, the Aramaic word MarYA is given instead. This word is understood by the Aramaic speaking people as meaning The Lord-Ya or, {The Lord-YHWH}, and in The Eastern Aramaic Peshitta & Western Aramaic Peshitto New Testament Scriptures, this same word MarYA is found in all the NT quotations of the OT passages which show this form of YHWH.[2]

One example is the case of the rendering of what should be "Yahuah of Life." Landau confused himself attempting to claim that title is Babylonian, because he seems unaware that he diminished the holy name of *Yahuah*; translating it as "Lord." There is no *Yahuah of Life* in any occult religion. That is nonsense. This really demonstrates how far modern scholarship has strayed from the Word.

We see the title "Lord of Majesty" just as we saw "Abba of Majesty" in use here. That is "Yahuah of Majesty." This becomes extremely evident in ***Revelation of the Magi*** in the account where Seth called "upon the name of the LORD *(3:2)*." That is exactly as Genesis 4:26, and Landau even uses all caps, which he well knows is rendering YHWH, יהוה, in Hebrew. Yes, our text not only uses *Abba* and *Yahusha*, but also *Yahuah*, about twelve times. That is a sign of inspired scripture.

"Lord (MārYā: YHWH, יהוה) of Life:" RotM 1:3, 8:8.
"Lord (MārYā: YHWH, יהוה) of Majesty:" RotM 3:1, 3:8, 29:5.
"The name of the LORD (MārYā: YHWH, יהוה):" RotM 3:2.
"Lord (MārYā: YHWH, יהוה) of Every Soul:" RotM 3:2.
"Lord (MārYā: YHWH, יהוה) of All:" RotM 17:5, 27:7, 32:1, 32:3.
"Lord (MārYā: YHWH, יהוה) of my holy virginity:" RotM 24:4 (Mary).

Scholars just cannot escape the facts. The name of *Yahuah* and His endearing title of *Abba* are entrenched throughout this publication. Anyone trying to debate some of these without recognizing that Landau, the translator himself, admits he was interpreting YHWH, just as Genesis, in the account of Seth calling upon the name of *YHWH*, is not offering an honest debate. They begin on a lie. The actual Hebrew name *Yahusha* and Greek equivalent is used as well. That is evidence that the ***Revelation of the Magi*** is a valid text. They are not testing it.

Additionally, this practice dates the same as the Peshitta Aramaic Bible, and the Syriac language firms the date of authorship to the first or second century for ***Revelation of the Magi***. When a text vets accurate and it dates itself, there is no question as to when it was created and who wrote it. Scholars who begin translating or commenting on a text, with the foundation that the original author is a liar, are simpleminded. They apply outlandish criteria (such as dismissing a text written by the Magi order with multiple authors, when they know the Bible has a similar dynamic in several books), which is evidence they are not offering credible criticism, and are hypocrites.

Content Compared to Old & New Testaments:

Finally, how does ***Revelation of the Magi*** compare to the Old and New Testaments? We will assess this in the following chart and encourage everyone to test this. This is not a small amount of data, and it presents in favor of this text. It is massive.

Revelation of the Magi	*Old/New Testament*
1:5 gift of majesty	*Jn. 4:10; Acts 2:38, 8:20, 10:45, 11:17; Rom. 5:15-17; 2Cor. 9:15; Eph. 3:7, 4:7; Heb. 6:4, Jas. 1:17*
2:1 nothing exists outside His will	*Jn. 1:3, Col. 1:16*
2:4 land of Nod	*Gen. 4:16*
2:7 expulsion from Paradise	*Gen. 3:23-24*
3:1 Enos and Seth began to call upon YHWH	*Gen. 4:26*
3:4 Noah delivered from the Flood	*Gen. 7:1*
3:5 Noah took books with him on the ark	*1En. 39:2, 68:1, 82:1, Jub. 7:39, 12:27, 21:10-11*
3:8 Lord of Majesty	*Is. 2:10, 19- 21; 24:14, 26:10; Mi 5:4; 1 Pet 1:16*
4:1 hidden mysteries	*Job 11:7, 12:22; Ps 78:2; Dn 2:22; Rom 16:24-25; 1 Cor. 2:7; Eph 3:9; Col 1:26; Rev 1:20, 10:7*
4:4 voice/word of the Father; light of the ray of His glory	*Jn 1:1-4; 1 Jn 2:14; Is. 55:11; Ho. 6:5*
by whose power and word all the worlds were set in order and established	*Gen 1; Ps 33:6; Jn 1:10; Heb 11:3; Col 1:16; 2 Pet 3:5; 2 Es 16:55*
4:8 God appearing in the bodily form of a human	*Is. 53:3; Jn 1:1-4; Phil 2:6-8; Col 2:9; 1 Tim 3:16*
4:9 His perfect riches that do not pass away, with His new world, with perfect salvation	*Is 59:19; Mt 16:27, 25:31; Mk 8:38; Lk 9:26; Jn 1:14*
6:2 the light of the star and about its glory, because he saw It in the Garden of Eden when it descended and came to rest over the Tree of Life	*Gen 2:9, 3:24; Rev 22:2, 14 1 En 32:3, Jub 4:23; 2 Es 8:52*
7:2 Every kingdom that will be divided against itself shall not stand.	*Mt 12:25-26; Mk 3:24-25; Lk 11:17-18*
7:3 the rib that was removed became a thorn	*Gen 2:21-23; Jub 3:5-7*
7:6 master made her a helper for me	*Gen 2:18; Jub 3:4*
7:8 filled with poison by the lie of the serpent	*Gen 3:1-5; 1 Tim 2:14*
8:1 among the holy watchers	*Dn 4:13, 17, 23; 1 En 1:5*
8:2 father whose mercy is mixed with discipline	*Dt 4:31; 1 Ch 7:13; Lk 6:36; 2 Cor 1:3*
8:5 the Evil One wanted to humiliate me with his fraud and be liberated from under my authority	*Mt 6:13, 13:19; 1 Jn 3:12; 1 En 32:6*
8:6 He shut his lying mouth and filled it with dust, and he tore off his feet so that he could not walk upon them	*Gen 3:14-15; Jub 3:23*
9:1 the reciters of the mystery of the majesty. And they will find great mercy and will pray, ask, and be heard	*Mt 6:6-7; Lk 12:3; Jn 16:24*
9:2 end times of that generation will be rebelling	*2 Es 15:6; 2 Tim 3:2-5*
9:2 they shall speak blasphemy unto the heavenly majesty	*2 Pt 2:10*
9:3 make painted idols and graven images, and shall even serve the sun and the moon, and they shall speak words of blasphemy	*Ex 20:4; Lev 26:1, 19:4; Ez 8:16; Jer 8:2; Dt 4:16, 5:8, 17:3, 27:15; Zep 1:5; Ho 2:18, 8:4, 13:2; Act 7:42*
9:5 (the deceiver) will make them desire the empty praise of great riches, pride, clothes, property, fornication, boastfulness, injustice greed, and various possessions	*Mt 5:19, 6:19; Mk 4:19; Rom 1:29; Col 3:5; 1 En 97:8*
10:2 nor could the clay be like the potter	*Is 29:16; Jer 18:6*
9:6 he will appear like a lover or a friend and entice them with reveling, drunkenness, impure and defiled feasts	*Dn 5:23, 23:2; Gal 5:19-21; Ep 5:18; 1 Pt 4:5; 1 En 69:27*
10:1 when you have eaten from the tree, you will become like your God	*Gen 3:1-5*
10:3 He will save me from destruction and raise me from the dust	*1 Sam 2:8; Ps 113:7*
10:4 descending to the darkness, He will strengthen me by His light He breathed into my nostrils	*Is 9:2, 51:14, 61:1; Mt 4:16; Lk 1:79; Jn 12:35 Gen 2:7; Is 2:22*
10:6 offering from your brother Abel...retribution for his blood from the hands of his brother who killed him	*Gen 4:3-12; 1 En 22:5-7*
10:7 Even to those who offend Him, he gives opportunity for repentance, and is gracious to them if they repent and seek it from Him	*Ex 20:6; Dt 5:10, 7:9; Pr 15:9; Is 30:18; Jr 9:24; Ps 33:18, 36:10, 119:132; Dn 9:4; Neh 1:5; Lk 1:50*
13:2 inhabitants of the world cannot bear to see the glory of the only Son of the Father of majesty	*Jn 1:14-18, 3:16-18, 5:19, 8:28; 1 Jn 4:9*

Revelation of the Magi	*Old/New Testament*
13:3 *the sake of the redemption of the lives of human*	*Jn 3:16; Ro 3:24, 8:23; Ep 1:7; Col 1:14; 1 Cor 1:30*
beings, because my Father has loved them, that they should not perish by the error in which they have persisted	
13:4 *even unto the death of a cross*	*Act 5:30, 10:39; Phil 2:8; Dn 12:2; Mt 19:29*
13:4 *For the sake of their salvation I will descend*	*Lk 18:30; Jn 3:16, 3:36, 5:24,6:40, 6:47*
to raise them up with me in love and indivisible	
peace if they shall believe in me without doubt	
13:5 *I have loved them that they may not perish*	*2 Pt 3:9; Lk 13:3-5*
Unless they repent and believe in me	
13:8 *I will be born like a human*	*Lk 2:11; Phil 2:7*
13:9 *my Gospel has been proclaimed by angels*	*Lk 2:8-15*
13:10 *I am everywhere, because I am a ray of light,*	*Mt 5:14; Jn 1:9, 3:19, 8:12, 9:5; Ep 3:9; 2 Cor 4:4*
whose light has shone in this world from the majesty of my Father	
14:5-8 *many forms that appeared to us: an infant,*	*Lk 2:12, 2:40, 1:79, 4:18; Jn 19:19; Ps 11:4; Is 9:2;*
a youth, humble, poor, unsightly, cross with person	*Jn 20:17; Heb 4:14, 8:1; Mt 19:28, 26:64, 27:52*
of light on it, went to Sheol and dead rose and worshiped Him, ascended in glory, opened the graves, raised the dead,	
ascended to the heavenly height and angels opened gates of heaven, angels and seraphs, Paraclete Spirit taking a crown	
15:1 *a voice with much light and unspeakable kindness*	*Ez 1:28; Act 22:9*
15:2 *No one knows the Father except the voice*	*Mt 11;27; Lk 10:22; Jn 1:18, 3:13, 14:6; 1 Jn 2:23*
bringing Forth the word of salvation	
15:3 *By the same voice and word the heavenly*	*Gen 1; Jub 2; 1 En 9:5, 14:3, 16:3; Ps 8:5;*
worlds and the lower ones of the Father of majesty	*Jn 1:1-4; Act 14:15; Ro 1:20; Heb 1:2, 2:7-9;*
came into being and were ordered; the angels,	*Col 1:16; Rev 14:7; 1 En 61:10*
powers, princes, authorities, even this world in which you exist	
15:4 *nothing exists outside the will of the Father of majesty*	*Jn 5:30, 8:28; Ro 4:17; Mt 3:17, 17:5; Mk 9:7;*
This is my beloved Son, sent of perfect love	*1 Pt 1:17; Ps 25:14; Jn 14:21; Lk 10:21*
This is the revealer of the secrets of the Father for His loved Ones	
As they can receive by the gift of His Son	*Jn 6:27; Heb 2:10*
17:9 *When you have seen Him, come and tell me,*	*Mt 2:7-8*
that I also may go to worship Him.	
15:5 *he who has told of new and perfect worlds to*	*Is 65:17, 66:22; 1 Cor 2:9*
those who are persuaded and believe in Him	*2 Pet 3:13; Rev 21:1-2, 3:12*
He is the image and form of the Father	*Mt 11:27; Lk 10:22*
15:6 *this is the only begotten Son, perfecting all*	*Mt 3:17; Mk 1:11; Lk 3:22; Jn 1:14, 1:18, 3:15-18;*
the will of His Father	*Heb 1:5; 1 Pt 1:17; 1 Jn 4:9, 4:34*
The world loves darkness more than Him	*Ps 45:7; Jn 3:19; Act 19:9; Heb 1:9; 2 Tim 3:4*
15:7 *Humbled and became a human being for the*	*Jn 3:16, 5:24, 6:40; Ro 4:24; Heb 5:9;*
salvation of human beings so that they would not perish	*1 Th 4:14; 1 Jn 5:13; Heb 4:3; Gal 3:22*
He put on, by His will, a body, a humble form, that with it he might slay death and take away the dominion	
of death to give eternal life to those who love Him and believe in Him	
15:8 *in whose name signs and portents take place*	*Mk 16:17*
through His believers	
The perfect Son, doing the will of Him who sent Him	*Jn 4:34*
The way and the gate of light for those who enter by it	*Ps 27:1; Jn 8:12, 9:5, 10:7-9, 12:46, 14:6*
He is in everything and is named and spoken of above all	*Act 17:24; 1 Cor 15:27; Heb 2:8; Col 1:18*
The bread of life that comes down from Me for believers	*Jn 6:33-35, 48, 51*
The sower of the Word of life	*Mt 13:3-18; Mk 4:14; Lk 8:10-15; Jn 4:36*
The shepherd of truth who gives himself as ransom for the flock	*Is 40:11; Mt 20:28; Mk 10:45; Jn 10:11*
He is the great priest	*Heb 4:14, 5:10, 6:20, 7:1, 8:1; 9:11*
By His blood absolves the worlds	*Ro 3:25*
He is a drink of the vine of life	*Jn 15:5*
15:10 *No one exists over Him or over His majesty to*	*Mt 28:18; Jn 10:30-36, 14:10, 20, 17:21*
speak of how He is, except me, and I and he, we are one	
17:1 *we arrived in the region of Jerusalem*	*Mt 2:1*
17:2 *its nobles and rulers were disturbed*	*Mt 2:2-4*
17:6 *Herod called and sent for the honorable elders*	*Mt 2:3-4*

Revelation of the Magi	*Old/New Testament*
17:6 Where is it written that the king Messiah and savior	Mt 2:5-6
and life giver of the worlds is to be born?	
18:1 We went and entered Bethlehem in joy	Mt 2:9-10
18:2 All of us went to the homestead in which	Mt 2:11
our guide was born	
18:8 We brought forth our treasures before Him	Mt 2:11
19:5 I shall be with you even until the end, and I am not	Ps 73:23; Mt 28:20; Jn 14:3
separated from you nor from all those who believe in me	1 Enoch 71:15-17
19:6 you will be witnesses for Me in the land of the East	Is 43:10-12, 44:8; Heb 12:1; 1 Th 2:10
together with my disciples	
19:7 when I have completed the will of my Father	Mt 26:64; Jn 1:51, 3:13, 8:21, 14:6; Act 7:56
regarding everything that He commanded me, I	
will go up in the glory in which I was with Him.	
I am with Him and have not become separated from the Father	Jn 8:16, 28, 38, 14:10, 20
19:8 in the hour that you shall see the sun darkened	1 En 51:1-2, 80:2-5; 2 Sam 22:8; Ps 18:7, 46:2;
in the daytime like night; and there is a great earthquake	Is 13:10; Jl 2:10, 31, 3:15; Am 8:9; Nah 1:5;
upon the earth, and the voice of the dead is heard	Zec 14:6-7; 2 Es 7:32-33; Mt 24:29; Mk 13:24;
from their graves	Act 2:20; Rev 16:18
19:9 see the heavens opened in glory before Me, and	Ps 80:15-17; Mt 26:64;
I am ascending in praise fitting for Me, and sitting at the	Mk 14:62; Lk 22:69; Jn 1:51; Ro 8:34; Ep 1:20;
19:9 right hand of the Father of majesty	Col 3:1; Heb 8:1,10:12; Jn 3:17, 12:47; 1 Jn 4:14
From whom I have been sent to save the world	
20:3 by your light and your word they were made perfect, and	Gen 1; Jn 1:3; Ro 1:20; 1 Cor 8:6; Heb 2:10;
all the worlds seen and unseen were brought to completion	Col 1:16-17; Jub 2
20:4 All the angles and powers worship You Yours is the place	Rev 7:11; Act 3:21, 13:39; Ep 1:11
of salvation which you will give to Your chosen ones.	
Yours is the ancient light	Jn 1:1-14, 8:12, 12:36; 2 Cor 4:6
You are the beloved fruit of the thought of the Father	Jn 14:10; Heb 1:3; 1 Jn 2:14
The revealer of hidden things	Dt 29:29; Jb 12:22; Dn 2:22, 47; Mt 11:25, 13:35;
	Mk 4:22; Lk 8:17, 10:21; Ep 3:9; 1 Cor 4:5
You are all, all is In you and nothing outside of your will	Jn 5:30, 6:39; Ep 4:6; 1 Cor 15:28
21:2 He comforted and said to us: ...do not be afraid	Is 41:10, 44:8
21:5 I shall send you some of my chosen ones who have been chosen	Is 66:19; Mt 28:19-20; Act 13:47
by me for your land. They shall speak and witness the truth with you	
21:6 I am never separated from you, nor from the presence of the Father	Mt 28:20; Jn 6:39, 14:3
I was sent to enlighten you	Is 42:6; Lk 2:32; Ro 2:19
21:8 Father does not have an image and form in this world	Jn 1:18, 14:10-11; 1 Jn 5:10
I am in my Father and my Father is in me	Jn 10:38, 14:10-11; 1Jn 5:10
21:9 Adam's sin, which became your downfall to Sheol,	Ro 5:12-16; Tit 1:2
death has had authority over you and error has reigned in deceit over your generations	
I have made known to you, your fathers, and even	Jn 12:36; 1 Th 5:5-8;
to that ancient race of yours, your freedom, because	1 Pt 2:9; Jm 1:25
you are from the race of light	Col 1:12, 20 times in D.S.S., Lk 1:79
All the worlds came into being for your sake	Is 45:18; Heb 11:3; 2 Es 7:11
21:10 I clothed myself in your form, that by it I	Is 49:7; Phil 2:7-8;
might bring to an end and destroy all those who	1 Pt 1:20
afflict you and your captors	Mt 12:42; Lk 11:31
I shall offer you to the Father, before Him as a pure and	Is 66:20; Mal 1:11;
perfect offering, since there are no blemishes of error on you.	Ro 12:1; 1 Pt 1:18-21, 2:5
I will set you free with love, truth, pure water,	Ps 102:20, 146:7; Lk 4:18;
and the birth of the Holy Spirit	Jn 8:36; 1 Cor 7:22; Gal 4:5; Heb 9:15
Brothers and believers, like infants in whom there	Mt 18:3; 1 Cor 14:20; Phil 2:15; 1 Jn 3:1
are no blemishes of evil	
21:11 Joy, redemption, fellowship of the Spirit, and	Ps 27:1; Is 61:10; Lk 20:36;
eternal Life shall be given to you through Me	1 Th 2:7; 1 Jn 1:7; Rev 1:5
Under the wings of the Father	Ps 36:7, 57:1, 61:4; Rt 2:12, 2 Es 1:30

Revelation of the Magi	*Old/New Testament*
22:2 Joseph and Mary, honored and blessed people	Mt 2:11
22:3 Mary will have a name, a memory and a blessing forever and ever	Lk 1:28, 42
23:1 O woman blessed among women	Lk 1:28, 42
23:3 this great gift and light of salvation is not yours alone,	Is 58:8, 62:1; Ro 6:23;
But is all for the heavenly and lower worlds	2 Cor 4:6
He is in the entire creation and enlightens it all	Jn 1:9; Ep 3:9
23:4 the forms with Him have been seen in every land,	Ps 65:5; Is 49:6; Lk 3:6;
Because He has been sent by His majesty for the	Act 13:47; Ro 1:16; Ti 2:11
Salvation and redemption of every human being	
24:1 Joseph and Mary turned back, rejoicing about all	Lk 2:19
these things that they had heard about the holy child	
24:4 O opener of my womb by your holy mercy, O	Lk 2:23
Lord of my holy virginity	
25:1 you were deemed worthy to be blessed among women	Mt 2:11; Lk 1:28, 42
25:2 Eve and her offspring will have hope and salvation,	Gen 2:9, 3:17, 22, 24; Rev 2:7, 22:14, 19
since by your person you have made her pass beyond	
the spear that fenced in the Tree of Life	1 En 24:9, 25:5
25:4 bring forth fruits of eternal salvation	Is 45:17, 46:13; Mt 25:46; 2 Tim 2:10; Heb 5:9, 9:12-15
26:3 I am everywhere	Jer 23:23; 1 Cor 15:28
I am Lord of the sun, and my light and word are more	Ps 89:15; Job 25:5; Is 2:5, 60:1; Jer 31:35; Act 26:13;
abundant by many times than the sun	Ep 5:8; 1 En 14:20
27:7 Kingdom of the Father of majesty	Mat 13:43; 1 Cor 8:6, 19:12
Sent Him for the healing of the worlds, to cure their	Ek 34:4, 16; Mt 4:24-27, 9:35, 10:8, 14:14,
sickness, because they could not be healed by one of	Mk 1:34, 6:56, Lk 4:40, 9:2,11, 10:9;
The ancient prophets, but only through the will	
Of the Son of perfect mercy	Act 5:15-16, 10:38, 19:12; Jam 5:15
27:10 He is the light that is all-sufficient and	Ep 1:18, 3:9, 5:9; 1 Tm 6:16; 1 Jn 1:5, 9
all-enlightening by His perfect love	
28:6 The faith of salvation increased in the land of	Ps 40:10, 65:5, 69:13, 78:22, 103:17; Act 14:9;
The East.	Ro 1:16, 13:11; Ep 1:13; 2 Tim 3:15;
	1 Th 5:8; 2 Th 2:13; 1 Pet 1:5, 9; Jude 1:3
29:1 Judas Thomas went down there by the will of	Act 1:13
Our Lord when He sent him	
The faith increased all the more in those who heard,	Act 2:43, 5:12, 6:8, 15:12;
through the many mighty works and signs that	Ro 1:8, 15:19; 2 Cor 12:12;
Judas Thomas, the apostle of our Lord, was doing there	Heb 2:4
29:4 Judas the Apostle recognized that the gift of our	Act 2:38; Ro 5:5, 15, 17, 20, 6:23; Ep 1:6, 3:7; 2;
Lord had overflowed upon them	Tim 1:6
The mighty works, the healings, the wonders,	Mk 8:6; Lk 19:37; Jn 2:11, 7:3, 20:30;
which He did in the sight of the Apostles	Act 2:22; Ro 6:26
29:6 Since everyone who believes in salvation and	Jl 2:32; Jn 10:29, 14:30; 1 Cor 15:2; Ro 6:9
with love receives the seal of my Lord Jesus Christ	
in truth, the Enemy does not rule over	
30:1 He went out to a spring of water and he took oil	Is 58:11; Mt 3:13; Mk 1:9, 26-28, 33, 3:23; Lk 3:16;
and gave praise over it	Jn 4:14; Act 1:5, 11:16, 13:24
30:2 Oil for salvation	Ps 23:5, 92:10; Is 61:3; Heb 1:9
30:4 The athletes of the contest defeat their enemies	1 Cor 9:25-27; 1 Tim 2:5
30:5 The victorious are crowned in the contest	Is 62:3; 2 Ti 2:5, 4:8
30:6 You fly over water like your twin, the Holy Spirit	Gen 1:2; Lk 3:22, 4:1; 1 Cor 12:3
30:7 Partner of the first born	Neh 10:36; Rev 1:5
30:9 Temples for your dwelling	Act 17:24; 1 Cor 6:19
31:1 He baptized them in the name of the Father,	Mt 28:19; Jn 3:22, 4:2; Act 2:38
And the Son, and the Holy Spirit	
31:2 Taking a whole loaf of bread, He gave praise, broke	Mt 14:19, 22, 15:36, 26:26; Mk 6:41, 8:6, 14:22, 16:19;
and gave first to the Apostle Judas and also to each of them	Lk 9:16, 22:19, 24:30, 51; Act 20:11, 27:35; 1 Cor 11:23-26;
Behold the consummation and sealing of your birth of salvation Ep 1:13	

Revelation of the Magi	*Old/New Testament*
31:3 They saw Him going up to heaven in glory	Ps 139:8; Mk 16:19; Lk 9:51; Jn 3:13, 6:62, 20:17; Act 1:11; Ro 10:6; 1 Tim 3:16; Heb 4:14
31:5 You alone have known your great name	Mt 1:21; Jn 20:31; Act 3:16; 2 Th 1:12; 1 Jn 3:23; Rev 19:12
31:6 You loved us with your great mercy that was for us, and everything the crucifiers brought upon You, you endured for our sake, being exalted above all sufferings and a kins-person of one who does not suffer	Is 53:5; Mk 8:31; Act 3:13; Ro 5:3; Gal 1:4; 2 Tim 2:3; Heb 12:2-3; 1 Pet 2:21, 5:10; Rev 1:9
31:6 we should have redemption by your grace	Ro 3:24, 5:2, 15-17, 21; Ep 1:7, 2:5,8; Heb 9:12
31:7 You are our advocate, and our guide, our Light, our Savior	Jn 14:26; 2 Cor 4:6; Phil 3:20; Heb 12:2; 1 Th 2:19; 1 Jn 2:1
31:8 You made us worthy in your mercy for your fellowship of everlasting life	Dan 12:2; Jn 3:36; Act 13:46; Ro 6:23; Gal 6:8; Ep 4:1; Phil 1:27; Col 1:10; 1 Tim 1:16; 2 Th 1:11
31:9 a multitude of brethren added to the faith day by day	Act 2:47, 11:24
31:10 Go out into the entire world and preach My gospel Go out to every place and preach the gift of our light and our Savior	Mt 24:14, 26:13; Mk 13:10, 14:9, 6:15; Act 10:36,42; 1Col 1:23; 1 Th 1:8; 1 Pet 1:12, 4:6; Act 13:47, 26:23; 2 Cor 2:14, 4:4-6; Col 1:6; Heb 6:4; Jam 1:17
32:1 through the Holy Spirit that was poured out upon them	Act 2:33, 38, 10:45; Ro 5:5; 1 Pet 1:12; 1 Jn 2:20, 27; Ti 3:6
32:2 Flee from the darkness and come to the light that does not pass away, so that you may live	Ps 27:1; Is 50:10; Act 26:16
Have refuge under the wings of our Lord Jesus	Ps 91:4; Ru 2:12
Great refuge on the last day from the fearsome judgement of fire that will come suddenly to purify the entire earth	Is 13:9; Zep 1:15, 18, 2:3, 3:8; Act 17:31; 1 Cor 4:5; 2 Pet 3:7, 2:9; Rev 6:17; 1 En 45:3-6
32:3 You shall be delivered by faith from the heat of the fire and shall enter the rest that is prepared for all the chosen and the believers	Is 57:2, 64:4; Zep 2:3; Mt 25: 34-41; Heb 4:3; 1 En 58:2-6, 69:27-29, 102:1
All who have believed in the child of perfect light and in eternal life	Jn 3:15-16, 5:24, 6:40, 47
In the kingdom of my Lord Jesus Christ, the Son of the Lord of All, in His heavenly majesty, in His new world	Mt 13:52; Jn 18:36; Act 8:12; 2 Tim 4:1; 2 Pet 1:11; Rev 12:10 2 Es 2:31; 1 En 103:1-4
32:3 His heavenly and great and never-passing-away light	Is 60:19-20; Dn 7:14; Mt 5:18, 24:35; Mk 13:31; Lk 21:33; 1 Jn 2:7-8; Rev 22:5
You shall rest forever, amen and amen	Is 14:3; Mt 11:28; 1 Th 4:17

Notice the abundant affinity to scripture in ***Revelation of the Magi*** compared to the Old and New Testaments. This book was written by one intimately familiar with scripture, as a prophet or priest would be. That is no liar, and no occultist, as none of them are that good. The claim that some scholars have made that they cannot prove authorship is impertinent. No one needs the name of the author which they do not have for some portions of our modern Canon even. That is hypocrisy. The accusation begins with a lie. It is meant to leave inspired texts in the questionable zone not because they have proven the book uninspired. No one can. The ignorance and inability of scholars to conduct research does not equate to a position in any sense. It is time to take ***Revelation of the Magi*** seriously, and begin to understand the many revelations, which abound within. We live in the days of increasing knowledge. If one will not embrace such, many will pass them by.

The Abundant Ancient Isles of
Gold, Frankincense, & Myrrh
Brought For More Than Little Boxes!

Ready to embark on an almost two-year excursion, the Maginoo kings,
princes, and Wise Men of prayer (magdasal) and reflective silence
(magiammo), prepare their gifts in the mountains of Ophir, Sheba, and
Tarshish. As the Queen of Sheba brought 4.5 tons of gold alone as well as
more store of frankincense and myrrh than the land of the Temple had ever
seen, twelve royals from her land would at least mirror her oblation. The
notion that they brought three little boxes from the Land of Gold and Spices
is unfounded. They likely each brought 4.5 tons which they could execute
with ease just as their Queen did a thousand years earlier.

Conclusion:
The Restoration of History &
Prophecy of the Magi Isles

It was a beautiful morning in the Land of the Magi. Just before dusk in 1982 in Hinoba-an on Negros Occidental, a joyful shout was heard: "Anak Ng Kamote! *(Son of a Sweet Potato!)*." One of the rice farmers of Negros was preparing their field for planting when they discovered what was not a sweet potato, but a large nugget of gold. These legends abound from that area, as well as areas of Mindanao, especially. In the shallow ground? He had no heavy equipment, nor even a pickaxe. This was not deep in the mountain but residual evidence of the ancient Land of Gold's alluvial deposits just below the surface.

How else would ancients mine gold when they had no such equipment as is needed to penetrate the mountains of South Africa, and other top gold-producing regions today? This was discovered in the shallow earth and not just in the mountains, leading to a gold rush, bringing in major mining companies who employed as many as 7,000 at their peak.[1] Of course, they exploited the land and people, leaving behind a wasteland; now appearing like a desert, in portions. Riddled with polarizing stories of politics and greed, academics have overlooked the part of the story that matters most. Alluvial gold deposits are proven to have existed in the Philippines just below the surface in the 1980's still.

In a recent blog titled "Dredging Under the Rice Paddies in the Philippines"[2] chronicling their gold identifying activities, a group called "The New 49'ers," in Angeles City writes of their experience finding gold, in the bedrock of riverbanks near Baguio. They claim to have found some in the sand of certain beaches. They report on dredging operations in the Bicol region as well. Interestingly, they write of Rice Paddy Dredgers who operate with their hands. Today, they have to go even deeper than in ancient times, but the precedence remains. For transport, they used wooden sleds attached to carabao, but that did not leave archaeology for anyone to find a thousand years later.

This soil was and is unique, and historically so, even in eyewitness and secondary accounts over thousands of years. Did they know this in the first century era of the Magi? Despite obvious scoffing from the uniformed, such as Pliny the Elder (who doubted that fact, yet still rendered geography identifying the Philippines), those who lived there and visited knew it was historic fact, documenting it many times.

In 43 A.D., Pomponius Mela charted the Philippines as this Land of Gold, describing it as having "golden soil" and "silver soil."[3] The Periplus of the Erythraean Sea notes that in 50 A.D., there were gold mines in the Philippines (also mapping it), and their coins were called "caltis," which matches the Filipino history of their

---

[1] *"Mining in Negros: A Story of Plunder, Destruction and Dislocations." By Karl G. Ombion and Edgar A. Cadagat. Bulatlat.com/Cobra-Ans, Vol. 2, No. 29. Aug. 25, 2002.* [2] *"Dredging Under the Rice Paddies in the Philippines." Dave McCracken's Adventures. Gold Mining Adventures. The New 49'ers. Retrieved 2024.* [3] *"Pomponius Mela, Chorographia Bk II, from Pomponius Mela's Description of the World." Translated by Frank E. Romer. University of Michigan Press. 1998. Sections 3.67-3.71.*

ancient gold coins called "piloncitos."[1] In 77 A.D., Pliny the Elder defines the Philippines as their "soil consists of gold and silver."[2] He also maps a route from China South to the Philippines very clearly for those who can read. He did not go there and his scoffing (thinking the golden soil is unbelievable) is impertinent. This historic fact is repeated in 300 A.D. by Solinus who wrote of *"...two islands, Chryse and Argyre. They are so rich in metals that a great many people have recorded that their soils are composed purely of gold and silver."*[3] These were all referring to the Philippines.

Concurrently and contemporaneously, these historians and cartographers were all describing this Land of Gold in the exact same way as the Magi, who also wrote in the first century. Not only did they map it, but they used similar language, such as "the last part of the inhabited world toward the East, beyond India, Southeast of China, under the Tropic of Cancer, beyond mainland Asia, islands, North of the Malay tip or Southern Headland, under the rising sun." The Magi isles are the same and they are affirmed by Psalm 72:10-15.

First Century Geography Defined, Only Undefined in Unacademic Scholarship:
43 A.D.: "...the so-called Islands of the Sun, so unlivable that the pressure of the atmosphere instantly sucks the life out of anyone who enters [Mela]."[5]
50 A.D.: "...the last part of the inhabited world toward the east, under the rising sun itself... After this region under the very north, the sea outside ending in a land called This... [Periplus of the Erythraean Sea]"[1]
77 A.D.: ""The first river that is known in their territory is the Psitharas, next to that the Cambari, and the third the Laros; after which we come to the Promontory of Chryse, the Gulf of Cynaba, the river Atianos, and the nation of the Attacori on the gulf of that name, a people protected by their sunny hills from all noxious blasts, and living in a climate of the same temperature as that of the Hyperborei..." [Pliny the Elder, route from China South to the Philippines][2]
124 A.D.: "where the rising of the bright sun itself is even visible... you turn further towards the eastern sea, your path leads you to the island of Chryseia, where the rising of the bright sun itself is even visible. Turning from there (West into the Indian Ocean) before the southern headland, you would immediately come to the island of mighty Colias... (Malay Tip) [Dionysius Periegetes]"[4]
First Century: RotM 2:4 These are kings, sons of Eastern kings, in the land of Shir, which is the outer part of the entire East of the world inhabited by human beings, at the Ocean, the great sea beyond the world, east of the land of Nod, that place in which dwelt Adam, head and chief of all the families of the world." (Affirming Psalm 72:10-15)

---

[1] *Periplus of the Erythraean Sea, ca. 50 C.E. § 63-64. This journey is detailed throughout sections 56-65!* [2] *Pliny the Elder, Natural History 1-11, § 6.23.6 - ca. 77 C.E. & Pliny the Elder, Natural History 1-11, § 6.20.2 - ca. 77 CE* [3] *Solinus, Polyhistor, 52.17 - ca. 300 CE.* [4] *Dionysius of Alexandria, Guide to the Inhabited World, § 58 - ca. 125 C.E.* [5] *"Pomponius Mela, Chorographia Bk II, from Pomponius Mela's Description of the World." Translated by Frank E. Romer. University of Michigan Press. 1998. Sections 3.67-3.71.* [6] *"Biblical Magi." Wikipedia.*

Also, understand this land where the sun rises is documented in *1 Enoch* and mega history as the Philippines. Many ancients even label the region of the Philippines as "subsolanus" on maps, which is the origin of the sun and the East wind. The Greek phrase interpreted "from the East" is a literal reference "from the rising sun." This is a famous region that cannot be suppressed.

The phrase "from the east" (ἀπὸ ἀνατολῶν, apo anatolon), more literally "from the rising [of the sun]", is the only information Matthew provides about the region from which they came.[6]

These were not fiction, but proven scientific, historic fact. For instance, King Solomon's navy returned with more gold in their first trip to Ophir *(about 15.75 tons, over $500 million value),* than the gold production leader, Egypt, was capable of producing in twenty years (according to the records of Queen Hatshepsut). They did not have modern, heavy mining equipment. The Queen of Sheba came with Solomon's navy, offering her added gifting (the equivalent) of about $168 million dollars in gold alone (which is 4.5 tons). She offered more frankincense and myrrh than the nation of the Temple had ever seen because she came from the Philippines, the Land of Gold and Spices.

Her oblation is the archetype and foreshadowing of the Magi's giftings. The pattern from Adam to the Queen of Sheba to the Magi era is indisputable. Modern scholars assume these Kings brought tiny presents, the size of their hands. This is such a minute, misconstrued scale compared to the truth, and is not precedence, but gross negligence. When the Land of Gold and Spices brings gifts, they are a mass amount in barrels and barrels measured in shiploads. The weight would be tons, not a Christmas present, which is another fraud they have attempted.

The Three Kings have nothing to do with Christmas gifts nor such a holiday which is not of Biblical origin, and they would never keep it. Gift-giving in December is the practice of Zeus, never the Bible. Jesus *(Yahusha)* was born on Shavuot in the late Spring in June, not in December. No one brought Him gifts at His birth. He also does not give gifts on His birthday, other than the Holy Spirit who came on Pentecost, the Greek for Shavuot. There were no Christmas Trees; the Prophet Jeremiah rebukes that pagan practice as idolatry *(10)*. Pastors and leaders are admonished by Jeremiah directly, by name, as "brutish" (stupid) for following this practice and leading their sheep to the occult. Mary well knew who the Queen of Heaven was as the Harlot of Babylon (which Mary never was), who Jeremiah rebukes five times. Why are these in this narrative at all?

The Greeks went to the Magi Isles as Mela was documenting an 800-year record of travel to their isles of gold and silver–Chryse *(Ophir in Hebrew)* and Argyre *(Tarshish in Hebrew)*. Josephus did not. Ptolemy did not. Magellan even corrected them directly in writing in Pigafetta's Journal, yet we have not found a single academic nor Bible scholar who even knows that. They change the Isles of Gold into a Peninsula (in fraud), that the British, colonial academia, and even scholars still cannot figure that out to this day. Their ignorance is not a position. The maps used by him and Columbus chart that in the Philippines as well. No mystery here.

These alluvial deposits cannot be dismissed, as they are the only condition in which the mass finds in ancient Ophir, Sheba, and Tarshish could be gathered. Anyone expecting an archaeological signature for a practice requiring nothing that would leave such, is as obtuse as a paradigm could behave. That ignorance has led to the misplacing of the Land of Gold and Garden of Eden for the past century. This was known to history, geography, science, linguistics and the Bible for thousands of years prior. It is no surprise the conquerors did not want the world to know they attacked the ancient land of Temple resources and that of the treasure of Adam set aside for the Messiah, brought by the Queen of Sheba and Three Kings in covenant. That would be a public relations nightmare indeed.

Adam was not a builder or freemason, that was Cain the Evil and his lineage who moved away from Adam's homeland. Applying Cain, the first builder of cities, as a litmus test to find fictional architecture never recorded in any historic account of Ophir, to Adam's righteous lineage, is dunderhead behavior.

Marco Polo even mentions in the thirteenth century a golden palace in Zipangu *(Philippines)* southeast of South China, as the Chinese Isles of Gold according to Kublai Khan.[1] The plethora of illiterate scholars who cannot read his simple geography is dumfounding. No gold palace ever existed in Japan *(known as Nippon or Nihon, not Japan locally)* in that era, and one with extremely thin gold leaf (not fitting his description), was not even built yet until after his time. However, one did exist in the Philippines in written history *[Pigafetta]*.[2] Polo mentions cannibals, which Japan is not known to have such legends. However, the Philippines has many, even those written by the Chinese. Japan does not make this claim, it is the British, in origin, who committed this fraud reinforced in illiterate academia.

Maps pinpoint Zipangu in the Philippines prior to Marco Polo *[Al-Idrisi, 1154]*.[3] Charts of his journey even do so *[Bowen, 1744]*,[3] and several maps for more than 500 years after his legend surfaced *[Fra Mauro, 1458; Toscanelli, 1474; Behaim, 1492; Hunt-Lenox, 1504; Jagiellonian, 1510; Schoener, 1520; Apianus, 1520; Ramusio, 1560]*.[3] Columbus corrected the Great Khan and Polo for not divulging that their Zipangu was the ancient Ophir of King Solomon.[4] This was known and only ignorant illiterates cannot seem to read the narratives and forget much information still there in the

---

[1] *"The Travels of Marco Polo." By Hugh Murray, F.R.S.E. 2nd Edition. Edinburgh, 1844. p. 272-273.* [2] *"The First Voyage Round the World by Antonio Pigafetta." 1522, translated by Lord Stanley of Alderley. p. 40, 110, & 114. "Magellan's Voyage Around the World By Antonio Pigafetta" By James Alexander Robertson. Vol. 1. U.S. 1906. p. 117.* [3] *All maps in full color, high resolution in Garden of Eden Revealed: The Book of Maps. Schwab/Zamoranos. 2024. www.OphirInstitute.com.* [4] *"The Life and Voyages of Christopher Columbus." By Washington Irving. pp. 22, 210, 205 & 352.* [5] *a. "Baths in 16th Century Philippines." By Beth Ocampo. Philippine Daily Inquirer. July 30, 2013. b. "When Did Philippine History Begin?" American Historical Association.*

accounts. They had purposely retired such facts into the halls of the secret occult circles who would benefit financially from such hidden knowledge in the colonial era, which continues in mindset. However, these are the Magi Isles.

Antonio Pigafetta notes these alluvial gold deposits on or just below the surface in his journal at least twice.[2] He also mentions the King of Butuan had a palace of gold.[2] Of course, modern archaeologists then demand that the Spanish and Americans proactively leave that gold palace as a museum, when they well know history exposes, they stole that gold. In fact, the Spanish erased all history of the Philippines, as not a fragment survives–not one! Padre Chirino in 1590[5] notes all Filipinos he encountered could read and write in their own language. Where are those documents they were writing and reading? One of them is our text, **Revelation of the Magi (RotM).** They were either stolen and remain hidden, or destroyed. Regardless, there are no surviving historical documents of the Philippines until now. Even the record of the conquerors preserves it as the Land of Gold and Garden of Eden in all of history with 6,000 years of maps, but this find affirms all that research.

Now we know, the Magi also provided this same geography and it is indisputable. The academic position remains a few etymologies and wordplay or less. We object to that being characterized as academic. There is one local ancient record in the Philippines until now, and it says much. A legal contract written in Baybayin on a copper tablet from before the Spanish was found and named "The Laguna Copperplate." That was the Magi society and **Revelation of the Magi** restores this history as well. A society that can write a legal contract on copper is not a barbarian culture. That accusation is ill-informed and plain stupid.

Some seek evidence of King Solomon's copper mines, which is not actually the Bible account, yet even those ignore that the Philippines remains #1 in copper on all of Earth as well. In fact, it is #5 in all resources on all of Earth, for that matter. How can an academic or scholar reject that land from consideration? Yet, they do. No one has been able to disprove this conclusion in the decade that we have been researching this. However, academia simply ignores it still.

When **Revelation of the Magi** appeared on the scene in English in 2010, it proved to be the restoration of the written history of the Philippines for the era of the first century B.C. to first century A.D. Documented history affirms this was written before the second century. Since that is the same criteria and date used to judge the New Testament fragments, **Revelation of the Magi** proves to be a historic account of the Filipino Magi and their journey to Bethlehem, their return, and the multiple revivals in their land, as a result. It also provides a record of the Apostle Thomas (that we did not have previously), which coalesces with the traditional writings that he arrived in India. In ancient terms, India includes both the Philippines and the Indies, and represents a far more vast region.

When **Revelation of the Magi** lays down the facts (like the word "Magi" is not Greek, but originates in the Philippines), this is quite a claim, indeed. However, it proves true. The ancient, royal class of the Philippines was the *MAGInoo*. When we discovered that word has two meanings from those languages, just like **Revelation of the Magi** says; we easily identified that *MAGdasal* means "prayer" and *MAGIammo* means "silence." It is difficult to imagine any scholar who would attempt to debate such concrete connection. It is undeniable.

When the names of the Magi and their fathers are recorded and some vet as Tagalog and other Filipino languages, this enters the realm of fact. When that includes the names of Ophir, Sheba, Tarshish, and several of Ophir's brothers, it would be insane to respond with the academic "nuh-uh." They love to say that. It matters not that academics and scholars failed to take this seriously while they sat in the seat of the scornful, thinking their "ignorance is bliss." The person who made up that phrase must have been ignorant. They manage flawed paradigms, fueled by willing ignorance, just as 2 Peter 3 warned would define this age. When gaggles of scholars acquiesce to set a foundation conceding to be stupid, this does not somehow rise to a level of brilliance to which they should be capable but refuse to embrace. It is time to expose the truth once and for all.

Though most scholars are not thought racist, this leads to the suppressing of an entire people in colonial racism. That includes Filipino theologians. Their history is obscured, and their purpose in prophecy becomes muddied when it never should have been. We owe this in origin to the Pharisees and the Vatican, who will likely defend their illiterate positions with a deepened ignorance, as we have already experienced on these topics. They are rendering themselves impertinent and that is their problem, not yours, nor ours. We can know the truth.

In the Philippines, we are told that the ancient Philippines was pagan, worshipping multiple gods, such as Bathala, Anitos *(demons)*, and Animism. Perhaps some of the tribes within did so, but to assume the entire nation of the Philippines was guilty of this sin is unfounded. Scholars and fake researchers who have not read any previous history on the topic tend to believe the Jesuit narrative on record, that the heavy embellishment and redefinition of this conquered people as savages must be the truth. It never is in that regard as they always apply leaven to such accounts, with the intention of justifying their stealing, killing, and destroying, which are the fruits of their father, the devil *(John 10:10, John 8:44)*.

How do we know the Magi knew the God of the Bible? Again, this has never been a mystery; Magellan's journey proved it was so. When Magellan asked Filipinos about their religion and God, they responded with an answer not mentioned in modern textbooks (in fraud). They said they had only one God and that their authentic worship was to worship *ABBA*. Who? How did Filipinos learn that *Abba* was a title for the Creator of the Bible? The Catholic Church does not want us to know this because they raped the Magi, and that tie is there in this text. They denigrated them and stole the very resources given to the Messiah, the Temple and to Yahuah in Adam's first sacrifice. They did not bring Jesus to the Philippines. They crushed His relationship with those of Ophir just as the Pharisees moved to have

Him executed, or so they thought. Abba of the Philippines is Abba of scripture. It is the way that *Revelation of the Magi* often refers to *Yahuah.*

This is representative of the ancient, authentic worship which does not require buildings and infrastructure, or affirmation of a first to second century date of authorship. Just as the Magi met monthly in the Cave of Treasures where Adam once resided, they maintained that authentic worship. They would have known of the title "Abba" from Jesus *(Yahusha)* Himself who used it in the Garden of Gethsemane and almost thirty times in *Revelation of the Magi.* That includes the Apostle Thomas, and Paul does twice as well. This is exactly what we should expect in the Land of the Magi and their history that affirms this. Produce the other land on all of Earth who can remotely challenge these proofs. They cannot.

Every representation of Jesus *(Yahusha)* in *Revelation of the Magi* matches scripture and we have charted its affinity to the Bible throughout. Occult writers deviate from scripture, changing the narrative, and scholars should know this. Our conclusion is: *Revelation of the Magi* passes the test of inspired authorship. It is not necessary to form a counsel to vote on its canonicity. As it proves accurate, it most certainly is an authoritative, historic account. It was indeed written by at least two authors over about a century and it can be affirmed in other writings, the use of the Syriac and especially its use of the name *YHWH, Abba,* and *Yahusha.*

We now have another witness to the prophecy of Jesus *(Yahusha)* in Matthew 12:42. This passage represents a people in relationship with Him directly. The Philippines once had that, but will restore it in the coming age. No one can suppress this any longer. As Filipinos or really, Magi of Ophir, learn their identity in Him and restore His ways, revival will erupt like nothing the world has ever seen. However, this will ignite and travel around the world. The Pope does not want this because it will not unite under him but against everything he stands for in the many abominations of his role, title, and function.

Matthew 12:42 KJV (Luke 11:31)
*The queen of the south shall rise up in the judgment with this generation, and shall condemn it: for she came from **the uttermost parts of the earth** to hear the wisdom of Solomon; and, behold, a greater than Solomon is here.*

Ezekiel 38:13 KJV
*Sheba (Philippines), and **Dedan** (D-D-N originally is Dodan, brother of Tarshish), and the merchants of **Tarshish** (Philippines), with all the young lions thereof, shall say unto thee, Art thou come to take a spoil? hast thou gathered thy company to take a prey? to carry away silver and gold, to take away cattle and goods, to take a great spoil?*

The Philippines is already revealing signs of its rising. It will have a voice on the world stage, which it will use to stand against corruption and the satanic world order all over. Before Matthew, Jesus *(Yahusha)* declared He would destroy those who afflict the Magi, as well as their captors, before they even had such. He predicted the conquest of the nation and its restoration on the world scene. This is the origin of His words in Matthew as He represents His close relationship to the Magi and their land of nativity. Wow!!!

Prophecy From Messiah to the Magi:
RotM 21:9 "And again, I have made known to you, your fathers, and even to that ancient race of yours, your freedom, because you are from the race of light."
21:10 "...I clothed myself in your form, that by it I might bring to an end and destroy all those who afflict you and your captors."
"...And I shall set you free with love, and with truth, with pure water, and the birth of the Holy Spirit..."

As the Magi are restored in Ophir, they will also usher in the return of the Lost Tribes of Israel, according to Isaiah. Even in recent news, the Philippines is building its own navy and shipyards once again.[1] For the dunderheads who cannot read (calling themselves scholars), Isaiah 60 is a promise to the Lost Tribes, and it is an End Times concept throughout (as we have covered). Anyone attempting to claim this passage speaks of the birth of Messiah is illiterate.

Isaiah 60:9 KJV
Surely the isles shall wait for me, and the ships of Tarshish first, to bring thy sons from far, their silver and their gold with them, unto the name of the LORD thy God, and to the Holy One of Israel, because he hath glorified thee.

These are not suggestions in prophecy, and we did not make them up. When Jesus *(Yahusha)*, Isaiah, and Ezekiel predict the rising of the Isles of the Magi in the Last Days, it is certain to occur. All doubt is removed, and no modern prophet is needed to determine this. We encourage everyone to watch the Philippines in this coming age but also, may we all restore His ways in our lives. He is more important than fabricated holidays and fictions of men that wish to deceive. He built no buildings nor organizations but defined His ekklesia as a gathering of two or more *(Matt. 18:20)*. The entire Bible has one main topic, pleasing the Father and the Son. There is no other more important. It is a relationship with Jesus *(Yahusha)* that matters, just as the Magi had.

This is perfectly instructed by our Savior when He tells us He will reject Christians on the Day of Judgment because they do not KNOW Him or He does not know them. The Vatican stands in the way of salvation, which is personal.

---

[1] a. *"Phl building own naval vessels." By Lade Jean Kabagani & Neil Alcober. Daily Tribute. Mar. 4, 2024. b. "PH to build new navy shipyards – Defense chief." By Priam Nepomuceno. Philippine News Agency. Nov. 6, 2024.*

Matthew 7:17-29 KJV

Wherefore by their fruits ye shall know them. Not every one that saith unto me, Lord, Lord, shall enter into the kingdom of heaven; but he that doeth the will of my Father which is in heaven. Many will say to me in that day, Lord, Lord, have we not prophesied in thy name? and in thy name have cast out devils? and in thy name done many wonderful works? And then will I profess unto them, I never knew you: depart from me, ye that work iniquity.

This is one of the saddest concepts in scripture that someone can actually believe they are saved, yet by His definition they are not. Salvation is defined in John 15 by our Savior Himself.

John 15:1-26 KJV

I am the true vine, and my Father is the husbandman. Every branch in me that beareth not fruit he taketh away: and every branch that beareth fruit, he purgeth it, that it may bring forth more fruit. Now ye are clean through the word which I have spoken unto you. Abide in me, and I in you. As the branch cannot bear fruit of itself, except it abide in the vine; no more can ye, except ye abide in me. I am the vine, ye are the branches: He that abideth in me, and I in him, the same bringeth forth much fruit: for without me ye can do nothing. If a man abide not in me, he is cast forth as a branch, and is withered; and men gather them, and cast them into the fire, and they are burned. If ye abide in me, and my words abide in you, ye shall ask what ye will, and it shall be done unto you. Herein is my Father glorified, that ye bear much fruit; so shall ye be my disciples. As the Father hath loved me, so have I loved you: continue ye in my love. If ye keep my commandments, ye shall abide in my love; even as I have kept my Father's commandments, and abide in his love. These things have I spoken unto you, that my joy might remain in you, and that your joy might be full. This is my commandment, That ye love one another, as I have loved you. Greater love hath no man than this, that a man lay down his life for his friends. Ye are my friends, if ye do whatsoever I command you. Henceforth I call you not servants; for the servant knoweth not what his lord doeth: but I have called you friends; for all things that I have heard of my Father I have made known unto you. Ye have not chosen me, but I have chosen you, and ordained you, that ye should go and bring forth fruit, and that your fruit should remain: that whatsoever ye shall ask of the Father in my name, he may give it you. These things I command you, that ye love one another. If the world hate you, ye know that it hated me before it hated you. If ye were of the world, the world would love his own: but because ye are not of the world, but I have chosen you out of the world, therefore the world hateth you. Remember the word that I said unto you, The servant is not greater than his lord. If they have persecuted me, they will also persecute you; if they have kept my saying, they will keep yours also. But all these things will they do unto you for my name's sake, because they know not him that sent me. If I had not come and spoken unto them, they had not had sin: but now they have no cloak for their sin. He that hateth me hateth my Father also. If I had not done among them the works which none other man did, they had not had sin: but now have they both seen and hated both me and my Father. But this cometh to pass, that the word might be fulfilled that is written in their law, They hated me without a cause. But when the Comforter is come, whom I will send unto you from the Father, even the Spirit of truth, which proceedeth from the Father, he shall testify of me: And ye also shall bear witness, because ye have been with me from the beginning.

In these days of increasing knowledge *(Dan. 12:4)*, may we all restore the message the Magi received and guarded for so long. For Salvation is the core; salvation in relationship with Jesus *(Yahusha)*. Shalom and Yah Bless.

INCREASING INSIGHT
THE REMNANT IS AWAKENING

Garden of Eden Revealed: 7" x 10"

Apocrypha: Vol. 1: 7" x 10"

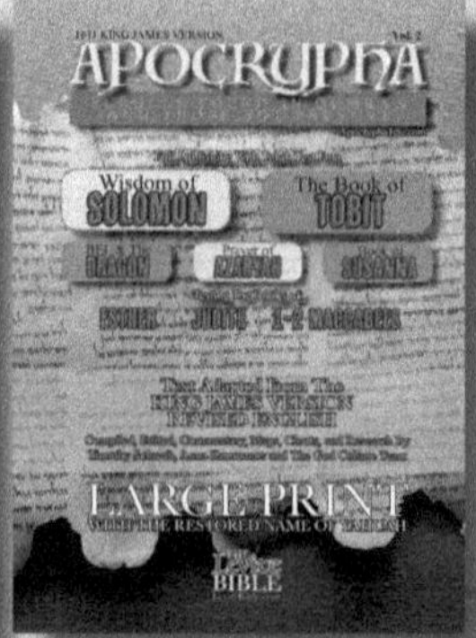

Apocrypha: Vol. 2: 7" x 10"

2nd Esdras: 7" x 10"

International: 

Philippines: 

Three Kings: 7" x 10"

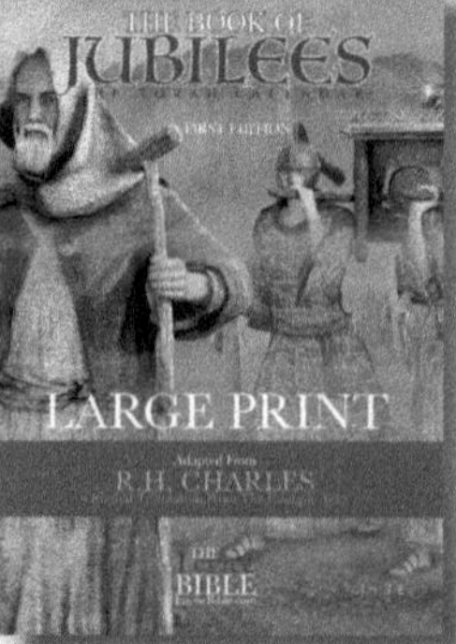

The Book of Jubilees: 7" x 10"

Bible History Illustrated: 7" x 10"

First Enoch: 7" x 10"

www.OphirInstitute.com

REST: Sabbath: 6" x 9" Paperback

The Full Case: 6" x 9" Paperback

Coffee Table Book: 10" x 12" Hardcover

Tagalog, Ilokano, & Small Group Study